THE CAMBRIDGE HISTORY OF SOUTHEAST ASIA

VOLUME TWO

From c. 1500 to c. 1800

THE CAMBRIDGE HISTORY OF SOUTHEAST ASIA

THE CAMBRIDGE
HISTORY OF
SOUTHEAST ASIA

VOLUME TWO

From c. 1500 to c. 1800

edited by

NICHOLAS TARLING

CAMBRIDGE
UNIVERSITY PRESS

PUBLISHED BY THE PRESS SYNDICATE OF THE UNIVERSITY OF CAMBRIDGE
The Pitt Building, Trumpington Street, Cambridge, United Kingdom

CAMBRIDGE UNIVERSITY PRESS
The Edinburgh Building, Cambridge CB2 2RU, UK www.cup.cam.ac.uk
40 West 20th Street, New York, NY 10011–4211, USA www.cup.org
10 Stamford Road, Oakleigh, Melbourne 3166, Australia
Ruiz de Alarcón 13, 28014, Madrid, Spain

The Cambridge History of Southeast Asia was first published in hardback
in two volumes in 1992, reprinted 1994
Volume One ISBN 0 521 35505 2 (hardback)
Volume Two ISBN 0 521 35506 0 (hardback)

The Cambridge History of Southeast Asia is first published in paperback
in four volumes in 1999
Volume One Part One: From early times to c. 1500
ISBN 0 521 66369 5 (paperback)
Volume One Part Two: From c. 1500 to c. 1800
ISBN 0 521 66370 9 (paperback)
These two volumes contain the contents of 0 521 35505 2 (hardback),
with additional supplementary material
Volume Two Part One: From c. 1800 to the 1930s
ISBN 0 521 66371 7 (paperback)
Volume Two Part Two: From World War II to the present
ISBN 0 521 66372 5 (paperback)
These two volumes contain the contents of 0 521 35506 0 (hardback),
with additional supplementary material

The set of four paperbacks, containing the complete contents of *The Cambridge History
of Southeast Asia*, ISBN 0 521 77864 6 (paperback).

Typeface Palatino 10/11 pt. *System* Penta [MT]

A catalogue record for this book is available from the British Library

National Library of Australia Cataloguing in Publication data
The Cambridge history of Southeast Asia.
Bibliography.
Includes index.
ISBN 0 521 66369 5 (Volume One Part One).
ISBN 0 521 66370 9 (Volume One Part Two).
ISBN 0 521 66371 7 (Volume Two Part One).
ISBN 0 521 66372 5 (Volume Two Part Two).
ISBN 0 521 77864 6 (set).
1. Asia, Southeastern – History. I. Tarling, Nicholas.
959

ISBN 0 521 66370 9 paperback

Transferred to digital printing 2004

CONTENTS

MAPS

NOTE ON SPELLING

The spelling of proper names and terms has caused editor and contributors considerable problems. Even a certain arbitrariness may have not produced consistency across a range of contributions, and that arbitrariness contained its own inconsistencies. In general we have aimed to spell place-names and terms in the way currently most accepted in the country, society or literature concerned. We have not used diacritics for modern Southeast Asian languages, but have used them for Sanskrit and Ancient Javanese. We have used pinyin transliterations except for some names which are well known in English in the Wade–Giles transliteration.

NOTE ON GENDER IN SOUTHEAST ASIAN LANGUAGES

Southeast Asian languages do not distinguish the sexes in general. Many references to individuals or groups of people in ancient indigenous sources leave it unclear whether women are meant or included. For example, we usually do not know whether a certain function is occupied by a male or a female. Even words borrowed from Sanskrit (which has genders corresponding to sex) are sometimes applied without observing this correspondence: Queen Tribhuwanā (sic) or Tribhuwanottungadewī is called *mahārāja* (a masculine word). These languages do not distinguish between brothers and sisters, but they do between younger and older siblings.

There also seems to have been little discrimination between sexes as far as functions are concerned. There were not only queens reigning in their own right in ancient Java, but also 'prime ministers', such as Airlangga's Mahārastrī *i* Hino with a name ending in '-Dewī'. As to Kĕrtanagara's four daughters, it seems that this king had no sons—at least they are never mentioned. Therefore what the sources tell us about the daughters provides no evidence of matrilineal descent. Apparently, both lineages were equally important. In some ways ancient Indonesian society was less 'sexist' than our own still is.

ABBREVIATIONS

AP   *Asian Perspectives*, Honolulu.

BEFEO   *Bulletin de l'École Française d'Extrême-Orient*, Paris.

BIPPA   *Bulletin of the Indo-Pacific Prehistory Association*, Canberra.

BKI   *Bijdragen van het Koninklijk Instituut voor de Taal-, Land- en Volkenkunde*, 's-Gravenhage.

BSOAS   *Bulletin of the School of Oriental and African Studies*, London.

FMJ   *Federation Museums Journal*, Kuala Lumpur.

JAS   *Journal of Asian Studies*, Ann Arbor.

JBRS   *Journal of the Burma Research Society*, Rangoon.

JMBRAS   *Journal of the Malay/Malaysian Branch of the Royal Asiatic Society*, Singapore/Kuala Lumpur.

JRAS   *Journal of the Royal Asiatic Society*, London.

JSEAH   *Journal of Southeast Asian History*, Singapore.

JSEAS   *Journal of Southeast Asian Studies*, Singapore.

JSS   *Journal of the Siam Society*, Bangkok.

MAS   *Modern Asian Studies*, Cambridge, UK.

MQRSEA   *Modern Quaternary Research in Southeast Asia*, Rotterdam.

TBG   *Tijdschrift van het Bataviaasch Genootschap van Kunsten et Wetenschappen*, Batavia/Jakarta.

VKI   *Verhandelingen van het Koninklijk Instituut voor de Taal-, Land- en Volkenkunde*, 's-Gravenhage.

PREFACE TO THE PAPERBACK EDITION

Two ideas came together in the project for a Cambridge History of Southeast Asia. One was the concept of the Cambridge Histories themselves. The other was the possibility of a new approach to the history of Southeast Asia.

In the English-speaking and English-reading world the Cambridge Histories have, since the beginning of the century, set high standards in collaborative scholarship and provided a model for multi-volume works of history. The original *Cambridge Modern History* appeared in sixteen volumes between 1902 and 1912, and was followed by the *Cambridge Ancient History*, the *Cambridge Medieval History*, the *Cambridge History of India* and others.

A new generation of projects continues and builds on this foundation. Recently completed are the Cambridge Histories of Africa, Latin America and the Pacific Islanders. Cambridge Histories of China and of Japan are in progress, as well as the New Cambridge History of India. Though the pattern and the size have varied, the essential feature, multi-authorship, has remained.

The initial focus was European, but albeit in an approach that initially savoured rather of the old Cambridge Tripos course 'The Expansion of Europe', it moved more out of the European sphere than the often brilliant one-author Oxford histories. But it left a gap which that course did not leave, the history of Southeast Asia.

Southeast Asia has long been seen as a whole, though other terms have been used for it. The title Southeast Asia, becoming current during World War II, has been accepted as recognizing the unity of the region, while not prejudging the nature of that unity. Yet scholarly research and writing have shown that it is no mere geographical expression.

There have indeed been several previous histories of Southeast Asia. Most of them have been the work of one author. The great work of the late D. G. E. Hall dates back to 1955, but it has gone through several editions since. Others include B. Harrison, *South-east Asia, A Short History*, London: 1954; Nicholas Tarling, *A Concise History of Southeast Asia*, 1966; and D. J. Steinberg, et al., *In Search of Southeast Asia*, 1971. The authors of these works faced difficult tasks, as a result of the linguistic diversity of the area; the extent of the secondary material; and the lacunae within it.

Given its diversity, Southeast Asia seemed to lend itself to the Cambridge approach. A magisterial single-volume history existed; others had also made the attempt. A single volume by several authors working together had also been successful. But a more substantial history by a larger number of authors had not been attempted.

The past generation has seen a great expansion of writing, but Southeast Asia's historiography is still immature in the sense that some aspects have been relatively well cultivated, and others not. The historical literature on the area has become more substantial and more sophisticated, but much of it deals with particular countries or cultures, and many gaps remain. A range of experts might help to bring it all together and thus both lay the foundation and point the way for further research effort.

The Cambridge approach offered a warning as well as an invitation. There were practical obstacles in the way of histories on the scale of the original European histories. They got out of hand or were never finished. A summation that was also to lead other scholars forward must be published within a reasonable time-span. It must not be too voluminous; it must not involve too many people.

Practical indications of this nature, however, coincided with historiographical considerations. There were some good histories of Southeast Asia; there were also some good histories of particular countries; but there was, perhaps, no history that set out from a regional basis and took a regional approach. This seemed worthwhile in itself, as well as establishing a coherence and a format for the volumes.

In almost every case—even when chapters are the work of more than one person—authors have been taken out of their particular area of expertise. They were ready to take risks, knowing that, whatever care they took, they might be faulted by experts, but recognizing the value all the same in attempting to give an overview. Generally contributors felt that the challenge of the regional approach was worth the hazardous departure from research moorings.

Authors invited to contribute recognized that they would often find themselves extended beyond the span of the published work which has made them well known. The new history did, however, give them a chance—perhaps already enjoyed in many cases in their teaching—to extend into other parts of the region and to adopt a comparative, regional approach. The publishers sought a history that stimulated rather than presented the last word. Authors were the more ready to rely where necessary on published or secondary works, and readers will not expect equally authoritative treatment of the whole area, even if the sources permitted it.

At the same time, the editor and the contributors have had, like any historians, to cope with problems of periodization. That is, of course, always contentious, but particularly so if it seems to result from or to point to a particular emphasis. In the case of Southeast Asia the most likely temptation is to adopt a chronology that overdoes the impact of outside forces, in particular the Europeans. The structure of this history is not free from that criticism, but the contributors have sought, where appropriate, to challenge rather than meekly to accept its implications.

A similar risk is attached to the division of the material into chapters. The scope of a work such as this makes that all the more difficult but all the more necessary. Sometimes the divisions appear to cut across what ought to be seen as a whole, and sometimes repetition may result. That has been allowed when it seemed necessary. But it may still be possible to pursue certain themes through the book and not to read it merely in chronological sequence. Within the four major chronological divisions, chapters are in general organized in a similar order. The work may thus in a sense be read laterally as well as horizontally.

Some topics, including treatment of the arts, literature and music, have been virtually excluded. The focus of the work is on economic, social, religious and political history. But it will still be difficult to pursue the history of a particular people or country. The work does not indeed promise to offer this; though it offers guidance to those who wish to do this in its apparatus, the footnotes and bibliographic essay to each chapter, the historiographical survey, the list of bibliographies, and the index.

*   *   *

The work was originally published in 1992 in two hardbound volumes. The paperback edition is a reprint in four volumes with minor revisions. While the work in its two-volume format has been quite widely welcomed, it is hoped that the new format will make it more accessible, and in particularly bring it more readily within the reach of those who teach and are taught about the region, as well as those who are simply curious about it. The four paperbacks may stand on their own, though it is also the case that the whole is more than the sum of the parts.

The first volume contains an essay on the historiography of Southeast Asia and Part 1 of the original Volume 1, 'From Prehistory to c. 1500 CE'. The present volume contains Part 2 of the original Volume 1, covering the years c. 1500 to c. 1800. The third paperback covers the region from c. 1800 to the 1930s, and the fourth the period from World War II to the late 1980s. It also contains a bibliography of bibliographies on Southeast Asia.

The periodization of the present volume caused much of the discussion among the contributors when the work was being prepared. That reflected the new approaches that scholars were adopting to what some called the 'early modern' phase and the new research that was inspired by and sustained them. Periodization implies a choice of emphasis, and it was felt that choosing c. 1500 as in some sense a starting-point was to imply, if not to insist, that the advent of the Europeans was so significant that it should form some kind of division in Southeast Asian history. It was argued that more emphasis ought to be placed on the fifteenth century itself, in particular on the impact of the expansion of Chinese trade in the early Ming.

The closing date of the present volume also aroused some discussion among us, and indeed led the editor to seek the contribution of Professor Kathirithamby-Wells. The original scheme again risked over-emphasis on the role of the Europeans, and the eighteenth century took on the overtones of 'decline' that it had acquired in European history and that still survived the earlier revisions of the great Dutch scholar-administrator J. C. van Leur ('On the Eighteenth Century as a Category in Indonesian History', in *Indonesian Trade and Society* The Hague and Bandung: van Hoeve, 1955, pp. 265–89). After the crises of the middle decades, however, this was a period of reconstruction and innovation for the mainland kingdoms, driven partly by competition among them. Island Southeast Asia itself witnessed economic expansion and the Dutch and Spanish realms became more coherent.

The wider debate, to which Professor Kathirithamby-Wells thus contributed, has continued. In part it has focused on the work of another contributor, Anthony Reid. At the time *The Cambridge History of Southeast Asia* was being prepared, he was engaged in his masterly work, *Southeast Asia in the Age of Commerce*, the first volume of which had appeared in 1988, and the second of which was to appear in 1993. That surveyed the whole region by way of major topics, also putting it into a chronological framework that emphasized the impact not only of the economic expansion of the fifteenth century, but also that of the economic decline of the later seventeenth century. For that he adduced a number of reasons, such as changes in the world's economy, perhaps, too, in its climate, the monopolistic pressure exerted by the Dutch Company, and the absolutism of Southeast Asian rulers. He offered an image of 'retreat' on the mainland.

Admiring the completed work, Vic Lieberman yet stressed the risk that it presented as valid for the whole region an interpretation that, stressing the impact of maritime trade, better fitted island Southeast Asia than the mainland: 'the thesis of a seventeenth-century watershed seems to be fundamentally inapplicable to the mainland' ('An Age of Commerce in Southeast Asia? Problems of Regional Coherence', *Journal of Asian Studies* 54, 3, August 1995, p. 801). He did not 'deny the value of regionwide syntheses', however. Indeed he suggested 'that the closest archipelagic analogies to Burmese, Thai and Vietnamese integration can be found in the early history of the Spanish and Dutch colonial systems'. Comparing them, he added, might oblige us 'to lay aside our recent distaste for colonial, as opposed to indigenous history' (pp. 804–5).

Lieberman has pursued this task in an essay entitled 'Mainland-Archipelagic Parallels and Contrasts, c. 1750–1850', which appears in a volume edited by Anthony Reid, *The Last Stand of Asian Autonomies. Responses to Modernity in the Diverse States of Southeast Asia and Korea* (Basingstoke: Macmillan, 1997). In that Reid himself writes on 'a new phase of commercial expansion in Southeast Asia, 1760–1850', while drawing attention to the increased cohesion of the three major mainland states in the period, and their pressure on the intermediate Lao, Shan and Khmer states, rescued only by European intervention in the nineteenth century.

The inclusion of Korea in that volume suggests another thrust in the study of the 'early modern' period, in advancing which Lieberman has again been influential. There were advantages, he argued, in putting the history of the mainland Southeast Asian states in the context of other states in the 'early modern' period. Nor should those states be confined to Asia: the comparisons and contrasts should be on a 'Eurasian' basis. In 1995 the School of Oriental and African Studies at the University of London con- vened a workshop called 'The Eurasian Context of the Early Modern History of Mainland South East Asia, 1400–1800', and revised versions of the contributions appeared in *Modern Asian Studies* 31, 3, 1997. Lieberman's own essay, which the other contributors were invited to critique, was enti- tled 'Transcending East–West Dichotomies: State and Culture Formation in Six Ostensibly Disparate Areas'.

This ambitious endeavour did not amount to dislodging the 'regional' thrust in the study of Southeast Asia, though it related to Lieberman's concern that such a thrust had tended to assimilate the experience of the mainland and the archipelago too closely. It suggested rather that historians and their readers should not allow their concern for the region either to ghettoise its history or to obscure the variety of experiences it contained.

In seeking to 'transcend' the 'East–West dichotomy', it had another positive aspect for the study of Southeast Asia, particularly in this period. The debate among our contributors had itself suggested the persistence of a division between what in the 1950s and 1960s were called, in terms put forward by John de Casparis and John Smail, 'Eurocentric' and 'autonomous' views of Southeast Asian history. Was there a tendency to overplay or to underplay the role of Europeans, particularly in the archipelago, in the first centuries of their presence in the region? The wish to 'transcend' an 'East–West dichotomy' was reinforced by Lieberman's initiative, but it was already under way, as he pointed out. The research of M. A. P. Meilink-Roelofsz, M. C. Ricklefs, Anthony Reid, J. Kathirithamby-Wells, Barbara Watson Andaya, and Leonard Andaya was producing a consensus that, 'while the Portuguese commercial impact was indeed limited, by c. 1700 the Dutch had helped to transform economic and political life, as well as certain aspects of cultural development, in critical sectors of the archipelago' ('Local Integration and Eurasian Analogies: Structuring Southeast Asian History, c. 1350 – c. 1830', *Modern Asian Studies* 27, 3, July 1993, pp. 557–8).

That work is well represented in the present volume, and it has been continued in yet more recent publications. The difficulty in 'transcending' the 'East–West dichotomy' was not merely an attitudinal one: it was also a question of sources. The written data available are mostly European in origin, though not all, as we are reminded by Yoneo Ishii's translations from the *Tosen Fusetsu-gaki* (*The Junk Trade from Southeast Asia* Canberra: Australian National University, and Singapore: Institute of Southeast Asian Studies, 1998); and while, at least in the case of the largest collection, that of the VOC, it is less prejudiced than much of the material offered by the archives of the imperial phase, it is still difficult to avoid adopting a 'Western' view. 'Even when relying primarily on European documents', however, as the Andayas have pointed out, 'some scholars have still been able to discuss the interaction between Europeans and native communities from an indigenous perspective, and to provide significant information concerning the ways in which local societies changed' (Leonard Y. Andaya and Barbara Watson Andaya, 'Southeast Asia in the Early Modern Period: Twenty-Five Years On', *Journal of Southeast Asian Studies* 26, 1, March 1995, p. 95).

In some cases, they add, 'it has been possible to integrate European material with indigenous writings in order to analyze key events and cultural concepts as a basis for understanding the "internal view" ' (p. 95). Their own work has advanced this approach: Leonard Andaya in *The World of Maluku: Eastern Indonesia in the Early Modern Period* (Honolulu: University of Hawaii Press, 1993), and Barbara Watson Andaya in *To Live as Brothers* (Honolulu: University of Hawaii Press, 1993). M. C. Ricklefs has pursued a somewhat similar course. European sources are essential in the study of early modern Javanese history, he argues, though they are but a first step. 'Deeper understanding can only be sought in Javanese sources' (*The Seen and the Unseen Worlds in Java, 1726–1749* Sydney: Allen & Unwin, 1998, p. 345). Without these voices, as Ann Kumar writes, 'any structure we may erect in the name of history is a silent shell, empty of human life' (*Java and Modern Europe* Richmond: Curzon, 1997, p. 4).

In these studies, historians are characteristically enough responding not only to the dictates of their discipline, but also to the wider changes in the society of which they form a part. In a post-Cold War world and in a phase of globalization, it was not surprising that it seemed possible to talk in terms of 'Eurasia'. Nor was it surprising that, as the struggle for national independence receded into the past, it was possible to pursue a more balanced view of the role of the Europeans. The end of the Vietnam War and the reunification of the state have been accompanied and followed by more sophisticated studies of its earlier history. Those have benefited from attempts to balance the 'Confucian' aspects of the state, traditionally emphasized in its historiography, and its 'Southeast Asian' nature. As a result the work of Keith Taylor, Nola Cooke and Li Tana offers us fresh insights into both Trinh and Nguyen Vietnam. The last-named published *Nguyen Cochinchina* in 1998 (Cornell Southeast Asia Program).

During the preparation of *The Cambridge History of Southeast Asia*, we were made aware of the current significance of gender studies. A note in Volume One reproduced on p ix above, pointed out that many references in ancient indigenous sources left it unclear whether women were meant or included. Barbara Watson Andaya has since tried to make some headway with the problem. Her recent articles include 'The Changing Religious Role of Women in Early Modern South East Asia', *South East Asian Research* 2, 2, September 1994, pp. 99–116; 'Women and Economic Change: the Pepper Trade in Pre-Modern Southeast Asia', *Journal of the Economic and Social History of the Orient* 38, 2, 1995, pp. 165–90; and 'From Temporary Wife to Prostitute: Sexuality and Economic Change in Early Modern Southeast Asia', *The Journal of Women's History* 9, 4, February 1998, pp. 11–34.

Nicholas Tarling 1999

FROM c. 1500 TO c. 1800

INTRODUCTION

The second part of this work covers the period from the late fifteenth century to the late eighteenth and early nineteenth centuries of the Common Era. The opening chapter places the region in an international context, affected by changes of which the advent of the Europeans was only one. The three chapters that follow outline the political, economic and social, and religious changes that Southeast Asia underwent. A fifth chapter surveys the region on the eve of the phase in which it came almost entirely under European political control.

In the period 1500–1800 Indians and Chinese, who had visited Southeast Asia since the early Common Era, came in far greater numbers. In the seventeenth century the Japanese became involved in Southeast Asian trade for the first time. But the latest and most formidable arrivals were the Europeans. Chapter 1 deals with the arrival and establishment of these groups in the region. It also deals with the interaction between the foreign and Southeast Asian communities, and the innovations and adaptations that resulted. These included the establishment of European-controlled cities and the emergence of mestizo communities. The chapter also discusses developments in shipbuilding and firearms technology that had important repercussions for Southeast Asian societies.

This period also saw a slow movement towards larger political groupings, which subsequently were to form the basis of modern nation-states. This is the focus of Chapter 2. Neither increased participation in international trade, nor the incursion of the Europeans, necessarily worked against the fragmentation that characterized the region. By 1600 the basis for future consolidation in Siam, Burma and Vietnam had been laid down, and the Spaniards had established a strong position in Luzon and the Visayas. The existence of small units in the island world helped the Dutch. Even the most potentially cohesive island, Java, was divided into distinct spheres.

Many of the economic changes that characterized the period date back, Chapter 3 argues, to the fifteenth century. This is true of the surge in international commerce that lasted into the early decades of the seventeenth century. Whole communities came to engage in cultivating pepper, cloves, cotton, sugar and benzoin, and became dependent on the international market, and large cosmopolitan port-cities emerged. In a region then short of population, the mobilization of labour was crucial. There were sophisticated methods for investing capital in trade and securing an adequate return. But capital and fixed property in private hands enjoyed less security over against the state than in early modern Europe. The need to counter Dutch pressure added to absolutist trends that in the end might be counter-productive. That pressure, and the reaction to it, are to be seen in the context of the economic crisis that marked the mid-seventeenth century in Southeast Asia as elsewhere. From the late seventeenth century, the direct involvement of Southeast Asian states with international commerce diminished. The Chinese communities secured new opportunities.

Chapter 4 takes up the account of religious developments in Southeast Asia from about 1500. European material, particularly from missionary sources, is used to survey indigenous beliefs in areas still in the sixteenth century little touched by world religions. The advance of Islam and Christianity, particularly in the island world, is then discussed. Their adaptation to the local context may be compared with that of Hinduism, Buddhism and Confucianism in the preceding phase. The eighteenth century, a time of disruptive economic and political change, was also a time of renewed religious activity.

Chapter 5 describes the region in the late eighteenth and early nineteenth centuries as it began to be drawn into a new phase of world economic development and of European political aspiration. On the mainland three new dynasties were founded—the Konbaung, the Chakri, and the Nguyen—but their policies and their prospects differed. In Java reaction to growing interference by the Dutch led to the Java War of the 1820s. In the other Indonesian islands their inactivity facilitated British commercial enterprise, in turn stimulating the development of a number of indigenous states, as well as an outbreak of adventurism and marauding. The temporary British occupation of Manila in the 1760s forced the Spaniards to reappraise their policy in the Philippines. The islands were increasingly opened to world trade, and substantial economic and social change resulted.

INTERACTIONS WITH THE OUTSIDE WORLD AND ADAPTATION IN SOUTHEAST ASIAN SOCIETY, 1500–1800

Southeast Asia in the period 1500–1800 witnessed important demographic developments which were to have significant consequences in the region. While the Indians and the Chinese had visited Southeast Asia regularly since the early Christian era, they were now coming in far larger numbers than previously. During the early seventeenth century the Japanese, new to the area, became involved in Southeast Asian trade in order to redress internal economic problems faced by the new Tokugawa shogunate. The newest and most formidable of the foreigners were the Europeans, who were determined to acquire a monopoly of the spice trade. The story of the circumstances which brought these foreign groups to the region and the manner in which they became established is an essential part of Southeast Asian history.

Equally important to the history of this period is the interaction between the foreign and Southeast Asian communities which brought innovations and adaptations in local society. The establishment of the European-controlled city, which created a unique mixture of foreign and indigenous elements in its physical structure, government, economic affairs, and inhabitants, was one such innovation in Southeast Asia. With its European administration and large foreign Asian population, the city presented local inhabitants with the opportunity to observe and participate in new economic activities, to adopt and adapt useful novel ideas, and even to establish sexual liaisons with the foreigners which produced the various types of mestizo or mixed racial/ethnic communities. These mestizo communities flourished in the cities and became the ideal intermediaries, helping to bridge the social, economic, cultural, and technological gaps which divided the foreign groups from the Southeast Asians.

The frequent interaction between Southeast Asians and foreign groups also led to transmission of ideas in shipbuilding and firearms technology. The Southeast Asian boat had evolved through contact with traditions of neighbouring lands, and local shipwrights continued to build new types of ships, modify existing ones, or abandon outdated designs in accordance with their needs. The vastly increased presence of European and foreign Asian shipping in Southeast Asian waters in this period provided the Southeast Asian with an ideal opportunity to learn new foreign shipbuilding techniques and to make crucial decisions regarding the feasibility of competing with particular foreign carriers or warships. The decisions taken were to have important repercussions on Southeast Asia's ability to maintain its dominance in both long-distance and regional trade.

The technology of firearms was introduced to Southeast Asia via China, India, and Turkey, but it was Europe which made the greatest impact on local firearms production in this period. While Southeast Asians had learned to manufacture their own cannon, handguns, and gunpowder, they and the rest of the world were left in the wake of the European as a result of a technological revolution in the late seventeenth century which took the European to the forefront in firearms technology. The Southeast Asians on the whole attempted to incorporate the latest ideas, but cultural factors hindered a total adoption of the new technology. An added obstacle was the policy of the European governments in Asia to deny outsiders access to this information, thereby reducing Southeast Asia's ability to maintain the pace of change.

This, then, is a story of certain innovations and adaptations which occurred in Southeast Asia as a result of the interactions between foreign groups and the local inhabitants between 1500 and 1800. The Southeast Asians received foreign groups with their new ideas, and they adopted and adapted those ideas which best suited their purposes. In the past such an approach had always been appropriate, and in this period there was little reason to believe that a selective response would not once again prove successful in strengthening and enriching Southeast Asian society.

THE COMING OF FOREIGN GROUPS

The Asians

Throughout their long trade and cultural relations, China has always regarded Southeast Asia as inferior in status. China was the Middle Kingdom, the Centre of the Universe, the superior and self-sufficient civilization. The non-Chinese 'barbarian' races sought contact with China to receive its beneficence in the form of knowledge and material goods. Objects from the outside world could therefore be regarded only as 'tribute', while reciprocal goods in exchange from the Chinese emperor were seen as 'gifts'. In keeping with this state philosophy, all foreign trade was entrusted to the Ministry of Ritual Affairs (Li bu). Chinese imperial governments actively discouraged the movements of their traders to foreign lands and regarded overseas trade as 'tributary trade', a concept which had originally applied to China's relations with its nomadic neighbours but later extended to all foreign groups. Soon after 1433, the date of the last of seven vast overseas expeditions known as the 'Ming voyages', the Ming emperors turned away from the sea and enforced a policy in which 'not even a little plank was allowed to drift to the sea'.[1] The state-initiated expeditions ended, and all overseas trade was placed under a ban, not to be lifted until 1567.

Despite the periodic central government decrees forbidding such trade, the southeastern provinces of Fujian, Guangdong, and Zhejiang were not significantly hampered in their traditional participation in overseas commerce. Fujian had been engaged in this trade since the ninth century and was the first to establish large settled communities in the 'Nanyang' ('Southern Ocean', the term used to refer to Southeast Asia). Quanzhou, the centre for Fujianese maritime enterprises between the ninth and the fifteenth centuries, was supplanted by Yuegang in Zhangzhou prefecture (later renamed Haicheng, as a new administrative seat in 1567) in the late fifteenth century, and in turn was displaced by Amoy (Xiamen) between the mid-seventeenth and the eighteenth centuries. Fujian's prominent role in overseas ventures was due to the availability of capital derived from land and labour from a large lineage organization. Prominent local families with capital from their landed estates usually funded a junk and would hire a relative or servant to become managing 'partner' to undertake the risky overseas journey. While the shipowner held the largest part of the investment on the ship, all the crewmen were also given the opportunity to join the partnership (*gongsi*). Others were consigned space on the ship for their goods in a commenda system. It was commonplace to regard the crew as merchants first and sailors second. Rural poverty, particularly after the mid-sixteenth century, was also a contributing factor in forcing many Fujianese to go abroad, and by the beginning of the seventeenth century they were found in increasing numbers in the Philippines, Japan, and the Indonesian areas. Canton (Guangzhou) in Guangdong province and Ningbo in Zhejiang were two other ports which played an important role in China's overseas trade.

The Eastern (*Dongyang*) and Western (*Xiyang*) Seas trade system was initiated in Fujian in 1567. At Yuegang passes were awarded annually to the overseas trade guild (*yanghang*) that outfitted junks which took one of two routes. The Western Seas route went along the Southeast Asian mainland coast from Vietnam to the Malay peninsula and ended at the entrepôt of Banten in west Java. The Eastern Seas route went via Japan, the Ryukyus, the Philippines, and the Indonesian islands and had its principal terminus in Manila. In the early seventeenth century the system was disrupted by the cruisers of the Vereenigde Oost-Indische Compagnie (VOC, the Dutch East India Company) which made the waters off Manila unsafe, attacked the Fujian coast, and blockaded Banten.

The disturbances created by Dutch activity on the China coast provided the opportunity in 1629 for an ex-pirate Zheng Zhilong to gain the favour of the provincial authorities and eventually control Fujian's overseas

---

[1] Leonard Blussé, 'Chinese commercial networks and state formation in Southeast Asia', paper presented to the Conference on Southeast Asia from the Fifteenth to the Eighteenth Centuries, Lisbon, December 1989, 3.

shipping. When the Manchus began their conquest of China, the south under the dominance of the Zheng, including the famous 'Coxinga' (Zheng Chenggong), remained loyal to the Ming and continued to trade to Southeast Asia. Nevertheless, there was a marked drop in the numbers of junks arriving in the region, which forced the Chinese trade agents already settled in Southeast Asia to adapt to local economic networks in order to survive. Many of those who had settled in Batavia after 1619 were forced to move either to the northern coastal towns of Java to continue their former intermediary functions, or to the interior to become tax farmers.

With the end of Ming resistance in 1683, the new Manchu Qing dynasty adopted a more positive attitude toward overseas trade which lasted for over a century and led to greater co-operation between the merchants and state officials. The desire for security and 'maritime defence' encouraged the Qing dynasty to lift the maritime ban in 1684. They realized that places such as Fujian were dependent on international trade for their livelihood, and maritime security could be jeopardized by discontented coastal provinces. It was this security factor, rather than the ideological reasons of trade with the outside world, which was the reason for the promulgation and the rescinding of bans on overseas activities.

The return of Chinese trade and migration led to the opening of Batavia's Ommelanden where the Chinese became involved in agriculture, especially in the establishment of sugar plantations. Those who had earlier moved to the north Javanese coasts and the interior of Java helped to monetize Java's economy, with the most prominent even becoming part of the nobility in the northern coastal towns. The Fujianese were joined in this period by those from Chaozhou and Quanzhou, with the former becoming involved in the lucrative Siamese rice trade and in building junks in Ayutthaya because of the lack of suitable timber in their home region. Their ships also brought large numbers of Hakka migrants to Southeast Asia. The increased emigration from China was a major factor in the imperial authorities' decision in 1717 to impose yet another ban on overseas trade. But this ban was a failure at the very outset: trade to Vietnam was barely affected and that to the Indonesian islands was resumed after five years. The ban was thus officially withdrawn in 1727. The lifting of the ban saw the resumption of Chinese trade and migration to Southeast Asia and the involvement of Chinese in new ventures. There were those who established gambir plantations in Riau, and others who opened tin mines on Bangka and the Malay peninsula and gold mines in Borneo. With these new enterprises Chinese settlements began to sprout in the interior, as well as in the coastal towns.

After the establishment of Spanish Manila in 1571, it became one of the principal destinations for Chinese migrants, with an estimated 630 junks arriving from southern China in the first thirty years. By 1586 the Chinese population of 10,000 dwarfed the approximately 800 Spaniards and Mexican creoles in the city. The growing disparity in numbers caused the Spanish authorities grave concern and so they created a separate Chinese quarter, known as the Parian, within the Spanish walled city, the Intramuros. After the old Parian was burned down, a new one was built in 1595 outside the walls for security reasons. The numbers of Chinese continued to grow despite massacres in 1603, 1639, 1661 and 1686, and in a number of other 'reprisals'. Attempts by the Spanish authorities after 1603 to limit the numbers of Chinese to 6000 through legislation proved unsuccessful, and by 1750 the Chinese population had risen to 40,000.

Batavia, founded by the Dutch East India Company in 1619, came to harbour another major concentration of overseas Chinese in Southeast Asia. It was the policy of the Company from the outset to attract a large population of Dutch freeburghers and Chinese. The former failed to come in sufficient numbers, and the Chinese were at first brought from coastal areas of China and from the northern Javanese port cities where Chinese communities had been established in earlier centuries. In 1620 junks began to arrive from China depositing hundreds of migrants, and with the resumption of China's official trade to Southeast Asia in 1683, the numbers of junks arriving annually in Batavia's roadstead grew from an average of three or four to about twenty. Many who came were illegal immigrants who were landed on the islands or isolated coastlines near Batavia and eventually found their way to northern Javanese ports. The new Chinese migrants were primarily from Amoy, Canton, Zhenhai, and Ningbo.

While the Dutch found the Chinese to be ideal settlers because of their diligence and ability to fulfil a great variety of tasks, they feared the sizeable Chinese population which dwarfed the European presence. Between 1680 and 1740 the Chinese population in Batavia doubled, with the Chinese accounting for 20 per cent of the total population or 50 per cent of the non-slave population. The office of Kapitan China was created by the Dutch in 1619 to administer the Chinese population, but the spectacular growth of the Chinese population in Batavia eventually led to the creation of other Chinese officials called 'lieutenants' and 'secretaries' to assist the Kapitan. By 1740 there were one captain and six lieutenants holding office in Batavia.

The third major area of Chinese concentration in Southeast Asia was in Siam, in the royal capitals of Ayutthaya, then Thonburi, and finally Bangkok. In the seventeenth century the Chinese lived both within the walls of Ayutthaya and outside. The Chinese quarter was located in the southeast corner of the city, while outside the walls the Chinese were concentrated to the south and the east. Only the Chinese and the Muslim trading communities had any substantial population in the city, and two of the finest streets ran through their quarters. Along these streets were the major public market and more than 100 two-storey houses of stone or brick with tiled roofs, which contrasted sharply with the vast majority of other buildings of bamboo and thatch. The Chinese community was so numerous that unlike the other foreign communities it had two leaders called *kapitan*, or by the Siamese noble title of *nai*. In addition to being traders and merchants, the Chinese were pig-breeders, artisans, physicians, and actors, with a fortunate few even becoming Siamese court officials.

The Chinese had a very favourable position in Siam because they were outside the system by which all freedmen (*phrai*) were registered in a specific district under a lord or noble (*nai*) and thus liable for corvée labour. The Chinese were therefore able to use the Siamese royal capital as a base and move freely throughout the country or go overseas and engage in trade or become wage-labourers. They came to manage successful commercial enterprises and were employed by the rulers to collect taxes or to run government enterprises, such as tin-mining and state overseas trade. Since the bulk of the latter trade was with China, the Siamese court used Chinese as port officials, captains and navigators of royal junks, and purchasers and sellers of overseas consignments for the king and the nobility. In addition to the offical tribute trade, Chinese merchants resident in Siam and China conducted an 'unofficial' trade by supplying products for the royal trade to China and assuring the delivery of tribute gifts to the Siamese court from the Malay vassal kingdoms. The most prominent Chinese came to serve as court officials in the Sino-Siamese tributary trade on behalf of the Ayutthaya court. Although such practices were condemned by the Chinese emperor elsewhere, he tolerated the Chinese serving the Siamese ruler as *Ratakusa-tibodi* (individuals charged with outfitting the royal junks for trade), interpreters, shipmerchants, shipmasters, and crewmen in the tributary trade.

When Taksin, the son of a Teochiu father and a Thai mother, was formally crowned in Thonburi in 1768, he was assisted by many Chinese from his father's home area of Chaozhou. Their trade provided the food and other resources necessary for Taksin to build his new capital at Thonburi on the Chao Phraya and to overcome the challenges of other Thai groups for dominance after the fall of Ayutthaya in 1767. Once Taksin was firmly in control, the Chinese helped to stimulate the local economy with their gold and silver and through their international trade. In recognition of their role, Taksin created a privileged group known as the *chin luang*, or 'royal Chinese', whose role was perhaps modelled after the *huangshang* or emperor's merchants in China. He relied on them to deal not only with commercial matters but also with political and military affairs. Along the Gulf of Thailand and in peninsular Siam, Taksin appointed *chin luang* as tax farmers, provincial governors, and military commanders.

A great advantage of the Chinese as royal trade agents was their familiarity with and acceptance into international Chinese commercial circles. Through their knowledge of the China market, their personal links with the mercantile groups in southeastern China, and concessions made by Chinese authorities to Chinese sailors and Chinese-style vessels whatever the ultimate ownership of the ship or the cargo, the Chinese became indispensable to the Siamese élite for the China trade. Since those Chinese who served as officials of the state automatically became incorporated into the Siamese system of ranking based on 'dignity marks' (*sakdina*), the Chinese provided with the position of 'captain' of a trade vessel or of a tax farm achieved sufficient marks to be classified as nobility. In the late eighteenth century Chinese headmen in lower Siam were given clientships by Rama I with equivalent powers to an autonomous ruler.

While Manila, Batavia, and Ayutthaya-Thonburi-Bangkok became the three major centres of overseas Chinese populations in Southeast Asia, Vietnam through propinquity and historical circumstances continued to be a focus of Chinese activity in this period. The port of Fai-fo (present-day Hoi An) was a major trading centre in South Vietnam in the early seventeenth century and consisted of two settlements, one Japanese and the other Chinese. By 1695 the Chinese were still prominent, serving the ten to twelve Chinese junks which arrived annually from Japan, Canton, Siam, Cambodia, Manila and Batavia. The Japanese, on the other hand, had disappeared from Vietnam and from many other parts of Southeast Asia, ending their short but spectacular involvement in the economic affairs of the region.

Toward the middle of the sixteenth century the continuous civil wars which had wracked Japan were coming to an end, and many of the lords (daimyo) began to devote their energies to overseas trade. The development of the domestic economy and the growth of towns gave birth to a wealthy class of merchants who also began to invest in international commerce. The first Tokugawa shogun, Ieyasu, encouraged foreign trade as a means of strengthening the finances of the shogunate. Japanese ships carrying the shogun's red seal increased in numbers in Southeast Asia, and they were welcomed by local rulers because they bore personal letters and gifts from the shogun himself. Between 1600 and 1635 more than 350 Japanese ships went overseas under the Red Seal permit system. They called into approximately nineteen ports, including Vietnam, Cambodia, the islands in the Malay-Indonesian archipelago, and Luzon in the Philippines. A measure of the importance of this Japanese trade was their export of silver. Between 1615 and 1625 an estimated 130,000–160,000 kilograms of silver was sold, amounting to 30–40 per cent of the total world output outside Japan.[2]

The Japanese were especially prominent in Ayutthaya, and by the late 1620s the trade between Siam and Japan was probably greater than Siam's total trade with other nations. Japanese sources indicate that between 1604 and 1616 some thirty-six Japanese ships issued with the official Red Seal permit were destined for Siam, the highest number authorized for any single country in those years A large colony of Japanese came to settle in Ayutthaya, with 1000–1500 living in the Japanese quarter of the city. King Sontham (r. 1620–8) had a personal Japanese bodyguard, and the Japanese adventurer Yamada came to wield considerable influence in the Siamese court. But in 1632 the new Siamese ruler Prasat Thong (r. 1629–56) massacred many of the Japanese in the city and forced others to flee the country. Thereafter the Chinese regained their dominance in the Siamese trade.

Between 1633 and 1636 the Tokugawa shogunate gradually closed Japan to foreign traders, but the links between Japan and Southeast Asia, especially Siam, remained open. Between 1647 and 1700 some 130 Siamese ships arrived at Nagasaki, and though the Siamese in 1715 were limited to one junk a year, it was a privilege denied many other nations. Other Southeast Asian areas benefited from Tokugawa policy which divided foreigners into three groups: the Chinese (To-jin), the Catholic Europeans, i.e. the Spaniards and Portuguese (Nanban-jin), and the Protestant Dutchmen (Kōmōi-jin, lit. 'red-haired people'). Among the To-jin was a special category for areas of Southeast Asia known as 'inner ports' (Okuminato). Ships

[2] Iwao Seiichi, 'Japanese foreign trade in the sixteenth and seventeenth centuries', *Acta Asiatica*, 30 (1976) 10.

from such places as Tonkin, Cambodia, Ayutthaya, Nakhon Sithammarat, Songkhla, Pattani, Melaka, and Batavia were therefore able to maintain trade with Japan.[3] One important consequence of Tokugawa policy forbidding Japanese abroad from returning home was the gradual amalgamation of the Japanese community into Southeast Asian society.

A third important foreign Asian group in Southeast Asia in this period was the Indians. Like their Chinese counterparts, the Indians had been trading to Southeast Asia since the early Christian era and had left a lasting impact on local culture. Indian overseas commercial ventures were mainly in private hands, since Indian states relied on agricultural production and internal commerce for their revenue. Nevertheless, there was considerable individual investment in overseas trade by rulers, administrators, and military officials who were content to leave control in the hands of merchants.

The high cost of building a ship and of obtaining a full cargo, as well as the danger of losing all through shipwreck, discouraged most merchants from purchasing more than one ship. Although an owner-merchant could go with his ship and cargo overseas, he usually appointed an agent to captain the vessel and to undertake all the necessary commercial transactions. The owner-merchant and the captain were allotted the largest cargo space, while the rest of the ship was parcelled out to small traders who accompanied their one or two bales of cotton cloth in the hope of gaining profit overseas. These smaller merchants were able to compete effectively alongside the few wealthier ones because they were satisfied with a lower profit margin and were able to establish their own personal networks in foreign ports. The ubiquity of the Indian trader, which so impressed Tomé Pires and other Portuguese observers in the sixteenth century, was a consequence of the practice of Indian ships bringing large numbers of these small Indian merchants with their goods. The sailors and ship's officers were also provided with space to carry trade goods which were sold abroad to supplement their wretched incomes. Unlike the Chinese, however, the Indians did not settle in large numbers in Southeast Asia in this period.

The vast majority of Indian traders to Southeast Asia came from three regions: the northwest (Gujerat), the south (Malabar and Coromandel), and the northeast (Bengal). In these areas there were a few major emporia serving as collection centres for a large well-developed inland trading system, while small individual ports serviced small specific interior trade networks. The importance of Gujerat lay in the strategic location of its ports lying at the confluence of a number of trading systems. Cambay in the sixteenth, Surat in the seventeenth, and Bombay in the eighteenth century linked the oceanic regional trade of Asia with the coastal and interior trade of India. Through links with the Portuguese ports of Goa and Diu, Gujerat became part of an international trade network which extended to China in the east and Europe in the west.

South India was a second major centre for Indian overseas trade. It was pepper which had made the Malabar coast attractive to international

---

[3] Yoneo Ishii, 'Seventeenth Century Japanese Documents about Siam', JSS, 59, 2 (July 1971) 164–5.

traders, and by the beginning of the seventeenth century the ports of Calicut, Travancore, and Cannanore had emerged as commercial centres. However, the Coromandel coast in southeast India proved to be even more successful in international trade than Malabar. Masulipatnam in the northern Coromandel and Nagapattinam in the southern Coromandel were the most prominent trading centres in that region. In the sixteenth century Coromandel Hindu traders, called 'Klings' by the Portuguese, frequented the ports of Portuguese Melaka, Aceh, and Banten where they had factors and agents. From these western ports they then sailed westward to the other islands in the Indonesian archipelago. Coromandel trade suffered from Dutch restrictions in the seventeenth century, but Perak, Kedah, and Johor on the Malay peninsula continued to be major terminal points of the Coromandel trade. In mainland Southeast Asia, the Coromandel merchants were active in Arakan, Ava, and Ayutthaya, with Tenasserim serving as a terminal for Mergui and a transit point to the ports on the Gulf of Thailand and Cambodia. Ayutthaya and its outlying provinces became a major growth sector in the Coromandel trade in the seventeenth century.

The decline in Coromandel's trade began in the final decade of the seventeenth century with the fall of the Qutb Shahs of Golconda. The nobility and the patrician merchants appear to have abandoned overseas commerce, and Masulipatnam in northern Coromandel survived with only a reduced amount of international trade. In southern Coromandel Porto Novo, the successor to Nagapatnam, San Tomé, and Cuddalore became the chief ports of the principal Tamil Muslim traders known as 'Chulias'. They reaffirmed links with the rulers of Kedah, Johor, Arakan and Ayutthaya, which had been forged in earlier centuries.

Bengal was the third major Indian area involved in Southeast Asia. In the sixteenth century Satgaon and Chittagong were the two major ports from which Bengal merchants sailed to the Southeast Asian areas, but in the seventeenth century they were replaced by Hooghly, Pipli and Balasore. Bengal's trade was directed principally to Aceh, the Malay peninsula, and to the Burmese and Thai coasts. The Bengal Muslim merchants who were prominent in this trade in the seventeenth century consisted of influential expatriate merchants from west Asia, and possibly from Surat and Golconda, as well as local Islamic communities who were converts from Hindu seafaring castes. Hindu merchants were also an important part of the Bengal trade, though they were less influential than the Muslims. As in the other areas of India, Bengal witnessed a decline in its overseas trade toward the end of the seventeenth century due to the political and economic chaos in the interior.

The Europeans

In addition to the foreign Asians, the Europeans formed another substantial presence in Southeast Asia between 1500 and 1800. The new European traders had a distinct advantage over their more established and more experienced Asian counterparts because they enjoyed support from their governments. Indeed, the earliest European ventures were those initiated

and funded by the Portuguese and Spanish royal houses, with the former
the first to undertake a systematic policy of finding a direct sea route
between Europe and the spice-producing areas of Asia. Since the fourteenth century Portuguese rulers had encouraged the successful trading
families of Italy, Spain and France to settle in Lisbon by granting them
special privileges. This policy succeeded in making Portugal the 'wharf
between two seas',[4] serving both the northern European and the Mediterranean states. By the end of the century there were an estimated 400–500
ships loading annually in the port of Lisbon. The enclaves of Genoese,
Venetians, Florentines, Flemings, French, and Germans established in
Portugal provided the expertise and capital which encouraged the Crown
to expand its trade links beyond Europe.

A major impetus for overseas expansion was the trade in spices—
pepper, cinnamon, and the highly-desired trinity of clove, nutmeg, and
mace. In the second half of the fifteenth century, Turkish control of the
Levant forced the traditional spice routes to move away from the Persian
Gulf to the Red Sea. The desire to escape this dependence on the Muslims
(an association which in Portugal had been strictly limited by law and
constantly condemned by the Church) and to participate directly in the
highly lucrative spice trade were important stimuli in Portugal's gradual
search for a sea route to Asia. In the first half of the fifteenth century Prince
Henry the Navigator encouraged a systematic programme of discovery,
which culminated in Vasco da Gama's successful voyage to the west coast
of India in 1498. The arrival in Asia was the culmination of Portugal's
'Glorious Enterprise' which had been motivated by a blend of religious
fervour, national pride, and commercial profit. Though the Portuguese had
not yet reached the home of the fabled clove, nutmeg, and mace in Maluku,
da Gama's cargo of spices 'together with the boughs and leaves of the
same' aroused considerable excitement in Portugal. To keep the new route
a secret, King Manuel of Portugal decreed in 1504 that, on pain of death,
complete secrecy must be maintained with regard to the new discoveries.
This ban appeared to have been successful, for not a single book on the
new information being collected on Asia by the Portuguese is known to
have been published during the first fifty years of the sixteenth century.

Affonso de Albuquerque became the architect of the Portuguese Asian
empire, or the *Estado da India*, with its administrative centre at Goa. It was
he who conceived of the strategy to control the vital nodes of the spice
route. This meant seizing Melaka, the principal collecting port of cloves,
nutmeg, mace, and Southeast Asian pepper; controlling maritime traffic
along the west coast of India; capturing Hormuz at the mouth of the
Persian Gulf; and conquering Aden, which was strategically located at
the entrance to the Red Sea. This grand plan nearly succeeded: the island
of Goa fell in 1510, to be followed by Melaka in 1511 and Hormuz in 1515.
Only Aden successfully resisted a Portuguese attack in 1513 and remained
outside direct Portuguese control.

The Portuguese Crown created a unique form of state capitalism. It

---

[4] B. W. Diffie and G. D. Winius, *Foundations of the Portuguese empire 1415–1580*, Minneapolis,
1977, 41.

became the sole entrepreneur investing the state's resources to create a trade monopoly in its overseas territories. The Crown monopoly in spices continued in Melaka until 1533 and in Maluku until 1537. But long before this time, the profitability of Crown capitalism was being questioned, and even the Crown began to realize that a steady fixed income free from the vagaries of the marketplace and the venality of its own people was desirable. Thus began the practice of granting concessions to individuals as rewards to buy and sell certain quantities of spices, with the only requirement being that they resell to the Crown one-third of the cargo at a fixed price. If the goods were transported in state ships, then an additional percentage of the freight had to be paid to the Crown. By the second half of the sixteenth century voyages were made in ships owned by the concessionaries themselves, with no royal expense involved.

The Crown trade, including the concessions awarded to various individuals by the king, was only one part of the Portuguese Asian commercial picture. Portuguese private trade was also able to prosper because it relied on products and exchange networks within the Asian region itself. The Portuguese never succeeded in finding a European product which was in demand in Asia, except for gold and silver and armaments, and they lacked the resources to control the existing production system in Asia. They therefore learned to participate in the Asian trade, quickly identifying Indian cloth as the essential item of exchange in the Southeast Asian area. Like the Asian traders, the Portuguese became involved in the peddling trade; they carried goods from port to port, buying, selling, and reselling, and creating profit in each transaction. The transition to the peddling trade was facilitated and even encouraged by the advice and assistance provided by rich Asian merchants residing in ports under Portuguese control.

Portuguese private trade operated in secondary ports of Southeast Asia and complemented the Crown and concessionary trade located in the major stapling centres of Goa, Melaka, and Macao. Private Portuguese merchants were mentioned in Timor in 1522, north coast Java in 1532, with a further 300 trading between Melaka and China and another 300 based in Pattani. Of the eight or nine Portuguese ships in the mid-sixteenth century sailing annually to Coromandel to purchase cloth, only one belonged to the Crown. By the fourth decade of the sixteenth century, Portuguese trade had to all intents and purposes become a part of the Asian system.

In comparison to that of the Portuguese, the Spanish enterprise in Asia was a modest affair, confined almost exclusively to the Philippines. It was very much in the shadow of the Spanish empire in the Americas, being under the direct jurisdiction of the Viceroyalty of Nueva España (New Spain, present-day Mexico). The earliest Spanish contact with Asia was in March 1521 when Magellan's expedition reached the Philippines. Though Magellan himself was killed at Mactan, his crew continued the journey to Maluku and eventually to Spain in 1522, thereby becoming the first to have successfully circumnavigated the globe. The return of the expedition revived the Spanish rulers' dream of reaching Maluku and monopolizing the lucrative trade in spices. Unfortunately, at the time that the expedition reached the Spice Islands, they learned that the Portuguese had been there since 1512. Despite Spain's attempts to include Maluku in its sphere of influence through the Treaty of Tordesillas of 1494, circumstances in Europe forced it to 'relinquish' its claims to Maluku in return for a payment of 350,000 cruzados by Portugal.

For the remainder of the sixteenth century, Spanish initiatives in Asia originated in the viceregal office in Nueva España and only indirectly from the Spanish Crown. In 1542 an expedition was outfitted from Mexico under the command of Ruy López de Villalobos. It was directed to go to the Islas del Poniente, or the Western Islands, a name which navigators after Magellan had given to the Philippine islands. Magellan himself had christened these islands 'San Lazaro' because he had sighted them on that saint's day, and it was Villalobos who honoured the Crown Prince Felipe of Spain by renaming the islands of Samar and Leyte in the Visayas, Felipinas, or the Philippines, a name which was later applied to the entire archipelago. Villalobos was instructed not to violate the arrangements with Portugal, but to investigate the products of the Western Islands. But this expedition, like those which went before, ended in failure.

In November 1564 another expedition of five ships and more than 400 men under the command of Miguel Lopez de Legazpi set sail from Natividad in Mexico with instructions to occupy the Philippine islands. Legazpi was ordered to

> sail with God's blessings to the Western Islands; not to Maluku . . . which according to existing agreements fall under the jurisdiction of the King of Portugal, but to other islands nearby such as the Philippines which lie within the demarcation of the King and are also rich in spices. The main purposes of this expedition are . . . the conversion of the natives and the discovery of a safe route back to Nueva España, that the kingdom may increase and profit from trade and by other legitimate means.[5]

From the outset of the Philippine venture, the Christianization of the natives was regarded as one of the most important priorities of the Spaniards.

Though the profit motive was still prominent, the economic prospects of the Philippines as a colony appeared to Legazpi to be bleak. The only marketable spice was cinnamon, which grew in the hostile Muslim-dominated island of Mindanao. The amounts available were not sufficient to sustain a Pacific trade with the Americas, and there was only a small quantity of gold. Furthermore, the natives were too poor to provide a ready market for manufactured products. In short, Legazpi informed the Spanish monarch that the Philippine colony could not be sustained by trade. But once the Spanish authorities in the Philippines had time to observe the local and international trade being conducted around them, they realized that there was in fact great potential for Spanish participation in the thriving economic link between these islands and China.

The move of the Spanish government from Cebu to Manila in 1571 was a decisive step in the establishment of direct trade ties between the Spaniards and the Chinese. By 1576 the Chinese were frequenting the port of

[5] Rafael Lopez, trans., *The Christianization of the Philippines*, Manila, 1965, document 5, 262.

Manila as they had done in pre-Hispanic times, but this time dealing with the Spaniards rather than with their former local trading partners. It was Legazpi who first suggested that a trade in Chinese silk could perhaps replace the loss of the trade in spices to the Portuguese. Thus began the galleon trade, where merchants from Macao brought Canton silk, cotton cloths, and other wares to waiting merchants from Acapulco, who offered their silver from the American colonies in exchange. So valuable was this Macao–Manila–Acapulco trade that the Spanish merchants from Nueva España settled in Manila in order to be able to supervise operations and assure the proper loading of the Chinese goods on the large Spanish galleons. The best years of the galleon trade were the last decades of the sixteenth and the first decades of the seventeenth century. In the peak year of 1597, the amount of bullion sent from Acapulco to Manila reached a total of twelve million pesos, a figure exceeding the total value of the official trans-Atlantic trade, although the normal value of the trade was still an impressive three to five million pesos. Despite the later restriction of a single galleon leaving annually from each of the two ports, the galleon trade remained a dominant force in the Spanish–Philippine economy until the late eighteenth century and was abandoned only in 1815.

The Philippines never provided Spain with the fabulous riches which it received from the gold and silver mines in America. But it was perhaps because Philip II of Spain was able to rely on a steady source of revenue from the Americas that he was willing to tolerate the losses sustained in the Philippines and magnanimously offer to make it 'the arsenal and warehouse of the faith'.[6] With this pronouncement the religious aspect of the colonization now took indisputable precedence in the Philippines. Restrictions on Spanish travel to the interior, because of the perceived dangers of a hostile population and environment, led the authorities to rely increasingly on the clergy to help govern and prepare the inhabitants in the interior for the acceptance of the 'Spanish' religion and state. Though the numbers of regular and secular clergy were not very high— perhaps some 400 in the whole of the Philippines during the sixteenth and seventeenth centuries—their leadership in both spiritual and secular affairs was a crucial factor in the maintenance of Spanish control.

Neither the Portuguese nor the Spanish economic efforts in Asia had fulfilled the early promise of fabulous riches from the East. Learning from their experience, the northern Europeans came to experiment with a new economic form in the hope of succeeding where the Iberian nations had failed. The seventeenth century was to bring the English and the Dutch into the Asian commercial scene and introduce a highly innovative trading idea: the joint-stock company. It had distinct advantages over other commercial ventures because it could maintain large fixed assets, exist beyond shifting groups of investors, and obtain exclusive trading rights from the state.

The English East India Company (EIC) was organized in 1600, two years before the formation of the United Dutch East India Company. It

---

[6] John Leddy Phelan, *The Hispanization of the Philippines: Spanish aims and Filipino responses, 1565–1700*, Madison, 1967, 14.

embodied the spirit of mercantilism in its manipulation of political power and privileges for commercial goals. Nevertheless, the EIC sought to avoid being dominated by the Crown or the aristocracy, even to the point of refusing to approve the membership of James I in 1624. From the beginning the EIC's policy was dictated by its own concerns, rather than those of the state. In like manner the Company's interests had a low priority for the early Stuart kings.

The first English voyages proceeded with great caution, and only after the safe return of each fleet was another outfitted. By the end of the second voyage (1604–6) the English realized that the English goods would not be profitable in the Malay-Indonesian archipelago, and that there needed to be a greater variety of products from Europe. They also learned through experience and through contact with Portuguese traders that Indian piece-goods were essential for any bartering in Southeast Asia. Thus in the third voyage in 1607 the English had instructions to establish trade with Surat or the Red Sea ports before going on to Southeast Asia. On this and subsequent voyages the EIC sought to develop markets for goods for the Europe-to-Asia trade, while seeking sources of Indian piece-goods for the archipelago.

Up to 1612 the English voyages were separately financed, with shareholders participating in a particular expedition. There was no co-operation among English factors handling different voyages, which resulted in a situation where there existed three rival English lodges in Banten. With the proliferation of trading factories in Asia, the EIC decided in 1615 to centralize its operations by placing all factories 'to the Northwards' (Gujerat westward) under Surat and those 'to the Southwards' (Coromandel eastward) under Banten. On the seventh voyage (1611–15) it founded factories at Masulipatnam, at Ayutthaya, and at Pattani. The Thai ruler was only too willing to allow the English to trade in his kingdom as a counter to the ever-growing strength of the VOC. In eastern Indonesia the EIC had successfully opened a factory in the kingdom of Makassar and gained control of the islands of Run and Nailaka in the Banda islands. By its presence in these sites it had obtained access to the cloves, nutmeg, and mace, thereby imperilling the attempted monopoly of these valued spices by the VOC. In 1623 the chief factor of the EIC and others at the English factory in Ambon were killed by the Dutch, ending for over a century any further English involvement in the Spice Islands.

The situation for the English in Batavia, where they had moved from Banten in 1619, became unbearable. In 1628 they finally received instructions to return to Banten where the sultan was said to be eager to have them back. Although the English factories in the Spice Islands, Ayutthaya, Pattani, and Japan were abandoned, the Banten factory continued to receive pepper from the east-coast ports of Sumatra and spices from Makassar. But the tiny English presence in the archipelago, harassed at every turn by the VOC, had little real chance of success. In 1682 the English were forced to abandon Banten, retaining only a small post in Bengkulen in southwest Sumatra. The EIC in effect retreated to the Indian subcontinent and made India its principal area of activity until the middle of the eighteenth century.

Throughout this early period the EIC was often at a disadvantage compared to other European traders. The English government opposed the export of bullion, even though this was the principal means of obtaining goods in Asia. Furthermore, private English trade was allowed to flourish because it was regarded as being complementary to EIC activities. In practice, however, EIC officials and their wives were able to enrich themselves through private trade at the expense of the Company. Finally, the EIC never exercised the degree of centralization of finances and administration in the seventeenth century which was such a prominent feature of its much more efficient rival, the Dutch East India Company.

The expansion of the Dutch into Asia was part of a commercial and technological revolution which transformed the Low Countries from a colony of Spain into one of the leading European nations in the seventeenth century. This 'Golden Century' of the United Provinces of the Netherlands was the culmination of a long process of capital accumulation dating back to the fourteenth century in the herring trade. From the highly successful fisheries, the Baltic trade, the carrying trade, and the much older river trade, the Lowlands accumulated vast capital resources. In addition, persecution of Calvinists by the Spaniards in the southern Netherlands led to an exodus of wealthy merchants and industrialists from Antwerp, Ghent, Brussels, and other cities who brought their riches and expertise to the north, especially to Amsterdam. It was they, with their long experience in the Portuguese enterprise, who were in the forefront in financing new commercial and trade ventures. The combination of capital and expertise enabled the northern Netherlands to become the centre for the leading European financiers.

The readiness of the Dutch to invest in new ventures to Asia was a natural progression in their growing involvement in world trade. The first Dutch fleet to reach the islands of Indonesia was in 1596 when three ships and a yacht anchored off Banten. There then followed similar voyages sponsored by a number of port towns in the Netherlands. In the six years of the 'Wilde Vaarten' (Free Navigation) of these competing companies, the profits made were less than two or at the most three months' profit in the herring fisheries. Nevertheless, the lure of the riches to be made in the spice trade attracted rival companies which threatened to destroy the profitability of the whole venture. Finally, in 1602, after much bargaining and compromising they were persuaded to amalgamate into the United Netherlands Chartered East India Company (Vereenigde Geoctroyeerde Oost-Indische Compagnie, VOC).

The directors of the Company, the *Heeren XVII* (Seventeen Gentlemen), initially instructed the VOC officials in Batavia to avoid unnecessary wars with native kingdoms, especially in 'the neutral places belonging to free nations, where we find the laws and do not have to bring them'.[7] However, under the powerful Governors-General Jan Pieterszoon Coen (1618–23, 1627–9) and Antonio van Diemen (1636–45), the directives of the *Heeren XVII* were generally ignored. In 1619 Coen seized Jayakatra

---

[7] P. Mijer, 'Punten en artikelen, in vorm van Generale Instructie', 26 April 1650, in *Verzameling van instructiën, ordonnaciën en reglementen voor de Regeering van Nederlandsch-Indië*, Batavia, 1848, 89.

(Jakarta) from Banten and established the city of Batavia, which became the VOC headquarters in Asia. He then removed the English from the Banda islands in 1623; the Portuguese from Maluku in 1605, Negombo and Gale in Sri Lanka in 1640, and Melaka in 1641; and the Spaniards from the northern part of Taiwan by 1643 and Maluku in 1663. Since these successes had helped secure the spice monopoly and contributed to the ousting of the English and Portuguese, the *Heeren XVII* raised few objections. Coen's policy of maintaining VOC power by the establishment of forts, garrisons, and warships was generally upheld. But by the second half of the seventeenth century, they were less tolerant of costly wars to enhance trade.

Learning from Portuguese experience, Coen pleaded with the *Heeren XVII* in 1619 for sufficient ships to enable the VOC to participate in the intra-Asian trade. His aim was not to dismantle the Asian peddling trade but to co-ordinate it to the VOC's advantage by retaining ships and capital within Asia, rather than repatriating them as was then the practice. By not issuing dividends to its stockholders in these early years, the VOC was able to preserve its capital in Asia and to create a fleet and a network of factories to participate in the profitable intra-Asian trade.

In addition to the creation of Asian capital, Coen was also instrumental in introducing a system of intelligence-gathering to assist the VOC against its European and Asian competitors. Economic accounts and local political reports were sent regularly to Batavia from Dutch posts throughout the Asian region. Important trade decisions were thus based on an analysis of economic and political intelligence stretching from Europe to the farthest outpost of the VOC trading empire. The VOC would sustain a loss in one area to eliminate a competitor, while making it up in another area by using crucial information on production shortages or political instability. With the VOC ships also becoming the dominant carriers of Asian trade, many kingdoms were dependent on the goodwill of the VOC to assure the continuing export of their products and the import of valued goods.

By 1640 the total VOC capital circulating in Asia, known as the 'Indies Funds', was as much as eight to ten million guilders, which equalled or exceeded the entire Portuguese investment in the pepper trade at its height. But although the sheer size of its investments, personnel and ships had an influence on the Asian peddling trade, the VOC did not displace this trade but simply operated with it. While the Company's organization was superior to the pedlar, its costs were higher. A shrewd pedlar who was satisfied with a smaller profit margin than the Company could operate successfully alongside the Company.

Through the joint-stock company, both the VOC and EIC were able to penetrate the Asian market and make a far greater impact on the local economies than either the Portuguese or Spanish Crown monopolies. Because of the dominance of the VOC, the English Company was never able to compete effectively in Southeast Asia. The VOC, on the other hand, through its Indies Fund, superior freight capacity, and its unique intelligence-gathering system, permanently altered trading patterns and affected the economic and political future of many Southeast Asian societies. Even though most European activities were confined to the coastal regions, frequent intercourse between the coast and the interior in many

Southeast Asian kingdoms meant that even the interior could not long remain insulated from the new ideas and pressures being introduced by the Europeans.

The principal attraction of Southeast Asia to foreign groups had always been the trade in spices and other exotic products. But in the period between 1500 and 1800, many also came to Southeast Asia driven by the higher ideals of national honour and religion, as well as by the more immediate concerns of security and survival. The search for a safe haven for trade and settlement in Southeast Asia was facilitated by the openness of local rulers to outsiders. The result was the establishment of large permanent foreign settlements in Southeast Asia. Many continued to participate in international trade, while others pursued occupations learned in their own lands or developed new skills to cater to the changing Southeast Asian economic landscape.

Because of the size of the foreign communities, especially in the cities of Melaka, Manila, and Batavia, there arose new foci of power which came to challenge the indigenous states in trade, in political influence, and in terms of loyalty from foreign and local groups. What assisted this process was the establishment of the European-controlled city in Southeast Asia. Within the walls, the protected suburbs, and the roadsteads or harbours of these cities, the Southeast Asian could witness the creation of a new urban form; the symbiotic relationship between the European, the Chinese, the mestizo or mixed ethnic group, and the local inhabitants; and the new shipbuilding and firearms technology of the European and the foreign Asians. These developments foreshadowed the type of colonial society which was to emerge in later centuries from the increasing disparity in resources and strength between the Southeast Asians and the foreign groups.

INNOVATIONS AND ADAPTATIONS IN SOCIETY

The European-Controlled City

Between 1500 and 1800 there were three European-controlled cities which attained great prominence in Southeast Asia: Portuguese (and later Dutch) Melaka, Spanish Manila, and Dutch Batavia. They came to symbolize to the Southeast Asian the new and growing importance not only of the Europeans but also the foreign Asians in the area. Though these cities shared a number of similar features, there were also differences which reflected the role which they had been given in the overall goals of their masters in Europe. Portuguese Melaka and Dutch Batavia were entrepôts serving the economic interests of the Portuguese Crown and the share-holders of the Dutch East India Company, respectively. The Portuguese enterprise had a decided religious thrust as a result of the *Padroado Real*, or the Royal Patronage, in which the Papacy had entrusted the conversion of heathen lands to the Portuguese Crown. Nevertheless, ultimately it was the profits from the spice trade which informed the activities of the Portuguese in their factories and customs houses. For the Dutch the establishment of Batavia had one basic purpose: to create a base and headquarters for the expansion of the Company's economic empire in Asia. Batavia also functioned as an entrepôt, but its principal role was to act as the administrative centre and the symbol of the Company's greatness and power in the Asian world. In marked contrast to the Portuguese in Melaka and the Dutch in Batavia, the economic impetus of Manila was clearly subordinated to cultural-religious imperatives, for imperial Spanish policy saw urban centres as a means of transmitting Spanish language, customs, and religion to the heathen worlds of America and Asia. But whatever the ultimate justification for the establishment and maintenance of the European-controlled cities, they served a useful function in providing the Southeast Asians with the opportunity to observe and learn from the activities of the foreigners resident in their midst.

These European-controlled cities occupied sites which were previously thriving local settlements. When the Portuguese fleet under Vasco da Gama first reached Calicut on the west coast of India in 1498, Melaka was already famous as an international emporium. It was located in the sheltered waters of the Straits of Melaka, a major waterway which linked East Asia to India, the Middle East, and Europe. Moreover, it was at the 'end of the monsoons', the winds which brought the traders from the west on the southwest monsoon, and those from the east on the northeast monsoon (see Map 2.2). The Portuguese thus seized the Malay city in 1511 and rebuilt it on the same site for good reason. Manila was already a thriving Muslim trading settlement of 2000 people located at the mouth of the Pasig River when the Spaniards arrived in 1570. Both Manila and the neighbouring settlement of Tondo were linked through Brunei to the international trade network centred in Melaka. The Spaniards' decision to conquer Manila and to use the site for the development of their own centre was based on Manila's established reputation in the trading world and its access to a rich agricultural interior. Batavia, formerly Jayakatra, was under a provincial lord who acknowledged the overlordship of the sultan of Banten. Its location close to the Sunda Straits, the only other opening through the western half of the archipelago, made it an ideal site for the Dutch who were already using the port extensively for their trading ships. Since the Straits of Melaka were closed off to the Dutch by the Portuguese, the former decided in 1619 to take control of Jayakatra, rebuild it as the main headquarters of the Dutch East India Company, and christen it 'Batavia' after the ancestors of the Dutch people.

By rebuilding on established sites, the Europeans were inheriting excellent locations and a trade reputation which they hoped to maintain. At first fortresses and buildings were erected in the native style, using wood, bamboo, and nipa palm thatching. Frequent fires led to a policy of using stone, bricks, and roof-tiles, which resulted in more fire-resistant, durable and imposing edifices. The new physical appearance of the European-controlled cities came to symbolize the strong and seemingly permanent presence of the Europeans in the region. In Manila the Spaniards adopted the grid design which had been used in Mexico City with its well-arranged streets and squares. Around the main plaza (*plaza mayor*) were found the cathedral and the municipal buildings, while in the smaller plaza (*plaza de armas*) were the fort and the royal buildings. The wooden palisades were replaced by a stone fortress at the northwest and southwest corners of the city, and in 1593 the city itself was enclosed by stone walls to form the Intramuros. Within these walls stood the equally grand monuments to the spiritual and secular authorities now ruling in Manila. It was no accident that the stone cathedral in Manila was long the most imposing building in the Philippines, though the sturdy but gracious palaces of the archbishop and the governor-general were also impressive. The hall of the colonial assembly (the *Audiencia*), the monasteries, the churches, and the private homes with their balconies, tiled roofs, inner courts, and iron grilles over windows and entrances, were all testimony to the new power exerting its will over the local landscape.

Batavia, too, underwent physical transformation to satisfy the requirements of security, the comfort of a familiar environment, and a style of architecture which would assert Dutch dominance in the surrounding landscape. The fort built at the mouth of the Ciliwung River was earlier sufficient to house many of the Dutch East India Company's buildings, such as the governor-general's residence, the workshops, the treasury, the garrison, the armoury, the counting houses, the prison, the meeting hall of the Council of the Indies, and the first church. The growth of the Dutch population eventually forced the authorities to create more housing outside the fort. As a result new fortifications were erected in 1645 to enclose the settlements on both the east and west banks of the river. With security ensured, the Dutch undertook to replicate Holland in the East by creating a system of canals (Figure 6.1). The river was straightened to form one large canal, with a number of other smaller canals encircling and criss-crossing the city. Along these canals stood the one- or two-storey brick homes of the more prominent citizens. Among the stone and brick structures, the most impressive was the town hall built in 1710 with its two storeys and large cupola, a fitting tribute to the dominance of the burgher element in the Company and the city.

In Melaka the Portuguese built their stone fortress on the site of the former palace of the exiled Malay sultan and placed a wall around the main centre, forming an Intramuros. Within these walls the large stone fortress dominated the city of mainly wooden and nipa-thatched houses in the first half of the sixteenth century. By the early seventeenth century the city boasted such large stone structures as the cathedral, the churches, the headquarters of the religious orders, the bishop's palace, and the town hall. In the centre was a small hill on which stood the stone church and the towers of St Paul and the Jesuit convent. In Melaka it was the massive fortress which dominated the landscape, an appropriate symbol of Portugal's long and, in the end, fruitless struggle to maintain an official spice monopoly through the use of force. After the VOC conquest of Portuguese Melaka in 1641, Dutch-style buildings were erected next to Portuguese ones, giving Melaka its distinctive atmosphere.

In keeping with the message conveyed by the durable and imposing European architecture, the superiority of the European was reinforced in other ways in these multi-racial cities. The Europeans controlled the guns,

Figure 1.1   One of the principal canals in Batavia along which were built imposing Dutch brick buildings.

From Johan Nieuhof, *Voyages and Travels to the East Indies, 1653–1670*, Singapore, 1988, opp. p. 266; reproduced courtesy Oxford University Press, Kuala Lumpur, Oxford in Asia Historical Reprints.

the ships, and a formidable army composed of a core of Europeans and a majority of native mercenaries who came from the various areas where the Europeans had posts. A typical example of the mix of the military force in a European-controlled city was Dutch Melaka in 1756. One battalion consisted of 240 Europeans, 100 native Christians, 77 Bugis, and a mixed group of 270 Malays, Indians, Portuguese, and Chinese.[8] Batavia, too, relied heavily on Asian mercenaries, as well as militia units organized into separate ethnic groups of Dutch, English, Danish, French, Portuguese and other Christians (presumably the *Mardijkers*, who were Asian slaves who had been given their freedom by the Portuguese on their becoming Christian). The division of the fighting forces into separate ethnic and racial groups was part of a deliberate Dutch policy to forestall any possibility of their combining against the authorities. In keeping with this policy, each group was assigned a specific residential district and encouraged to maintain its own language, dress, religion, and custom. The Spaniards in Manila relied principally on recruits from the local Filipino communities, their most famous mercenary force being the Macabebe Pampangans.

[8] Barbara Watson Andaya, 'Melaka under the Dutch, 1641–1795', in K. S. Sandhu and Paul Wheatley, eds., *Melaka: The transformation of a Malay capital c. 1400–1980*, Kuala Lumpur, 1983, I. 210.

The Europeans quickly stamped their authority on the cities. There was some attempt to build upon earlier political structures, but the different needs and aims of the Europeans inevitably led to changes. Melaka no longer had a Malay sultan, but the Portuguese retained the Malay offices of *bendahara*, *temenggong*, and *syahbandar* and assigned them different functions. The *bendahara* was no longer the chief Malay civil official likened to a prime minister; instead he was now an Indian merchant in charge of the civil and criminal affairs of the Indian population. The *temenggong* retained his former judicial functions of adjudicating in disputes and punishing offenders, but now his jurisdiction was limited only to the Minangkabau subjects living in areas outside Melaka. The office of *syahbandar*, an important position dealing with international trade in the port, was taken completely out of the hands of the Malays and made into a European office. Affairs of the various ethnic groups in the city were regulated by one of their own people appointed by the Portuguese with the title of *kapitan* or captain. In Manila and Batavia nothing of the former native administration was retained, although the Dutch in Batavia and Melaka (after it was seized from the Portuguese in 1641), also adopted the practice of appointing captains of foreign groups.

Portuguese Melaka was headed by a captain and a council, who were assisted by a factor, a judge, scribes, market inspectors and constabulary officials. Melaka's administration was responsible to the Viceroy and the council of state based in Goa, the headquarters of the entire Asian Portuguese enterprise known as the *Estado da India*. In addition to the royal administration, there were two other types of institutions which were regarded as the twin pillars of Portuguese colonial society: the *Senado da Camara* (town or municipal council) and the *Santa Casa de Misericórdia* (Holy House of Mercy). Since Portuguese overseas appointments of governors, bishops, and magistrates were rarely for more than three years, these institutions provided the needed continuity in administration. The tasks of the councils were vast and varied. In Melaka the council controlled the finances of the city, priced all provisions, established correct weights and measures, maintained the fortress and other public facilities, and acted as a court of first instance. The *Misericórdia* was responsible for the sick and needy and maintained hospitals in Portugal's overseas settlements.

In Manila the Governor-General of the Philippines was appointed by the Viceroy of Nueva España and was ultimately responsible to the Council of the Indies in Spain. He was guided by royal orders and edicts known as the *Recopilación*, or the 'Laws of the Indies', which were transmitted through the Council, as well as other laws applied generally throughout the Spanish colonies. In addition to his administrative status, the governor-general wielded vast military, ecclesiastic, and legislative powers in his position as captain-general, viceregal patron under the *Patronato Real*, and president of the Philippine *Audiencia*. The *Audiencia* was created in 1583 to serve as a supreme court of the colony, an advisory body to the governor-general, and as a check on his powers. But the last function was not often exercised since the governor-general had sufficient powers to have the members imprisoned or sent to distant provinces.

Manila's authority extended to the provinces, where a system of *encomiendas* was introduced. The *encomienda* was a quasi-feudal right granted by the king to favoured individuals to obtain tribute or service from inhabitants of a 'pacified' area. In return the *encomendero* was entrusted with the task of assuring the physical and spiritual well-being of his wards. By the end of the sixteenth century the system was replaced by a provincial administrative structure consisting of the *alcaldia-mayor* in pacified areas, and *corregimientos* in unpacified and strategic areas. These provincial governments mirrored the central government in Manila, with the *alcalde-mayor* (governor) exercising executive, judicial, and military powers. Below the provincial governments were the municipal governments which were principally in the hands of native leaders, the *datus*. They were heads of the traditional villages who had been incorporated into the Spanish administrative structure and given the Spanish title of *cabeza*, meaning 'head'. One was then chosen to be the principal head with the Spanish title of *gobernadorcillo* ('little governor').

In 1619 Batavia was developed as the headquarters of VOC activities in Asia. Supreme power was invested in the High Government (*Hoge Regering*), consisting of the governor-general and the Council of the Indies. Batavia appointed the officials and the commanders of garrisons who manned Company posts scattered throughout the region. Each post was a smaller version of Batavia but with relatively fewer Europeans. As we have seen, regular political and economic reports were sent by these outposts to Batavia, which then became the basis for major decisions taken by the governor-general and the Council of the Indies. Batavia was ultimately responsible to the body of directors in Amsterdam, the *Heeren XVII*, which in turn had strong links with the States-General. But, as in Portuguese Melaka and Spanish Manila, the authorities in Batavia exercised considerable initiative and independence because a message and reply between Europe and Asia often took two to three years.

The European governments ruled over cities which were noteworthy for their large foreign Asian population with only a minimum of native inhabitants. Although pre-European cities in Southeast Asia were also renowned for their cosmopolitan nature, these new cities reflected the expansion of the Europeans to all parts of Asia. Groups from China, India, Japan, Persia, and the many different areas in Southeast Asia were all represented. But because these cities had been created at the expense of some local lord, the Europeans initially could not rely upon the support of the inhabitants. The Dutch in Batavia not only forbade any Javanese or Sundanese from entering the city, but also banned the purchase of Javanese slaves because of security risks. In Manila the Spaniards took the precaution of forbidding the local people and foreign Asians from settling within the Intramuros. Before the gates closed at nightfall, all Chinese, Japanese, and Filipinos, except for a handful of municipal employees, retail traders, and household servants, had to leave the city. The Portuguese in Melaka were equally wary of the Malays whose loyalty to their exiled lord, now based in Johor-Riau at the southern end of the Malay peninsula, was still strong.

Because of their distrust of the local inhabitants, the Europeans came to depend increasingly upon the Chinese to develop their cities. Eager to succeed in their new homelands, the Chinese migrants quickly carved a niche for themselves and became the sole suppliers of goods and services to the European cities. In Manila Chinese silver and goldsmiths could faithfully copy any jewellery brought from Spain. Chinese capacity to absorb new skills and to perfect them was evident in the creation of religious art, bookbinding, and even in the making of saddles, bridles, and stirrups, where they soon surpassed their Spanish teachers. In addition they brought other skills from their homeland, where they were bakers, carpenters, druggists, market gardeners, ceramic makers, tobacco dealers, dyers, hatmakers, weavers, locksmiths, tailors, etc. Attempts to remove Spanish dependency on the Chinese by transferring some of the occupations to other groups failed, mainly because there were many in authority who profited from their links with the Chinese and were willing to provide protection and patronage. Some Chinese became established in market gardening in the outskirts of Manila, supplying the city with a reliable source of fresh food. Only in their role as middlemen did the Chinese impinge directly on the local inhabitants. They went directly to the producers in the provinces to exchange silk and cotton goods for food and other products, and then sold them at a considerable profit in the cities. So popular did Chinese cloth become among the Filipinos that the Spanish government feared locally manufactured cloth would disappear.

In Batavia the Chinese performed many of the same functions as in Manila, since they essentially became the retail traders of this cosmopolitan city. But like their counterparts in Manila, they also engaged in agriculture, establishing sugar estates in the city environs. To encourage the Chinese to establish market gardens and other agricultural ventures, the Dutch offered incentives in the form of exemption from poll tax, guaranteed purchase of products by the Company, and the establishment of minimum prices. The Dutch decision to afford legal protection to property was a further incentive to acquire land, leading to the rise of a Chinese property-owning middle class. The Company's hope of developing the agricultural potential of Batavia's surrounding lands led to Dutch possession of more agricultural land, but most of it was then leased to Chinese who worked it with Javanese labour.

While the Spaniards in Manila eventually excluded the Chinese from the Intramuros, the Dutch lived together with them in Batavia. This decision was taken to safeguard the Chinese from hostile local inhabitants and thus ensure a steady flow of income to the Company from Chinese entrepreneurial activity. The Company was always careful not to impose too burdensome a tax on the Chinese, lest they flee and live under a Mataram or Banten lord whose taxes were lower. By the beginning of the eighteenth century the numbers of Chinese in central Java had increased greatly. One contemporary observer remarked that 'there is not a river, harbour, bay or creek navigable for shipping, which does not have a customs post [tollgate], of which the keeper is invariably Chinese'.[9] So important were the Chinese to the economy that both the Javanese and the

---

[9] Peter Carey, 'Changing Javanese perceptions of the Chinese communities in Central Java, 1755–1825', *Indonesia*, 37 (April 1984) 8.

Dutch attempted to protect them through laws. According to Javanese code laws, the fine for killing a Chinese was twice that for killing a Javanese. The Dutch, too, made certain that the Chinese were protected by signing treaties with the Javanese rulers which placed the Chinese under Company jurisdiction. These measures were nevertheless totally ignored when the Company believed its interests were threatened by the Chinese.

In Portuguese Melaka the Chinese were not as prominent in the economic life of the city as in Manila and Batavia. That role was filled by Indians who had the advantage of close ties with the Portuguese both in the Indian subcontinent and in Melaka. The importance of the Indians in Melaka is confirmed by the practice of appointing one of the Indian merchants to be the *bendahara* in the new Portuguese administrative structure. Most influential were the Hindu Tamils from the Coromandel, known as Klings, whose considerable expertise in the Asian trade helped the Portuguese to integrate successfully into the system. After the Dutch seizure of Melaka in 1641, there was a noticeable shift in the influence of foreign Asians in the city. The Indians were suspected of sympathy for the Portuguese and accused of 'smuggling' Indian piece-goods despite Dutch restrictions. Their favoured place was now taken by the Chinese, whom the Dutch always believed to be essential for the prosperity of any city. In 1641 there were only 400 Chinese in Melaka, but by the middle of the next century the number had grown to 2000. Some were involved in masonry and carpentry, but apparently the majority of the Chinese were shop-owners and teahouse proprietors. The Dutch were able to gain substantial revenues by taxing the Chinese for gambling, pig slaughter, and wearing a queue.

In addition to the Chinese, another group which flourished in the European-controlled city was the mestizo communities. Liaisons between foreign men and local women had become more common in this period because of the large established communities of foreign males who rarely brought their womenfolk with them to Southeast Asia. The hybrid nature of the European city encouraged the mixing of groups through formal or informal arrangements, and so the city became a symbol of a development which was spreading throughout Southeast Asia at this time. For the Chinese, Indian, or European private trader, there were advantages in obtaining a Southeast Asian wife in a society where blood ties established trust and facilitated exchange. The women provided their foreign husbands with an entrée into local society which was essential to trade. Moreover, the women themselves often engaged in the negotiations for the purchase of desired products for their husbands.

The process of 'indigenizing' foreign groups could scarcely be avoided because of the types of activity in which these groups were engaged and because of government policies. Chinese and Indians quickly learned that there was more profit in obtaining products at the source, and so made it a practice to go frequently into the countryside. Spanish and Dutch policy of encouraging agricultural activities among the Chinese further contributed to increased Chinese contact with local inhabitants. When the Spaniards offered to grant Chinese who converted to Christianity permission to live outside the Parian, a sizeable number did so and settled in areas near

Manila and closer to local villages. They were exempted from paying an annual tribute to the Spaniards for a period of ten years and allowed to move freely in the interior. Baptismal books from certain Manila churches in mainly Chinese districts in the early seventeenth century indicate that many Chinese males between twenty to forty years old became Christian as a preliminary to marriage with Filipinas. From about 1629 baptisms of infants begin to appear in the registers, almost all of Chinese fathers and Filipino mothers, as the first generation of a Filipino-Chinese *mestizaje* or mestizo community became established. As the population of Manila increased, Spaniards, Chinese, and Japanese came to live in the native *arrabales* or suburbs. The frequent interaction of these groups and the Filipinos eventually led to the mixing of the races and the rise of a distinct group by the mid-seventeenth century.

The Europeans who settled in Southeast Asia rarely returned home and thus became an important source of urban mestizo communities in the cities. Although many high-ranking officials brought their women to Asia, they were the exception. The private trader, the clerk and copyist, and the common soldier were too poorly paid to afford the passage for European women and therefore sought companions from local communities. Other factors prevented the migration of European women to Asia. The Portuguese overseas territories were regarded as a 'frontier land of conquest', and few white women dared venture to the East. Rarely were there more than a dozen women on a ship from Europe carrying between 600 and 800 people.

Because of the difficulty in obtaining white women to help establish Portuguese settlements in Asia, Affonso de Albuquerque encouraged Portuguese to marry Indian women of Aryan origin who had been converted to Christianity. He saw these marriages and the offspring of such unions as a basis of a loyal population which would solve Portugal's chronic shortage of labour in its overseas territories. This policy was condemned by many in the Church and in the government, but the common soldier and lowly official in the Portuguese overseas posts welcomed this ruling, some even regarding it as being too rigid. In defiance of the stated guidelines, they married local woman whatever their status or origin. Those who married in the East were allowed to leave the royal service and become *casados*, or married men. To support themselves the *casados* normally engaged in trade, and it became a common phenomenon of port cities to have quarters inhabited by the *casados*, their Asian wives, and their Eurasian children.

Through their Asian wives, the *casados* tended to become more involved with indigenous society than with their own. Their children came to learn the language and the culture of the mother and, less perfectly, the religion, language and culture of the father. It was this Indo-Portuguese group which came to facilitate commerce between the European and the local population. In the seventeenth century the Dutch relied heavily on them as intermediaries and interpreters, and many Dutchmen chose Indo-Portuguese Christian women as wives. By the seventeenth century this mestizo culture was prevalent in the European-controlled cities and in most Asian trade ports.

The Dutch East India Company faced the same problem as the Portuguese in attempting to bring white women to Asia. In the early years spinsters and girls from orphanages were sent to the East. Some thirty-six white women were sent in 1609 with the hope of establishing permanent Dutch colonies. It soon became apparent, however, that those who came were not the respectable women that the authorities had hoped would immigrate. The unsatisfactory experiment with the early shipments of white women to the East forced the directors of the Company to admit that 'it was of no use for the man in the street and expensive and prejudicial to the interests of the Company to send Dutch women'.[10] By 1652 the Dutch established a policy which remained in force for the next 200 years to restrict the immigration of white women.

The Company was thus forced to adopt the earlier Portuguese practice of creating a loyal corps of individuals from the offsprings of marriages between Dutchmen and Asian women. The men were Company soldiers and officials who had served their five-year tour of duty and wished to remain in the East. Upon swearing an oath of loyalty and obedience to the Company's laws, and upon agreeing to engage only in business activity approved by the Company, these freeburghers were allowed to remain in Asia. In 1617 the *Heeren XVII* decreed that the freeburghers could marry only with the Company's permission and only with Asian or Eurasian women. Permission would be granted on the condition that these women first became Christian, and that their children and slaves 'in so far as possible' be raised as Christians. At first only Maluku was open to the freeburghers and their families, but they were later allowed to go to Batavia, Melaka and a few other places. To keep the freeburghers in Asia and fulfil the original intention of establishing colonies, in 1639 the Company forbade them to return to Europe while still married. As reinforcement of this policy, Asian and Eurasian women were also forbidden to go to Europe. The practice of grooming sons to become members of Dutch society in Asia or Europe, while preparing daughters for life as wives of officials in Asia, reinforced the policy's intention of keeping Eurasian women in Asia.

It is no surprise, therefore, that women and their children in Dutch colonial society exhibited many of the traits of indigenous Southeast Asian society. Even the very few white Dutch women in Batavia who were born and raised in the East preferred to speak a creole form of Portuguese in preference to their halting Dutch. Since many of the Dutch soldiers and a few merchants had also married Indo-Portuguese women, this unique culture was continued in the Dutch settlements. In commenting on the married women in Batavia, a seventeenth-century Dutch observer made no distinction in the behaviour, dress, and demeanour of the Asians, Eurasians, or Europeans:

---

[10] Leonard Blussé, 'Batavia, 1619–1740: The Rise and Fall of a Chinese Colonial Town', JSEAS, 12, 1 (1981) 166; Jean Gelman Taylor, *The Social World of Batavia: European and Eurasian in Dutch Asia*, Madison, 1983, 9, 12.

They adopted—or retained—such Oriental habits as squatting on their hams on the floor, instead of sitting on chairs and they ate their curry with their fingers instead of with spoon and fork. They spoke little or no Dutch among themselves, but only a bastard form of creole Portuguese . . . Whenever they went to church or appeared in public, they were decked out with silks, satins and jewels, and were followed by a train of slaves; but at home they squatted around in their shifts or in the most transparent of underclothes.[11]

At home these women behaved in a Southeast Asian way, but in public they attempted to be European in dress and demeanour.

Children born of foreign males and Southeast Asian women were not a new phenomenon in the region, but it was the size and prominence of such mestizo groups in this period which was noteworthy. The existence of large communities of Chinese and European men in the midst of Southeast Asian society encouraged intermarriage. By contrast to the past, however, children from such marriages were no longer automatically absorbed into Southeast Asian society, especially where the father was an important foreign merchant or official. The fathers now had the alternative of raising their children, but most often their sons, in their own communities. These mestizo children were socially located between the cultures of their foreign fathers and their Southeast Asian mothers, and not totally accepted by either. Yet their very presence half-way between these societies made them ideal intermediaries in trade, diplomacy, and in the transmission of ideas between the two cultures. It was in cities such as Melaka, Manila, and Batavia that these mestizo communities were most prominent and successful in this role.

Aside from the slaves, the lowest rung of the social and economic ladder in the European-controlled city was occupied by the local inhabitants. There were some 12,000 native Filipinos living in Manila's suburbs in 1609, many of whom found employment as craftsmen, small merchants, market gardeners, domestic servants, soldiers, and wage labourers in the city. In a letter to the Crown in 1729, the archbishop of Manila wrote: 'We find in this country many who are skillful and who can practise all the trades and who can supply us with all the necessary supplies but they will never be able to do this as long as there are so many Chinese.'[12] Despite the archbishop's advocacy for greater participation of the local inhabitants in the life of Manila, he was unable to uproot the deeply entrenched Chinese-Spanish interests defending the status quo.

In Batavia there were relatively few Javanese or Sundanese living within the city walls. A population count in 1673 revealed that 2024 were Dutch, 726 Eurasian, 2747 Chinese, 5362 Mardijkers (free Portuguese-speaking Indonesian soldiers), 1339 Moors (Indian Muslims) and Javanese, 611 Malays, 981 Balinese, and 13,278 slaves, a total of 27,068.[13] The Company and the Chinese would occasionally recruit both Javanese and Sundanese

[11] Comments were made by Nicholas de Graaff and paraphrased by C. R. Boxer in *The Dutch seaborne empire 1600–1800*, London, 1965, 225.

[12] Maria Lourdes Diaz-Trechuelo, 'The role of the Chinese in the Philippine domestic economy' in F. Alfonso, ed., *Chinese in the Philippines*, Manila, 1966, I. 177, 181.

[13] Susan Abeyasekere, *Jakarta: A history*, Singapore, 1987, 19.

through their local lords for seasonal work in the sugar plantations established in the environs in Batavia or for some public building project in the city. But, as the population figures indicate, most of the manual labour in the city was done by slaves brought from various parts of the archipelago and from Dutch posts elsewhere in Asia.

The Malay population of Melaka lived on the coast south of the fort and along the river under their own leaders. Their primary function appears to have been the supplying of rice, fruit, vegetables, and fish to the city, but they were also employed as craftsmen and ordinary labourers in the shipyards, factories, and the various religious and civic bodies in Melaka.

Despite the limited role of the local inhabitants in the European-controlled cities, their daily interaction with foreign groups exposed them to a number of new ideas. Through direct observations and active enquiry, the Southeast Asians assessed foreign objects and techniques and selected those which were the most useful and practical for their purposes. This pragmatic stance, bred of centuries of exposure to outside influence, had been successful in strengthening Southeast Asian society in the past, and it was an attitude which was again adopted in this period. Some of the most far-reaching of these ideas were in the field of shipbuilding and the production of firearms, technological developments which had important implications for the future of Southeast Asia's long-distance trade and warfare.

Ship technology: The carrier and the warship

Southeast Asia's long contact with the Arabs, Indians, and the Chinese was principally by sea, and therefore it was inevitable that many nautical ideas and techniques were transmitted. It must be stressed, however, that the record of shipbuilding techniques before 1800 is sparse, since shipwrights' plans were not written down and the archaeology of shipwrecks has barely begun. The absence of archaeological and other reliable historical evidence makes it difficult to determine the extent of the interaction between the shipbuilding traditions of Southeast Asia and those of its principal trading partners in the Indian Ocean and China. But while there was an exchange of ideas, some of the developments in the Southeast Asian ship were a response to specific environmental features.

As far as is known, Southeast Asia's pre-fourteenth century boatbuilding traditions evolved from the dug-out canoe. Over time, planks lashed with vegetable material were gradually raised higher and higher on both sides of the keel. These sewn-plank boats used a lashed-lug technique, in which the planks are carved out so that pieces of wood, or lugs, protrude on the inner side; holes are drilled in the lugs to take ties which attach the planks to the ribs of the boat. These boats were unique to Asia, although they resemble early Scandinavian boats. Many of these boats in Southeast Asia had a detachable animal or dragon head and tail on their prows to symbolize the *nāga*, the sacred snake which assured the fertility of the land. The use of such boats in warfare was linked with fertility rites, since the shedding of blood was a crucial aspect in the impregnating of the soil with the god's fecundity.

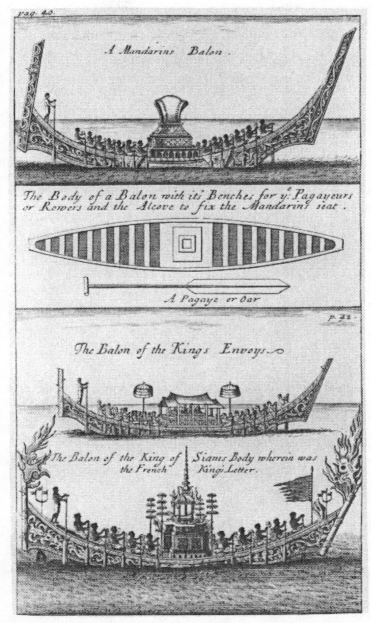

Figure 1.2   Three long-boats from Siam used here for ceremonial purposes.
Similar boats were also used for war, with the sides protected by shields.
Note the use of the dragon or *naga* head at the prow.

From Simon de la Loubère, *The Kingdom of Siam*, London, 1693, reprinted Kuala Lumpur, 1969,
opp. p. 40; reproduced courtesy Oxford University Press, Kuala Lumpur, Oxford in Asia Historical
Reprints.

From the basic dug-out canoe, another common Southeast Asian boat was developed: the outrigger canoe, known as the *kora-kora* in Maluku and *caracoa* in the southern Philippines. One of the earliest detailed descriptions of such a boat is from north Maluku in 1537. The boat was egg-shaped in the middle with both ends sloping upwards, and it could sail forwards and backwards. No nails or caulking were used; instead the keel, ribs, and fore and aft timbers were lashed by the black horsehair-like fibre (*gamuto*) from a palm, either areng (*Arenga*, Labill.) or sago (*Metroxylon*, Rottb.). Small holes were made through which the cords could pass, and they were then tied to the grips inside. Planks were joined edge-wise with wooden dowels and were caulked with the fibre of the *baru* tree (*Hibiscus tiliaceus*). The Dutch at the end of the sixteenth century noted a similar practice in Banda in which coir was used for caulking the boat's seams, and joints were smeared with a lime mixture.

Some 10–12 thwarts or cross-beams extended outward between two and nine metres on each side, depending on the bulk of the boat. To these beams were attached two or three rows of floats where additional paddlers sat. At the very end of the cross-beams were wooden forks to which were tied other thicker and larger bamboo poles for support against listing. Platforms of split bamboo with walls and roofs of local material were built on the outrigger beams, which could be enlarged to carry more passengers or cargo. As in the long-boat, the prow carried a detachable neck and head of a serpent with the antlers of a deer. Among the largest of this type of outrigger canoe was the north Malukan *juanga*, which could have four banks of fifty paddlers on each side, with another 100 men on the platform in the boat.

There were some variations in the outrigger canoe. The single outrigger was favoured by some because of its better performance in the open sea, and perhaps because it may have served some practical function such as making it easier to cast a fishing net. Another variation was the replacement of one of the outriggers with another canoe. These large double canoes and single outriggers with a large platform built over the hulls using certain types of rigs were still in use at the time of the arrival of the Europeans in the sixteenth century. A separate development in boatbuilding traditions was the raft which, along with the dug-out, was the principal mode of transport in the rivers of Southeast Asia.

When the Dutch first arrived in the busy port of Banten at the close of the sixteenth century, they noted a number of boats which were common throughout the region. The first was the *perahu*, a name which was generally used for a small undecked boat. At Banten the *perahu* had a house-like structure built over part of the hull to serve as a shelter. It also had a large mainmast and a foremast with bamboo booms. The sails were made of a type of palm or rattan matting and sometimes even of woven palm leaves. Some six men sat in the front of the *perahu* and would row if necessary, while two men remained in the back to work the two rudders placed on either side of the boat. There was also a bamboo rudder under the middle of the *perahu* which was kept in place by a rope. There was another boat called the *katur* which impressed the Dutch for its speed. It was a basic dug-out with a round keel, pointed bows, and a double

Figure 1.3 A *kora-kora* or *juanga* from Banda, showing the double outriggers with four banks of rowers on each side, the shelter with other rowers and dignitaries, and the upper deck with the warriors. A swivel-gun is placed prominently at the front of the boat, and a dragon or *naga* head is attached to the prow.

From I. Commelin, *Begin ende Voortgang*, 'Eerste Schip-vaerd der Hollanders', Amsterdam, 1646, I. opp. p. 22; facsimile Uitgaven Nederland N.V., in co-operation with N. V. Het Parool, publishers, Amsterdam; N. Israel, antiquarian and publisher, Amsterdam; and B. de Graaf, antiquarian and publisher, Nieuwkoop, Z.H.

outrigger. It had such a large sail that the Dutch marvelled that it did not overturn in the wind. There was also a trader called a *jong*, which had a bowsprit and in some cases a forked mast, as well as a mainmast and a foremast. There was an enclosed upper deck stretching the whole length of the *jong*, part of which formed a special cabin for the captain. Below the main deck were compartments where the goods were stowed, with access through two openings on either side of the ship. The capacity of the largest *jong* which the Dutch saw in Banten was estimated to be not more than forty tonnes, though they commented that those from China and Pegu were far larger.

The *jong* was a specialized cargo-carrier which appears to have been a descendant of an earlier long-distance ship which the Chinese called *kunlun bo*. It was reported to be the principal carrier of exotic products to China and was also engaged in direct trade to India. From Chinese records of the third and eighth centuries CE and from excavations of two wrecks found in China, one dating from c.1271, the following reconstruction of the features of the *kunlun bo* can be made: its size was usually about fifty metres in length with a carrying capacity of 500–1000 people and a burden of 250–1000 tonnes; absence of iron in fastening; V-shaped hull with a keel;

Figure 1.4   **A.**   A type of *perahu* from Banten with its mat sail and shelter.
B.   An outrigger canoe from Banten known as a *katur*, whose sail was so
large that the Dutch marvelled that it did not overturn in the wind.
C.   A Banten *jong*, showing the opening in the lower deck where goods were
stowed.

From I. Commelin, *Begin ende Voortgang*, 'Eerste Schip-vaerd der Hollanders', Amsterdam, 1646, I.
opp. p. 78; facsimile Uitgaven Nederland N.V., in co-operation with N. V. Het Parool, publishers,
Amsterdam; N. Israel, antiquarian and publisher, Amsterdam; and B. de Graaf, antiquarian and
publisher, Nieuwkoop, Z.H.

pointed, basically symmetrical stems and sterns; strakes and frames joined
by wooden dowels; several layers of planks; no bulkheads; double, quarter
rudders; rigging with multiple masts and sails; and no outriggers. Carv-
ings on Southeast Asian monuments up to the fourteenth century show
local boats with tripod or bipod masts, quarter rudders, the canted square-
sail and a type of lug-sail, and outriggers. The difference in description
between the Chinese and the Southeast Asian evidence may be due to the
fact that the former is referring to a long-distance carrier, while the latter
depicts a more familiar local boat not meant for the open sea.

All the features of the *kunlun bo* were found in the *jong*, which sixteenth-
century Portuguese sources called a *junco*. They described the *jong* as larger
than the Portuguese ship (which had a burden of 300 to 400 tonnes), very
tall and sheathed with four layers of planks, making it impervious to
Portuguese gunfire. Other contemporary accounts state that the *jong* had
an average burden of 400 to 500 tonnes; used no iron, with the planks of
the hull edge-fastened by the use of wooden dowels inserted into the
seams; and contained multiple sheathing, two lateral rudders, and multiple masts, usually two to four of the canted square-sail and the lug-sail

types, plus a bowsprit. Unfortunately, to date there have been no archaeological finds of *jongs* exactly fitting these historical descriptions.

The size and special requirements of the *jong* demanded access to expertise and materials not available everywhere. Consequently, the *jong* was mainly constructed in three major shipbuilding centres: north coastal Java, especially around Rembang and Cirebon; south coast Borneo (Banjarmasin) and adjacent islands; and Pegu on the Gulf of Martaban. A common feature of these three places was their accessibility to forests of teak (*Tectona grandis*, Linn.); this wood was highly valued as shipbuilding timber because of its resistance to the shipworm. Southern Borneo's supply of teak would have come from north Java, a short journey southward on the Java Sea. For the various types of smaller Southeast Asian boats the different areas had their own boatbuilding villages and traditions, many of which persist to the present day.

There was a new development in shipbuilding techniques as a result of mutual borrowings between the Chinese and Southeast Asians. The Chinese *chuan*, better known in the West as 'junk', evolved from the raft and had a flat or slightly rounded bottom without keel, stern or sternpost; a transom stem and stern; no ribs or internal frames; and solid transverse bulkheads. It used local matting for sails attached to bamboo, a practice which is believed to have originated from Southeast Asia.[14] From a combination of South China's boatbuilding techniques and those of Southeast Asia emerged a hybrid tradition which one scholar has termed the 'South China Sea tradition'. What he argues is that the Chinese techniques, which had proved adequate for their principally riverine and coastal navigation, underwent change as a result of contact with ocean-going vessels of the Southeast Asians. Thus the Chinese created long-distance trade junks, which combined Chinese features (such as partitioned watertight bulkheads, axial rudders, and iron fastening for planks) with those of the *kunlun bo* (V-shaped hulls with keel, rigging of multiple masts and sails, multiple sheathing of hulls, stem and stern posts). The earliest such hybrid ship found in an archaeological site in Southeast Asia is dated sometime in the first half of the fifteenth century.[15] With the increase of the junk trade to Southeast Asia and the practice of having the junks built in the region, there was a natural progression to the amalgamation of characteristics of both the Southeast Asian and the Chinese ship.

The increasing use of the hybrid *chuan* by both Chinese and Southeast Asian traders was encouraged by Chinese imperial policy. In Chinese ports junks and their cargo were taxed at a lower rate than Western and other ships. As long as the specifications of a Chinese junk were met, Chinese officials cared little about the foreign origins and ownership of the vessel. This measure encouraged all merchants to ship goods to China on junks, and in the seventeenth century even the Dutch employed Chinese junks crewed by Chinese in the Batavia–China trade. The Thais

[14] Paul Johnstone, *The Sea-Craft of prehistory*, Cambridge, Mass. 1980, 191.
[15] Pierre-Yves Manguin, 'The trading ships of insular Southeast Asia: New evidence from Indonesian archaeological sites', *Proceedings Pertemuan Ilmiah Arkeologi*, 5 (July 1989) 213–16.

were especially encouraged to maintain Chinese-style craft in their trade with China, since fee and tariff concessions were granted to these vessels in both China and Siam. The increasing demand for Chinese-style ships encouraged Southeast Asian shipwrights to build the hybrid *chuan*, a task made easier because of their familiarity with many of the indigenous features of the ship. The hybrid *chuan* was very popular in the seventeenth and eighteenth centuries; it had all the advantages of the *jong* as well as the official encouragement of the Chinese imperial authorities, and this led to the gradual relegation of the *jong* to inter-island trade. The latter's demise was hastened also by the arrival of the specialized carriers and warships of the Europeans.

Three particular European crafts came to make an impression in the Southeast Asian world. The first was the Mediterranean galley, which was adapted by the Spanish and the Portuguese for use in the Philippines and eastern Indonesia. It was long and narrow, with a length of seven or eight times its breadth; the vessel narrowed considerably fore and aft. It had a deck running the whole length of the boat and was propelled by long oars. A special deck was built for the fighting men, and along the whole length of the galley were placed shields to protect the rowers and the soldiers. The Dutch in the late sixteenth century commented on a Banten version of a galley, which had a galley built at the stern. The slave rowers sat confined below deck, while the soldiers stood above deck ready for combat. The Banten galley had two masts and was armed with four small cannon placed at the bow.

The second type of European craft introduced to Southeast Asia was the cargo carrier, especially the Dutch *fluyt* or fly-boat. It measured between thirty and forty metres, had a full section, almost flat bottom, a high proportion of keel length to overall length, and a rounded hull suited to bulk transport. The fly-boat successfully challenged the *jong* and the hybrid *chuan* in the carrying trade of Southeast Asia.

The third type of European vessel was the armed merchant ship, a combination of warship and cargo carrier. It was constructed to carry cargo, but its gundecks and structure were also reinforced to take the weight of heavy artillery and to withstand the tremors which resulted from the recoiling of fifteen to twenty cannons firing simultaneously. The technological breakthrough which had enabled the building of the armed merchantman gave the Europeans a considerable advantage over their competitors. Not only could they absorb protection costs in the carrying trade, but they could simultaneously prevent their competitors from participating in certain areas.

The Southeast Asians were aware of the advantages of European ships, and there was a steady transfer of construction detail from European to Southeast Asian shipwrights. As iron became cheaper, iron fastenings were used; the Western square sterns were borrowed from sixteenth-century Iberian models. Local shipwrights were capable of building European-type ships since they had suitable timber, skilled shipwrights, sufficiently trained artillery personnel, and access to guns through their own foundries or through purchase from foreign sources. Pegu, for

example, maintained its shipbuilding reputation well into the late eighteenth century. One of the ships built for the English in 1787 served both as
a man-of-war and a merchant ship and was eventually converted to carry
convicts to Australia. It was still in operation in 1897 when it made a final
voyage from Australia to England and 'surprised everybody and made but
little water'.[16]

On the whole, however, Southeast Asians built few larger vessels with
European features but continued to rely mainly on Asian prototypes which
they adapted for trade or war. The Vietnamese frequently employed junks
for these purposes. The Trinh in north Vietnam had 500 large junks each
carrying at least three cannon, and one sixteenth-century Jesuit observer
regarded these vessels as the equal of any European ship in Asian waters
at that time. In the archipelago the various types of two-masted *perahu*
were preferred for their lightness and speed, and they could be easily and
conveniently adapted for carriage or warfare. The large trade vessels, such
as the Malay *gurab* and *pancalang*, and the Bugis-Makassar *padewakan* and
penjajab, were converted in times of war by installing swivel-guns (*rantaka*).
The larger *gurab* had two guns fore and fifteen on each side, while the
smaller carried two fore and ten on each side. Even the smallest native
craft had at least three swivel-guns on each side. The guns were attached
to the bulwarks of the boats and could be turned, lifted, or lowered by
means of a wooden handle inserted in a hollow tube in the breech end of
the guns. They were intended to injure and kill, much like the traditional
arms, rather than to sink enemy boats.

The increasing domination of long-distance trade by the Chinese,
Indians, and Europeans did not provide the incentives for further modifi-
cation of Southeast Asia's own carrier, the *jong*, which had in any case
already produced the successful hybrid *chuan*. Moreover, the growing
risks associated with the arming of merchant vessels, not only by the
Europeans, but now also by the Indians and Chinese, made overseas trade
much less attractive. International traffic to Southeast Asia was rising,
and attractive profits could be made in local ports free from the hazards
and risks of long-distance trade. The *jong* continued to be used, but now it
was smaller and involved almost exclusively in trade in the coastal areas of
Southeast Asia. In addition various types of *perahu* and 'sampans', a vague
term used to describe a whole range of cargo ships adapted from a foreign
model, became the major carriers in local trade. The Southeast Asians
relinquished their role in long-distance trade; they chose to rely on their
superior knowledge of local waters and their small, light, and fast vessels
armed with swivel-guns to carry on their regional trade in defiance of the
heavier armed but slower European and foreign Asian ships.

Innovations in firearms technology and land warfare

China, the Middle East, and Europe were the three major sources of the
new firearms technology which reached Southeast Asia. The evolution of

[16] W. H. Coates, *The old 'Country Trade' of the East Indies*, London, 1911, 100.

this technology occurred in China, beginning with the use of incendiaries in Taoist ritual. From incendiaries the technology progressed through the stages of flame-throwing weapons (fire lances), explosives (bombs launched from trebuchets), rockets, and finally barrel guns and cannon. The discovery in the thirteenth century of a fast-burning gunpowder mixture, high in nitrate, of sufficient propellant force to send off a projectile from a narrow metal bore set the stage for the production of cannon and small firearms.

Knowledge of this new technology was brought by the Mongols to India, the Islamic world (Arabs, Turks, Persians), and Europe. The Ottoman Turks perfected the large siege cannon and created muskets in the sixteenth century which were considered the equal of the Spanish musket, then the finest in Europe. The Europeans improved cast-iron cannon in the seventeenth century, and standardized and mass-produced them in the eighteenth. They concentrated on light and mobile artillery, rather than on the large siege cannon which preoccupied the Turks. But it was in handguns that the Europeans excelled. In Germany in the mid-fifteenth century a matchlock mechanism was invented which enabled a continually burning match to ignite the gunpower mixture to fire a bullet from the barrel of a handgun. The matchlock arquebus was the result, an unwieldy gun which required one hand to hold the barrel and another to adjust the match and pull the trigger. But the matchlock mechanism was simple, cheap, and fairly foolproof, and remained the principal handgun until it was replaced by the flintlock in the late seventeenth century.

By the sixteenth century firearms technology was not yet universally or even generally applied in the armies of China, Europe, or the Islamic lands. The new technology still had to demonstrate its superiority over traditional arms and be incorporated in established war tactics in each area. Perhaps the greatest obstacles to the widespread use of firearms was cultural opposition. In China Confucianism was only barely tolerant towards things military, and the Confucian officials believed it beneath them to devote their energies and skills to the development of firearms. In the Islamic lands of the Middle East, the creation of light cavalry armed with recurved bows arose naturally in the nomadic environment. As long as such skills were being produced and the cavalry was effective, there was little reason to adopt the new firearms. In Europe there was initial reluctance to adopt the use of cannon and small firearms because this meant a challenge to the traditional warrior, the armed knight, and a whole way of life. But prior to the greater acceptance of firearms, the introduction of the steel crossbow had already demonstrated the vulnerability of the armed knight and the growing prominence of the unskilled common soldier who, with a powerful weapon, was the equal of or superior to the noble armoured knight on horseback. The European world was thus far less reluctant than the Chinese or the Islamic world to adopt firearms.

Cultural factors do not appear to have prevented the Southeast Asians from expressing keen interest in the new technology. In the sixteenth century they purchased guns from foreigners and enticed or forced gun-founders to remain in their lands to reproduce these new weapons. Gunfoundries in Pegu and Ayutthaya provided some of the firearms found in Melaka when it was taken by the Portuguese in 1511. In Ayutthaya it was the Chinese and in Pegu the Indians who appear to have been the first to establish foundries. The Burmese readily adopted firearms and incorporated special corps of gunners into their armies. After the Burmese capture of the port city of Syriam from Portuguese adventurers in the early seventeenth century, the surviving Europeans were forcibly resettled in villages northwest of Ava in upper Burma and were later joined by a thousand Indian Muslim sailors and gunmen. These captives and their descendants became the backbone of Burma's artillery corps and musketeer forces. To bolster the firepower of its own units, Burma followed a policy of hiring short-term mercenaries for specific campaigns.

Although the figures provided by the Burmese sources seem to be inflated, they provide an indication of the proportion of guns to soldiers. In a Burmese royal order of 1605, a fighting force of 1000 men was to be 'adequately equipped with weapons including guns and cannon'.[17] Another royal order dated 1637 describes a typical armed unit with 1000 men, 10 cannon, 100 guns, and 300 bows. So well-established were gun units within Burma by this time that, in addition to a foreign (feringi) gun group, there were many other local gun units, all of which were given an area of land to inhabit. In the outfitting of one unit of 100 gunners, each man was issued with a gun and all necessary supplies. They were well-trained and encouraged to improve their marksmanship, 'provided they do not practice on live targets'.[18] The division of the Royal Bodyguard of Bayinnaung in the invasion of Ayutthaya in 1568 was said to have 4000 Kala Brin-gyi (Portuguese) gunners and another 4000 Kala Pathi (Muslim Indian) musketeers, figures which may well be exaggerated especially for the 'Portuguese'. So valued were firearms that Burma's port officials were entrusted with the task of procuring foreign guns and gunners. Burma had its own foundries and gunpowder mills, but it preferred to replace its obsolete guns and to obtain European gunpowder through periodic arms purchases at the coast.

The Chinese brought firearms technology to the Thais, but by the sixteenth and seventeenth centuries the latter looked to Europe for the latest developments. A Portuguese from Macao was brought into the service of the ruler of Ayutthaya in the seventeenth century to cast cannon, although the Thais were already capable of producing their own. A treatise on the casting of cannon is believed to have been furnished by a seventeenth-century Dutchman to the governor of Sukothai. It describes the composition of the metal, provides a diagram of the proportions of the weapon, explains the methods of loading and firing, and has sketches of ramrods, cleaning rods, and gun mounts. The pair of cannon sent to Louis XIV by King Narai in the seventeenth century was described by the French as 'six feet long [1.82 metres] made of malleable iron, beaten while cooling . . . inlaid with silver, mounted on carriages also inlaid with silver'.[19] The

---

[17] Than Tun, trans., *The royal orders of Burma, AD 1598–1885*, I, Kyoto, 1983, order dated 16 Feb. 1605, 16.

[18] Ibid., Order dated 24 July 1638, 103.

[19] C. A. Seymour Sewell, 'Notes on some old Siamese guns', JSS, 15, 1 (1922) 5.

French regarded them as well-made, and they were used in the storming of the Bastille on 14 July 1789.

The demand for cannon for the wars against the Burmese could not be met by the foundries in Ayutthaya, and so they were imported, especially from the Europeans, or seized from conquered areas. The paintings on some of the beautiful lacquered bookcases now housed in the Vajiranana Library in Bangkok show Thai soldiers with muskets and cannon in battle against the Burmese. What is distinctive is the sight of cannon attached to a timber tripod and trestle to attain the right elevation. When a cannon was brought into service, a special ceremony was held to inscribe its name on the barrel. Among some of the names bestowed on cannon were: 'The Lao who plays polo', 'The Javanese who performs the kris dance', 'The Annamese who wields the spear', 'The Shan who plays in the vanguard', 'The fierce Farang [foreigner] who shoots straight', 'The Chinese who disembowels', 'The Burman who thrusts with the lance', 'The Makassar who destroys the camp', and 'The Bugis who runs amok'.[20] On each barrel the calibre of the weapon and the amount of gunpowder required were inscribed; it was prudent of the Thais to adopt this measure, since the wrong quantity and mixture of gunpowder in an imperfectly made cannon often caused explosions and the loss of the gunner's life.

The importance of good gunpowder was recognized early by the Thais. A treatise dating back to 1580 prescribes the various mixtures to produce incendiary rockets; to discharge flames to frighten elephants, horses, and footmen; to produce 'murk and darkness'; and to shoot men and animals with soft bullets so as not to kill them. The ability of the Thais to produce these varying strengths of gunpowder demonstrates a good knowledge of its propulsive force. The Thais were equally competent in the production of handguns. In Trailok's laws of 1454 determining civil and military status there are obvious interpolations from perhaps the late sixteenth or the seventeenth century which list occupations such as a corps of artillery with large and small firearms, gunfounders, and gunpowder-makers. The Thais became so well known for their production of firearms and gunpowder that the Japanese shogun Ieyasu, founder of the Tokugawa dynasty, requested muskets from the Ayutthaya ruler in 1606, and muskets and gunpowder in 1608.

A major incentive to the Thais in the production and incorporation of the new weaponry in their armies was the persistent threat from the Burmese between the sixteenth and the early nineteenth centuries. In an attempt to stop the advance of a Burmese invading force in 1760, the ruler of Ayutthaya sent two armies, one by land and another by sea. The land and the sea forces were divided equally into 30,000 men with 2000 guns. The guns in the land force were mounted on carriages and on elephants, while those in the sea force were placed on warboats. When Ayutthaya was finally captured in April 1767, the armoury of the city contained 1000 muskets inlaid with gold and silver tracery and more than 10,000 ordinary muskets; the famous twin cast bronze cannon; 'guns for dismantling city walls; guns for repelling enemy attacks; guns embossed with figures of

[20] Ibid., 10.

dragons and seamonsters; guns constructed for mounting on carriages, at the bow of war boats, and on elephants; and breech-loading guns'.[21] In total there were 3550 various sorts of firearms, most of copper or bronze, but some of iron. In addition there were 50,000 shells of various size which were manufactured in China, Laos, Europe, India, Ayutthaya and the Yun country of northern Thailand.

Vietnam was another mainland Southeast Asian state which came to produce and use firearms on a relatively large scale in warfare. By recovering guns from Portuguese, Spanish and Dutch shipwrecks in the sixteenth and seventeenth centuries, and by employing European gunsmiths, the Vietnamese had come to learn about the latest European developments which they then applied to their own foundries. A Portuguese mestizo, João da Cruz, offered his services to the Nguyen family in south Vietnam and established a foundry in Hué to build guns in the European way. The Vietnamese quickly applied the new techniques to their own considerable skills in casting. In the late seventeenth century, they cast two bells of 500 pounds (230 kilograms) for the Christian churches in Ayutthaya at the request of Phaulkon. When the Vietnamese asked the English to send a gunfounder in 1678, it was not to learn about founding but to assess European techniques. They were able to recognize quality workmanship, and in 1689 the Nguyen lord refused to accept from the English two cannon which had certain flaws. At another time only seven of twenty cannon sent by the English were deemed to be of acceptable quality.

The armoury of the Trinh lord in north Vietnam in the seventeenth century contained some fifty to sixty iron cannon from falcons to demi-culverins. There were two or three whole culverins or demi-cannon and some iron mortars. The largest weapon was a locally cast bronze cannon of some 3500–4000 kilograms, which was considered by a European observer to be ill-shaped and more for display than combat. Cannon were so highly valued in the north that the Trinh lord had the sole right to purchase them, and guards were posted along rivers and major road intersections to prevent their export. Around the Nguyen court in the south were some 1200 bronze cannon of different calibres. Some bore the Spanish or the Portuguese coat of arms, while others—most likely of local manufacture— were beautifully crafted in the form of dragons, sphinxes, and leopards.

In the archipelago Aceh developed a reputation for the possession and use of large cannon and firearms through its association with Turkey. In the sixteenth century the Ottoman ruler sent 500 Turks, among whom were gunners, gunfounders, and engineers, along with large bombards and ample supples of ammunition, to the ruler of Aceh to assist in an attack on Portuguese Melaka. Although only two ships of the original fleet reached Aceh sometime in 1566 or 1567, this was only the first of a number of shipments of guns which Turkey was to send to Aceh. A Portuguese source in 1585 noted the presence of Turkish bronze cannon of all calibres,

---

[21] 'Burmese invasions of Siam', translated from the Hmannan Yazawin Dawgyi, compiled under order of Bagyidaw, 1829, *Journal of the Siam Society, Selected Articles*, vol. 5, part 1, Bangkok, 1959, 50.

gunners, naval personnel, and engineers capable of fortifying and besieging fortresses. Among the Turks were those who taught the Acehnese to
make their own guns. The Turks also transmitted to their Acehnese allies
their preoccupation with gun size. One of the cannon founded in Aceh so
impressed the Portuguese by its size that it was sent as a gift to the king of
Spain. By the early seventeenth century Sultan Iskandar Muda of Aceh
boasted an arsenal of possibly 2000 pieces, among which were 1200 bronze
cannon of medium calibre, and 800 other guns such as swivel-guns and
arquebuses. Although Aceh produced its own cannon and guns, its rulers
in the seventeenth century preferred to obtain European firearms, especially those beautifully damasked and bejewelled guns which were brought
as gifts by travellers and traders.

In Java the ancient and respected craft of kris-making provided the
technical skills which were applied to the making of guns. Both cannon
and handguns required special expertise and may have been made by the
same individuals. The craftsman's spiritual power was said to be transmitted to the guns, evoking thereby the same reverence for these new
weapons as for the kris. By the beginning of the seventeenth century the
Javanese in Surabaya were producing their own bronze cannon, and by
mid-century Mataram had the capacity to manufacture some 800 muskets
in a period of three months.

The Bugis and Makassar people of south Sulawesi adapted quickly to the
introduction of firearms because of the frequency of wars between them.
As one Frenchman observed in the early seventeenth century: 'There are
no people in India more nimble in getting on Horseback, to draw a Bow, to
discharge a Fuzil [musket], or to point a Cannon.' He also described
cannon in Makassar which were so big that 'a Man may lie in 'em and not
be seen'. Nevertheless, he believed that these cannon were of little use
since the powder was not of sufficient strength to fire a heavy projectile.[22]
When the Dutch captured the Makassar royal citadel of Sombaopu in 1669,
one of the prizes was the pride of the Makassar armaments, the locally-
made cannon named 'The Child of Makassar' (*Anak Makassar*). Like many
other large cannon in the archipelago, it proved unwieldy and its fire
ineffective because of the lack of good gunpowder. The Dutch also seized
33 large and small bronze and 11 cast-iron cannon, 145 bases (a type of
handgun), 83 breech-loading gun chambers, 60 muskets, 23 arquebuses,
127 musket barrels, and 8483 bullets. Although it is impossible to know the
origin of these armaments, local sources stress that the Makassar people
were already manufacturing muskets sometime in the late sixteenth or
early seventeenth century. By the eighteenth century their neighbours the
Bugis were producing guns of such straight bore and fine inlay work that
they attracted the admiration of Europeans.

The Malays were another ethnic group in the archipelago noted for the
possession and use of firearms. When the Portuguese captured Melaka in
1511, they found a large number of cannon and other firearms among
which were esmerils (small wrought-iron swivel-guns), falconets (cast-

[22] N. Gervaise, *An historical description of the kingdom of Macasar in the East Indies*, London, 1701, 72.

bronze swivel-guns larger than the esmeril), and medium sakers (long cannon or culverins between a six and a ten pounder). The Portuguese believed that these captured firearms were not of local manufacture and were probably made in the foundries of Pegu and Ayutthaya, known for their production of small artillery. However, Malay gunfounders were compared favourably with those of Germany, who were then the acknowledged leaders in the manufacture of firearms, and the Malay gun carriages were described as unrivalled by any other land, including Portugal. An Italian participant in the attack mentioned the presence of heavy cannon in Melaka which caused considerable loss of Portuguese lives. Though the Malays were eventually defeated, they were described as 'most valiant men, well trained in war, and copiously supplied with every type of very good weapon'.[23]

Even the Minangkabau from the interior of Sumatra appeared to have manufactured sufficient quantities of firearms to satisfy their own needs and those of their neighbours. Iron and steel were produced in local forges, but by the eighteenth century they became more reliant on the Europeans for their supplies. Their matchlock arquebuses were described in the eighteenth century as having barrels which were 'well-tempered, and of the justest bore'.[24] The barrel was made by rolling a flat bar of iron around a rod and beating the edges together to form the bore. But while the Minangkabaus had mastered the art of manufacturing guns, they were less successful in producing gunpowder. They used the same proportions of charcoal, sulphur, and saltpetre as the Europeans, but often the mixture was improperly corned because of the small quantities made and the haste in the preparation of gunpowder intended for immediate use.

Southeast Asians had known about firearms before the sixteenth century, but it was the arrival of the European and Turkish guns and gunners that showed them the effectiveness of these new weapons. At first Southeast Asians readily purchased or were provided with various types of armaments, from heavy Turkish cannon to smaller hand-held arquebuses. Southeast Asian rulers encouraged foreign gunfounders to establish foundries in their lands so they could learn more about the new technology. Many already possessed translations of foreign manuals explaining the principles and the process of manufacturing firearms and gunpowder. Once the principles were explained, local craftsmen were able to apply their own skills in kris- and sword-making or in the casting of bronze Buddha statues to create their own cannon and small handguns.

Despite the ability of some Southeast Asian gunfounders to supply their own armies and even export to neighbouring lands, they were at a considerable disadvantage in relation to European gunmakers, whose technology quickly outstripped all others by the eighteenth century. In the previous two centuries, it was possible for Southeast Asian rulers to capture European soldiers or seamen or accept 'renegades' to manufacture guns and gunpowder in their kingdoms. With the mass-production of new cast-iron cannon in the late seventeenth century, the relationship

---

[23] *Lettera di Giovanni Da Empoli*, with introduction and notes by A. Bausani, Rome, 1970, 138.
[24] William Marsden, *A history of Sumatra*, reprint, Kuala Lumpur, 1975, 347.

between the gunner and his gun was no longer one of a special craftsman with his work of art. Fewer people were now required in the manufacture of firearms, and only a few highly-skilled individuals possessed the increasingly complex knowledge necessary to produce the sophisticated arms in the later seventeenth and the eighteenth centuries. It was no longer feasible for Southeast Asian rulers to depend upon captured or even hired European or foreign Asians and expect them to reproduce guns of the same quality as those manufactured in Europe or in European foundries in Asia.

The much more reliable wheel-lock and flintlock mechanisms used in muskets, which were becoming common in seventeenth- and eighteenth-century Europe, appear to have been admired but not reproduced in Southeast Asian foundries. So vast was the gap between the quality of handguns manufactured in Southeast Asia and those in Europe that one English observer in the early nineteenth century remarked that the wheel-locks and flintlocks were a 'complex machinery far beyond their [Southeast Asians'] skill'.[25] With mass production and the rapid changes in technology, the Europeans quickly unloaded obsolete armaments on to Southeast Asians as new and more effective weapons were created. For Southeast Asians, these outdated guns were sufficient for their war requirements, and so there was little incentive to enter into a technological arms race with the Europeans.

Southeast Asians gradually abandoned their efforts to maintain their own independent source of firearms because of the difficulty of obtaining consistent up-to-date knowledge. Although there were always Europeans who were willing to teach the Southeast Asians what they knew, most of those who came to Southeast Asia were not specialist gunsmiths or gunfounders. It is highly unlikely that the occasional 'renegade' who sought safety or employment in a local court would have possessed the skills of the founders in Europe or even of those Europeans and Eurasians in Asia who had made gunfounding a family concern. Excellent bronze guns were being cast at the Indo-Portuguese foundries at Goa and Cochin in India by the master gunfounder, João Vicente, in the first half of the sixteenth century. The Dias and Tavares Bocarro family, the principal cannonmakers in Goa from 1580 to 1680 and perhaps longer, were renowned for their excellent work. Yet the technology which lay so close to Southeast Asia remained out of reach because of the natural tendency for craftsmen to protect their industrial secrets, and because European governments explicitly forbade the transference of knowledge in the production and the use of firearms.

Where the absence of true expertise was sorely evident was in the production of gunpowder. The mixing of the gunpowder ingredients to the right proportion of charcoal, sulphur and saltpetre had taken years of experimentation by the Chinese. The Europeans were able to adopt the successful formula and then adjust the nitrate content to provide the necessary explosive power for the various types of new weaponry. In the sixteenth century the manufacture of good gunpowder was a highly

[25] John Crawfurd, *History of the Indian archipelago*, Edinburgh, 1820, I. 191.

respected skill which required a solid understanding of the new guns being developed. Founding techniques were still so imperfect that an overcharge could cause a cannon to burst, while the wrong mixture would not have the propulsive force to send off a ball. The Turks attempted to overcome the problem by engraving on the cannon breech the correct ball size and the weight of powder to fire the projectile, and, as we have seen, this practice was adopted to some extent by the Thais.

For the Southeast Asians newly introduced to the whole firearms technology, the fearsome consequences of an improperly charged cannon made them wary. Southeast Asians continued to maintain their own gunpowder mills, but they preferred to purchase their gunpowder from Europeans. Thus, by the eighteenth century, Southeast Asians had abandoned the attempt to keep pace with new developments in the production of both firearms and gunpowder, and came to rely increasingly on supplies provided by the Europeans.

The new firearms technology did not transform tactics in Southeast Asian warfare. Instead, in many cases the new weapons simply reinforced traditional weapons in established war strategies. In Java massed battles were rare because the main fighting occurred between the vanguards comprising the Javanese headmen and important officials. In this fierce but short combat the death of a few of the leaders was sufficient to send the followers fleeing to safety. Rarely were there many casualties, nor did the battles last longer than two hours. In the battle between leaders the traditional weapons of pikes and krises were used, rather than firearms. Krises were regarded as repositories of spiritual power, and the pitting of one kris-wielding leader against the other was in essence a battle of spiritual potency. Until the musket could achieve the same reverent and exalted status as the kris, it could not replace the latter as an essential weapon of the Javanese prince and nobleman.

Only one-fifth of the number of men brought to the field in a Javanese army consisted of fighting men, the rest being support units. Of these fewer than 10 per cent would normally have a gun. Japara in 1677 had an army of 1576 fighting men and only 79 guns, which were normally kept under guard by the ruler and issued only in times of war. These few firearms were effective against an enemy unaccustomed to the noise and range of the new weaponry. Even more important was the fact that a few firearms in the hands of specialized marksmen could create an immediate advantage by causing the death and wounding of some of the noblemen forming the enemy's vanguard. The fall of a leader was usually sufficient to cause his men to panic and flee. Cannon were less important in Javanese warfare, although on occasion they proved invaluable in creating breaches in heavily fortified stockades. In general, however, sieges were rare, and the skirmishes of small vanguards of special warriors left little place for field artillery.

Among the Bugis-Makassar people, the manner of fighting resembled that of the Javanese. When the king ordered the people to assemble for a war expedition, he distributed clothes, arms, powder and lead. There were some guns available, but those issued with them also carried a sword. After the powder was exhausted, they reverted to their swords and krises for close combat. Only the principal warriors, who were on the whole noblemen or princes, wore chainmail armour. The use of iron armour, believed to have been borrowed from the Portuguese, encouraged local development of firearms with their superior penetrative power. While the Bugis-Makassar soldiers continued to rely on the pike, the sword, and the bow, among the élite troops there was an increasing reliance on the musket to counter the practice of using chainmail armour. In 1695 of the assembled army of about 25,000 gathered to pay obeisance to the Bugis prince Arung Palakka, only his personal bodyguard were fully equipped with chainmail armour, golden helmets, firelocks (matchlock arquebuses) and two rounds of ammunition.

In the Malay areas the stockade or *kubu* was an essential component of warfare. The *kubu* had walls on three sides consisting of rows of palm trunks filled with earth. The fourth side backed onto a mountain or a jungle to enable the defenders to escape if the enemy succeeded in breaching the walls. The *kubu* was not intended to be heavily defended by guns nor to house a large number of people for long sieges. It provided a temporary shelter and respite from the fighting and was meant to discourage further action by the enemy. The key element was mobility, and so the *kubu* was quickly manned and abandoned as circumstances demanded. This method of warfare made siege cannon and other heavy guns of little value.

In the archipelago the ambush, the unexpected raid, and the surprise dawn attack, were established tactics. At times armies were brought together on the battlefield, but the death of a few leaders and soldiers appeared to have been sufficient to slake the thirst for blood in compensation for an insult or killing which had caused the war. Even when 'large' Javanese campaigns occurred in the seventeenth and eighteenth centuries, encouraged by Dutch firepower, the actual casualties caused by the local people among themselves were often small. A notable exception occurred in the few sieges of well-populated cities, such as Melaka in 1511 and Makassar in 1669. The presence of guns enabled both defenders and besiegers to inflict casualties at a distance without the actual confrontation in battle which appear to have been crucial in the resolution of conflict.

Because of the nature of warfare in the archipelago, only firearms which contributed to existing tactics were readily adopted. One of the most common and effective weapons used by maritime kingdoms was the swivel-gun. It was a light, manoeuvrable cannon ideally suited to the small stockades. The U-shaped upper part of the swivel-gun held the trunnions of the gun, while the pointed foot was attached in the walls in the embrasure of the fort. At the breech end of these guns was a hollow tube about fifteen centimetres long in which was fitted a wooden spike or handle for turning, raising, or lowering the muzzle. In *kubu* or stockade warfare the swivel-gun, known locally as *rentaka* or *lantaka*, merely added a new weapon to traditional fighting and required little radical change of tactics. The swivel-gun proved to be especially suited to the design of Southeast Asian boats and to the requirements of naval combat.

The matchlock arquebus was another weapon which was quickly adopted. Its use was often limited to special corps of foreign mercenaries or a hand-picked local élite fighting force, usually the personal guards of the

Figure 1.5 **A.** A Malay brass swivel cannon, called Lela. The barrel was usually 180 cm long. The finest were made in Brunei.
B. An ornamental swivel gun with a 'monkey's tail'. All Malay swivel guns were loaded and fired from the breech. The 'monkey's tail' helped the gunner to aim.

From Mubin Sheppard, *Taman Indera: A Royal Pleasure Ground*, Kuala Lumpur, 1972; reproduced courtesy of Oxford University Press, Kuala Lumpur. Originals in the Sarawak Museum.

king. The physical encumbrance of the arquebus, the long delay in reloading, and its inability to function in wet conditions, quickly outweighed the shock advantage of its noise and penetrative force. An arquebus was found to be useful only in the first salvo, for the Southeast Asians do not appear to have adopted the volley technique which employs several ranks of musketeers firing in turn to maintain a continuous hail of fire. The lack of sufficient guns and good gunpowder may have been too great to permit the use of such tactics. Instead, they attached a sharp pointed object at the end of the arquebus to transform it to a bayonet for close combat once the single volley had been fired. Swords and daggers were often issued to arquebusiers for this purpose.

The powerful mainland states, which in this period were engaged in a struggle for dominance in the region, demonstrated a greater initiative in

Figure 1.6   Three soldiers from Banten armed with the traditional spear, sword
and shield, as well as with a matchlock. The soldier in the middle wears
chainmail armour which consists of iron plates linked together with rings.

From I. Commelin, *Begin ende Voortgang*, 'Eerste Schip-vaerd der Hollanders', Amsterdam, 1646, I.
opp. p. 72; facsimile Uitgaven Nederland N.V., in co-operation with N. V. Het Parool, publishers,
Amsterdam; N. Israel, antiquarian and publisher, Amsterdam; and B. de Graaf, antiquarian and
publisher, Nieuwkoop, Z.H.

the use of this new weaponry arising out of the necessity to keep abreast
or ahead of their traditional enemies. But even in these states, there is little
evidence that firearms had resulted in new battle techniques which revolu-
tionized established ideas of warfare. In the reign of the Burmese monarch
Bayinnaung in the mid-sixteenth century, guns were successfully integrated into the infantry and elephant units, with musketeers and artillerymen
in a ratio to other troops of 1:2 or 1:3. During the Burmo-Siamese wars of
the sixteenth to the early nineteenth centuries, the Burmese placed heavy
cannons on artifically created mounds or on high towers as siege weapons,
to good effect. In 1564 Ayutthaya quickly surrendered to the besieging
Burmese forces because it had no defence against the array of large-calibre
cannon brought against it.

As a matter of survival against the Burmese, the Thais were as assiduous
as their arch-enemies in adopting firearms in the battlefield. Cannon were
fired at the enemy from a distance and, if the enemy did not panic and
flee, the armies drew closer to each other to fire their muskets and arrows.
One contemporary French account claimed that close combat between the
armies rarely occurred since there was a great reliance on war elephants.
These elephants carried a few guns about one metre long which shot one-
pound (454-gram) balls. Since only the more prominent leaders would
fight on elephants, battles often depended, as in the archipelago, on a

Figure 1.7   Battle between Pegu and Ayutthaya: a duel between princes on elephants and armies with spears, swords and shields. The outcome of the duel was often a critical factor in the morale of the opposing armies.

From I. Commelin, *Begin ende Voortgang*, 'Oost-Indische Reyse', Amsterdam, 1646, III. opp. p. 22; facsimile Uitgaven Nederland N.V., in co-operation with N. V. Het Parool, publishers, Amsterdam; N. Israel, antiquarian and publisher, Amsterdam; and B. de Graaf, antiquarian and publisher, Nieuwkoop, Z.H.

duel or a limited skirmish between the princes and noblemen of the warring armies.

The civil wars in Vietnam encouraged the production and use of firearms. A Jesuit observer in 1631 commented on the proficiency of the Vietnamese in handling both cannon and arquebuses:

> The Cochin-Chinese have now become so expert in the managing of them [artillery and arquebuses] that they surpass our Europeans; for indeed they did little else every day but exercise themselves in shooting at a mark. They are so good they could hit with the artillery better than others would with an arquebus. And with arquebus, too, they are good. They go daily to the fields to practise.[26]

For the field artillery the Vietnamese relied on small cannon which could be borne on the backs of the soldiers and fire a four-ounce (112-gram) shot. One man carried the barrel, measuring about 2 metres, while another took

---

[26] C. R. Boxer, 'Asian potentates and European artillery in the 16th–18th centuries: a footnote to Gibson-Hill', JMBRAS, 38, 2 (1965) 166.

the carriage, consisting of a round piece of wood about 10 centimetres thick and the same length as the barrel. In action, one end of the carriage was propped up by two legs or by a fork about one metre off the ground, and the cannon was placed on the carriage, lying in an iron socket with a swivel. The gunner could thus control and adjust his aim, aided by a short stock resting against his shoulder. These small cannon were used to clear a pass or to disperse enemy forces waiting to repel a crossing. The soldiers were all taught to make their own gunpowder with little 'engines' to mix the ingredients and to make whatever quantity required. But the Vietnamese suffered the same poor results with their gunpowder as their neighbours. The cause was attributed to the poor corning of the powder which produced unequal lumps.

In the wars between the Nguyen and the Trinh in the seventeenth century, the latter kept ready a force of seventy or eighty thousand men, armed with swords or thick, heavy matchlocks with barrels of 1 to 1.2 metres in length. Soldiers were provided with hollow bamboo to protect the barrel of the gun from dust when it was hanging on a rack in the house, and another larger lacquered bamboo case to protect the entire gun from the elements while on the march. The Vietnamese were considered among the quickest of any nation in the loading and firing of their muskets. In four motions they were able to draw their ramrod, insert the powder and lead, ram the charge down, remove the rod and replace it, and then fire at first sight very successfully. Every soldier carried a leather cartridge box containing small sections of bamboo filled with powder and shot. Each of these sections was sufficient for one charge and could be neatly poured down the barrel of the musket. An Englishman at the same period required some twenty motions to load and fire.

By the middle of the eighteenth century, firearms had become a permanent part of Vietnamese warfare. When the Tayson forces routed the Chinese army sent in aid of the Le emperor in 1789, the leader of the Tayson is described as entering Thang-long (Hanoi) with 'his armour . . . black from the smoke of gunpowder'.[27] Many fleeing Chinese were also killed by mines, demonstrating Vietnamese familiarity with their use.

Despite the varying use of guns in combat, all Southeast Asians were convinced of the spiritual powers which these weapons could bring to battle. Europeans were constantly amazed at the numbers of cannon, large and small, which they found in Southeast Asian arsenals; some were too tiny to be weapons. When the Portuguese seized Melaka in 1511, they claimed to have found some 3000 cannon in the city. Most had never been fired, which elicited disdainful European comments regarding the quality of the locally-produced guns. However, the production of large quantities of guns was often intended for spiritual rather than physical combat. One of the sights which puzzled and amused Europeans was the local practice of dismounting a cannon from its carriage, upending it with its barrel in the air, and then tying it to the pole of a house. These cannon were obviously never fired nor employed as field guns. They became instead representations of the sacred stone of the local deity, a local version

[27] Charles B.-Maybon, *Histoire moderne du pays d'Annam (1592–1820)*, Paris 1919, 298.

of the Śiva linga and therefore the repository of powerful protector spirits.

During the final stages of the siege of Ayutthaya by the Burmese in 1767, the ruler of Auytthaya ordered that the great cannon called *Dvaravati*, 'which had been regarded from ancient times as the guardian of the city, should after the customary propitiatory offerings had been made to the presiding spirit',[28] be brought out to be fired at the enemy. When the powder failed to ignite after a number of attempts, the Thais regarded this as a sign of the removal of the protection of the guardian spirit and the end of Ayutthaya. Another greatly revered cannon which had been cast under Narai, and given the name *Phra Phirun* (a rain god), was thrown into the lake after the seizure of Ayutthaya. When Taksin finally reconstituted the Thai state and established his own dynasty, he cast another *Phra Phirun* in 1777 in his capital city of Thonburi 'to be an emblem that the kingdom had recovered from its reverses and had regained its former greatness'.[29] Frequently flowers and incense were placed on these cannon to appease the spirits. Even cannon in use in the field could elicit a similar response among their users. One small three-pounder was especially revered by the Burmese because of its reliability, and so it was sprinkled with fine scents and dressed with beautiful cloth. At one of the battles near Prome in 1755, the Burmese ruler consented to the offer of liquor and meat to the spirit of the *Yan Bon Khwin* cannon.

The Makassar people, too, had their guardian cannon, the *Anak Makassar* (Child of Makassar), whose qualities were praised in a panegyric to the Makassar fighting forces in the war against the Dutch in 1666–9. For the Javanese the effectiveness of the cannon was not measured by its destructive capacity but by its ability to amass spiritual power for the benefit of the community. It is not surprising that among the guns which the Javanese possessed was a wooden cannon which they said had descended from the heavens. The Mataram state cannon, *Guntur Geni*, was fired only to assemble the community, to summon the nobles when the Susuhunan was angry, or to announce the death of a dignitary.

The Southeast Asian decision to adopt firearms for their spiritual potency is in character with the history of the area. The practical value of this new technology on the battlefield was not ignored, but its adoption was not a matter of great concern except perhaps in the warring states of Burma and Siam, and in Vietnam with its own internal wars and its long history of armed conflict with the Chinese. By contrast the spiritual nature of firearms was immediately recognized by all as being in keeping with their perception of the inter-relationship between the material and spiritual spheres of life.

There was, therefore, only a partial adoption of the new firearms technology in Southeast Asia and a tendency to rely on imports rather than on locally-produced guns and gunpowder. But even if Southeast Asians had devoted time to perfecting their understanding of firearms, new advances in Europe would have quickly outstripped the pace of developments in Asia. By the eighteenth century the Europeans had established

[28] 'Burmese Invasions of Siam', VI, 46.
[29] Seymour Sewell, 'Notes', 23.

superiority in the production of great quantities of reliable cast-iron cannon and of the much lighter and more reliable flintlock muskets. The close relationship between the producer and the gunner which had characterized earlier centuries no longer held by the eighteenth century. While it may have been possible earlier for Southeast Asian rulers to seize European gunners and expect them to reproduce the armaments which they were using, this was no longer possible by the eighteenth century, as we have seen. The Southeast Asians were now dependent upon the goodwill of the Europeans for their supply of guns and gunpowder. Since the latter were unwilling to provide the Southeast Asians with the means to challenge them, the consequences were predictable. In the early nineteenth century the Burmese arsenal consisted of some 35,000 muskets, most of which were rejects from the English and French armouries. The situation was similar or worse in the other parts of Southeast Asia, signalling the beginning of a European technological monopoly in arms production and supply in the region.

SUMMARY AND CONCLUSION

In the period between 1500 and 1800, local and international circumstances contributed to the arrival in Southeast Asia of an unprecedented number of foreign Asian and European merchants who settled permanently in the region. The new foreign presence differed from that in former centuries by creating economic and political entities outside the control of a Southeast Asian lord. Within these unique urban settlements, the foreign element dominated; only a peripheral role was allotted to the local inhabitants. The partnership forged between the European government and the foreign communities, mainly Chinese, created successful port-city states in Portuguese Melaka, Spanish Manila, and Dutch Batavia which came to challenge the political and economic authority of neighbouring Southeast Asian states.

As in the past, the Southeast Asians regarded the strong foreign presence as an opportunity to exchange ideas and goods which would ultimately benefit the community. In this regard the European cities— with their novel form of government, architecture, technology, and way of life—were a constant source of wonder and a useful model for the local inhabitants. The mestizo communities, being located physically, physiologically, and culturally midway between the European or foreign Asian and the Southeast Asian, proved ideal mediators in the flow of ideas between groups.

As a result of the frequent interaction of the various groups within the European-controlled cities and in smaller outposts, the life of the Southeast Asian was affected. Foreign advances in shipbuilding and firearms production were greatly admired, but the extent to which the Southeast Asians adopted this new technology depended upon their perceived needs. The situation in long-distance trade had changed dramatically with the introduction of new cargo ships and the armed merchantmen of the

Europeans, and with the financial advantages of using Chinese-style junks for the China trade. Furthermore, there were now too many risks in the open sea and too much competition from the government-supported European ventures and from the growing Chinese junk trade. The Southeast Asians therefore concentrated on the commercial traffic within the region and abandoned the long-distance Southeast Asian *jong* for the hybrid *chuan* and for smaller, faster, and more manoeuvrable boats.

A similar pragmatic decision was made with regard to the adaptation of firearms to Southeast Asian warfare. There was a true appreciation of the effectiveness of the new weapons, and the Southeast Asians invested time and effort to develop their own arms and gunpowder. Ultimately, however, the new weapons were used to reinforce traditional ways of fighting rather than to transform the tactics of warfare. In the mainland states there were successful attempts to integrate corps of musketeers and gunners into the armies. Nevertheless, these new guns were employed in traditional war tactics where the war elephant, pikes, swords, and spears were still the dominant weaponry. In the archipelago the new arms technology was admired but used selectively in the traditional battle where the initial skirmish could decide the outcome, and where stockades (*kubu*) were regarded as temporary shelters which could be as easily abandoned as defended. One important use which Southeast Asian rulers had for the new weapons was to harness their spiritual powers for the benefit of the kingdom. This led to the practice of accumulating large numbers of decorative and unuseable guns, and to the tendency to venerate certain cannon as palladia of kingdoms. Southeast Asians were true to their character in regarding both the spiritual and the temporal spheres as being intertwined, hence employing the cannon to fight the enemy on both fronts.

Between 1500 and 1800 Southeast Asians adapted new ideas from the outside world in the same way as they had done in the past. The nature of these adaptations, which involved selective borrowing within an accepted cultural framework, had always been successful in the past. Nevertheless, it was already becoming apparent by the late eighteenth century that this traditional response toward new technological advances in shipbuilding and firearms production was inadequate in face of the threat from the Europeans. The strength of Southeast Asian culture had always been its ability to select outside ideas and to adapt them to accepted practice. But in the nineteenth century this formula proved inadequate to prevent the gradual loss of Southeast Asia's economic and military dominance to foreign groups.

BIBLIOGRAPHIC ESSAY

On foreign groups in Southeast Asia

The Asians
On the Chinese a dated but still useful general work is Victor Purcell, *The Chinese in Southeast Asia*, London, 1965. For a background on the Chinese

traders and migrants who came from Southeastern China, especially from
Amoy, to Southeast Asia in the seventeenth and eighteenth centuries,
see Ng Chin-keong, *Trade and society: the Amoy network on the China coast
1683–1735*, Singapore, 1983. A summary of pre-twentieth-century Chinese
activity in Thailand can be found in chapter one of G. William Skinner's,
Chinese society in Thailand: an analytical history, Ithaca, 1957. Two studies on
the Chinese involvement in Southeast Asia, specifically on the Sino-
Siamese trade, are Jennifer W. Cushman, 'Fields from the Sea: Chinese
Junk Trade with Siam during the Late Eighteenth and Early Nineteenth
Centuries', Ph. D. thesis, Cornell University, 1975; and Sarasin Viraphol's
Tribute and profit: Sino-Siamese trade 1652–1853, Cambridge, Mass., 1977.
One of the few sources on the Chinese in Cambodia is W. E. Willmott,
'History and sociology of the Chinese in Cambodia prior to the French
Protectorate', JSEAS, 7, 1 (March 1966). Leonard Blussé, *Strange Company:
Chinese settlers, mestizo women and the Dutch in VOC Batavia*, Dordrecht,
1986, is a collection of articles on various aspects of Chinese presence
in Batavia and on Java. For a useful periodization of Chinese involvement
in trade to Southeast Asia and Chinese impact on local societies, see
Leonard Blussé, 'Chinese commercial networks and state formation in
Southeast Asia 1600–1800', paper presented to the Conference on Southeast Asia from the Fifteenth to the Eighteenth Centuries, Lisbon, December
1989. See also Peter Carey, 'Changing Javanese perceptions of the Chinese
communities in Central Java, 1755–1825', *Indonesia*, 37 (April 1984). More
spotty in quality is another collection of articles by different authors edited
by Felix Alfonso, Jr, *The Chinese in the Philippines*, Manila, 1968, I: *1570–
1770*; II: *1770–1898*. One particularly interesting article in vol. I of
this collection is Maria Lourdes Diaz-Trechuelo's, 'The Role of the Chinese
in the Philippine Domestic Economy'. A well-researched book on the
Chinese and the Chinese mestizo community in the Philippines is Edgar
Wickberg, *The Chinese in Philippine Life, 1850–1898*, New Haven, 1965.

For the Japanese, see Iwao Seiichi, 'Japanese Foreign Trade in the
Sixteenth and Seventeenth Centuries', *Acta Asiatica*, 30 (1976), for a
summary and discussion on the Japanese trade to Southeast Asia in this
period. A more detailed study is R. L. Innes, 'The door ajar: Japan's
foreign trade in the seventeenth century', Ph.D. thesis, University of
Michigan, 1980. An interesting examination of Japanese sources regarding
Southeast Asian trade, especially with Thailand, is Yoneo Ishii, 'Seventeenth century Japanese documents about Siam', JSS, 59, 2 (July 1971).

For the Indians see M. N. Pearson and Ashin Das Gupta, eds, *India and
the Indian ocean, 1500–1800*, Calcutta, 1987, for articles on the importance
of Southeast Asia in the wider world of Indian trade. See especially
S. Arasaratnam, 'India and the Indian ocean in the seventeenth century',
which provides a discussion on the various arms of the Indian trade and
the role of each region of India in this trade in the seventeenth century. A
similar focus and intent for the sixteenth and eighteenth centuries are
found in this same volume in M. N. Pearson, 'India and the Indian ocean
in the sixteenth century'; and in Ashin Das Gupta, 'India and the Indian
ocean in the eighteenth century'. For an interpretative essay placing India
within the broader canvas of world trade, see K. N. Chaudhuri, *Trade and*

civilizatirn in the Indian ocean: an economic history from the rise of Islam to 1750, Cambridge, UK, 1985. A contemporary account of Indian trading activities in Southeast Asia at the beginning of the sixteenth century can be found in Armando Cortesão, ed. and trans., *The Suma Oriental of Tomé Pires*, 2 vols, London, 1944.

The Europeans

Donald F. Lach's five-volume work entitled *Asia in the making of Europe*, Chicago, 1965–77, focuses on Asian contributions to European civilization and contains English summaries of many obscure European accounts of activities of early explorers and administrators in Asia. Holden Furber, *Rival empires of trade in the Orient, 1600–1800*, Minneapolis, 1976, discusses the individual European trading companies' structures and their trade in Asia in the seventeenth and eighteenth centuries. For a more recent discussion of Asian and European trade in Southeast Asia, consult a collection of articles edited by P.-Y. Manguin and G. Bouchon entitled *Asian trade and civilisation*, Cambridge, 1989.

For the Spanish, there is J. H. Parry's *The Spanish seaborne empire*, London, 1966, which describes Spanish overseas expansion, while J. H. Elliot, *Imperial Spain, 1469–1716*, Harmondsworth, 1963, provides a general background for understanding the motivations and the activities of the Spanish overseas officials. For an account of Spanish explorations to Asia and the Pacific, see O. H. K. Spate, *The Spanish Lake*, Canberra, 1979.

For the Portuguese, B. W. Diffie and G. D. Winius, *Foundations of the Portuguese empire 1415–1580*, Minneapolis, 1977, provides a general account of the Portuguese nation and its efforts to establish an overseas empire. It also contains a detailed discussion of the workings of the *Estado da India* and of Portuguese activities in Asia. C. R. Boxer, *The Portuguese seaborne empire*, London, 1969, complements the previous study in his discussion of the official and unofficial lives and works of the Portuguese and their descendants in Portugal's world-wide empire. For a study of the various Portuguese intra-Asian trade routes and the value of each route in the sixteenth century, see Luis Filipe F. R. Thomaz, 'Les Portugais dans les mers de l'archipel au XVIe siècle', *Archipel*, 18 (1979); P.-Y. Manguin, *Les Portugais sur les côtes du Viet-Nam et du Campá*, Paris, 1972; and George B. Souza, *The survival of empire: Portuguese trade and society in China and the South China Sea, 1630–1754*, Cambridge, UK, 1986.

For the northern Europeans the story of the rise of the Dutch nation as a European maritime power in the sixteenth and seventeenth centuries is discussed in B. Vlekke, *Evolution of the Dutch nation*, New York, 1951; Charles Wilson, *Profit and power*, London, 1957, and Pieter Geyl, *The Netherlands in the seventeenth century, 1609–1648*, 2 vols, New York, 1961. A more recent and stimulating account of Dutch society in the seventeenth century is Simon Schama's *The embarrassment of riches: an interpretation of Dutch culture in the golden age*, London, 1987. C. R. Boxer, *The Dutch seaborne empire*, London, 1965, provides a descriptive account of Dutch society and government overseas, while O. H. K. Spate, *Monopolists and freebooters*, Canberra, 1983, examines the Dutch and English voyages to Asia and the Pacific in the seventeenth and eighteenth centuries. The structure and the

economic activities of the English East India Company are documented in
K. N. Chaudhuri, *The trading world of Asia and the English East India Company
1660–1760*, Cambridge, UK, 1978. A good collection of articles on the
various European East India Companies can be found in L. Blussé and
F. Gaastra, eds, *Companies and trade: Essays on overseas trading companies
during the Ancien Régime*, London, 1981.

For an account of the intra-Asian trade, the classic study is still M. A. P.
Meilink-Roelofsz, *Asian trade and European influence in the Indonesian archipelago between 1500 and about 1630*, The Hague, 1962. Kristof Glamann's
Dutch-Asiatic trade, 1620–1740, 's-Gravenhage, 1981, 2nd edition, focuses
on the products which were sold in Europe in order to reconstruct the
relative value of specific items in the Dutch trade with Asia.

On innovations and adaptations in Southeast Asia

The European-controlled city
A readable account of the life of the Portuguese community in Melaka is
the article by I. A. Macgregor, 'The Portuguese in Malaya', JMBRAS, 28, 2
(1955). One of the most valuable pictures of Melaka at the time of the
Dutch conquest in 1641 is Joost Schouten's report of his visit to Melaka
dated 7 September 1641, which forms part of P. A. Leupe's *The siege and
capture of Malacca from the Portuguese in 1640–1641*, published in the
JMBRAS, 14, 1 (1936). Dutch Melaka is described in a lively style by
Barbara Watson Andaya in her 'Melaka under the Dutch, 1641–1795' in
K. S. Sandhu and Paul Wheatley, eds, *Melaka: the transformation of a Malay
capital c. 1400–1980*, 2 vols, Kuala Lumpur, 1983, I. 195–241. For Batavia
the most valuable work remains F. de Haan's *Oud Batavia*, Batavia, 1922. A
more recent work which examines the social history of Batavia and
present-day Jakarta is Susan Abeyasekere, *Jakarta: a history*, Singapore,
1987. The best single work on Manila is Robert R. Reed, *Colonial Manila: the
context of Hispanic urbanism and process of morphogenesis*, Berkeley, 1978.

The mestizo or 'mixed' communities
An interesting study of the mestizo groups in Batavia is Jean Gelman
Taylor, *The Social world of Batavia: European and Eurasian in Dutch Asia*,
Madison, 1983. It traces the origins and development of the Eurasian
population in the Dutch-controlled city of Batavia, with an emphasis on
the role of Asian and Eurasian women in the creation of a unique Betawi
culture. C. R. Boxer, *The Portuguese seaborne empire*, London, 1969, and *The
Dutch seaborne empire*, London, 1965, devote chapters to the special mestizo
community which arose from the Portuguese policy to encourage mis-
cegenation in their colonies. Boxer, *Race relations in the Portuguese colonial
empire, 1415–1825*, Oxford, 1963, provides a detailed study of the creation
of the mestizo communities and the racist issues which arose in Portuguese overseas territories. A recent study of this community is by Ronald
Daus, *Portuguese Eurasian communities in Southeast Asia*, Singapore, 1989.
Edgar Wickberg, *The Chinese in Philippine life, 1850–1898*, New Haven,

1965, contains excellent sections on the Chinese mestizo. See also Jesus
Merino's 'The Chinese Mestizo: general considerations' in Alfonso Felix,
Jr, ed., *The Chinese in the Philippines*, Manila, 1968, II: *1770–1898*, 45–66.

Shipping and navigation
For an introduction to early shipbuilding traditions in different parts of the
world, see Paul Johnstone, *The sea-craft of prehistory*, Cambridge, Mass.,
1980. A reconstruction of the earliest Southeast Asian ship and the type of
long-distance ships which the Europeans found in Southeast Asia in the
sixteenth century is found in P.-Y. Manguin, 'The Southeast Asian ship: an
historical approach', JSEAS, 11, 2 (September 1980). On the latest archaeological finds on Southeast Asian ships, especially of the hybrid 'South
China shipbuilding tradition', see P.-Y. Manguin, 'The trading ships of
insular South-East Asia: New evidence from Indonesian archaeological
sites', *Proceedings Pertemuan Ilmiah Arkeologi*, 5 (July 1989). For a discussion
of the more ordinary boats found in the archipelago, see Adrian Horridge,
The perahu: traditional sailing boat of Indonesia, Singapore, 1985, as well as his
Outrigger canoes of Bali and Madura, Indonesia, Bishop Museum Special
Publication 77, Honolulu, 1987. See Virginia Matheson and Barbara Watson Andaya, *The Precious Gift: Tuhfat al-Nafis*, Kuala Lumpur, 1982, for a list
of the types of ships which were used in Malay waters. An excellent
discussion of boatbuilding and navigation techniques in the Philippines is
William Henry Scott, 'Boat-building and seamanship in classic Philippine
society', in Scott, *Cracks in the parchment curtain*, Quezon City, 1982.

Descriptions of other Southeast Asian vessels can be gleaned from
reports of contemporary European official documents or travellers' accounts.
A short discussion of Maluku boats based on seventeenth-century Dutch
archival sources can be found in G. J. Knaap, 'Kruidnagelen en Christenen: De Vereenigde Oost-Indische Companie en de bevolking van
Ambon 1656–1696', Ph.D. thesis, Utrecht University, 1985. One especially
important collection is I. Commelin, *Begin ende Voortgang van de Vereenigde
Nederlandtsche Geoctroyeerde Oost-Indische Compagnie*. 4 vols, Amsterdam,
1646, which provides not only excellent descriptions of various types of
boats which the Dutch encountered in Southeast Asian waters at the end
of the sixteenth and early seventeenth centuries, but also beautiful illustra-
tions of the different craft.

A general overview of Indian shipping and shipbuilding methods is
found in Radha Kumud Mookerji, *Indian shipping: a history of the seaborne
trade and maritime activity of the Indians from early times*, Bombay, 1957. K. N.
Chaudhuri, *Trade and civilization in the Indian ocean: an economic history from
the rise of Islam to 1750*, Cambridge, UK, 1985, contains a more recent
discussion on ships and navigation of Indian traders in this period. The
type of Indian ships which sailed to Southeast Asia in this period is
discussed in Clifford W. Hawkins, *The dhow, an illustrated history of the dhow
and its world*, Lymington, 1977.

Regarding the Chinese junks and sampans which were in use in Southeast Asia, see Jennifer W. Cushman, 'Fields from the sea: Chinese junk
trade with Siam during the late eighteenth and early nineteenth centuries',

Ph.D. thesis, Cornell University, 1975. On the early development of Chinese ships and their contribution to the world of shipping and navigation, see Joseph Needham, *Science and civilisation in China*, IV: *Physics and Physical Technology*, part 29 'Nautics', Cambridge, UK, 1971, 376–699.

Firearms and warfare
A monumental work on the evolution of gunpowder and various types of firearms is Joseph Needham's *Science and civilisation in China*, V: *Chemistry and Chemical Technology*, part 7, 'Military Technology; The Gunpowder Epic', Cambridge, UK, 1986. From this early beginning, one can trace the evolution of firearms and battle tactics in Europe, the Muslim lands, and Asia in the works of Carlo M. Cipolla, *Guns and sails in the early phase of European expansion 1400–1700*, London, 1965; James D. Lavin, *A history of Spanish firearms*, London, 1965; John Francis Guilmartin, *Gunpowder and galleys: changing technology and Mediterranean warfare at sea in the sixteenth century*, Cambridge, UK, 1974; and Geoffrey Parker, *The military revolution; military innovation and the rise of the West, 1500–1800*, Cambridge, UK, 1988. India's contribution to firearms technology can be found in the works of O. P. Jaggi, *Science and technology in medieval India*, Delhi, 1977; and Iqtidar Alam Khan, 'Early use of cannon and musket in India, AD 1442–1526', *Journal of the Economic and Social History of the Orient*, 24, 2 (1981). A concise account of firearms and battle tactics in Japan, much of which had relevance to Southeast Asia, is Sugimoto Masayoshi and David L. Swain, *Science and culture in traditional Japan, AD 600–1854*, Cambridge, Mass., 1978.

The material on firearms and battle tactics in Southeast Asia has not been collected in a compendium, such as those which exist for China, Japan, and India. One of the more general accounts which attempts to place Southeast Asian developments in the wider context of firearms developments in other parts of the world is C. R. Boxer, 'Asian potentates and European artillery in the sixteenth to the eighteenth centuries: a footnote to Gibson-Hill', JMBRAS, 38, 2 (1965). Others are much more specific and often deal only with one group of people, such as Manuel Godinho de Eredia, 'Description of Malaca, and Meridional India and Cathay', trans. J. V. Mills, JMBRAS, 8, 1 (1930), on the Malay manner of warfare and their armaments in the early seventeenth century. On Siam there is C. A. Seymour Sewell, 'Notes on some old Siamese Guns', JSS, 15 (May 1922), which provides the history and some technical details on guns and gunpowder-making in Siam. For Burma, despite the lack of material on the technical aspects on the production of firearms, there are numerous references to the use of guns and gunpowder in Than Tun, ed and trans., *The royal orders of Burma, AD 1598–1885*, Kyoto, 1983–8. See also Victor B. Lieberman, 'Europeans, trade, and the unification of Burma, c. 1540–1620', *Oriens Extremus*, 27, 2 (1980). Vietnam's early adoption and use of firearms is documented in Charles B.-Maybon, *Histoire moderne du pays d'Annam (1592–1820)*, Paris, 1919. A seventeenth-century account of the skills of the Vietnamese gunners, their training, and the establishment of gunfoundries is contained in Alexander de Rhodes (trans. Solange Hertz), *Rhodes of Viet Nam. The travels and missions of Father Alexander de Rhodes in*

China and other kingdoms of the Orient, Maryland, 1966. For the use of firearms and the making of guns and gunpowder in the archipelago, the information is scattered in a number of works. Luc Nagtegaal's 'Rijden op een Hollandse Tijger: De Noordkust van Java en de V.O.C. 1680–1743', Ph.D. thesis, Utrecht University 1988, discusses Javanese warfare, the production of guns and gunpowder, and the place of firearms in battle tactics. For a similar discussion on Aceh, see Denys Lombard, *Le Sultanat d'Atjeh au temps d'Iskandar Muda, 1607–1636*, Paris, 1967; for the Bugis and Makassar peoples, see Leonard Y. Andaya, *The heritage of Arung Palakka: A History of South Sulawesi (Celebes) in the Seventeenth Century*, The Hague, 1981; for Sulu and Magindanao, see James Warren, *The Sulu zone, 1768– 1898: The dynamics of external trade, slavery, and ethnicity in the transformation of a Southeast Asian maritime state*, Singapore, 1981; and for Maluku, see Hubert Jacobs, *A treatise on the Moluccas*, Rome, 1970.

POLITICAL DEVELOPMENT BETWEEN THE SIXTEENTH AND EIGHTEENTH CENTURIES

The immense cultural diversity of Southeast Asia and the linguistic skills required to approach the sources have tended to encourage localized rather than general studies of the region. The yawning gaps in our knowledge, the difficulties in interpreting information and the very real differences within even the larger divisions of 'island' and 'mainland' do not facilitate efforts to draw the Southeast Asian past together. What can the highly literate, Sinicised élite of seventeenth-century Vietnam have in common with the more oral, Muslim courts of the Malay states? Is it possible to conceive of a Shan community in the hills of upper Burma as sharing in any sense the same world as villagers on a small isolated island in eastern Indonesia? At times it seems that the more closely one approaches the material, the more elusive a common history becomes. Yet the longer view may make the task less formidable. From a contemporary vantage-point the most significant development of the pre-modern period is the slow movement towards the larger political groupings which were to form the bases of later nation-states. This movement was by no means irrevocable, nor was it everywhere apparent. But whereas throughout Southeast Asia the 'states' at the beginning of the sixteenth century only generally approximate those we know today, three hundred years later the current shape of Southeast Asia is clearly discernible. It is the process which brought this about which we shall now examine.

THE POLITICAL LANDSCAPE

Reconstruction of early Southeast Asian history has understandably focused on those places which have left tangible evidence in the form of monuments or some kind of documentation. In effect this has encouraged an interpretation of Southeast Asia's past as a progression from one 'great state' to another. But the historical dominance of an Angkor or a Pagan can sometimes lead us to forget that they were a coalescence of local power centres, and that whatever cohesion they attained was at best tenuous. It was the political fragmentation of Southeast Asia which often struck early

European commentators. Marco Polo saw north Sumatra as a place where 'there are eight kingdoms and eight crowned kings . . . every kingdom has a language of its own'; in the same vein a Portuguese, whose country had been under one monarch since the eleventh century, remarked that the Laos appeared to have 'so many kingdoms'.[1]

The 'polycentred' nature of pre-modern Southeast Asia is traceable to a number of factors. First, it is useful to remember that much of the region, even into modern times, has been occupied by peoples who are basically tribal. The essence of a tribal grouping is that it is normally 'not a political organization but rather a socio-cultural-ethnic unity'.[2] Fission into segments, frequently hostile to each other, is common, although these segments can readily act together against any shared threat from outside. But because tribal segments tend to see themselves as equivalent, and because they are often economically and socially self-sustaining units, the normal 'political' condition tends towards disunity rather than towards a permanently organized state.

A second consideration is the potential for division which results from the character of leadership in most Southeast Asian societies. Influence over others can be due to inherited rights, but it more frequently reflects personal standing and exceptional ability, subsumed in the notion that some individuals possessed of extraordinary 'fortune' or 'luck' will be able to control the vagaries of fate. This deep-rooted attitude to leadership coexists with the concept that certain lineages are innately superior because of their descent from some great ancestor. Thus the archetypal Malay hero who had become entrenched in folk legend is known as 'Hang Tuah' (the fortunate lord), while Ramathibodi of Ayutthaya (r. 1491–1529) is described as one of the 'most fortunate kings'. Similarly a Shan chronicle attributes the success of a local saw-bwa (tribal head) to his complex but favourable horoscope 'when Lagana was in the realm of Fasuddho . . . and because Venus was together with Lagana'.[3]

Frequently the 'luck' of such a person was made evident to others by the discovery of some unusual object in which was vested a supernatural quality. Javanese babads (verse chronicles), for example, relate the story of a coconut owned by a palmwine tapper. Any individual who drank the milk of this coconut was destined to become the founder of a future royal house in Java. The winetapper, however, allowed the future Lord of Mataram to drink the milk in his place, and it was thus that the dynasty which ruled central Java during the seventeenth century was founded. The importance of holding such sacred objects is especially apparent in traditions associated with the Bugis and Makassarese communities of Sulawesi. Here legends describe how the special aspects of the original founder were recognized when he or she came across an item such as a rusty ploughshare, a seed or an unusually shaped stone. These then became the

---

[1] Henry Yule, ed. and trans., *The Book of Ser Marco Polo*, 3rd edn, London, 1926, II. 284; C. R. Boxer, *South China in the Sixteenth Century*, London, 1953, 70.

[2] Marshall D. Sahlins, 'The segmentary lineage: an organization of predatory expansion', in Ronald Cohen and John Middleton, eds, *Comparative Political Systems; Studies in the Politics of Pre-Industrial Societies*, New York: American Museum of Natural History, 94.

[3] Sao Saimong Mangrai, *The Padaeng Chronicle and the Jentung State Chronicle Translated*, Michigan Papers on South and Southeast Asia, no. 19, University of Michigan, 1981, 250.

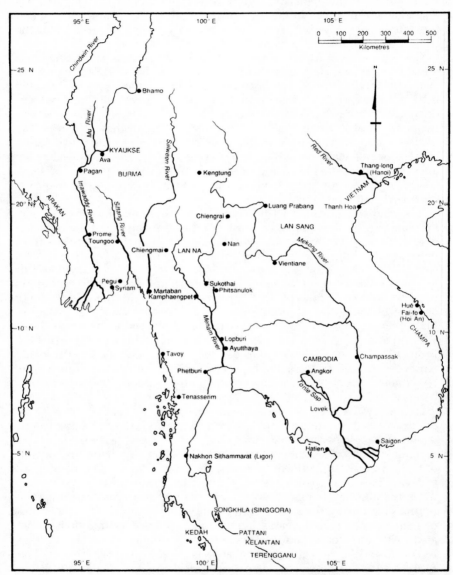

Map 2.1   Mainland Southeast Asia, 1500–1800.

palladium (*gaukang*) of the community and the person who held it the ruler. Throughout Southeast Asia an individual who was successful in obtaining control of these power-laden objects was capable of mounting a formidable challenge to potential rivals.

The proliferation of localized areas of authority was also a reflection of Southeast Asia's geography. The extensive river basins of the mainland and Java may seem conducive to human settlement, but villages were often separated by wide stretches of forest and by hilly ranges, so that few people travelled regularly outside their own district. This social world was even more limited as one moved away from more populated areas. The mountain chains dissecting the highlands, the network of rivers cutting through dense jungle, the inhospitable swamp forests along the coasts, the thousands of islands scattered across the archipelago, all served to encourage the growth of communities which were physically distanced from each other. Styles of dress, social customs and particularly language fostered a local identification with a particular area. In the Philippines today, for instance, eighty languages are still spoken, and on the island of Panay alone there are said to be about forty separate dialects.

The societies which developed naturally from a fragmented environment were infused by attitudes which conceived of the landscape as an array of power-points, each the realm of one or more divinities regarded as manifestations of potent forces within the earth. From Assam to the easternmost islands of the archipelago, clusters of kinship-bonded communities were inextricably linked to ancestor spirits associated with mountains, trees, rivers, caves, rocks and to particular areas under the sway of supernatural deities. As Paul Mus has cogently put it, 'the locality itself is a god'.[4] In some areas this delineation of a 'locality' was clearly determined by landmarks like prominent mountains or watersheds, and the Semai of the Malay peninsula still commonly claim a 'land' that takes its name from a recognized geographical feature such as a small stream. Elsewhere more formalized territorial divisions were established. A royal decree from fourteenth-century Burma, for instance, lays down that 'boundary demarcations are always to be respected', and when the Portuguese first arrived on the island of Ternate in eastern Indonesia they noted that the local people 'keep boundaries and landmarks all over their territories, domains, places, villages and towns'.[5]

Ritual ceremony conducted at sacred spots within these boundaries helped to weld the community together. A missionary travelling in Dai Viet (Vietnam) in the latter part of the seventeenth century described the solemn oath of loyalty taken in each village by the officials. Sworn under the aegis of local guardian spirits, this oath promised the most terrible of punishments for those who broke it. An even more potent means of reiterating communal bonds was the offering of life, either animal or human, to powerful territorial spirits. In the early nineteenth century an

---

[4] *India Seen from the East: Indian and Indigenous Cults of Champa*, trans. I. W. Mabbett and D. P. Chandler, Monash Papers on Southeast Asia, no. 3, Melbourne, 1973, 13.

[5] Than Tun, trans., *The Royal Orders of Burma, A.D. 1598–1885*, I, Kyoto, Center for Southeast Asian Studies, 1983, 4; A. Galvão, *A Treatise on the Moluccas (c. 1544)*, ed. and trans. Hubert Th. Jacobs, Rome: Jesuit Historical Institute, 1971, 105.

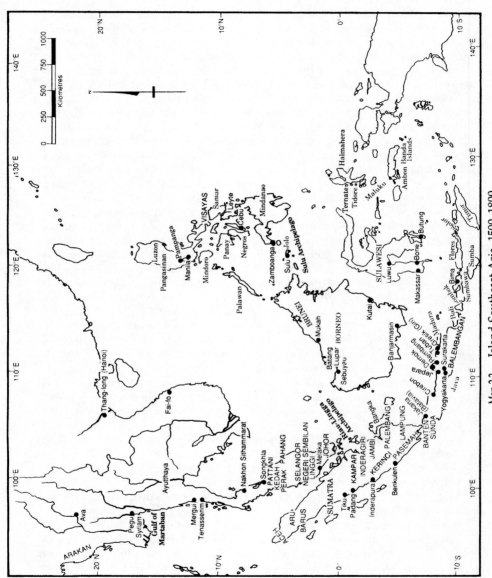

Map 2.2 Island Southeast Asia, 1500–1800.

old ceremony was still practised at Ba Phnom in Cambodia whereby a slave or criminal was sacrificed, the victim's head being impaled and offered to the major cult figure, a fertility goddess, while other parts of the body were offered to gods at other cult sites.

A sense of identification with a particular community was also encouraged by rivalries with neighbouring groups. Usually such feuding occurred because of competition over economic resources, with the aim of gaining control of a strategically placed river junction, a stretch of jungle known to produce certain exotic timbers, or a locality famed for its gold or rubies. In this environment intrusion by one group into an area regarded as properly belonging to another could be a serious crime. Amongst the aboriginal jungle dwellers, the so-called *kubu* of Sumatra, who specialized in collecting valuable forest products, death was the punishment for any individual who trespassed into the territory where he or she had no collecting rights. Slave raiding was another source of inter-communal conflicts. It is probable, for instance, that in early times Cham coastal groups thrived on the slave trade, and the place of such expeditions in Philippine society is suggested by the fact that in all the major languages of the archipelago the word *mangayaw* means 'to raid enemy territory'. Among a number of peoples raiding was also necessary to obtain victims for ritual sacrifice. In Burma, for instance, *myosade* is the name specifically given to a human victim buried alive under the foundations of a great building in order to provide a guardian spirit. Revenge was also a compelling motive for feuding, while among groups such as the Iban of Borneo or the Abung of Sumatra the taking of heads in raids was necessary in order to demonstrate manhood and obtain a wife.

In a discussion of the movement towards greater political entities in Southeast Asia, the potential for friction between communities deserves attention. While such friction could foster the localization of loyalties, it could equally serve as a stimulus for greater co-operation among groups as they sought to withstand attack by a predatory neighbour or themselves prey upon a weaker one. The unity established during these periods might subsequently fall apart, but memories of amicable relations could well be revived. Alliances, even if short-lived, could often allay old rivalries, and legends frequently recall the erection of a boundary stone to symbolize an agreement between two previously hostile communities. Gradually, too, traditions could develop which facilitated the resolution of future grievances. Certain sites such as the graves of ancestors might be designated as places where disputes could be settled by negotiation and discussion, with the decision sealed by an impressive oath. Among numerous archipelago groups it became customary to divert violence into mock battles. Ritual cockfighting, which sanctioned the death of a victim and the letting of blood, could thus serve as a symbolic means of expressing and defusing hostility between opposing factions.

The binding medium in the creation of bonds between communities was always kinship, usually formalized by a ceremony whereby two leaders accepted each other as brothers. The links which this new-found fraternity could bring about are well illustrated by a Shan chronicle's description of an alliance between two brothers, rulers of the Khun (Kengtung) and Lu peoples: 'When heat [mortal danger] comes from the Laos, let the Khun state be the fence, let the Lu state be the roots and yams; when cold [danger] comes from the Chinese, let the Lu state be the fence, let Kengtung state be the roots and yams'. The ancient custom by which two men could become brothers by together drinking each other's blood (called *thwethauk* in Burma) was legitimized in Theravāda Buddhist society by the *dhammathat* law books, and it was the *thwethauk* relationship which frequently bound a Burman overlord to his powerful vassals. The ability of such rituals to transform the most distant stranger into a kinsman is suggested in an early Spanish account of the Philippines when 'the Indian sucked the blood of the Spaniard and vice versa' and they thus became brothers.[6]

The cultural and geographic environment of Southeast Asia had a fundamental influence on the manner in which the polities of the region evolved. Confederations of communities which saw themselves as equivalent were found in many parts of Southeast Asia when the Europeans reached the region at the beginning of the sixteenth century. Relations between leaders and followers mirrored the obligations of kinfolk, and leadership itself was based on the belief that certain individuals were imbued with special qualities and had a relationship with the gods and spirits which enabled them to perform feats beyond the capabilities of ordinary mortals. In areas more exposed to outside influences, most commonly from India or China, this indigenous pattern had been overlaid by one which laid greater stress on hierarchy and which more clearly identified a dominant centre and its subordinate satellites. Yet the analogy of the family was still constantly invoked to explain and justify the resulting overlord–vassal relationships. Like a parent, the overlord should give protection, assistance and occasionally a stern rebuke; in return, the vassal/child should return loyalty, respect and service. The ideal of personal and continuing reciprocity which grew out of concepts of kinship lay at the heart of the Southeast Asian polity, and it could well be argued that whatever 'structure' can be discerned in most early kingdoms was ultimately based on the bonds of family. It was the exchange of women which made these bonds tangible, for the children that resulted from subsequent unions became a living symbol of irrevocable kinship. In the early sixteenth century in Ternate, for instance, the king was surrounded by 'four hundred women' and high ranking chiefs supplied him with sisters, aunts, cousins, nieces, and daughters and 'some are designated for this while they are still in their mothers' wombs'.[7]

A type of authority which resolved potential conflicts through reliance on personal loyalty to a high-ranking elder, chief, ruler or overlord could, at its best, function well. The possibility of fragmentation, however, was always present. The parent–child relationship imposed a clear hierarchy which might in some cases be unacceptable, and ties of kinship could well involve conflicting loyalties. Even the most solemn oath of allegiance could

[6] Pedro Chirino, *The Philippines in 1600*, trans. Ramon Echevarria, Manila, 1969, 235; Mangrai, *The Padaeng Chronicle*, 234.
[7] A. Cortasão, ed. and trans., *The Suma Oriental of Tomé Pires*, London, 1944, I. 215; Galvão, *A Treatise*, 89.

not easily be inherited or transferred. The typical Southeast Asian 'kingdom' was a coalescence of localized power centres, ideally bound together not by force but through a complex interweaving of links engendered by blood connections and obligation. Leadership, conceived in personal and ritual terms, required constant reaffirmation. On the death of each ruler, there-fore, his successor's authority had to be reconstituted with a renewal of marriage bonds and a vow of loyalty. This was especially true if he had more than one wife. While the women surrounding a leader were an important political statement, they could also yield an abundance of potential heirs, whose claims they could work to support. As states became larger, the liminal period between the death of one king and the installation of the next could often prove to be a time of crisis.

The possibility of retreat from centralized control was the greater because local loyalties remained a feature of all Southeast Asian states, and normally considerable autonomy was retained by regional centres. A prime example is the kingdom of Ayutthaya, which at the end of the fifteenth century dominated the central Menam basin. The territory under Ayutthaya's control, however, was divided into a number of graduated *muang* or settlements, each under its own governor. The latter might acknowledge the overlordship of Ayutthaya and drink the sanctified water of allegiance to show their loyalty, but as royal relatives and *muang* lords their status could be almost equivalent to that of the ruler. The governor of Kamphaengpet, remarked Tomé Pires, was 'like a king' inside his own territory.[8] Independence naturally increased with distance from the cen-tre, and although a law of 1468–9 claims that twenty kings paid Ayutthaya homage, its hold sat lightly on distant Malay Muslim tributaries such as Pahang, Kelantan, Terengganu, and Pattani. These areas essentially acted as autonomous states and as long as appropriate gifts were sent regularly to Ayutthaya there was little interference in their affairs. Similarly loose ties between centre and periphery were found in the kingdoms of the island world, and the sense of independence which this localization of authority encouraged is clearly expressed by the great Malay history, the *Sejarah Melayu*. In the words of a Melaka noble: 'As for us who administer territory, what concern is that of yours? For territory is territory even if it is only the size of a coconut shell. What we think should be done we do, for the ruler is not concerned with the difficulties we adminstrators encounter, he only takes account of the good results we achieve.'[9]

SOUTHEAST ASIA DURING THE SIXTEENTH CENTURY

The sixteenth century saw developments which were to have far-reaching effects on the political evolution of Southeast Asia. One prominent feature of the period is the continuing expansion of international commerce and the consequent rise of new exchange centres. On the mainland, settle-ments such as Pegu on the Burmese littoral were prime beneficiaries of the

---

[8] *Suma Oriental*, I. 109.
[9] C. C. Brown, ed. and trans., *'Sejarah Melayu* or Malay Annals', JMBRAS, 25, 2 and 3 (1952) 66.

increased traffic, and a desire for greater participation in seaborne trade may have prompted the shift of the Khmer capital south to Lovek (near modern Phnom Penh) about 1504. It was in the island world, however, where the proliferation of trading centres was most apparent, fuelled by a growing world demand for the region's products. The western archipelago had long been part of a wider commercial world, but now the expanding market for fine spices encouraged Javanese, Malay and Chinese traders to deal directly with sources of supply in the eastern islands. As a result, this previously little-frequented area became integrated into a commercial network which stretched to China, India and into Europe itself.

The rise of new ports was further stimulated by the arrival of Europeans in search of spices and by the Portuguese defeat of Melaka in 1511 which saw the flight of Muslim trade to other centres. It was the patronage of local and foreign Muslims, coupled with the rise of pepper-growing, that led to the emergence of Banten in west Java and of Aceh on the northern tip of Sumatra. Other examples of flourishing settlements which had once been of minor importance come readily to mind. Pattani, on the east coast of the Malay peninsula, was a strategic meeting point for Malay and Chinese vessels; across the sea in Borneo the newly Islamized port of Brunei grew to provide an entrepôt for the southern Philippines and the islands of eastern Indonesia.

Some centres in the western archipelago rose to prominence because Melaka's fall also meant the fragmentation of Southeast Asia's most prestigious maritime state. The refugee Melaka dynasty, located in the Riau-Lingga archipelago or in peninsular Johor, now found it more difficult to maintain its hold over its vassals on the peninsula and the east coast of Sumatra. Though a nineteenth-century Malay account recalls that 'in this period all Malay kings ranked below Johor', the descendants of the Melaka dynasty never completely regained their former status and the sixteenth century saw the breakaway of former dependencies such as Perak on the west coast of the Malay peninsula.

The loosening of ties between overlord and vassal was equally apparent on Java's north coast, where a number of harbours were well placed to benefit from participation in the spice trade and the diversion of Muslims from Melaka. By the early sixteenth century these towns were identifiably Islamic, and their links with the interior Hindu-Buddhist kingdom of Majapahit, their nominal suzerain, were weak. Several coastal lords, like Patih Yunus of Demak, had Chinese blood and had gained their position because of personal ability rather than inherited rights. The lord of Japara was even said to be the son of a slave from Borneo. It was probably around 1527 that a coalition of these ports, led by Demak, defeated Majapahit and established their own independence.

In the political development of Southeast Asia the widening participation in international trade had significant repercussions. For established centres such as Ayutthaya, it brought a confirmation of their dominant position. Already favoured by its geographical site, Ayutthaya had been able to take advantage of growing maritime commerce as a result of administrative reorganization under King Trailok (r. 1448–88). A new ministry, the *Mahatthai*, was established to supervise civil matters and to oversee foreign affairs and trade. In the early sixteenth century some Portuguese ranked Ayutthaya with the most powerful continental empires in Asia, and its prosperity was such that later Thai chroniclers regarded this period as a golden age.

Other ports with more recent origins similarly found that the wealth which came from commerce enhanced their status, raising them well above areas with less access to major maritime routes. On the island of Samar in the eastern Philippines, for instance, cloth could be obtained only through intermittent trading contact with outsiders. When Magellan's ships arrived in 1521 only the chiefs wore cotton, while the clothes of the ordinary people were made of bark cloth. In Brunei, however, Magellan's men found a court where even the servants wore gold and silk. The ostentatious lifestyle there was obviously a major reinforcement to claims by the Brunei ruler to stand as the region's overlord.

On another level the rise of small but thriving exchange centres gave a new impulse towards the development of larger groupings, especially in the Philippines and eastern Indonesia. In these areas there had previously been little need or incentive to move towards the formation of 'kingdoms', but a more commercialized environment made increasingly obvious the value of some form of economic and political co-operation in order to strengthen links with wider trading networks. Perhaps the best illustration of this process is Makassar in southwest Sulawesi: during the sixteenth century it grew from a legendary association of the symbolic 'nine' small communities into the focus of regional commerce. A similar process can be traced in a number of other places, like Manila, where by 1570 several *barangay* or villages had grouped together under the authority of two Muslim *datu* (village leaders), who were themselves linked through kinship ties with the court of Brunei.

To a considerable extent, therefore, the economic climate of the early sixteenth century nurtured the movement towards political consolidation, a movement apparent not only among coastal ports, but among prominent interior centres as well. In the Tai-speaking world Ayutthaya may have dominated the Menam basin but to the north was Lan Na with its important *muang* of Chiengmai and Chiengrai, while eastwards lay Lan Sang which included much of modern day Laos and was focused on two *muang* at Luang Prabang and Vientiane. But throughout Southeast Asia an equally important factor in the centralizing process was the reputation for religious patronage which normally accompanied the rise of a commercial centre. It was in these wealthy and populous places that religious scholars gathered, and where the symbols of spiritual prestige—impressive buildings, saintly graves, sacred relics—were most likely to be found. The leadership of Demak on Java's north coast, for example, was based not only on its trading prosperity but on its fame as a centre for Islamic studies and protector of the venerated mosque associated with the first Muslim teachers on Java. The great Buddha statue which was erected at Luang Prabang in 1512 was a source of pride for local Lao, but it also elevated the *muang's* status in the wider Buddhist world.

To a considerable extent the growth of trade and a common religious heritage promoted links between different centres, providing a basis for

closer relationships. It has been argued, indeed, that until the end of the
sixteenth century Lovek and Ayutthaya saw themselves not as separate
polities but as participants in a shared hybrid culture.[10] In Tai-speaking
areas a similarity of dialects encouraged monks to travel between *muang* to
preach at leading monasteries, bringing learned scholars from quite distant
places together. In 1523 Chiengmai was said to have sent sixty copies of
the Tipitaka (the Buddhist canon) and a venerable teacher to Lan Sang,
while the king of Lan Sang was himself educated by two monks, one of
whom came from Nan in eastern Lan Na and the other from Chiengmai.
These links were reinforced by the exchange of women between ruling
families. In 1546, for example, the king of Lan Sang succeeded in Chiengmai because there was no male heir, but he took the two daughters of the
previous ruler as his wives.

In the archipelago, too, the widespread use of Malay and an acceptance
of the Islamic faith fostered continuing interaction between many coastal
trading centres. The travels of ancestors, heroes, kings and religious
teachers between courts which shared basic cultural elements is a recurring theme in local legends. According to Javanese tradition, for instance,
the holy man most closely associated with Surabaya came from Champa,
while in about 1524 the ruler of Demak received his title of sultan at the
hands of a saintly teacher from Sumatra. European sources support the
impression that people of ambition and knowledge moved easily between
these cosmopolitan ports. The lord of Gresik, said Tomé Pires, was a
merchant who was related to the former Melaka king and had himself been
born and raised in Melaka. With this kind of exchange it was possible for
some Malays to see themselves as part of a culture which extended beyond
parochial loyalties. As a noble in the *Sejarah Melayu* remarks, 'Is the Sultan
of Pahang or the Sultan of Perak different from [the Sultan of Melaka]? All
of them are our masters when all is well.'[11]

Yet despite the similarities which helped to draw many Southeast Asian
communities into a mutually beneficial association, competition to attract
trade and control resources also fed continuing rivalry between them. The
Melaka epic, the *Hikayat Hang Tuah*, even describes Inderapura on the east
coast of Sumatra as not truly 'Malay', while Brunei is seen as an 'alien
country'. It was often through the emotive language of religion that this
rivalry was most clearly articulated. Among Buddhist kings frequent
reference was made to the concept of the Universal Monarch, the *cakka-*
vatti, who has obtained his position because of the great merit he has built
up in previous lives and the charismatic glory (*pon*) he has attained in this
one. His rule is characterized by the readiness with which other states
acknowledge him as king and by his possession of sacred objects such as
white elephants, magical horses and women of supernatural power from
whom emanate rays of glowing light. A common Buddhist iconography
accepted throughout most of the mainland meant 'precious objects' were
not now simply of local significance but had a wider value as sources of
intense spiritual power. According to a Portuguese observer, the king

---

[10] David Chandler, *A History of Cambodia*, Boulder, 1983, 80.
[11] Brown, *'Sejarah Melayu'*, 204.

of Ayutthaya would undergo the 'most severe trials' to acquire as many elephants as possible, and Thai and Burmese chronicles are replete with stories of raids which not only depopulate an entire region but carry off holy images, sacred books and teachers. In an environment where several Buddhist kings aspired to become *cakkavatti*, refusal to surrender a white elephant or a set of the Tipitaka was interpreted as a direct challenge.

In the area covered by contemporary Burma (Myanmar) rivalry between developing religious and political centres was complicated by a heritage of ethnic fragmentation. The revival of Mon strength in the fifteenth century had brought a renewed patronage of Buddhism, enhancing the status of the Mon capital at Pegu. Meanwhile, the locus of Burman prestige, Ava, steadily declined. Previously the dominant centre of the Irrawaddy basin, renowned for its sponsorship of Buddhist scholars and its possession of holy scriptures and white elephants, it was now the target of continuing raids by various Shan tribal groups. The latter had developed more cohesive and hierarchical societies than had most hill peoples, in part because of their wet-rice agriculture, and a number of areas were well known as centres of Buddhist study. In Kengtung, for example, some monasteries are said to date from the mid-fourteenth century. Though called simply *saw-bwa* by Burman rulers, the chiefs of Kengtung were entitled by their own people 'lords of the earth' and were regarded by them as kings. In the process of expansion it was perhaps inevitable that such places should look with envy at the more favourable location of lowland areas, and the early sixteenth century was distinguished in Burmese history by the downward Shan thrust. In a desperate move to hold back Shan raids, the ruler of Ava yielded to them progressively more territorial control, but in vain. By 1527 Ava was in Shan hands. The king was killed and a Shan prince placed on the throne, an event which precipitated the flight of Burman refugees southwards to the relative safety of Toungoo on the Sittang River.

The ethnic fragmentation which characterized Burma is, of course, far more pronounced in the archipelago, and to this was added the economic competition which often undercut the slow trend towards larger political unities. This was especially true when centres were in proximity, produced similar products and drew from the same trading network. The relations between the numerous ports along Java's north coast provide a classic example. For a brief period after Majapahit's defeat, Demak was able to establish its suzerainty over rival harbours and even to expand it across the seas to Palembang in Sumatra and Banjarmasin in Borneo. However, the supremacy of Demak rulers was never completely secured, and by the 1550s their position was already under challenge from neighbouring lords. During the late sixteenth century the remarkable success of the newly emergent Mataram in central Java may have been facilitated because of the inability of the coastal rulers to overcome their rivalry and mount any co-ordinated action.

In island Southeast Asia during the sixteenth century the expression of competition in religious terms was accentuated by the spread of Christianity and the importation of hostilities between Muslims and Christians. In eastern Indonesia, where Portuguese missionaries were most active, some kings readily agreed to baptism in the belief that this would ensure them spiritual power and European assistance against their traditional (Muslim) enemies. Throughout the archipelago the Portuguese goal of winning souls as well as gold meant many Muslims perceived them as a danger to their religion as well as a commercial challenge. At intervals, therefore, attempts were made by Islamic states to invoke *jihad* or holy war and to forge a coalition to drive out the infidels. Portuguese Melaka was a prime target and between 1513 and 1529 alliances involving Johor, Aceh, most of Melaka's former vassals, and even Jepara on Java's north coast unsuccessfully attacked the town twelve times. During the 1560s the anti-Christian mood received some encouragement from Turkey which was involved in its own 'holy war' against Christendom.

Despite the recurring calls for a religious crusade, however, relations between the Christian Portuguese and local Muslim kings were always governed by pragmatism. On the one side, Europeans needed to buy and sell, while for their part native rulers often saw a European connection as an important ingredient in commercial success. During a campaign against unbelievers in the 1580s, for instance, the devout Muslim ruler of Banten in west Java forbade trade by the Portuguese, but it was not long before they were permitted to return. The call to holy war against the Europeans was thus only rarely effective. Far more significant were the entrenched rivalries between centres which had existed long before the European arrival or which had developed as a result of the period's heightened economic activity. Now such rivalries could frequently be justified by calling the enemy's religious beliefs into question. Aceh's hostility was directed as much against the commercial challenge of Johor as against the Portuguese, and a seventeenth-century Acehnese poem depicts the Johor prince as an infidel, a sun worshipper, a follower of the prophet Moses.[12]

This is not to imply, of course, that European influence can be overlooked, but it is important to emphasize that in the pre-modern period the experiences of the mainland and the islands diverged quite markedly. In the first place, European interest in the mainland was limited. It was not seen as a source of spices, and it was the aim of dominating this trade which had brought the Portuguese and Spanish to the region. Second, although Europeans actively frequented ports such as Pegu and Ayutthaya, they never controlled a mainland centre that could be compared with Melaka, and thus never exerted the same influence on established trading patterns. Third, the population and economic resources of the states on the mainland far outweighed those of the Europeans in the region. Occasionally an ambitious Portuguese or Spaniard might propose seizing power in one or another kingdom, but the authorities never considered the dubious gains worth the risks such an enterprise would involve. One scholar has put the case quite forcibly: 'Siam and its continental neighbours remained entirely outside the Portuguese imperial design and charted their own destinies during the sixteenth century.'[13]

---

[12] G. W. J. Drewes, ed. and trans., *Hikayat Potjut Muhamat: an Achehnese Epic*, The Hague, 1979, 9.

[13] Donald F. Lach, *Asia in the Making of Europe*, Chicago and London, 1965, I. book 2, 571.

The implications of this statement are well illustrated in an examination of developments in Vietnam. Unlike any other Southeast Asian people, the Vietnamese had experienced centuries of Chinese domination which, while infusing their lives with aspects of China's culture, had also enabled them to conceive of themselves as clearly non-Chinese. A close examination of the laws promulgated under the fifteenth-century Le kings has in fact pointed to a greater sense of a nation-state than is apparent in Chinese legal codes of the same period.[14] This sense of a distinct identity may have been encouraged by Vietnam's move south into the Cham areas after 1471, for Chams were commonly regarded by the Vietnamese as morally and culturally inferior, with whom intermarriage was undesirable. Yet the fragile underpinnings of central control in Southeast Asian kingdoms meant that fragmentation was always possible, even in a relatively unified state such as Vietnam. The Chams bitterly resented their subservience, and in 1504–5 there was a major Cham uprising. At the same time less able Le rulers found it impossible to contain the challenge of ambitious individuals. Between 1505 and 1527 eight kings were installed, six of whom were assassinated by rival aspirants to the throne. In 1527 the head of one of the most powerful regional families, the Mac, succeeded in deposing the Le ruler and installing himself instead, but he was confronted with the continuing opposition of other families who pressed for a restoration of the Le. One of these, the Nguyen clan, gained a foothold in the south central area while the Mac remained in control of the delta region. When both sides appealed to the Chinese as mediators, Beijing ruled that the Mac should govern the north and the Le with their protectors the south. By the middle of the sixteenth century, therefore, hints of a future division in Vietnam were already apparent.

Europeans were not directly involved in these hostilities, although Nguyen Kim's son later successfully used Portuguese cannon against his enemies. The exploitation of Western weaponry was more pronounced in the Menam basin, where the movement towards the creation of a single territorial entity under Ayutthaya's domination was already well in train. Indeed, some scholars have already discerned the genesis of the wider cultural-political unity which lies at the heart of the modern Thai state. Three hundred years earlier the terms 'Syam' and 'Tai' may have referred only to the people of Sukothai,[15] but now when outsiders spoke of 'Syam' they clearly meant Ayutthaya and the territory under its control. Local sources, which differentiate between the 'Tai' of Ayutthaya, the 'Tai Yuan' of Lan Na and the Lao of Lan Sang, also point to an emerging 'Siamese' identity, and sixteenth-century Portuguese descriptions make a clear distinction between Lao traders and the Siamese. The European presence in Ayutthaya simply fed into this continuing process of state development, mainly due to the military technology they introduced at a time when Ayutthayan kings were attempting to assert their superiority over often

[14] See Nguyen Ngoc Huy and Ta van Tai, *The Le Code, Law in Traditional Vietnam— A Comparative Sino-Vietnamese Legal Study with Historical-Juridical Analysis and Annotations*, Athens, Ohio, 1987.

[15] L. P. Briggs, 'The appearance and historical usage of the terms Tai, Thai, Siamese and Lao', *Journal of the American Oriental Society*, 69 (1949) 62; Wyatt, *Thailand*, 89.

reluctant vassals. In a climate where military organization was receiving closer attention, European weapons were attractive because they could be effectively combined with traditional fighting methods to give the possessor a distinct advantage, even if it was simply to inspire terror through the noise of explosives. Thus a contract made with Ramathibodi in 1518 allowed the Portuguese to trade in Ayutthaya, Ligor, Tenasserim and Pattani in return for guns and war munitions, and a number of Portuguese mercenaries were attached to the Ayutthayan army.

However, it was in Burma where European military technology apparently had its greatest appeal, and may have made a measurable contribution to the resurgence of Burman strength. The founders of a new dynasty originating from Toungoo, Tabinshwehti (r. 1531–50) and his successor Bayinnaung (r. 1551–81), aimed from the outset to recreate a centralized state in the Irrawaddy basin, and the advent of the Europeans was thus timely. Experts in gunnery were recruited into royal service, and during successful attacks on the Mon capital of Pegu in the late 1530s and on Martaban in the 1540s several hundred Portuguese mercenaries were reportedly deployed. While it would be wrong to overestimate the effects of European firearms, local chronicles speak with awe of the 'great guns' by which Tabinshwehti could 'smash the [Shan] *saw-bwas*' warboats to splinters' since they 'had no cannon or large mortars'.[16] By the late 1550s most Shan states had accepted Bayinnaung's overlordship and in 1558 he even defeated Chiengmai, which had successfully resisted the armies of Ayutthaya eleven years earlier. So impressive were his victories that one eminent Thai prince, the viceroy of the northern provinces, was even willing to attach himself to this seemingly invincible conqueror. Besieged by Bayinnaung's army, Ayutthaya fell in August 1569 and by 1574 Vientiane in Lan Sang was also in Burman hands. For the first time in history Burman rulers had been able to subdue the 'great arc of Tai-speaking peoples', and from Chiengmai to Ayutthaya splendid new pagodas built at Bayinnaung's direction proclaimed the power of the king whom the Mons referred to in awe as the 'Victor of the Ten Directions'.[17]

The success of Bayinnaung, however, did not depend solely on military strength. He acted as a model Buddhist king, distributing copies of the Tipitaka, feeding and ordaining monks, and building and repairing monasteries and pagodas. Continued efforts were made to encourage commerce as laws were collated, judicial decisions collected and weights and measures became more standardized. Officials were appointed to supervise merchant shipping and Bayinnaung himself sent out ships to undertake commercial voyages. He also directed his attention to resolving the longstanding Burman–Mon rivalry by bringing Mon princesses into the palace and by taking Mon chiefs as his brothers. Finally, Bayinnaung saw himself as part of a wide diplomatic world, exchanging missions with Bengal, Sri Lanka, Portuguese Goa and China. All these actions were in the tradition of great Burmese kings. What made Bayinnaung's rule

[16] Victor Lieberman, 'Europeans, trade and the unification of Burma, c. 1540–1620', *Oriens Extremus*, 27, 2 (1980) 213.

[17] Victor Lieberman, *Burmese Administrative Cycles. Anarchy and Conquest, c. 1580–1760*, Princeton, 1984, 32–3.

exceptional was the extension of his overlordship hundreds of kilometres from his capital at Pegu into areas like Lan Sang which had never before known Burman control. For the Portuguese in mid-century it was no longer Ayutthaya but Pegu which was 'the most powerfullest monarchy in Asia, except that of China'[18] and it was not lightly that Bayinnaung termed himself the King of Kings.

European involvement in mainland Southeast Asia did not affect the overall direction of political developments during the sixteenth century, although in some cases it may have hastened the movement towards a greater centralization of authority. In island Southeast Asia, however, the impact of the European presence was far greater. In part this was because most 'states' Europeans encountered were smaller than were those on the mainland, and therefore more easily dominated. Even in the larger kingdoms European influence was extensive because of their attempts to gain trading advantages through alliances with local rulers, whom they mistakenly believed had powers similar to kings in Europe. But the notion that a 'state' was a permanent structure controlled by a 'government' to which obedience was automatically due was not shared by many of the societies with which the Portuguese came in contact. When Kampar and Aru, two of Melaka's foremost vassals, asked for friendship with the Portuguese shortly after the conquest of 1511, they were expressing a widely held view of the overlord–vassal relationship. It was essentially a temporary one, and the client state was fully entitled to transfer allegiance should a more desirable patron emerge. In the words of a Bugis text from Sulawesi, 'We are like birds sitting on a tree. When the tree falls we leave it and go in search of a large tree where we can settle.'[19]

The European conception of a state was also inappropriate in much of the archipelago where a type of political entity had evolved which enabled several kingdoms to join together and yet maintain a fundamentally equal status. A prime example of this kind of entity was among the islands of northern Maluku (the Moluccas). Here the myth of an original family of rulers was constantly reshaped in accordance with changing political realities so that the cultural and spiritual unity of the area retained a consistent relevance to the present. In 1522, however, the Portuguese established a fort on the island of Ternate, and in a continuing search for compliant allies they became deeply involved in local affairs, frequently supporting their own candidates in succession disputes or when thrones fell vacant. At the same time they encouraged their royal clients to extend beyond the traditional bounds of the Maluku world and to establish control over places with which Maluku had no historical or cultural bonds. The resulting polities, though far more extensive than their predecessors, were inherently fragile because they had been created in a way which was quite alien to the processes by which 'states' had hitherto developed in this part of Southeast Asia. While the unity of the Maluku islands themselves remained intact, the seventeenth and eighteenth centuries witnessed

---

[18] Ibid.
[19] Leonard Y. Andaya, *The Heritage of Arung Palakka. A History of Southwest Sulawesi (Celebes) in the Seventeenth Century*, The Hague, 1981, 113–14.

increasing reliance on force in order to maintain what were in essence artificial links between the centre and the periphery.

In a sense these developments reflected a growing impatience with the protracted process by which loyalty to an overlord had been built up in the past. Now the ambition to control labour and economic resources inflated the goals of individual chiefs who, with access to greater wealth and military resources, could assert their superiority in a matter of years. In 1512 the ruler of Aceh was simply 'a knightly man among his neighbours', but by the middle of the century the control of his descendants stretched down both coasts of Sumatra, and campaigns in the name of Islam had already been launched against the Bataks of the interior. It appears that the assistance of Turkish mercenaries may have been instrumental in Aceh's success, but contemporary Portuguese writers also felt that they had contributed to the growing dominance of some centres over others. According to the Portuguese chronicler João de Barros, there were once twenty-nine kingdoms along the coasts of Sumatra, 'but since we became involved with these oriental states, favouring some and suppressing others according to the way they received us . . . many have been absorbed to the territory of their most powerful neighbours'.[20] Perhaps the most formidable display of the determination to create a 'state' even in the face of resistance was manifested following the Spanish arrival in the island of Cebu in 1565. Their vision of a united Christian colony owing allegiance to one centre had no precedent in the history of the Philippine archipelago, but it was ultimately to furnish the framework for the modern Philippine state.

While it is already possible to see the implications of the European presence, political development in the island world also had an impulse of its own. In Java, for instance, the Portuguese exerted no influence on the renewed move towards centralization which occurred in the latter part of the sixteenth century. In many ways such a move was predictable, for Java was geographically and culturally more unified than the rest of the archipelago, and even in the fourteenth century the poet Prapanca had extolled the notion that 'the whole expanse of Java-land' should be under the rule of one king. During the 1580s a vague figure known as Senapati moved to establish himself in the interior and expand his control towards the coast. According to later traditions, Senapati had fallen asleep on the Lipura stone, believed to mark Java's centre, where he had received a vision of the dynasty he would found. On a later journey to the bottom of the sea the Princess of the Southern Ocean had even promised him the assistance of all the Javanese spirits. Yet any effort to establish an overlord in Java had to contend with the localization of power and the personal nature of leadership which infused all of Southeast Asian society. Whether the dominance of one centre was achieved by persuasion or force, the kind of state which resulted was fraught with tensions.

---

[20] Mark Dion, 'Sumatra through Portuguese eyes; excerpts from João de Barros', *Decadas da Asia*', *Indonesia*, 9 (April 1970) 144.

THE CYCLE OF FRAGMENTATION AND UNITY

One of the major reasons for the tendency to fragmentation in all Southeast Asian kingdoms was the difficulty of transferring political power from one generation to another. The potential for conflict was particularly great in larger states where kings were likely to have numerous children by several women and where the rewards for success were high. In theory, succession should be settled harmoniously within the royal clan by an agreed selection. However, the increasing inability to reach a mutually acceptable decision as states became more politically complex necessitated the introduction of laws of succession. According to sixteenth-century reports from Ayutthaya, for example, there had been an attempt two hundred years earlier to regulate succession by providing that on the death of a king his brother should inherit the throne, rather than his son. A practice had also been introduced of appointing a secondary king, who would be regarded as heir. Nonetheless, smooth succession in the Thai as well as the Burmese state was a rarity. Burma had to be forcibly reunited in 1551 after the death of Tabinshwehti, and Bayinnaung was in fact no blood relation to his predecessor, but the husband of Tabinshwehti's sister.

Though Islamic states more clearly identified the elder son as the legitimate heir, disputes between a royal prince and his uncles, younger brothers of the dead ruler, remained common. Complications could arise because of claims and relationships derived from local cultures which were often unrecognized by imported Indian or Muslim law codes. In Bugis-Makassar society the husband of a woman who nursed a royal prince became his *patarana*, and the ties between the two could frequently be stronger than between the child and his true father. Throughout the region, too, a special bond was established between those who as babies had been fed from the same mother. To use the Malay term, they became 'saudara susu' or milk brothers. Tabinshwehti's mother had been Bayinnaung's wet nurse, and in 1688 it was a 'milk brother' of the Ayutthayan king who acted as regent and then succeeded to the throne. Added to these factors was the ever-present possibility of the emergence of the 'extraordinary leader' whose claim to rule could be justified not by royal blood but by his exceptional powers and possession of special objects. A Balinese *babad*, for instance, tells the story of the ancestor of a ruling clan in northern Bali who becomes ruler because he holds a powerful magic kris which not only becomes his adviser and confidant, but enables him to become a *cakkavatti*, a Universal Monarch.

The very personalized nature of royal authority meant that the death of a king or a period of weak rule was often a time of crisis as princely factions and their supporters jockeyed for power. In this process royal women are commonly depicted as playing a crucial role. The *Sejarah Melayu* describes how the dowager queen attempted to poison the Melaka ruler in order to obtain the throne for her grandson, the ruler of Pahang; Thai chronicles attribute the death of Phra Yot Chau (r. 1546?–48?) to the sorcery of his father's concubine who seized the throne for her lover. Women who had

been the initial fulcrum of an alliance between lord and vassal are frequently seen as contributing to its breakdown. Indigenous accounts often
attribute an attack on a neighbouring community not to hopes of acquiring
greater prestige or economic advantage, but to the resentment suffered by
a society over the treatment of one of its high-ranking women. According
to tradition, the *bayin* (independent sovereign) of Ava in the late sixteenth
century revolted against his brother/overlord in Pegu because his daughter, wife of the crown prince, was struck by her husband/cousin, and blood
was drawn. She sent the bloodstained handkerchief to her father, who
promptly rebelled. With minor variations the same story is found in Thai
accounts. Even the offering of a woman can be subsequently interpreted as
a factor in the collapse of a previously flourishing state. Javanese legend
says that Senapati presented a beautiful concubine to his enemy the king
of Madiun, who then neglected the defence of his realm, thus allowing
himself to be overcome by Senapati's forces. Indeed, according to an Old
Javanese text, at the end of the *kaliyuga* (the present age) all women 'long
to be the cause of a dreadful war'.[21]

It was at times of political upheaval that the Southeast Asian state was
particularly vulnerable, because any decline in general prosperity or even
an unusual and unwelcome event was attributed to supernatural anger at
the failings of the ruler. Sickness, an eclipse, late rainfall, a volcanic
eruption, earthquake, the discovery of a deformed elephant—events
which in normal circumstances could be explained away—were now
interpreted as evidence of royal ineptitude. Even kings could share this
view. When no rains fell in Vietnam in 1467, Le Thanh Ton (r.1460–97)
said, 'I am a person without merit . . . I am the father and mother of the
people, sick at heart. If I do not dispense wide grace and generous
forgiveness, then how can genuine blessings reach the people?'[22] In part
Le Thanh Ton's despondency was also due to the popular belief that a king
should be able to foretell and avert disaster, and in Vietnam one of the
tasks of Confucian scholars was to interpret the meaning of occurrences
such as the appearance of a new star. It was no coincidence that during his
reception at the Vietnamese court Alexander of Rhodes 'began talking
about eclipses to pass the time' and his prediction of an eclipse three days
before it happened was greeted with wonder. In the early sixteenth
century in Ternate the king was said to be 'an excellent astrologer', and
according to legend Senapati had told the ruler of Pajang that the appointment of an astrologer was vital to the maintenance of royal power.

The task of such a person was to foretell the future and produce the
magic mantra which would prevent the occurrence of disasters like
drought or famine. The more powerful the kingdom, the more vulnerable
it was to the effects of such events, for the continuing warfare which
maintained a great state placed a heavy burden on peasant society. It was
the peasants who supplied the ranks of the armies, it was their crops and
cattle which were seized for supplies, and it was they who could be carried

---

[21] B. Schrieke, *Indonesian Sociological Studies*, II, The Hague and Bandung, 1955, 72.
[22] Stephen Young, 'The law of property and elite prerogatives during Vietnam's Le dynasty
1428–1788', *Journal of Asian History*, 10 (1976) 16.

off by opposing armies to be sold as slaves in distant lands or to increase the manpower of rival kings. In Burma the chronicles describe how the ruler of Ava, on hearing of the Shan approach in 1527, devastated the countryside, filling in wells and breaking down irrigation canals to make a barrier between himself and the Shans. In Cambodia Spanish observers of the late sixteenth century remarked that with increasing attacks from the Thai, 'the women work the soil while their husbands make war'.[23] Rarely are peasant voices heard in the sources, but occasionally they found a spokesman. A poem written by a sixteenth-century Vietnamese poet, for instance, tries to depict the distress brought about when people were taken from their villages to swell armies, and were thus unable to maintain their canals and dykes or to plant their crops.

> How monstrous are the great rats
> Which pitilessly deceive and steal
> There is nothing more in the fields but dried up rice germs
> Not another grain in the granaries
> The peasant, bent with weariness, sighs
> The peasant's wife, emaciated, never ceases to weep
> Nothing is more sacred than the life of the people
> But you do it terrible harm.[24]

Given the right leader, most societies were able to justify the argument that an unworthy king should be deposed. An exception, perhaps, was found in the Malay areas where peasant rebellion is comparatively rare. The word *derhaka*, treason against the ruler, is found in Old Malay inscriptions as early as the seventh century and the belief that rebellion would result in the most terrible of punishments was deeply embedded in Malay culture, to be reinforced by later teaching that ultimately Allah himself would punish the wicked king. Unless led by a prince of the royal house, Malays were generally reluctant to oppose the ruler, and it is surely significant that the great folk hero of the Malays, Hang Tuah, is willing to kill his friend rather than be disloyal to his king.

In Java, on the other hand, it has been said that the essential folk hero is the rebel, and rebellion is a favourite theme in both oral and written tradition.[25] A hold on royal power was never guaranteed because the divine effulgence which rulers were believed to possess could leave one individual and pass to another, designating him as the rightful king. This in effect resembles the Sino-Vietnamese concept of the 'mandate of heaven' that in theory at least could pass from the highest in the land to the lowest. In Vietnam rebellion could also be justified because the Confucian classics themselves, while stressing the loyalty which should be given to the emperor, also set high standards for 'benevolent government'. The philosopher Mencius (372–289? BC) even condoned the killing of inept

---

[23] Chandler, *History of Cambodia*, 86.
[24] Cited in Thomas Hodgkin, *Vietnam. The Revolutionary Path*, London, 1981, 73.
[25] Supomo Surohudojo, 'Rebellion in the *kraton* world as seen by the *pujangga*', in J. A. C. Mackie, ed., *Indonesia: the Making of a Nation*, Canberra: Australian National University, Research School of Pacific Studies, 1980, 563–77.

kings who had lost 'the hearts and minds' of their people.[26] During the
first years of the sixteenth century, when the prestige of Le kings reached
its nadir, peasant rebellion was a frequent occurrence. Between 1510 and
1516 there were at least eight uprisings, the most serious in 1516, when
a pagoda keeper declared himself to be a descendant of the Trinh and a
reincarnation of Indra (de Tich). His alleged miracles gained him thousands of followers, and at one point the rebels captured the capital of
Thang-long (Hanoi) and proclaimed their leader king.

Throughout most of Southeast Asia it was this kind of local holy man
who commonly provided the focus of resistance to the ruler. In the
Theravāda Buddhist countries kings could be accused of *acaravipatti*, or
failure of duty, but only a person regarded as possessing abnormal abilities
and sacral power would voice such criticism. The sources yield scattered
evidence of rebellions led by these figures, *weikza* in Burman or *phu mi bun*
in Thai. In 1579 a rebellion broke out among the mountain people of the
extreme south of Lan Sang, led by a holy man who claimed to be a
reincarnation of a previous ruler. He marched on Vientiane with a considerable following and forced the ruler to flee. Two years later another holy
man in the countryside near Ayutthaya led a rebellion in which the
minister of civil affairs, the *Mahatthai*, was slain.

An added impulse to rebellion was the wideheld expectation that the life
of even the mightiest kingdom was dictated by time. Among Javanese it
was commonly believed that some kind of catastrophe, probably the fall of
a dynasty, would occur with the passing of each Javanese century. Similar
beliefs can be found in mainland states. In 1638 in both Ava and Ayutthaya
there was great rejoicing when ruling kings successfully survived the
thousand-year cycle of the Buddhist Era, but a poem written in Ayutthaya
in the late seventeenth century warns that its downfall will inevitably come.

Nonetheless, while crisis years could foster expectations of dynastic
collapse, it still required particular conditions and a leader of considerable
influence to activate actual revolt. For the most part peasants who were
dissatisfied took service under another lord, sought refuge in a monastery
or disappeared into the crowded coastal ports. Southeast Asian historians
have been unanimous in identifying the control of people as a key to the
retention of political control, a view which local sources themselves reflect.
In the words of a Malay *hikayat* (story), 'It is the custom of kings that they
call themselves kings if they have ministers and subjects; if there are no
subjects, who will render homage to the king?'[27]

The ruler's control over people could be crucial in stemming the tendency towards fragmentation because it was ultimately the principal
means of determining the hierarchy between competitors for power,
whether they were royal princes or vassal kings. The language of authority
frequently reflects the value placed on manpower. Seventeenth-century
Filipinos defined the word 'Datu', as 'he who has vassals', and in the Thai
areas military officers were called by the number of people theoretically

---

[26] Alexander Woodside, 'History, structure and revolution in Vietnam', *International Political
Science Review*, 10, 2 (1989) 149.

[27] A Bausani, *Notes on the Structure of the Classical Malay Hikayat*, trans. Lode Brakel, Centre of
Southeast Asian Studies, Monash University, Working Paper no. 16, 20.

under their command, like 'Lord of a Thousand Men' (Kun Pan) and 'Lord of a Hundred Men' (Kun Sen). While death in battle, sometimes on a large scale, was certainly not unknown, a victorious king generally preferred to transport prisoners back to his own territory to augment the population under his control. As long as he could command greater human resources than his rivals he would be able to maintain his superiority. In the words of a Persian visitor to Ayutthaya, 'They have no intention of killing one another or inflicting any great slaughter'.[28] But although the population of defeated states might be carried off, the typical Southeast Asian pattern was to leave tributary kings in power, with the requirement that they send regular gifts and appear at court to make personal obeisance. Despite their conquest by Vietnam, for instance, the Chams retained their own ruler and continued to receive some recognition from Peking well into the sixteenth century. In this type of situation there was no way of preventing a vassal king from increasing the manpower at his command and then mounting a challenge to his overlord.

It was a combination of relative autonomy and demographic recovery which enabled Ayutthaya to cast off Burmese control in the latter half of the sixteenth century. The Burmese left no occupying force in Ayutthaya after the pillage of 1569, and appeared content simply to accept the homage of its kings. They had, however, taken away large numbers of prisoners and for many years Ayutthaya felt the effects of the lack of population. Between 1570 and 1587, for example, the Khmers attacked Ayutthaya six times, no doubt wreaking revenge for earlier Thai invasions. But in 1585 and 1586 the heir to the Ayutthaya throne, Naresuan, was able to rally local forces and declare his independence from Burma. He not only strengthened the city's defences but set in motion reforms which enabled Ayutthaya to retain a tighter hold over its subjects. Expeditions by the Burmese were thrown back, and the defeat of a major offensive in 1593 meant Ayutthaya was once again free.

In a little more than sixty years the balance on the mainland had swung back again in favour of Ayutthaya. Its former rivals, Lan Sang and Lan Na, had suffered considerably at the hands of Bayinnaung and Lan Na was never able to regain its former authority. While Lan Sang, less affected because of its geographical isolation, managed a partial recovery, it too was unable to repeat the challenge it had made to Ayutthaya in the first half of the sixteenth century. Ayutthaya reasserted itself as the dominant Thai state, signalling its new position by a successful attack on the Khmer capital at Lovek in 1594. In desperation, the Cambodian king appealed to the Spanish at Manila, asking for military assistance in exchange for submission to the Spanish Crown. With the failure of this effort there was nothing to stop continued Thai incursions and the eventual enforced submission of Cambodia to Ayutthaya's control.

The triumph of Ayutthaya was a reflection of Burma's fragmentation. Large-scale military expeditions proved impossible to sustain from the capital at Pegu, and there was considerable loss of manpower as villagers fled to escape military service. Regional towns, their populations swollen

---

[28] John O'Kane, trans., *The Ship of Sulaiman*, London, 1972, 90.

by the influx of refugees, were all too ready to assert their independence. Just as serious was the fact that the delicate relationship which Bayinnaung had built up between different ethnic groups began to fall apart. In 1594 an alliance between Mons and Ayutthaya threw back Pegu's forces and the Ayutthayan king Naresuan succeeded in taking the entire southeast coast, even threatening Pegu itself. The final blow to the dynasty came when the *bayin* of Toungoo entered into negotiations with the ruler of Arakan to mount a joint attack on Pegu. By 1600 Burma had once again broken into a number of realms, assuming the 'general appearance of the early sixteenth century before Tabinshwehti started his work of unification'.[29]

In Vietnam, too, internal divisions were becoming more apparent as the compromise mediated by China in the mid-sixteenth century collapsed. The Nguyen were challenged by an even more powerful clan, the Trinh, as both tried to oust the Mac and establish themselves as defenders of the Le. In an effort to maintain his position, the Nguyen leader in 1558 accepted the position of governor of the southern region which bordered on the Cham areas and was thus at the limits of Vietnamese settlement. By 1592 the Trinh had managed to push the Mac back to the mountains on the Chinese border, but this did not lead to greater unity between the Nguyen and Trinh. The latter remained in theory champions of the Le, but it was they who appointed the mandarins, administered revenues and supplied the queens who became mothers of princely heirs. In 1599 the Trinh head assumed the title of *vuong* or prince, and this then became hereditary in his family. The Nguyen simply refused to accept this assertion of supremacy. By 1627 open warfare had broken out between the two families, and it ended only with an uneasy truce in the 1670s.

At the end of the sixteenth century certain clear trends on the mainland can already be seen. Notwithstanding periods of fragmentation, the basis for future consolidation in Siam, Burma and Vietnam had been laid down, and these states had already signalled their potential for domination over the Lao and Khmer. In the island world, however, such trends are not nearly so apparent. In the Straits of Melaka, Johor, Aceh and Portuguese-controlled Melaka remained at odds; Java was divided between the Mataram-dominated interior, Sunda, Hinduized areas like Balambangan in the east, and the Islamicized coastal ports; Brunei was regarded as a leader in the Borneo region; and Balinese forces were sufficiently strong to expand into the neighbouring islands of Lombok and Sumbawa, where they were to clash with the growing strength of Makassar. The presence of the Europeans further complicated the picture. Manila had been confirmed as the Spanish base for their Christianizing effort in the Philippines, and a strong position had already been established in Luzon and the Visayas. In the southern archipelago, however, they faced continued opposition from powerful Muslim centres. It was at this point that new actors appeared on the stage. The English were soon eclipsed by the newly formed Dutch East India Company (Vereenigde Oost-Indische Compagnie, VOC), which in 1605 made apparent its intentions of becoming the pre-eminent European power by capturing the island of Ambon from the Portuguese. In May 1619

---

[29] Lieberman, *Burmese Administrative Cycles*, 45.

the VOC governor-general, Jan Pieterszoon Coen, forcibly seized control
of the west Javanese town of Jayakatra, renamed it Batavia and immediately set out to transform it into the hub of the Dutch trading network. The
most skilled astrologer would at this point have been hard-pressed to
predict future developments. Certain centres in the archipelago could be
identified as having more commercial power or greater cultural influence
than others, but it was still very much a polycentric world. To a considerable extent the political and economic shifts of the seventeenth
and eighteenth centuries were to determine which of these areas would
ultimately emerge as leaders in the region.

THE CENTRES OF POWER IN THE
SEVENTEENTH CENTURY

In explaining the rise of the great Southeast Asian kingdoms of the seventeenth century, local chronicles are inclined to attribute the emergence of
such states to the 'luck', the prestigious descent and the personal abilities
of the ruler. A modern historian, while acknowledging the achievements
of individuals, might be more inclined to suggest that the prime factors
were geographical. During the seventeenth century the natural advantages enjoyed by some areas became particularly apparent, for increasingly
the power of a kingdom came to be determined not merely by commercial
wealth but by the ability to marshal large numbers of people who could be
supported by the resources of the state itself. In the sixteenth century the
kings of Burma had considered the delta town of Pegu as the most
desirable site for a capital, but a hundred years later the centre of government was moved back to Ava, which dominated the rice-growing basin of
Kyaukse as well as the Mu River irrigation system. In Java, too, the
sixteenth century had for a brief time seen the locus of economic power
shift to the coast, but after the establishment of Mataram no kings were
ever tempted to move away from the fertile regions of the centre. By
contrast, the vulnerability of areas dependent on imported food became
apparent when the sea lanes were cut. In 1640–1 the VOC laid siege to
Melaka and after a blockade of seven months the Portuguese finally
surrendered. By this time, however, the inhabitants were so emaciated
that mothers were even said to have exhumed their young for food. In this
context it can be noted that, despite the rise of Aceh as one of the great
Indonesian states during the seventeenth century, its reliance on rice
supplies from Minangkabau, Siam and Burma to feed its population has
been identified as a possible reason for its later decline.[30]

The correlation between the growing of wet-rice and the development of
dominant state structures is not coincidental. First, wet-rice can support
a far higher population than the lower-yielding hillside and rain-fed
varieties, or the sago and root crops which were a staple diet in most of
the eastern Indonesian islands. Second, because wet-rice growers are

---

[30] Denys Lombard, *Le Sultanate d'Atjeh au Temps d'Iskandar Muda 1607–1636*, Paris, EFEO,
1967, 61.

more sedentary, they are much easier to tie to a central authority. In seventeenth-century Burma it was possible for a royal edict to order the collection of rice 'from over two hundred villages', and in Java a Dutch envoy remarked that 'each family brings ten bundles of padi, every village delivers an amount to the king's receivers'. It is not surprising that the Pampangans in western Luzon, transformed by the Spanish from itinerant traders and fishers to settled rice-growing peasants, became so closely involved with the Spanish, who contrasted their loyalty with the swidden agriculturalists of the forested hills and the roaming 'vagabonds' whose lack of any fixed abode prevented any exaction of tribute. These were views which many Southeast Asian kings would have shared. A Burmese edict of 1598, for example, commands each soldier to remain at the place 'where his ancestors had lived for generations before him' and in Ayutthaya the forests were seen as the home of 'ungoverned' people who should be persuaded to come out and plant rice fields.[31]

For European governors and Southeast Asian rulers alike, large settled populations supported by abundant amounts of food were seen as the key to authority and power. In Ayutthaya, indeed, it was the ownership of rice fields, albeit at times theoretical, that provided the basis for the formal gradings in noble status (sakdi na), and in Vietnam rulers had traditionally rewarded their followers by gifts of land. From the centre's point of view, it was important that as much rice as possible was produced. The aim was not only the maintenance of existing fields but their extension. A Burmese regulation of 1643 makes it a requirement for palace guards not on duty to cultivate the fields, while Javanese traditional law specifically laid down that 'a person asking permission to work a wet-rice field [sawah] but not carrying out the task so that the field lies fallow must repay the equivalent of the rice harvest of the entire field'. It was the consequent density of population which struck a Dutch envoy to the Mataram court in 1648. He spoke of 'the unbelievably great rice fields which are all around Mataram for a day's travel, and with them innumerable villages'.[32]

Not all states, of course, were able to fulfil the potential which a large population accorded them. Vietnam is a case in point. Here the annual flooding of the Red (Hong) River delta had been controlled since early times by damming and irrigation. The demographic results of this were apparent in a census dating from the fifteenth century which records over three million people living in the delta. Their larger, more organized population had enabled the Vietnamese to overrun the Cham areas, and still in the late seventeenth century an Englishman who had long traded in the region marvelled at the numbers of villages and the push of crowds in the streets of the capital 'even though they are reasonably large'. Internal feuding and the outbreak of war between the Nguyen and Trinh

---

[31] Than Tun, Royal Orders, I. 8; Lorraine M. Gesick, 'Kingship and Political Integration in Traditional Siam, 1767–1824', Ph.D. thesis, Cornell University, 1976, 16.

[32] M. C. Hoadley and B. Hooker, An Introduction to Javanese Law: A Translation of and Commentary on the Agama, Tucson, 1981, 174; H. J. de Graaf, De Vijf Gezantschapreizen van Ryklof van Goens, The Hague 1956, 52.

in 1627, however, absorbed the energies of the country for nearly four decades, resulting not in the growth of a more settled peasant population but in their dispersal and flight. Even so, the early seventeenth century saw the Nguyen lords effectively taking over control of the Mekong delta as Vietnamese pushed into Khmer-speaking areas and established their own customs house near modern-day Ho Chi Minh City.

The size of the population any centre could command had far-reaching political effects. It was not simply that these places were capable of amassing the economic resources which reinforced their claims to supremacy over their neighbours. They also commanded substantial armies which could compel the obedience of recalcitrant vassals. The point can be made clearly by comparing the armed forces of Johor, the most prestigious of the Malay states but one without any agrarian base, with those of the Trinh. In 1714 the Dutch estimated that Johor could bring to battle 6500 men and 233 vessels of all types. In Vietnam, by contrast, the Nguyen army was tallied at 22,740 men, including 6410 marines and 3280 infantry. The same pattern is apparent in the other rice-producing states. In 1624 the ruler of Mataram was said to have augmented his army by as many as 80,000 soldiers and in 1635 an order was proclaimed in Burma to raise the strength of the armed forces to an unrealistic but presumably ideal figure of 885,000 men. Aceh, which did not have a rice base, is a partial exception, but it drew heavily on its interior peoples to provide manpower, and was able to put to sea galleys which allegedly carried about four hundred men each.[33]

In the seventeenth century these large armies were most commonly deployed to shore up compliance with the hierarchy which the vassal–overlord relationship entailed. In many cases the offer of protection and the prestige of a powerful patron was no longer sufficient recompense for the acceptance of a lower status, since many so-called 'vassals' had considerable standing of their own. The Shan state of Kengtung, for example, was regarded by Ava as a tributary which, though permitted a degree of autonomy, was ultimately subservient to its overlord in the lowlands. Nothing of this, however, emerges in Shan chronicles which describe how Kengtung in its turn acted as protective suzerain to nearby *saw-bwas*. The ruler of Kengtung 'was possessed of great glory and power without peer, and there was no one, either within or without the state, to rebel against his authority, nor did he go to submit to the ruler of Ava'.[34] In order to incorporate the many centres like Kengtung into larger political systems, the seventeenth century saw a greater reliance on force than ever before. The kind of cultural strains which this could introduce is suggested in a nineteenth-century chronicle which relates how Bayinnaung forbade the 'evil' and 'heathen' practice of burying a Shan *saw-bwa's* slaves, horses and elephants with him. In so doing, of course, he was condemning his vassals to perpetual poverty in the world beyond death.

[33] Leonard Y. Andaya, *The Kingdom of Johor 1641–1728*, Kuala Lumpur, 1975, 333; Charles Maybon, *Histoire Moderne du Pays Annam (1592–1820)*, Paris, 1920, 111; Schrieke, *Indonesian Sociological Studies*, II. 147; Than Tun, *Royal Orders*, I. 49; Lombard, *Le Sultanat*, 85–6.
[34] Mangrai, *The Padaeng Chronicle*, 185.

A RENEWAL OF THE MOVEMENT TOWARDS
CENTRALIZED CONTROL

By the early seventeenth century, Siam and Burma were reaffirming their position as the two strongest political and economic powers in the region. For neither, however, was the path easy. In Ayutthaya Naresuan may have left behind a relatively strong core but the Thais still felt threatened by their neighbours. In 1622 the Khmers decisively routed Thai forces, and Ayutthaya lost four or five thousand men. There were also recurring rebellions in a number of southern tributary states, sometimes surprisingly successful. In 1634 Pattani forces were able to defeat those of Ayutthaya, and it has been suggested that the assertion of Thai control in the peninsula was accomplished only by recourse to European arms and military advisers. During the latter part of the century the Thai missions sent to France by King Narai in 1684 and 1687–8 were apparently directly aimed at obtaining assistance against insurrections in the south.

In Burma, too, though the process of reunification was quick to take hold, it entailed nearly a generation of warfare. The son of Bayinnaung by a minor wife began to attract a following of refugees, and by 1597 he was extending the areas under his control west towards Pagan and north to Ava. Repeated military success ensured his standing as a man of *hpon* (charismatic glory) as he moved against the Shans, and by 1606 his forces had conquered almost the entire Tai region west of the Salween River. His son Anaukpetlun (r. 1606–28) completed the process, extending Burmese sovereignty from Kengtung in the east to Arakan in the west, and from Bhamo in the north to Tavoy and Chiengmai in the south. According to stories told a hundred years later, Anaukpetlun's military prowess was such that he could conquer his enemies simply by laughing, and at news of his coming 'men, gods, monsters and ghosts' vanished in terror.[35]

From the 1660s, when wars between Ayutthaya and the Burmese were renewed, there was a continuing rivalry between them for control of territory and resources. Not only did the demands for tribute from dependencies grow greater, but there was also far less tolerance of any signs of disloyalty. The type of semi-autonomy which had characterized vassal states two or three centuries before could now be sustained only in the case of considerable geographical separation. The area of modern Laos, for instance, was ultimately able to survive because it was considerably removed from the centres of Burmese and Thai control, and was shielded by its environment. A Genoese traveller remarked on 'the mountains and inaccessible precipices that surround it on every side like so many ramparts that none can force their way through and which thus serve as a protection against the insults of their enemies'.[36] Though in the seventeenth century it was divided into three separate kingdoms, centred on Vientiane, Luang Prabang and Champassak, the frequent quarrelling between them did not destroy the sense of being different from their Thai neighbours to the south. A long history of regional sponsorship of Buddhism, and the

---

[35] Lieberman, *Burmese Administrative Cycles*, 56.
[36] Cited in Wyatt, *Thailand*, 121.

possession of revered objects like the statue of the Emerald Buddha, also served to reinforce a sense of local pride. Furthermore, it appears that to a significant extent the powerful neighbours of the Lao, the rulers of Vietnam and Ayutthaya, were prepared to recognize its separate identity. Boundaries were set up between Lan Sang and Vietnam with the provision that those who lived on houses on piles were to be regarded as Lao subjects, and those whose houses were on the ground were Vietnamese. In 1670 another frontier marker, sanctified by the consecration of a Buddhist shrine, was set up to reaffirm the borders with Ayutthaya.

Geographical distance thus enabled the Lao kingdoms to survive. The old state of Lan Na (Chiengmai), which had considered itself the equal of both Lan Sang and Ayutthaya in the sixteenth century, was not so fortunate. More accessible from both Ayutthaya and Ava, it became a victim of the increased rivalry on the mainland and the demands of overlords on their vassals. Though subservient to the Burmese and with a governor installed by Ava, Chiengmai did not easily set aside memories of its former independence and was always ready to break away. In 1660, hearing (incorrectly) that Ava had fallen to the Chinese, the governor sent an envoy to Ayutthaya to ask that he be accepted as a vassal. However, when the Siamese took over control (seizing in the process the famed Buddha Sihinga image) they were soon ejected by Burmese forces. By 1664 Chiengmai was again under Ava's suzerainty. But the Burmese, like the Thais, appear to have adopted the policy that 'once a vassal, always a vassal' and the punishment for Chiengmai's defection was harsh. Ava's control was now considerably stricter, with the regular installation of Burmese rather than local governors and frequent calls on local manpower to fill the ranks of Ava's armies.

Though Ava permitted its Tai vassals in the highlands to retain the rank of *pyi* or sovereign state, this was nonetheless a limited autonomy. Between 1613 and 1739 the Burmese launched at least ten campaigns to enforce control in the Tai uplands. But here there was a common religious language, so that patronage of local monasteries and the appointment of learned monks could be used to reinforce the centre's authority. The strains were far greater in areas where cultural and religious links were weak, like those between Ayutthaya and the mixed Malay-Thai culture of the southern isthmus. In the fifteenth century the Malay state of Kedah, along with its neighbours, had been able to pacify two masters by acknowledging the distant overlordship of both Melaka and Ayutthaya. In the changed mood of the seventeenth century, however, the Thai king Prasat Thong (r. 1629–56) demanded that the Raja of Kedah come personally to Ayutthaya and pay him homage. Although the Kedah ruler was excused when he feigned illness, his court was presented with a small image of Prasat Thong and told that homage should be paid to it twice daily, something that would have been anathema to a Muslim king.

The attitude towards the vassal–overlord relationship in the previously lightly governed Malay shadow areas was becoming stricter; a particularly graphic example of this is the case of Songkhla (Singgora). In 1651 the ruler, a Muslim, refused to come to Ayutthaya to swear public allegiance to the Thai king. In one of the many fierce campaigns which followed, a Thai fleet of 120 ships was despatched, each vessel smeared with human blood and hung with human heads to terrify Songkhla into obedience. By 1679 its ruler had finally complied with the order to go to Ayutthaya to pay personal homage. While he was in the Thai capital, however, King Narai (r. 1656–88) ordered almost all Songkhla's inhabitants carried off. Its fate is vividly depicted in a rare eighteenth-century Thai map which shows a deserted city with tigers prowling in the environs.[37] The continuing effort to incorporate these areas into Ayutthaya's cultural ambit is suggested by the fact that in 1689 the viceroy of Ligor, a Malay, was replaced by a Thai.

The greater reliance on force to create new political structures was also evident in the island world, where it had been an integral part of European intrusion into the area. When the Spanish led by Miguel Lopez de Legazpi landed in Cebu in 1565 to find their peaceful overtures rejected, they opened fire on the local settlement. On the island of Luzon, Manila was taken by force, and during an attack in 1570 as many as 500 people may have been killed with 1500 houses burned. In the early years of Spanish colonization natives were often compelled to submit and accept Christianity, with the alternative frequently being death or enslavement. Some Spanish observers noted with distress the degree to which force was used to extract local compliance. 'If no tribute is given', said one commentator in 1573, 'the houses and lodges are burnt with no attention being paid to instructions',[38] and by the 1580s some Filipinos were saying that to be baptized meant to become a slave. The death and impalement of leaders of local rebellions remained a harsh reminder of the Spaniards' military superiority.

In the Indonesian areas the Dutch used even more force to attain their goal of commercial dominance and to provide 'an example' to native kings. With a charter which enabled it to act virtually as a sovereign state, the power of the VOC was made dramatically clear within a few years of its arrival. In 1621 the town of Banda was destroyed because of local resistance to the imposition of a nutmeg monopoly. Thirteen of the leaders were executed, beheaded and quartered and 24 others imprisoned and tortured. Of 15,000 Bandanese only about 1000 were left and Banda itself became a colony settled by Dutch and mestizo concessionaires.

The commercial competition which was a major reason for the European presence also encouraged local states to increase their control over people and resources. Aceh is a foremost example of the manner in which force could be used to compel submission. During the reign of Sultan Iskandar Muda (1607–36) a series of campaigns was launched on neighbouring states along the coasts of Sumatra and on the Malay peninsula. The effective end of Acehnese expansion only came in 1641 when its arch-enemy, Johor, allied with the Dutch in their successful siege of Portuguese Melaka. For nearly thirty years, however, the mere whisper of a possible Acehnese attack had been sufficient to panic whole communities.

What made Aceh particularly feared was recourse to force on a scale never before experienced in the Malay world. During Iskandar's attack on

---

the peninsular states Kedah was ravaged, the capital demolished, and the remaining inhabitants carried off to Aceh. The following year another five thousand people were taken from Perak. A Frenchman visiting Aceh at the time reckoned that around 22,000 prisoners had been taken away from the areas Iskandar had conquered, but the lack of food in Aceh meant that most of them 'died naked in the streets'. The small kingdoms along the southern Sumatran coasts understandably feared the same fate, and only a promise of protection from both the Dutch and the English was sufficient to dissuade the ruler of Jambi from moving his capital far into the interior.

Other newly emergent centres of archipelago trade, such as Banten in west Java and Makassar in Sulawesi, were also determined to establish their superiority over surrounding states. The territorial expansion of Banten in Java was limited because of the existence of Mataram, but when the Dutch arrived in 1596 its control already extended into the Lampung region of southern Sumatra and it was in the process of attacking Palembang. The Dutch commander, indeed, was promised 'the best' of any booty taken if he would render Banten assistance in this campaign. In after years Banten rulers continued to maintain a tight hold over their vassals, and in 1678 an expedition was sent to punish the lord of one area because he had been so bold as to hold a tournée on a Saturday and 'according to Javanese custom' no one was permitted to sponsor such an occasion except 'emperors, kings and independent princes'.[39] Further east another powerful state, Makassar, drew considerable benefit from Portuguese assistance in building up its military strength. Newly converted to Islam, its ruler found little difficulty in transforming traditional rivalries towards Makassar's Bugis neighbours into a crusade against unbelievers. By the 1640s Makassar was suzerain of all the small states of southwest Sulawesi, and had extended its dominion over the entire island of Sumbawa. During the years of warfare, Bugis and Makassarese soldiers, dressed in their chain-mail armour and carrying muskets which they themselves had made, acquired for themselves a formidable reputation for ferocity and courage which 'surpasses that of all other people in the Eastern Seas'.[40]

Dominating the archipelago, however, was Mataram, where already by 1600 the basis had been laid for future expansion. Under Sultan Agung (r. 1613–46) Mataram extended its power to the northern coast and to the island of Madura, finally defeating its most serious rival Surabaya in 1625. Eastern Java had not been totally subdued, Banten remained independent and successive campaigns against the Dutch in Batavia had failed. Nonetheless, by the time Agung died, Mataram's control had been confirmed over the heartland of central Java and most of the northern ports. For the first half of the seventeenth century Palembang, Jambi and Banjarmasin were also regarded as Javanese vassals, despite treaties made independently with the Dutch East India Company.

Historians have pointed to Agung's reliance on consensus and consultation to maintain the links between Mataram and its vassal states, but should this fail force was the principal means of compelling obedience.

---

[39] J. A. van der Chijs et al., eds, *Dagh Register Gehouden int Casteel Batavia*, 31 vols, 1887–1931, 1678, 629.
[40] William Marsden, *A History of Sumatra*, reprint, Kuala Lumpur, 1966, 209.

When Pajang rebelled in 1617, the city was destroyed and its entire population moved to Mataram. Two years later Tuban was also completely destroyed. The Dutch claimed that after Agung's campaign against Surabaya, 'not more than 500 of its 50–60,000 people were left, the rest having died or gone away because of misery and famine'.[41] While Javanese armies do not appear to have used Western military technology to the same extent as Ava or Makassar, Agung's success reportedly owed much to the recruitment of Portuguese advisers who taught his commanders how to make gunpowder. Certainly Javanese chronicles see military supremacy as a major reason for Mataram's victories. In the words of a *babad* of the early eighteenth century:

> They began to make cannon . . .
> The Adipatis all marched out
> Taking with them the great guns.[42]

Suzerainty of the Javanese interior over the coast was not new. What does appear to be different in the seventeenth century was the degree of force now necessary to maintain this overlordship. A century before, coastal rulers had regarded themselves as the equal of the interior kings; memories of this former independence were not easily forgotten. Even fifty years after the conquest of Surabaya, many coastal regencies saw themselves as merely 'occupied' by the central Javanese. To a casual observer it might seem as if the governors subject to Mataram had considerable autonomy, but in many respects this was illusory, for no longer were the coastal ports able to maintain an essentially separate existence; the chronicles regularly record how regents from areas like Surabaya and Cirebon came to offer personal obeisance, 'offering life and death'. Regardless of the privileges accorded such regents, they were still required to render account to their overlord of all happenings in their domains and to ensure that his orders were carried out. In addition, the marriage ties which so often helped to temper overlord–vassal tensions were increasingly absent in Java because Mataram rulers tended to choose wives from among the ladies of their own court.[43] For the coastal lords the reality of their relationship with Mataram was a constant humiliation and it is significant that when Mataram's superior force declined after Agung's death they were only too ready to defy the centre, necessitating further use of force. The dismissal of regents for some real or imagined crime became a relatively common occurrence, and between 1694 and 1741 at least five coastal lords who had opposed the Mataram ruler were executed.

---

[41] Schrieke, *Indonesian Sociological Studies*, II. 148.
[42] M. Ricklefs, *Modern Javanese Historical Traditions*, London: School of Oriental and African Studies, University of London, 1978, 36–7.
[43] Luc W. Nagtegaal, 'Rijden op een Hollandse Tijger. De Noordkust van Java en de V.O.C. 1620–1742', Ph.D. thesis, Utrecht University, 1988, 93.

KINGSHIP AND CENTRALIZATION IN THE
SEVENTEENTH CENTURY

The death of these lords, killed by their king, points to a continuing question in Southeast Asian statecraft—to what degree should royal power be shared? In most states, accepted attitudes towards the decision-making process had always placed a high value on consensus. The same traditions which allowed any respected individual to contribute to discussion in village debates had been maintained as state structures became more elaborate. In the assemblies of nobles which governed Malay states, for instance, rules for correct behaviour guaranteed speakers a fair hearing: 'When people are talking in the Assembly . . . let no one interrupt a conversation between two persons.' To facilitate joint agreement, all information should ideally be shared: 'The raja must speak of all things, whether good or evil, to his nobles; the nobles should also tell the raja all things.'[44] Even a court like Java, which Europeans saw as autocratic, retained the notion of the free exchange of ideas between king and his advisers.

Popular views of the king's supernatural powers notwithstanding, when he met with his nobles his proverbial relationship (to use Malay imagery) should be that of a tree to its roots, of fire to its fuel, of a captain to his crew. Yet in actuality the ruler was often at loggerheads with both his nobles and his family, and should they oppose him he could easily be outnumbered. Throughout Southeast Asian history there are repeated instances of a cabal of powerful individuals acting against the ruler. In Ayutthaya, for example, Prasat Thong had been made king in 1629 when as *kalahom* (the principal minister) he and his court following took control of the army and seized power. On the *kalahom's* recommendation, the nobles then sentenced the king to be executed. In 1651 it was the Assembly of Nobles of Perak, led by the *bendahara* (chief minister) who quite independently of the king murdered representatives of the Dutch East India Company as they were delivering a letter to court. By 1655, when a boy ruler came to the throne, the *bendahara* and his associates were in complete control. Despite Dutch protests to Perak's overlord, Aceh, he was never brought to justice.

The balance could also be weighted against the ruler because nobles had extensive resources of their own. The twenty-member council or *Hlutdaw* of Ava, for instance, was made up of senior ministers and secretaries who, with additional assistants, supervised most aspects of the country's economy. Court politics were therefore characterized by factional struggles as rulers attempted to align themselves with powerful nobles in order to gain a secure hold on the throne both for themselves and their heirs. It is these struggles that lay behind the succession disputes which occurred in most centres with almost monotonous regularity. In 1631 the son of the Nguyen ruler, though overcoming a challenge from his brother supported by a

---

[44] Cited in B. Andaya, *Perak, the Abode of Grace: A Study of an Eighteenth Century Malay State,* Kuala Lumpur, 1979, 29.

group of Japanese from Fai-fo, felt it necessary to imprison four other half-brothers, sons of royal concubines; in Ayutthaya during 1656 three kings ascended the throne in a little more than two months before Narai was finally installed the following year.

In their efforts to retain power, rulers constantly laboured to increase their own resources vis-à-vis potential rivals, and the course of the seventeenth century thus sees a growing tendency to concentrate trade in the hands of the ruler and his agents. Royal participation in trade not only became commonplace; in many places the ruler's commercial activities completely dominated those of his relatives or nobles. In Ayutthaya in the seventeenth century 72 per cent of all ships mentioned in Dutch sources (excluding foreign vessels) was registered in the king's name. As time went on many rulers, encouraged by the duty European traders were willing to pay, extended the range of royal monopolies. Previously these had covered only rare items like elephant tusks and gems, but they now came to include profitable everyday products such as pepper, rattans and deerhides. Advantageously priced goods, duties and obligatory gifts further swelled the royal treasuries. A Brunei manuscript, for instance, specifies that the sultan should pay only 80 per cent of the ordinary price for any goods he bought, while at the same time receiving 10 per cent toll from all sales in his port. The same text cites the case of a Chinese captain wishing to avoid paying extra duty on his vessel; to do so he had to present the *syahbandar* (head of the port) with a gift of 100 reals, but the ruler received seven times that amount.

It was not only through trade that the wealth of kings grew. It was usual in most states for the property of foreigners or individuals lacking the protection of another noble to revert to the king. When an owner of a house died, a Spanish visitor to Cambodia remarked, 'all that is in it returnest to the king and the wife and children hide what they can and begin to seek a new life'.[45] In Ayutthaya the custom whereby half a man's property was to go to the king after his death was said to have been introduced only in the reign of Ekathotsarat (r. 1605–10). From 1629, during the reign of Prasat Thong, these exactions had increased even further, and now 'when a noble dies, his wife and children are taken into custody'. The same ruler found other means of increasing royal revenues, for he also 'demanded that all subject lands and cities under the Siamese crown list their slaves . . . he had the fruit trees counted everywhere in his kingdom, and placed a tax on each of them'.[46] This tendency to increase impositions from the centre appears to be widespread. In 1663 the ruler of Banten, whose control extended up into the Lampung region in south Sumatra, required all his subjects to plant five hundred pepper vines and bring the crop to Banten.

The growing wealth of kings also helped distance them from the common man. In sixteenth-century Cambodia 'anyone be he ever so simple may speak with the king', and according to tradition the Melaka

---

[45] Chandler, *A History of Cambodia*, 82.
[46] Jeremias Van Vliet, *The Short History of the Kings of Siam*, trans. Leonard Y. Andaya, ed. D. K. Wyatt, Bangkok: Siam Society, 1975, 88, 96.

hero Hang Tuah was shocked when he arrived in Turkey to find he would not be received by the ruler, for 'in the Malay states it is always the custom for a king to receive envoys'.[47] But as the splendour of a ruler increased, he became increasingly less available to his subjects, a tendency which is particularly apparent on the mainland. A Thai decree of 1740 reiterates the king's status as 'the highest in the land, because he is godlike' and like the rulers of Vietnam and Ava, he was rarely seen in public. While kings in the island world may never have assumed the same status as their mainland contemporaries, court hierarchy was still strictly observed and rulers eagerly seized upon the novelty items brought by trade in order to enhance their standing in relation to their peers; now kings wore glasses, ate Dutch bread, drank Spanish wine, wore Japanese brocade and might even, like the ruler of Banten, be entertained by a Portuguese trumpeter. They would have found little surprising in the fact that King Narai of Ayutthaya had an Indian cook and wore Persian clothes, for by this means he was adopting the 'proper manners, fine food and drink and clothing worthy of a mighty ruler'.[48]

In the effort to be seen as a 'mighty ruler', great attention was given to the royal audience. In Mataram, for instance, all coastal lords were required to present themselves at court on specific occasions such as *Garebeg Mulud*, the celebration of the Prophet's birthday, and to absent oneself was regarded as a rebellious act. It was at such times that the king's wealth, his high status and his pre-eminence amongst his kindred and nobles were publicly demonstrated. In these ritual statements a particular place was reserved for the presentation of tribute, the amount and value of which was established by tradition and sometimes carefully prescribed. A text from Brunei thus spells out the products which should be presented by local chiefs—sago from Mukah, padi from Sebuyau, cotton from Batang Lepar, gold from Melanau; in Burma written accounts were kept of the amounts paid in tribute by vassal states, presumably to identify defaulters. In Vietnam missions from Cambodia and the Lao states took the form of 'uncivilized' goods like jungle products, while return gifts from the emperor—paper, porcelain and cloth—were a symbol of his superior standing. Perhaps the most elaborate tribute was that paid to Ayutthaya, where at least from the fifteenth century vassals had been required to present with their gifts two beautifully crafted trees of gold and silver flowers, possibly derived from Hindu-Buddhist legends of magic trees which exist in the golden age of the cycle and which will grant any wish asked of them. The value of such gifts was considerable; according to the *Sejarah Melayu*, one sent from Pasai to Ayutthaya was worth a bahara of gold (about 170 kilograms).

As important as the value and nature of the gifts was the manner of presentation, for the purpose of such occasions was not only the confirmation of the ruler's superior position but the consolidation of ties between overlord and vassal. The ceremony by which vassals affirmed their loyalty

---

[47] Chandler, *A History of Cambodia*, 81; Kassim Ahmad, ed., *Hikayat Hang Tuah*, Kuala Lumpur: Dewan Bahasa dan Pustaka, 1971, 468.
[48] O'Kane, *Ship of Sulaiman*, 156.

could take various forms. In the Bugis and Makassarese states, for instance, each noble in turn drew his kris and performed a frenzied dance known as the *kanjar*, meanwhile loudly avowing his fidelity. In Vietnam Alexander of Rhodes noted that while swearing their oath of loyalty participants were categorized as to the clarity of their voice, for it was this which determined the length and quality of the robes they would be given. Elsewhere a common practice was to require the ritual drinking of water which had been impregnated with power by the chanting of a special formula or by dipping weapons into the container. Should an oath taken under such conditions be broken, it was believed that a terrible curse would fall on the guilty party. So strong was the belief in the potency of these oaths that during the course of the seventeenth century Ayutthaya consistently pressed independent tributary rulers to drink the water of allegiance, even though in theory they were not required to do so.

The insistence on a public display of subservience which was a feature of the foremost Southeast Asian states in the seventeenth century not surprisingly gave rise to tensions when able princes and ministers were required to humble themselves before an inept or unimpressive king. In a number of cases the recurring conflict between ruler and nobles was fuelled by the introduction of measures intended not only to concentrate more power in royal hands, but to ensure that this power would be passed on to the ruler's chosen successor.

SEVENTEENTH-CENTURY ADMINISTRATIVE REFORMS AND MANPOWER CONTROL

In Ayutthaya the reforming process had begun as early as 1569 following the trauma of the defeat by the Burmese. Naresuan had strengthened the capital at the expense of the provinces, and this trend had continued. Some provincial ruling houses had been almost eliminated, and considerable provincial manpower had been taken under royal control. In every town *yokkrabat* (spies) were appointed as officials of the central government to submit reports on the conduct of the town governor. Another move concerned the position of the ruler's relatives. The royal princes were not, as previously, appointed to govern provincial towns but were required instead to live within the capital city so that they could be more closely controlled.

Considering the close association between Ayutthaya and Burma, it is not surprising to note somewhat similar reforms undertaken by Ava. During the seventeenth century, particularly in the reign of Thalun (r. 1629–48), Burmese kings concentrated princely appanages around the capital, bringing them under much closer supervision. No longer could high-ranking princes rule in virtual independence at a place like Prome or Pegu; now the administration of distant areas was carried out by officers who were clearly appointed by the centre and responsible to it. The king was still cognizant of his kinship obligations, he was still linked by marriage to important officials and territorial leaders, and patronage was still an important tool of government. Nonetheless, the cumulative effects of Thalun's reforms was to reduce the opportunities for princes and nobles to exercise independent power.

Despite the changes which Le Thanh Ton had introduced in fifteenth-century Vietnam in order to increase royal authority, the power which could be wielded by strong Vietnamese nobles had become all too apparent. The battle for supremacy between the Nguyen and Trinh remained unresolved, even though both recruited assistance from Europeans. The Trinh launched massive campaigns against the south in 1643, 1648, 1661 and 1672 but, despite superior forces, they found victory eluded them. The division of Vietnam had already been symbolized by the construction of two great walls north of Hué in 1631, and by the late 1670s an uneasy truce brought the establishment of two separate administrations.

Within these two spheres the assertion of central control remained a preoccupation. Steps had already been taken to try to prevent the crystallization of local power, for Alexander of Rhodes noted that royal relatives were not permitted to hold administrative offices, and no mandarin could govern the province where he had been born. In the seventeenth century it appears that the major challenge to the authority of the Trinh and Nguyen came not so much from nobles as from village leaders whose independence had been nurtured by years of civil war. Successive edicts passed during this period attempted to restrict their activities and bring them more firmly under the state's supervision. Local officials, for instance, were no longer permitted to act as private judges and only the village chief had the power to settle lawsuits. From 1660 taxation and manpower quotas were established for each village, and it was the chief and elders who were required to ensure that these were duly submitted. Similar policies were also followed in the Nguyen-controlled areas, although in a more ethnically mixed population it was harder to discourage Vietnamese from taking on 'undesirable' Khmer customs. The examinations held by the Nguyen also reflected their less traditional environment. While still required to know the Confucian classics, candidates underwent an oral test and were questioned on practical matters as well, including military matters.

In their search for a means of reaffirming the centre's pre-eminence, both Trinh and Nguyen found a ready tool in Confucianism. The support which religion could give to the ruler was as apparent in Vietnam as elsewhere in Southeast Asia, but Confucian ethics had suffered considerably during the years of civil war when military skills had been more highly valued. In the new mood of the seventeenth century, however, district leaders in the north were required to be successful Confucian scholars who could act as models for proper behaviour and provide instruction in Confucian tenets. In 1669 the Trinh declared that the new title of the village leader was henceforth to be *xa quan* (village mandarin) rather than *xa truong* (village chief). A new moral code for village life was issued in 1663 entitled 'The Path for Religious Improvement' which stressed political fealty and the attributes of a good subject.

Underneath the exhortations of the Nguyen and Trinh was the basic desire of all Vietnamese governments to strengthen the centre's hold over manpower. It has been said, indeed, that the legal code of the Le dynasty displays a much greater interest in this aspect of government than does its Chinese counterpart. Reforms in Ayutthaya and Ava reflect the same goal. According to the chronicle given to the VOC official van Vliet, during the early seventeenth century the king of Ayutthaya promulgated laws requiring all commoners (*prai som*) to be registered under a leader (*nai*), who could be either a noble or a royal prince. A tattoo on the wrist identified the *prai som* of any individual *nai*, to whom they owed six months' service. In return, the *nai* would assume general responsibility for their welfare, particularly for any repayment of debt. The king also had servicemen of his own, known as *phrai luang*, and they too were required to undertake service for six months of the year, either in the army or in some other area. Women and monks, though exempt from service, were nonetheless registered so that when a monk returned to the world he would return to the service of his *nai*; registration of women helped determine to which *nai* the children should belong. The problem kings faced was that royal service was regarded as more onerous than service to a *nai*, and there was therefore a constant trickle of *phrai luang* into monasteries or to the protection of nobles and princes. The constant threat that the balance between king and nobles might be upset saw continuing efforts to prevent the erosion of royal manpower. One means, for instance, was to separate the *phrai* from their *nai* by bringing the latter into the capital and keeping his people in the provinces.

A similar concern over control of manpower can be seen in Burma, where the non-slave population was divided into those who were not obligated to provide the king with regular labour (*athi*), and *ahmu-dan* who were required to supply soldiers for the army as well as numerous services for the king, whether as a soldier, a palace servant or a labourer on an irrigation canal. During the first half of the seventeenth century the numbers of *ahmu-dan* in upper Burma rose considerably because large sections of Pegu's population were forcibly moved to the north, being concentrated particularly around the capital. It has been estimated that possibly 40 per cent of the population within a 200-kilometre radius of Ava now owed service to the king. Successive royal decrees appear preoccupied with the compiling of lists of servicemen, incorporating new measures to ensure that they did not change occupations or evade duty 'since it is very easy for a Burmese serviceman to be lost in a Burmese community in this extensive territory under Burmese control'.[49]

The degree of administrative reform which has been traced in the mainland states is far less apparent in the archipelago. Under Iskandar Muda and his son-in-law, Iskandar Thani (1636–41) the privileges of the royal family and nobles in Aceh were substantially curtailed. Royal princes, previously stationed in outlying areas as governors, were replaced by officials responsible to the ruler. These officials, with the title *Panglima*, were appointed every three years. They were required to report annually and were periodically inspected by the ruler's representatives. Punishment for dereliction of duty was severe; the *Panglima* of Tiku, for instance,

[49] Than Tun, *Royal Orders*, 69; Lieberman, *Burmese Administrative Cycles*, 96–105.

had his hands and feet cut off when found guilty of charges brought against him. Within Aceh itself Iskandar Muda is credited with laying down the divisions into *mukim* or parishes which were later to be grouped into larger administrative units. But his major concern was a potential challenge from his own nobles, the *orang kaya*, and against them he took strong measures. They were not permitted to build houses which could be used for military defence, nor to keep cannon of their own. A register was kept of firearms, which had to be returned to him and any who dared to oppose him were immediately executed.

The impact of Iskandar Muda's reforms was short-lived. The death of Iskandar Thani brought a restoration of influence for the *orang kaya* who were instrumental in installing queens to rule in Aceh until the end of the century. By the 1680s a Persian visitor described Aceh as a collection of satrapies, where 'every corner shelters a separate king or governor and all the local rulers maintain themselves independently and do not pay tribute to any higher authority'. In the rest of the island world other examples of significant administrative reforms are rare. Amangkurat I of Java (r. 1646–77) did attempt some centralization of royal influence by tightening his control over provincial administration and particularly over the north-coast ports. The most important cities were placed under one or more *syahbandar*, with several officials called *umbal* given charge over the interior. Japara, for instance, had four *syahbandar* and four *umbal* to supervise the hinterland. These new appointments considerably reduced the power of the coastal lords, making it less possible for them to oppose the king. But to strengthen his position Amangkurat resorted to assassination of large numbers of opponents, including nobles, princes and religious teachers, and the hostility this engendered simply exacerbated the tendency to resist undue intrusion by any central authority.

A number of reasons can be put forward for the slower rate of centralization in the island world and the greater difficulty in controlling populations. Geographic differences provide one obvious contrast. More characteristic of maritime than of mainland Southeast Asia, for instance, is the so-called 'Sumatra-type' polity, typified by a centre at a river mouth with the areas of production and often of settlement located at a considerable distance upstream. Again, a kingdom made up of a scattering of islands is far less amenable to central control than is the floodplain of a large river basin such as the Irrawaddy or the Menam.

A second problem was the semi-nomadic nature of many societies which was particularly marked in maritime Southeast Asia. Those Javanese living in areas producing wet-rice may have been relatively more settled than peoples in other areas, but movement both internally and to other islands was still common. Javanese lords certainly had a general idea of the numbers of people over which they claimed suzerainty, but the term *cacah*, often translated as 'household', should be seen not as a firm population figure but as a hopeful indication of numbers of families from which tax might be extracted. Traditional *cacah* figures continued to be cited, but they became increasingly unrealistic as villagers moved away to avoid burdensome demands for tribute and labour. In Java as elsewhere most rulers offered rewards to interior groups who captured fleeing subjects or slaves, but in Palembang the Pasemah people had the special status of *sindang*, signifying freedom from corvée and tax, in return for acting as border guards and capturing any royal serviceman (*kapungut*) discovered attempting to escape to the west coast. The kings of Palembang, however, like most other rulers in the archipelago, were heavily dependent on the co-operation of local authorities in the supervision of manpower and organization of corvée. Indeed, the extent to which village elders and family heads were able, in return for royal titles and gifts, to deliver large numbers of people to provide service for the king is remarkable.

Their labour, however, was always conditional. Should the ruler's demands exceed a certain level, he would find his people simply melting away. Nor was it simply a matter of individual flight. Whole communities could move, drawn by more attractive economic conditions or escaping from unwelcome exactions, punishment or sickness. The Suku Pindah (the moving tribe), so called because for generations they had moved back and forth between Palembang and Jambi, were by no means unusual. This kind of 'avoidance protest'[50] is well illustrated in the Philippines as the Spanish administration continued its campaign to move the population into towns where they could be Christianized and made subject to taxes and tribute. In mid-century at least one Spanish observer felt that the 'unconquered' Filipinos, whose numbers were constantly swelled by fugitives from the lowlands, might still exceed Spanish subjects. In addition, many Filipinos, though Christianized, were only nominally pueblo-dwellers. In 1660 a Spanish friar admitted that so-called 'towns' in Negros frequently consisted of only a church and a few huts where the Filipinos stayed when they came to town on a Sunday; they sometimes lived as much as half a day's travel beyond the township. More than a generation later another priest lamented that 'the innate desire of these savages is to live in their caves and their forests'.[51]

But perhaps the most dramatic demonstrations of group flight were the great migrations of Bugis and Makassarese nobles and their followers in the wake of continued disturbances during the course of the century, especially after the Dutch combined with the Bugis leader Arung Palakka (r. 1669–96) to defeat Makassar in 1669. As many as two thousand individuals could be included in one fleet, and because of their reputation as fighters and traders most kings were ready to receive them. In Sumbawa, Flores, Java, Madura, Borneo, Sumatra, the Malay peninsula and even Ayutthaya, refugees from Sulawesi established Bugis and Makassarese communities. Islands such as Kangian off the coast of Java and Siantan in the South China Sea became Bugis-Makassarese strongholds, and in the early eighteenth century Bugis even succeeded in claiming control of the underpopulated region of Selangor, a territory under Johor on the west coast of the Malay peninsula.

As the Bugis diaspora shows, one of the continuing difficulties in controlling manpower in the archipelago was that there were simply so many places where a runaway could find refuge and where he and his

---

[50] The term is used by Michael Adas, 'From footdragging to flight: the evasive history of peasant avoidance in South and Southeast Asia', *Journal of Peasant Studies*, 13, 2 (1981) 65.
[51] Angel M. Cuesta, *History of Negros*, Manila: Historical Conservation Society, 1980, 42, 111.

family would be welcomed. In 1651 Amangkurat I of Java forbade any of his subjects to travel outside Java. Since it would have been impossible to maintain a watch over Java's entire coastline, there is little likelihood that any such measure could have been successful. In the words of the ruler of Palembang in 1747, 'it is very easy for a subject to find a lord, but it is much more difficult for a lord to find a subject'.[52]

A further complication in the Indonesian archipelago was that native states were now competing for manpower and resources with the expanding presence of the VOC. The Dutch took Melaka from the Portuguese in 1641 and during the course of the seventeenth century they effectively eliminated all other European competition, eventually relegating the English to a single post in Benkulen in west Sumatra. In pursuit of their commercial aims, the Dutch became heavily involved in local affairs, especially on Java. Despite a siege in 1628–9, Sultan Agung of Mataram had failed to conquer Batavia. The dynasty's consequent loss of prestige was not restored by the extreme policies adopted by Agung's son Amangkurat I, and omens and dire prophecies of impending collapse were increasingly reported as the end of the Javanese century in 1677 CE approached. In 1670–1 a Madurese prince, Trunajaya, allied with the crown prince, religious figures and Makassarese refugees to launch a full-scale rebellion in east Java. By 1676 he controlled most of the coastal areas. There seems little doubt that had developments been allowed to run their course a new royal house, presumably headed by Trunajaya, would have assumed power. However, at this point the VOC reluctantly decided that its interests would be best served by some form of intervention to support the existing 'legitimate' Mataram line, especially as the rebels had begun to show signs of being anti-Dutch. In 1677 Amangkurat and the VOC concluded a military alliance, and by the end of 1680 Trunajaya was dead, killed by Amangkurat II (r. 1677–1703) himself. Two years later the Dutch also became involved in a succession dispute in Banten, and shortly afterwards its king became a VOC vassal.

Throughout the rest of the archipelago the Dutch were also discovering that it was almost impossible to pursue commercial goals without involvement in regional affairs, an involvement which was made the more likely by the lodges and factories established wherever the VOC saw commercial opportunities. These enclaves, where the Dutch claimed extra-territorial rights, were frequently regarded by local societies as a refuge if the exactions of kings or nobles became too great. But the Dutch also complained of the flight of criminals, debtors and deserters to the shelter of some neighbouring court, and it became common for treaties signed between the VOC and their allies to include a clause on mutual exchange of runaways. In many places long arguments developed over whether the children of a liaison between an Indonesian mother and a Dutch father were local or 'Dutch', and VOC officials were often prepared to engage in drawn-out negotiations to retain authority over their 'subjects'. Another sensitive issue concerned control over foreigners, notably Chinese. Those who had adopted Islam and married Indonesian women were generally

<hr/>

[52] VOC 2699, Resident of Palembang to Batavia, 13 March 1747 fo. 51.

regarded as being under local jurisdiction, but the arrival of large numbers of migrants following disturbances in China during the sixteenth and seventeenth centuries meant that in an increasing number of courts the question of 'Dutch' versus 'local' Chinese remained unresolved.

The island world differs further from the mainland in that some cultures actively encouraged their men to leave. The one which comes most readily to mind is that of Minangkabau where the inheritance of land and family goods through the female line impelled young males to leave the village (*merantau*) to make a living. Extensive migration led to a marked increase in Minangkabau settlements in Linggi and Negeri Sembilan on the west coast of the Malay peninsula, and along both coasts of Sumatra. Minangkabau rulers made no effort to summon their people back, but a sense of group identity remained strong and still in the late eighteenth century Minangkabau communities in the peninsula received their leaders from their original homeland. While its resemblance to great mainland kingdoms such as Ava is slight, the claim of Minangkabau rulers to exercise a vague overlordship over all Sumatra was widely accepted, though never supported by resorting to arms. It is difficult to overestimate the extraordinary respect with which the kings and queens of Minangkabau were regarded by the people of the archipelago. Even a text from as far away as Bima accepts the general Sumatran view that they were of the same origin as and equal to the kings of Turkey and China.

THE CREATION OF THE 'EXEMPLARY CENTRE'[53]

By the mid-seventeenth century hundreds of years of exposure to stories of the splendour of great rulers in distant lands had furnished Southeast Asians with a perception of kingship as the epitome of powerful government. Burmese kings built their religious buildings according to Sinhalese designs and a panegyric commissioned in Aceh in the early seventeenth century was apparently modelled on the *Akbarnama*, a Persian text extolling the reign of the Great Mogul. Powerful though such examples were, however, Southeast Asians could also draw on their own much nearer past. It was in Pagan that Tabinshwehti was crowned king of upper Burma, while an eighteenth-century Vietnamese historian notes that the usurper Mac Dang Dung 'maintained all the Le laws and systems, and did not dare to change or abolish any of them' because he was afraid of possible rebellions from the people 'who were full of memories of the old dynasty'.[54] Nor was the heritage of Angkor lightly laid aside. According to a Portuguese account, the temple complex was 'rediscovered' in the late sixteenth century by a king who was 'filled with admiration' at its splendours. Ayutthayan rulers were equally anxious to link themselves with the mixed Thai-Khmer traditions of the period before 1569, and a seventeenth-century chronicle makes Angkor a creation of the first Ayutthayan king.

[53] The phrase is from Clifford Geertz, *Islam Observed. Religious Development in Morocco and Indonesia*, New Haven, 1968, 36.
[54] Yu, 'Law and Family', 34.

Prasat Thong even had a plan of Angkor Wat copied to use as the basis for two new buildings, and talked about giving the name of Yasodhara to one of his palaces.[55]

In the western archipelago, memories of Melaka also remained powerful incentives to the restoration of Malay control in the straits long after its conquest by Portugal. A seventeenth-century Malay scribe, copying out the old Melaka law codes, noted wistfully that these were compiled 'in the days when Melaka was still strong'. Johorese expectations of their alliance with the VOC in 1602 are suggested by a popular Malay *hikayat* which depicts Malays and Dutch together defeating the Portuguese and then ruling jointly over a newly emergent Melaka. In Java the passage of time had enhanced Majapahit's reputation as an example of centralized power. Malay sources of the period extol the ruler of Majapahit, whose sovereignty extended from the interior of Java 'to the shores of the southern ocean' and to whom the kings of Banten, Jambi, Palembang, Bugis, Makassar, Johor, Pahang, Champa, Minangkabau, Aceh and Pasai had all allegedly paid homage. In the seventeenth century Javanese sources depict Trunajaya urging Sultan Agung's grandson to move to Majapahit 'so that the whole island of Java may know your Highness has established his court there'.[56]

The collective effect of such potent examples was becoming increasingly apparent by the mid-seventeenth century. It is probable that the number of 'kingless' communities, where government continued to be carried out by councils of elders and heads of clans, far outnumbered the 'kingdoms'. But for the most part these were interior peoples, like the Bisayas of Brunei of whom a Spaniard remarked, 'they have no lord who governs them and whom they obey, although in each settlement there are some important persons'.[57] Only in a few coastal areas had these kingless societies managed to retain power. For example, prior to its destruction by the Dutch, Banda had been ruled by an 'oligarchy of elders' made up of village leaders who met frequently in councils to deal with problems and settle disputes. To a growing extent, however, Southeast Asians themselves were coming to see the lack of kings as a characteristic of lesser peoples. Nandabayin of Pegu (r. 1581–99) was allegedly greatly amused when he heard that Venice was a free state without a king, and English traders in Jambi found they had a powerful argument in their claim that their Dutch rivals had no monarch; VOC officials themselves admitted that for local people, 'this is the point around which the compass turns'.[58]

The identification of several key states as 'power centres' in the seventeenth century is not simply a construct of a modern historian, for in the seventeenth century a number of rulers boasted that they stood high above their neighbours. In Ava the ruler held an elaborate ritual to make himself 'king of kings' in order to subdue 'all the other one hundred kings'; the

[55] Michael Vickery, 'The composition and transition of the Ayudhya and Cambodian chronicles', in A. J. S. Reid and David Marr, eds, *Perceptions of the Past in Southeast Asia*, Singapore, 1979.

[56] M. C. Ricklefs. 'Six Centuries of Islamization on Java' in N. Levitzion, *Conversion to Islam*, New York, 1979, 110.

[57] John S. Carroll, 'Berunai in the Boxer Codex', JMBRAS, 55, 2 (1982) 3.

[58] J. W. J. Wellan, 'Onze Eerste Verstiging in Djambi', BKI, 81(1926) 376.

Thais boasted that since the time of Naresuan 'they had never been subject to any other prince of this world'. A Makassar chronicle sees only Aceh and Mataram as its equals, while the ruler of Aceh considered himself to be 'the most powerful monarch in the world'. In 1667 Amangkurat I of Mataram referred to himself as the one 'to whom all the kings of the Javanese and Malay lands pay homage'.[59]

The hierarchy which these rulers perceived was to a considerable extent accepted by their neighbours. The Khmers, for instance, gradually came to take on the Thai view that they were inferior, and even incorporated into their own histories Ayutthaya's accounts of its victories over Cambodia, accounts which do not mention a Khmer revival in the early seventeenth century. What Khmers remembered was the defeat of Lovek in 1594 and their forced acceptance of Thai overlordship during the eighteenth century. According to legend, Lovek contained two sacred statues inside which were holy books containing special secret knowledge. It was to obtain these that the king of Siam attacked and defeated Cambodia. 'After reading the books, the Thais became superior in knowledge to the Cambodians.'[60]

The assertion of a hierarchy of states within Southeast Asia is matched by a growing tendency to see the centre as 'civilized' and those who live outside this environment as 'wild'. The epithet of 'wild' applied particularly to groups who had not accepted the dominant religious faith and whose lifestyle clearly contrasted with that of the capital culture. The Vietnamese made no sustained effort to spread Confucian customs into the highlands, and the fifteenth-century Le code, while allowing these areas to follow their own laws, had forbidden intermarriage between Vietnamese and hill tribes. Thai and Burman histories also saw Kachins, Karen, Chins, Lahus, Lawas and other illiterate, animist hill peoples as 'barbaric', and talk of country people 'loafing around'. In the Philippines the growth of this attitude can be linked with the separation between Christian and 'pagan', for 'barbarians' were those who lived away from organized communities and who were not amenable to the teachings of the Church. One priest felt that

> the mode of living of these Bisayans . . . appears to oppose all that is rational justice. They make the greatest effort to live like savages, as far as possible from the church, priest, governors and their own *gobernadorcillo* [petty governor] so as to live in freedom without God and without obedience to the king.[61]

The perception of those who do not share the mainstream culture as inferior is also a measure of their irrelevance to the centre. Similar expressions of contempt are far less apparent in those states where minority groups retained an important political or economic role. In the seventeenth century the king of Champa had a wife from the highlands, and in Cambodia when the hill tribes came down to present their tribute, flutes

[59] Than Tun, *Royal Orders*, I. 28; van Vliet, *Short History*, 81; W. Ph. Coolhaas *Generale Missiven van Gouverneurs-Generaal en Raden aan Heren XVII der Verenigde Oostindische Compagnie*, The Hague, 1960–85, I. 103; Schrieke, *Indonesian Sociological Studies*, II. 222.
[60] Chandler, *History of Cambodia*, 84.
[61] Bruce Cruikshank, *Samar 1768–1898*, Manila, 1985, 42.

were played softly and the gifts enumerated as the 'uncles' (the Cambodians) received the willing tribute of their 'nephews' (the hill tribes) and in return presented their chiefs with swords and the titles of Fire King and Water King. Johor and other Malay states continued to rely on the skills of the *orang laut* (the non-Malay sea peoples) for patrols and the collection of ocean products well into the eighteenth century. *Orang laut* leaders therefore retained an influential voice in government. In one Johor chronicle from the early eighteenth century, for example, the head of the *orang laut* is included in conferences concerning delicate matters of state. Whereas the request of a Gwe Karen for an Ayutthayan princess was rejected because he came of 'a race of forest dwellers', Dutch sources from the same period demonstrate how the king of Jambi was related to *orang laut* chiefs through his womenfolk. The gradual displacement of animist groups which occurred through the eighteenth century is a reflection of wider political and economic changes which were to affect the entire region.

THE FRAGMENTATION OF THE EIGHTEENTH CENTURY

None of the great centres of the seventeenth century survived into modern times. By the early 1800s new dynasties ruled in Burma, Siam and Vietnam; in the island world Banten and Makassar had both lost their status as independent entrepôts, Mataram was divided into two, and Aceh had been torn by two generations of civil strife. In tracing the reasons for these developments in mainland Southeast Asia, it could be argued that the very process of centralization contained within itself the seeds of fragmentation. Only a powerful centre could maintain its position in the face of the cumulative tensions induced by continuing efforts to tighten supervision of people and resources. Whenever the dominance of the capital was questioned, it was reflected in the steady seepage of manpower away from royal control. In societies where the king was heavily reliant on his armies to maintain his own standing against potential opposition, this loss of manpower was serious, especially if it coincided with conflicts over succession or the sharing of power.

In Ayutthaya the drift of population from the centre may have begun as far back as the 1630s, and the continuing incorporation of foreigners into royal service reflects the need of successive rulers to strengthen their position in relation to other manpower-controlling groups. At the same time the problem of kingly succession had never been resolved. In 1688 a group of Ayutthaya nobles, apparently alienated by King Narai's patronage of foreigners, acted to remove a Greek adventurer, Constantine Phaulkon, who had been appointed *Mahatthai*. The leader of the cabal, a noble who was Narai's foster brother, was made regent on behalf of the dying king. He quickly moved to have Phaulkon arrested and beheaded and on Narai's death assumed the throne himself. But while the dynasty he founded endured eighty years, it faced undercurrents of opposition. There are several references to village rebellions led by 'holy men', and the succession of King Borommakot (r. 1733–58) was only secured after a battle with rival princes which involved several thousand men. The Malay tributaries grew increasingly restive, and on several occasions it was necessary to despatch armies to subdue the rebellious peninsular states.

Burma was if anything more prey to internal division. Between 1660 and 1715 there were at least eleven attempts to usurp the throne, and as a result the *hlutdaw* came to exert a much greater influence in the selection of rulers. In 1695 an English visitor considered that the two most powerful ministers in fact 'ruled the kingdom', and by the turn of the century the 'royal business' was considered insufficient to warrant a daily meeting between the king and his council. The ruler's failure to resolve a dispute in the Buddhist monkhood over matters of doctrine contributed to the general atmosphere of unease. Not surprisingly, those vassal states that had never willingly accepted Ava's overlordship began to fall away. Chiengmai was lost in 1727, and in 1739 the Shan state of Kengtung drove out a *saw-bwa* appointed by Ava. Added to this was the fact that many royal servicemen were evading their obligations by avoiding registration, commuting their service through payments, entering the monkhood or placing themselves under the protection of other princes or nobles. In Ava the king's militia was seriously under strength as *ahmu-dan* and *athi* alike attempted to be registered as debt slaves in order to escape royal service. Indications of the centre's concern are seen in the periodic checks ordered to ensure that 'undesirables' did not enter monasteries, and a royal decree of 1728 which prohibits menial labourers in the palace from being ordained as Buddhist monks. Those escaping from debts or service could also, however, place themselves under village leaders, rebel monks or bandits who had set up their own centres of localized power in opposition to the centre. Everywhere representatives appointed by the central government were becoming victims of peasant discontent, and between 1727 and 1743 the governors of Martaban, Tavoy, Syriam, Toungoo and Prome were all killed or driven out by local rebels.

The beginning of the end came with the rebellion of Pegu, which had recovered after the devastation of the late seventeenth century but was subjected to a heavy tax burden. In 1740 its leaders declared their independence. Twelve years later, after continuous raiding of the Irrawaddy basin, a southern army which included representatives of several ethnic groups and was led by a prince of Shan descent stood outside the walls of Ava. In early 1752 after two months of siege the city fell, the king fled, and the Toungoo dynasty ended. Just fifteen years later the same fate befell Ayutthaya, where yet another succession dispute had broken out. In 1760 a new ruler in Burma, the founder of the Konbaung dynasty, threw the rejuvenated strength of Burmese might against Ayutthaya, an attack which was renewed by his sons, and Ayutthaya fell in 1767. The Thai capital, however, suffered far more than Ava had done; it was as if the hostilities of the last two centuries had finally found full expression. Its buildings were torched and pillaged, its inhabitants killed or captured. Deprived of a king and a focus of government, Ayutthaya broke up into five separate regions. For the first time in nearly four hundred years the Menam basin was once more politically fragmented.

But it was in Vietnam where the challenge to the existing order was greatest. Efforts by the Trinh to exert greater control over village leaders had been unsuccessful, and many peasants were refusing to be drafted for military service. In 1711 the centre had been forced to allow the village to allot public land within its own jurisdiction, and by the 1730s even the census records were not being maintained properly. The ability of the landed and privileged to escape tax payments meant that the burden was carried by ever fewer people who were at the same time the ones least able to pay. Reforms aimed at taxing private land and widely used items like salt were ineffective, and by 1713 less than one-third of the population under the Trinh were subject to taxation. In 1730 officials were appointed to induce wandering peasants to return home, but only a decade later it was calculated that one-third of the villages were deserted.

The flight of manpower meant both a decline in cultivation and a breakdown in provincial administration. In six provinces in 1721 financial problems compelled the Trinh to abolish the position of the commissioner responsible for checking the growth of undue local power, and as a result the incidence of corruption and oppression in village government markedly increased. Censors reported that 'in the villages the notables, using thousands of tricks, ruling arbitrarily, grabbing other people's property to enrich themselves, oppressing the poor, despising the illiterate, avail themselves of the least opportunity to indict people and bring suits against them'.[62] Lack of food and ineffective officialdom in turn contributed to an increase in peasant rebellion as wandering peasantry organized themselves into bands of local insurgents. Contemporary accounts depict a time of terrible famine, when 'people roamed about, carrying their children in search of some rice, lived on vegetables and herbs, ate rats and snakes'. In this climate the continuing rule of the Trinh was difficult to justify, and in a rebellion in the southern delta peasants carried banners proclaiming 'Restore the Le, destroy the Trinh'. It was not long, however, before some voices were even raised against the Le, whom intermarriage had made simply part of the Trinh clan. As elsewhere in Southeast Asia, people with special qualities, monks, scholars and holy men, emerged to assume leadership of peasant rebels. Some groups succeeded in establishing independent domains where they anulled debts, redistributed land and abolished taxation. One revolt, led by a Confucian scholar and made up of many thousands of peasants, was even able to defeat two Trinh generals.

In the Nguyen-controlled territory, official corruption and the dwindling of foreign trade similarly combined with famines to bring about a collapse of the tax base. Scholar-officials clearly warned the Nguyen that 'the people's misery has reached an extreme degree'. As the century progressed, revolts grew in intensity. In 1771 three brothers from the hamlet of Tayson in south central Vietnam emerged as leaders of what was to become the most effective resistance movement yet seen in Southeast Asia. Despite the fact that the government it established did not last, the Tayson rebellion not only succeeded in reuniting north and south Vietnam but also signalled the end of the old Confucian order.

Much of the island world in the mid-eighteenth century was also in

[62] Yu, 'Law and Family', 224.

disarray. It would be easy to attribute this to the influence of the Europeans—on the one hand the Spanish, now suzerain over most of the Philippines except for the Muslim south, and the VOC, which was not only overlord of Java, but had built up a network of alliances which linked it with kingdoms from the north of Sumatra across to the eastern islands. However, the question of the effects of the European presence must be approached with caution, for local society retained its own dynamics. A prime example of an event which had far-reaching implications, but in which the Dutch played only a minor part, concerns a case of regicide in Johor in 1699. The nobles, refusing to tolerate any longer the king's excesses, together plotted his assassination. Although the *bendahara* was duly installed as ruler, and although Johor quickly recovered economically, Malay society was deeply divided. Many *orang laut*, whose relationship with the Johor dynasty stretched back to the days of Melaka, simply refused to serve under the new order. The divisions created by the crime of *derhaka* (treason) opened the way for the seizure of the throne in 1718 by a Minangkabau prince who not only claimed to be the son of the murdered ruler but brought with him the imprimatur of the queen of Minangkabau. At this point a large party of Bugis refugees arrived in the area, allied with the displaced Bendahara, and drove the Minangkabau prince out. As a result of these events, a new political arrangement came into being in Johor, whereby the Malay sultan took secondary place to the Bugis raja muda. In time the trauma associated with the regicide faded, but for many Malays the new dynasty located on the island of Riau remained a permanent reminder that the Melaka line had ended.

In assessing the impact of the Europeans on political developments in the archipelago one must also remember that their numbers were never great. In concluding commercial treaties, VOC officials dealt almost exclusively with the ruler and his court, and this meant that outside Java comparatively few areas were deeply touched by the Dutch. It is equally useful to note the limited European presence in the Philippines. As late as 1800 there were almost no Spanish posts at altitudes higher than 150 metres, and except in the central plain of Luzon few Spaniards lived more than fifteen kilometres from the sea. For most Filipinos in the lowlands, their only European contact was with the clergy, who were the linchpin of the Spanish administration, yet their numbers too were small. In Samar in the western Visayas, a province of more than 13,000 square kilometres with an official population in 1770 of 33,350, there were only fifteen priests. While priests acted as local schoolteachers, doctors, archivists, linguists, and spiritual advisers for town-dwellers, there were many small communities of baptized Christians who saw a priest only once a year.

Interaction between Spaniard and Filipino was frequently eased because the Spanish friars, who spent their lives in isolated posts, often developed a considerable understanding of local society. The same comment also applies to VOC officials, many of whom had been born in the Indies and easily adopted local symbols of leadership to enhance their own standing, employing the kingly insignia of umbrella and betel box and even on occasion the golden *gelang* (anklets) of Malay royalty. In their correspondence governors-general exploited the terminology of kinship, addressing rulers as 'son' or 'grandson' and referring to themselves as a 'father'. In the exchange of gifts, the Dutch in many cases acted like an overlord accepting tribute. The small island of Roti in eastern Indonesia, for instance, sent wax, slaves and rice to Batavia, while the governor-general responded with 'civilized' products such as muskets, fine cloth, gold and silver batons, and Dutch gin. During the conclusion of a treaty on Timor, Dutch and Timorese signatories even sealed the treaty by drinking one another's mingled blood.

On the other side, the desire of locals to absorb these outsiders in the way they understood best is suggested by the numbers of Europeans adopted as sons or brothers, accorded high titles and presented with robes of honour. An eighteenth-century Javanese *babad* attempts to bring the Dutch into the fabric of Javanese history by transforming the famed Governor-General Jan Pieterszoon Coen (1619–23, 1627–9) into Mur Jang-kung, son of Baron Sukmul of Spain and a princess from Pajajaran. The latter's flaming genitals mark her as an *ardhanariciwari*, possession of whom can make even the poorest man king. Mur Jangkung vows to wreak revenge when he learns that the Pangeran of Jakarta banished his mother because he could not sleep with her. Loaded with beer, wine, bread and war materials, Mur Jangkung's fleet arrives in Java. He successfully takes Jakarta, thus regaining his birthright and installing his descendants (the Dutch) as the legitimate successors of Pajajaran and the proper rulers of west Java.

Nonetheless, the Dutch could never be just another indigenous power: they were different in the determination with which they pursued their very specific goals, and the assumptions on which they formulated policy were often incomprehensible to local peoples. But while for many archi-pelago communities the advent of the Dutch had brought hostility and conflict, there were numerous others for whom the VOC was a powerful and protective friend. The Bugis leader Arung Palakka, for instance, assisted the Dutch in the attack on his old enemy Makassar. When the combined Dutch and Bugis forces were successful, Arung Palakka was installed as overlord of all Sulawesi with the title *Torisompae* (the Venerated One) previously held by the Makassar king. In return for Dutch support, he agreed to expel from his lands all other European traders. Now when the Bugis performed the *kanjar* and swore their oath of loyalty, they did so not only before their own king but the Company as well. 'Look at me, Commissaris!' proclaimed one Bugis lord as the drums were beaten and he danced his allegiance, 'let me meet the enemies of the Company and I shall fight them sword in hand!'[63]

Another example of an area where association with the Dutch left memories of a *zaman mas*, a golden age, comes from the Malay peninsula where the state of Perak had long been threatened by outside powers like Aceh and Ayutthaya because of its extensive tin deposits. In 1746 the ruler signed a treaty with the VOC which granted the Dutch a monopoly of all Perak tin in return for protection. Although there were periods of tension,

[63] J. Noorduyn, 'The Bugis auxiliaries from Tanete in the Chinese War in Java, 1742–1744', in C. M. S. Hellwig and S. O. Robson, eds, *A Man of Indonesian Letters. Essays in Honour of Professor A. Teeuw*, Dordrecht, 1986, 279.

particularly when the Dutch made attempts to negotiate a lower tin price, the treaty endured until the demise of the Company in 1795.

What these two cases illustrate is the degree to which the Dutch could and did influence the course of local politics in pursuit of trading advantages. For both Arung Palakka and the Perak court, Dutch friendship was crucial; without it, Arung Palakka would not have been able to avenge the humiliation of defeat and regain his homeland; if left to itself, Perak would probably have fallen under the control of a stronger neighbour like Selangor. In the changing relationships between states, and in the power struggles within them, the role of the VOC was often decisive. Lacking support from Dutch forces, for instance, the family which ruled the pepper-producing state of Jambi would have been replaced in the 1690s; the measure of the king's unpopularity is indicated by the extent of population movement away from his jurisdiction and his descent into that anomaly in Southeast Asia, a king with no subjects. Similarly the region of Lampung in the southern part of Sumatra would have fallen under the control of Palembang during the eighteenth century had not the VOC acted to safeguard the interests of its vassal Banten. A converse situation prevailed on the west coast of Sumatra, where the Dutch encouraged the spread of Minangkabau authority following the VOC's successful military expeditions against the Acehnese in 1666 and 1667. In a treaty signed in 1668, Minangkabau was confirmed as the overlord of the west coast from Barus to Manjuta; the Dutch representative at Padang was appointed 'stadthouder' on behalf of the Minangkabau ruler.

Dutch anxiety to ensure that local power structures favoured their presence often meant real shifts in traditional patterns of authority. On a number of islands in eastern Indonesia, for instance, the Dutch passed over ritually superior 'religious' figures when recognizing rulers or regents because they felt such people were not amenable to political control. Instead, they tended to regard as legitimate those figures whom they perceived as 'secular'. By so doing they often elevated individuals who in fact merely held a lower rank in the priestly hierarchy. Another example of the way authority was reshaped comes from Barus, on the west coast of Sumatra. Here jurisdiction was shared between two kings, an 'upstream' and a 'downstream' raja (both of whom actually lived downstream). In order to further their access to camphor supplies in the interior, where both rulers had connections, the VOC played one against the other. In 1694 the Dutch abolished the dual·rajaship, although the effective division of authority between upstream and downstream eventually re-emerged with the position of raja rotating between the upstream and downstream families.

The question often arises as to why the Dutch were able to maintain their position in the island world for so long. In part, the reason lies in the profusion of small political units which had always been a feature of the island world and which the VOC helped to perpetuate by working to prevent regional alliances which might form the basis of an anti-Dutch coalition. Furthermore, the Dutch were always able to find one Indonesian group to use against another because local rulers themselves often saw a VOC alliance as a means of gaining an advantage over some long-time enemy. It was thus never possible for any anti-VOC alliance to maintain enough sustained support to ensure success. In the course of the seventeenth and eighteenth centuries various calls were made to rally Muslims against the infidels, but these were insufficient to overcome a tradition which had stressed localized loyalty rather than joint action. A test case came in 1756–7 when Bugis forces from Riau blockaded Melaka. For the better part of a year the town lay helpless, and the siege was only lifted when a fleet arrived from Batavia in mid-1757. Yet neither then nor in 1784, when the Bugis attacked once more, was Malay support against the Dutch forthcoming.

All these permutations of the Dutch presence can be seen in Java after 1680. Though Trunajaya was killed, rebellions against the centre continued. Amangkurat II was able to maintain his position against the challenge of his brother mainly because the Dutch were willing to assist him as the 'legitimate' heir. By doing so they publicly demonstrated that a king who could not rally sufficient popular support to remain upon the throne could yet be maintained by VOC armies. The Dutch continued to shore up their clients through the eighteenth century in the face of continuing unrest. In 1740 a rebellion initially involving Batavian Chinese also turned against the dynasty, and again the court appealed to the Dutch. VOC help, however, had a heavy price. Javanese kings repaid their debt by progressively ceding the coastal areas of Java to the Dutch. Finally in 1749 the entire kingdom of Mataram was signed over, and Pakubuwana II (r. 1726–49) thus became a vassal of the VOC. This new relationship was effectively symbolized when he was installed by the governor-general with the Dutch Resident sitting beside him. An influential faction in the court, however, refused to accept Pakubuwana's authority, and in an effort to prevent continued strife in the royal family the Dutch in 1755 divided central Java between Surakarta and Yogyakarta.

The words put into the mouth of Pakubuwana's rival encapsulate the major problem raised by colonial control:

> My lord, it is not fitting.
> Are you not aware
> that the role of a ruler
> carries the obligation to reign only?[64]

What the VOC wanted was kings and officials who would actually carry out instructions given to them, and would act as executors of the Company's desires. Seduced by titles and emoluments, threatened with exile or dethronement, or simply browbeaten, the indigenous élite became the means by which colonial authority was maintained. To some extent this pressure was felt wherever the Dutch signed a commercial contract, but in some areas the effects were more disruptive than others. In eastern Indonesia, for example, strenuous efforts were made not only to enforce a trading monopoly but also to compel production of particular spices. A great programme of 'extirpation' was set in place, whereby in return for regular payments to a number of kings the VOC acquired the right to

[64] M. C. Ricklefs, *Jogjakarta under Sultan Mangkubumi 1749–1792. A History of the Division of Java*, London, 1974, 41.

destroy clove trees on all islands except Ambon and other areas under their control. The VOC requirements for manpower for such expeditions, the infamous *hongitochten*, naturally aroused bitter resentment among local people and placed heavy strains on the loose relationships which had traditionally existed between the Maluku region and culturally separate groups like the Papuans. The same pattern can be traced in Sumatra. When pepper prices fell and people moved to grow cotton instead, the Dutch pressed those kings bound to them by treaty to order the '*extirpatie*' of all cotton bushes. Inevitably kings and local chiefs who agreed to carry out Dutch policies came to be seen as harsh and punitive.

Not surprisingly, it was the peasants of Java and the Philippines who felt the effects of European demands most keenly. In both places villagers were required to grow certain crops and to sell them to the Dutch or Spanish at set prices. A major source of resentment was the labour requirements, which often meant long absences from home and for which minimal compensation, if any, was made. Understandably, resentment was often directed at those seen to be the agents of extortion. In 1726 a Priangan regent was killed by one of his subjects because the price the latter now received for his coffee was so low that he despaired of ever climbing out of debt. The point was, of course, that it was the Dutch who had reduced the amount paid for coffee; the regent was simply passing the reduction on.

In the Philippines the original granting of *encomiendas* (the right to collect tribute) to individual Spaniards had been deemed a failure by the mid-seventeenth century so that by 1721 virtually all had reverted to the Crown. Nonetheless, many of the abuses which had led to criticism of the private *encomienda* persisted. The Spanish administration, constantly in need of funds, leant heavily on Filipinos to supply labour and finance for their national endeavours. In theory workers were supposed to be paid, but this was rare; they were usually supported by stipends of rice from their own villages. Despite government attempts at reform, Filipinos were often drafted for private rather than state labour, or sent to work at places far removed from their village. Still in the 1770s people were fleeing in Samar from the exactions of a governor who asked them to build boats and fortifications without providing adequate rations or time to tend their fields.

Another Filipino grievance was the requirement that certain products be sold to the government, often below the market price, to which was added the collection of tribute and numerous other taxes. The division of the Philippines into parishes administered by religious orders increased the burden carried by ordinary Filipinos, who also supported the clergy by contributing to their stipends and by supplying food and labour. Indeed, the Church often made a healthy profit by selling goods received as alms. In 1704 the *sanctorum* tax to defray the costs of administering the sacraments was imposed over all Spanish-controlled territory. Faced by this array of exactions, the hill people in some areas spoke of an evil spirit called *Tributo* that roamed around the mission towns and ate people up.[65]

---

[65] William Scott, *Cracks in the Parchment Curtain*, Quezon City, 1982, 36.

It was the Spanish-supported élites who were the key to the successful working of this system. Christianized native *barangay* leaders, the *datu* of pre-Spanish times, had been incorporated into the colonial administrative structure and given the title *cabeza*, or head. Members of this largely hereditary élite, termed generally the *principales*, took turns in filling the position of municipal 'little governor' (*gobernadorcillo*), the highest native official in the Spanish bureaucracy. In return for new titles, enhanced status, and privileges, the *principalia* class was expected to help organize labour services and taxation payments. In the process, however, they had to take on the role of buffers between the Spanish régime and the Filipino peasant, and to work closely with the friars in maintaining order; a priest in Samar reported that when a man had failed to come to Mass, 'I sent the Datus to whip him'.[66] The ambiguity of the *principalia* relationship with ordinary Filipinos is particularly evident in the numerous rebellions which broke out against Spanish rule. Sometimes they took on the role of spokesmen for discontented peasants; *principales*, for instance, led a revolt in 1745 which protested against the encroachment of friar estates into peasant land. On the other hand, local élites could be seen as an extension of Spanish government. Diego Silang, who led the uprising of 1762 which followed the British capture of Manila, though himself of *principalia* stock, was opposed to a group whom he saw as the instruments of oppression.

Over a hundred participants in the Diego Silang rebellion were hanged, while others were flogged or imprisoned. Their fate points to a prime reason for the Spanish domination of the Philippines and the successful Dutch manipulation of local politics—the effective and frightening use of force. The inability of the Spanish to subdue the Muslim south is clear evidence that European-led troops were by no means invincible, but their successes remained impressive. It is useful to remember that in Java between 1680 and 1740 the VOC suffered only three defeats, and it had been the hope of harnessing this force which had led many Southeast Asians to seek a greater association with the Europeans. In the *Babad Tanah Jawi* a pretender to the throne is thus advised to call on the Dutch, whose military skills are available in exchange for 'a few promises'. But those who attempted to render Europeans amenable to their wishes were to find that it was like 'riding a tiger'. By their intrusion into the region, Europeans had fundamentally altered the manner in which its history was to develop. Yet in the process they unwittingly provided the basis for the growth of a shared frustration which was ultimately to bring together groups which might otherwise be divided by language or culture or traditional rivalries. As early as 1577, a Filipino had called out to an attacking band of Spaniards, 'What have we done to you, or what did our ancestors owe yours, that you should come to plunder us?' Nearly two hundred years later the same anger was expressed by a group of Demak peasants who pulled a Dutch envoy off his horse, shouting, 'Stop, you Dutch dog, now you will be *our* porter!'[67]

[66] Cruikshank, *Samar*, 37.
[67] Scott, *Cracks in the Parchment Curtain*, 20; Luc W. Nagtegaal, 'The Dutch East India Company and the relations between Kartasura and the Javanese northcoast c. 1680–1740', in J. van Goor, ed., *Trading Companies in Asia 1600–1830*, Utrecht, 1986, 76. The image of the tiger is taken from the title of Dr Nagtegaal's thesis, 'Rijden op een Hollandse Tijger'.

CONCLUSION

While there are identifiable continuities between the sixteenth and eighteenth centuries, a survey of the period also suggests that significant changes were under way. In the first place, there had been a marked trend towards a greater centralization of authority, particularly among the mainland states. A combination of prosperity, administrative reform, and control of labour had enabled a number of centres to confirm their ascendancy over their neighbours, so that by the eighteenth century the typical Southeast Asian state was not so much a confederation of nearly equal communities as a hierarchically organized polity where the component parts paid some kind of allegiance to a dominant centre. An important aspect of the expansion of political authority was the creation of a 'capital culture'. Distinctive features of dress, language and custom which had once been key aspects in a community's separate identity now came to be seen as variations of the dominant culture which emanated from the political centre. Even in Burma, where ethnic differences were more pronounced, the resurgence of the Konbaung dynasty was based at least in part on a wide acceptance of Burman hegemony and Burman cultural values. Though some borders were to see adjustment in later years, in essence the political bases of contemporary Thailand, Burma, Vietnam, Cambodia and Laos had already been laid down.

In the island world the process of centralization was not nearly so apparent, facing as it did formidable obstacles of geography and wide cultural variation. The peoples of the Philippines still thought of themselves very much as 'Cebuanos' or 'Tagalogs', and to these localized loyalties was added the deeper divide between the Christianized north and centre and the Muslim south. Nonetheless, significant changes had taken place. The Spanish administration had helped to impose a degree of political uniformity, blurring some of the regional differences existing before the conquest, and their emphasis on the development of Manila gave it a pre-eminence which has survived to the present day. Nor is it difficult to point to features of the Malay-Indonesian archipelago which were to be of critical importance in the creation of contemporary nation-states. The trading network which had long served to link areas as distant as Timor and Melaka was not broken, despite VOC efforts, while the Dutch dependence on Malay as a medium of communication reinforced its position of lingua franca, and promoted its use in places where it had previously been little heard. At the same time the dominance of Java had been enhanced by the concentration of Dutch interests in Batavia, contributing to a polarity between Java and the outer islands that has continued into modern times.

Despite a foreshadowing of later developments, however, the eighteenth-century island world appears far more culturally and politically fragmented than does the mainland. In Vietnam, Siam and Burma the impulse towards centralization was so strong that within a generation all had recovered from the fragmentation of the eighteenth century. In the archipelago, on the other hand, even the most potentially cohesive region, Java, was by

1755 divided into distinct spheres. These differences between island and mainland are reflected in the historiography of Southeast Asia. By the seventeenth century the perception of a 'country' had enabled outsiders visiting mainland states to produce books such as de la Loubère's *Description of the Kingdom of Siam*, and the *History of the Kingdom of Tonkin* by Alexander of Rhodes. The concept of a 'national' history was also developing among indigenous scholars. The first history of Dai Viet had been written under the Tran in 1272; seventeenth-century Thai texts began to divorce Ayutthaya's history from that of Buddhism; in Burma U Kala in 1711 produced an encyclopaedic work aimed at providing a complete account of his country's past. It is rare, however, for chronicles in the island world to look beyond a dynasty or a specific cultural group, and modern scholars still grapple with the problem of writing a broader history that is not biased in favour of one area. While it has proved quite possible to reconstruct the collective past of particular societies—Pampangans, Javanese, Malays, Taosug—the great difficulty has been to synthesize regional studies on to a larger canvas, particularly given the lack of documents from so many areas. Yet it is important to continue to examine not merely the contrasts but the shared features which ultimately enabled political unities to be created from immense diversity. Only this wider view can assist in the reconstruction of a regional history in which all Southeast Asians are seen as true participants.

BIBLIOGRAPHIC ESSAY

Thailand and Laos

David K. Wyatt's *Thailand. A Short History*, New Haven and London, 1982, is a detailed study by a leading scholar containing material unavailable elsewhere. It is also the only complete analysis in English of Lao history in this period, and contains a helpful guide for further reading. Wyatt lists a number of contemporary European accounts, but of these the most valuable is probably Simon de la Loubère, *The Kingdom of Siam*, ed. D. K. Wyatt, Kuala Lumpur, 1969. Lorraine M. Gesick, 'Kingship and Political Integration in Traditional Siam, 1767–1824', Ph.D. thesis, Cornell University, 1976, discusses the question of tributary relations. A view of Siam from one of its Malay vassals is *Hikayat Patani: The Story of Patani*, ed. A. Teeuw and David K. Wyatt, The Hague, 1970. A seventeenth-century history of Siam based on Thai sources is Jeremias van Vliet, *The Short History of the Kings of Siam*, trans. Leonard Andaya, Bangkok, 1975.

Burma

Burma remains one of the Southeast Asian countries least researched by modern Western scholars, but an important interpretation of the pre-nineteenth-century period has come with the publication of Victor B. Lieberman, *Burmese Administrative Cycles. Anarchy and Conquest, c. 1580–1760*, Princeton, 1984. Although this has superseded all other accounts,

G. E. Harvey's *History of Burma*, London, 1925, can still be read because it so clearly reflects a chronicle viewpoint. The first three volumes of Than Tun's translation of the *Royal Orders of Burma, AD 1598–1885*, Kyoto, Center for Southeast Asian Studies, 1983–8, provide an invaluable source for the preoccupations of the Burmese court.

Cambodia

Available sources for Cambodian history between the sixteenth and eighteenth century are not numerous, but a good survey is David Chandler, *A History of Cambodia*, Boulder, 1983.

Vietnam

Vietnam between the sixteenth and eighteenth centuries has not attracted much attention among Western scholars. Charles Maybon's *Histoire Moderne du Pays d'Annam (1592–1820)*, Paris, 1920, is now very dated; Thomas Hodgkin, *Vietnam. The Revolutionary Path*, London, 1981, has a clear Marxist standpoint but nonetheless presents a sympathetic and readable account of this period. A study by Keith W. Taylor, 'The literati revival in seventeenth century Vietnam', JSEAS, 18, 1 (March 1987), looks at changes in the bureaucracy. Alexander of Rhodes' account of missionary work has been translated by Solange Hertz as *Rhodes of Vietnam*, Westminster, Maryland, 1966. The eighteenth century is discussed in Dang Phuong Nghi, *Les institutions publiques du Vietnam au XVIIIe siècle*, Paris, 1909. Insun Yu, 'Law and Family in Seventeenth and Eighteenth Century Vietnam', Ph.D. thesis, University of Michigan, 1978, contains valuable material not found elsewhere, while Gerald C. Hickey, *Sons of the Mountains: Ethnohistory of the Vietnamese Central Highlands to 1954*, New Haven, 1982, provides a view of the centre from the 'underside'.

The Philippines

The Spanish move into the Philippines is covered in the still valuable work by John L. Phelan, *The Hispanization of the Philippines: Spanish Aims and Filipino Responses 1565–1700*, Madison, 1959, which can be read together with Nicholas P. Cushner, *Spain in the Philippines: From Conquest to Revolution*, Quezon City: Institute of Philippine Culture, 1970. More stress on the Filipino reaction is given in Eric A. Anderson, 'Traditions in Conflict. Filipino Responses and Spanish Colonialism, 1565–1665', Ph.D. thesis, University of Sydney, 1977. Sources dealing with religious history are given in the bibliographic essay for Chapter 9, but H. de la Costa, *The Jesuits in the Philippines 1581–1768*, Cambridge, Mass., 1961, includes considerable information on political developments. The Philippines is also well served in the translation of contemporary documents, notably by E. H. Blair and J. A. Robertson, *The Philippine Islands 1493–1898*, 55 vols, Cleveland, 1903–9. While there is no recent synthesis of pre-nineteenth-century Philippine history, a number of local studies have appeared: Angel

Martinez Cuesta, *History of Negros*, Manila, 1980; Rosario Mendoza Cortes, *Pangasinan 1572–1800*, Quezon City, 1974; Bruce Cruikshank, *Samar 1768–1898*, Manila, 1985; Bruce L. Fenner, 'Colonial Cebu: an Economic-Social History, 1521–1896', Ph.D. thesis, Cornell University, 1976; John Larkin, *The Pampangans: Colonial Society in a Philippine Province*, London, 1972; Ana Maria Madrigal, *A Blending of Cultures: the Batanes, 1686–1898*, Manila, 1983. Cesar A. Majul, *Muslims in the Philippines*, Quezon City, 1973, is a full account of Spain's dealings with the Muslims of the south. Dennis Roth, 'The Friar Estates of the Philippines', Ph.D. thesis, University of Oregon, 1974, and David Routledge, *Diego Silang and the Origins of Philippine Nationalism*, Quezon City: Philippine Center for Advanced Studies, 1979, provide the background to major peasant uprisings in the eighteenth century.

Borneo, Sumatra and the Malay World

The most detailed study of Brunei is Donald E. Brown, *Brunei: The Structure and History of a Borneon Malay Sultanate*, Monograph of the Brunei Museum Journal, 2, 2 (1970). Robert Nicholl, *European Sources for the History of the Sultanate of Brunei in the Sixteenth Century*, Brunei, Brunei Museum, 1975, is a collection of translated Spanish and Portuguese documents, while John Carroll, 'Berunai in the Boxer Codex', JMBRAS, 55, 2 (1982), is a most interesting late-sixteenth-century Spanish description of the Brunei court, and Amin Sweeney, ed., 'Silsilah raja-raja Berunai', JMBRAS, 41, 2 (1968), is a genealogical history of its kings.

A survey of Malay history is contained in Barbara Watson Andaya and Leonard Y. Andaya, *A History of Malaysia*, London, 1982. Detailed studies of particular states are Leonard Y. Andaya, *The Kingdom of Johor, 1641–1728*, Kuala Lumpur, 1975; Barbara Watson Andaya, *Perak, The Abode of Grace: A Study of an Eighteenth Century Malay State*, Kuala Lumpur, 1975; R. Bonney, *Kedah, 1771–1821: The Search for Security and Independence*, Kuala Lumpur, 1971. Few of the relevant Malay court chronicles relating to this period have been translated into English. C. C. Brown, '*Sejarah Melayu* or Malay Annals', JMBRAS, 25, 2 and 3 (1952), an account of Melaka up to the early sixteenth century, remains essential reading for anyone interested in understanding Malay culture. A wider study written by a descendant of one of the Bugis migrants to Johor is Raja Ali Haji, *Tuhfat al-Nafis (The Precious Gift)*, Kuala Lumpur, Oxford University Press, 1982 which has been edited and translated by Virginia Matheson and Barbara Watson Andaya.

The most complete study of early seventeenth-century Aceh is Denys Lombard, *Le Sultanat d'Atjeh au Temps d'Iskandar Muda 1607–1636*, Paris, 1967. JSEAS, 10, 3 (Dec. 1969) contains several relevant articles relating to the seventeenth century. For an overview, see J. Kathirithamby-Wells, 'Forces of regional and state integration in the western archipelago, c. 1500–1700', JSEAS, 18, 1 (March 1987). Jane Drakard, *A Malay Frontier. Unity and Duality in a Sumatran Kingdom*, Ithaca: Cornell University Southeast Asia Program, 1990, looks at the previously little researched area of Barus. Christine Dobbin, *Islamic Revivalism in a Changing Peasant Economy.*

Central Sumatra 1784–1847, London and Malmö: Scandinavian Institute of Asian Studies, 1983, is a finely crafted study of Minangkabau society during the eighteenth and early nineteenth century. J. Kathirithamby-Wells, *The British West Sumatran Presidency (1760–85): Problems of Early Colonial Enterprise*, Kuala Lumpur, 1970, considers the situation on the west coast. The best contemporary account of Sumatra, focused on the west coast, is William Marsden, *A History of Sumatra*, reprinted Kuala Lumpur, 1966.

Java

The material for Java is considerable, but has been covered in detail in M. C. Ricklefs, *A History of Modern Indonesia*, London, 1981. He has drawn from his own research, notably *Jogjakarta under Sultan Mangkubumi 1749–1792*, London, 1974, and *Modern Javanese Historical Traditions*, London, 1978, the latter being a translation of a Surakarta chronicle. Earlier work by Dutch scholars has also provided indispensable material for the reconstruction of Java's history. H. J. de Graaf and Th. G. Pigeaud, *De Eerst Moslimse Vorstendommen op Java. Studien over de Staatkundig Geschiedenis van de 15e en 16e eeuw*, The Hague, 1974, is a detailed compilation of all that is known about the northern coastal ports. This should be followed by H. J. de Graaf's important studies—*De Regering van Panembahan Senapati Ingalaga*, The Hague, 1954; *De Regering van Sultan Agong, vorst van Mataram 1613–1645, en die van zijn Voorganger Panembahan Seda-ing-Krapjak, 1601–1613*, The Hague, 1958; *De Regering van Sunan Mangku Rat I Tegal Wangi, Vorst van Mataram, 1646–1677*, 2 vols, The Hague, 1961–2; *De Vijf Gezantschapreizen van Ryklof van Goens naar het hof van Mataram 1648–1654*, The Hague, 1956, which is a valuable account of Mataram by a VOC envoy. B. J. O. Schrieke, *Indonesian Sociological Studies*, 2 vols, The Hague, 1957, touches on a number of important themes in Javanese history which remain to be developed, while Somersaid Moertono examines the nature of Javanese kingship in his *State and Statecraft in Old Java: a Study of the Later Mataram Period, Sixteenth to Nineteenth Century*, Ithaca: Cornell University Southeast Asia Program, 1968. Luc Nagtegaal, 'Rijden op een Hollandse Tijger. De Noordkust van Java en de V.O.C. 1680–1743', Ph.D. thesis, Utrecht University, 1988, examines the relations between the centre and the coast and the way political relationships in Java were affected by the growing Dutch presence.

Eastern Indonesia

The secondary sources for eastern Indonesia are limited. Leonard Y. Andaya, *The Heritage of Arung Palakka: A History of Southwest Sulawesi (Celebes) in the Seventeenth Century*, The Hague, 1981, brings together material relating to Bugis-Makassar history and its implications for the rest of the region. James Fox, *Harvest of the Palm. Ecological Change in Eastern Indonesia*, Cambridge, Mass., 1977, is an anthropological study focusing on

Roti and Savu, but makes frequent use of VOC sources, as does another anthropologist, Ch.F. van Fraassen, 'Ternate, de Molukken en de Indonesische Archipel', Ph.D. thesis, University of Leiden, 1987. An interesting Portuguese account by Antonio Galvão dating from the mid-sixteenth century has been translated by Hubert Th. M. Jacobs as *A Treatise on the Moluccas (c. 1544)*, Rome: Jesuit Historical Institute, 1971. Willard Hanna, *Indonesian Banda. Colonialism and its Aftermath in the Nutmeg Islands*, Philadelphia: Institute for the Study of Human Issues, 1978, is a readable account of the Dutch assumption of control in Banda, while Gerrit Knaap, 'Kruidnagelen en Christenen. De Verenigde Oost Indische Compagnie en de Bevolking van Ambon 1656–1696', Ph.D. thesis, Utrecht University, 1985, examines the way in which the Dutch governed Ambon.

CHAPTER

3

ECONOMIC AND SOCIAL CHANGE, c. 1400–1800

It has been conventional to assume a new era began in Southeast Asia in 1500 with the arrival of Europeans, if for no better reason than that the sources become much richer and more accessible at this point. If one looked back from the age of high imperialism it was also obvious that the expansion of European empire in Asia began with Vasco da Gama and the discovery of a sea route from Europe to India. If we take our viewpoint from Southeast Asia, on the other hand, it is clear that the rapid social changes transforming the region were already in full flight before 1500, with the upsurge in international commerce of which the arrival of the Portuguese was a consequence, not a cause. The explosion of energy from the new Ming dynasty in China a century earlier is a more appropriate starting point for this new era of economic expansion, since it had some causal relation with a new dynasty in Vietnam, the decline of the 'classical' empires of Angkor and Majapahit, and their replacement by a string of new maritime city-states. Although most evidence about economic and social matters comes from a later period, we will therefore have to go back to 1400 in tracing the reasons for many of the changes.

POPULATION

To understand the impact of the major economic trends in the period it is necessary to have some impression of population levels. Contemporary estimates of population are extremely unreliable, but a combination of the more plausible of them with backward projection from somewhat more reliable and abundant nineteenth-century estimates yields roughly the order of population in 1600 shown in the table on page 463.

One of the characteristics of Southeast Asia before 1750, in contrast to adjacent India and China, was a low population density. Most of the region was still covered with jungle as late as 1800, so that attacks by tigers were not uncommon even on the outskirts of substantial population centres. Although overall density was probably not much above five per square kilometre (in contrast with more than thirty for India and China) most of the 20 to 30 million people of Southeast Asia were concentrated in a dozen trading cities and in the centres of wet-rice agriculture in the Red (Hong) River delta, the Mandalay area of upper Burma, the flood plains of the lower Irrawaddy, Pegu, Salween, Chao Phraya and Mekong rivers, Java (the northern coastal plain and the Mataram area), Bali, and south Sulawesi. Outside these areas a sparse population for the most part practised shifting agriculture in the lower slopes of what seemed a limitless jungle expanse.

The puzzle about pre-modern Southeast Asian population is why it remained so low, in contrast with its neighbours and with its own extremely rapid rise after 1800.[1] The answer does not appear to be wretched health and nutrition. Southeast Asians were relatively fortunate in their secure food-supplies, and they seemed to European and Chinese visitors to be relatively healthy and long-lived. Marriage was virtually universal, and most women appear to have embarked on child-bearing by their late teens. Although divorce was easy and frequent, it presented few barriers to subsequent remarriage. Children were much loved and indulged.

A number of factors may have kept birth-rates low, though none of them can be confirmed confidently from the available evidence. Shifting cultivation typically entails a high female work-load, difficult to combine with more than one child unable to walk. Breast-feeding in Southeast Asia has traditionally continued for two or three years, with resultant lengthening of post-partum amenorrhaea to about twenty-nine months. Abortion appears to have been a normal practice in the pre-Christian Philippines and continued to be so in many other animist areas of Southeast Asia. Belief systems before the acceptance of Islam and Christianity often did not forbid premarital sexual activity, and gonorrhea may in consequence have become endemic in some areas, causing a severe reduction in fertility—as has been the case in some animist areas of the archipelago in this century.[2]

Much the most important factor inhibiting population growth, however, was probably the instability of residence brought about by warfare and raiding, voluntary and forced migration, the pioneering of new cultivation areas, and corvée obligations. Of all the possible factors keeping birth-rates down, it is these that can most readily be seen to have changed in the nineteenth century as wars became less frequent and colonial and other states established zones of relatively stable conditions. Prior to 1750, periods and zones of peace were the exception, and they almost certainly gave rise to rapid population growth both through high birth-rates and immigration.

Southeast Asian warfare was not particularly costly of lives on the battlefield, but it was enormously disruptive of the domestic and agricultural pattern. Because rulers perceived their power in terms of human rather than territorial resources, their object in war was always to capture

---

[1] The best recent discussion of this phenomenon is Norman Owen, 'The Paradox of Population Growth in Nineteenth Century Southeast Asia: Evidence from Java and the Philippines,' JSEAS, 18 (1987).

[2] Anthony Reid, Southeast Asia in the Age of Commerce, I: The Lands Below the Winds, New Haven, 1988, 158–62; Norman Owen, 'Population and Society in Southeast Asia before 1900,' unpublished paper, 1988, 3–7.

as many of the enemy as possible, to take home to populate their dominions. Much larger numbers were mobilized for war than in comparable European campaigns—the kings of Burma, Vietnam, Siam and Java might each mobilize over a hundred thousand men—sometimes a majority of the available adult male population. They had to bring their own provisions, or else forage from the enemy territory they traversed. Hunger and disease were inevitably the result of these unwieldy campaigns. If the war went badly, the odds were against the soldiers ever returning to their families. As was said of Burmese–Thai warfare in the sixteenth century, 'these people bring so much damage to their enemies, ravaging all the plain, pillaging or burning all they encounter; but in the end they never return home without leaving half of their people.'[3] For the defenders, a common response to a force which came by sea was to abandon the settlement and flee into the surrounding forest until the attacker had done his plundering and departed. Hence families needed to be able to travel light, with little of their wealth in fixed property and with a minimum of children who could not run on their own.

Some wars of the period were so devastating in the mortality they caused that there can be no question that population declined sharply as a result. The Pegu area of lower Burma, the glittering centre of the vast empire of Bayinnaung (r. 1551–81), was destroyed and depopulated in the 1590s by vengeful Burman kings. Even if Floris' claim that this period 'coste the lyves of many millions of Peguers'[4] is much exaggerated, there is no doubt that the population was not restored for a century or more. In 1757 the Mons of lower Burma suffered another bout of defeat and depopulation by Burman rulers. Siam was twice laid waste by Burman armies, in 1549–69 and again in the 1760s, in each case losing the majority of the population in the immediate vicinity of the capital. When W. A. R. Wood wrote of these events in the 1920s[5] it was widely believed that Siam had barely then regained the population it had had before the onset of the Burmese wars in the 1550s. When Siam did reconstruct its population after these events, it was largely by bringing great numbers of captured Laos, Cambodians, Mons and Malays to central Thailand. Malaya was similarly devastated by the conquests of Sultan Iskander Muda of Aceh in the period 1618–24, with Pahang in particular never recovering its relative prominence after its capital was destroyed and 11,000 men taken captive by the victorious Acehnese. In Java the constant wars of succession between 1675 and 1755 ensured that each revision of the conventional *cacah* figures of households subject to corvée was downward rather than upward.[6]

The pattern of Southeast Asian population before 1750, therefore, was almost certainly one of dramatic ups and downs. Periods of strong rule able to guarantee internal security ensured rapid population growth by

---

[3] Pierre du Jarric, *Histoire des choses plus memorables advenues tant ez Indes Orientales, que autres pais de la descouverte des Portugais*, Bordeaux, 1608–14, I. 620–1.

[4] *Peter Floris, His Voyage to the East Indies in the 'Globe', 1611–1615*, ed. W. H. Moreland, London: Hakluyt Society, 1934, 53. Also du Jarric, *Histoire des choses* I. 618–23; III. 842.

[5] *A History of Siam*, London, 1924, reprinted Bangkok, 1959, 146.

[6] M. C. Ricklefs, 'Some Statistical Evidence on Javanese Social, Economic and Demographic History in the Later Seventeenth and Eighteenth Centuries,' MAS, 20, 1 (1986); Reid, *Age of Commerce*, I. 17–18.

natural causes and by immigration, as happened in fifteenth-century Vietnam, sixteenth-century Burma, seventeenth-century Siam and Laos, Aceh in 1550–1640, Makassar in 1600–60, and Dutch-controlled areas of Java after 1650. Such periods of steady growth were probably almost balanced by terrible setbacks such as those sketched above. Only after 1750 in Java and the Philippines, and after 1820 in most other parts of Southeast Asia, did stability and security begin to appear the norm rather than the exception, so that population increases of more than one per cent a year became general.

Estimated Southeast Asian Population about 1600

Region	Population ('000)	Density (per km²)
Vietnam (north and centre)	4,700	18.0
Cambodia-Champa	1,230	4.5
Laos (both sides of Mekong)	1,500	4.2
Burma	3,100	4.6
Siam (without Northeast)	1,700	4.3
Malaya (incl. Pattani)	500	3.4
Sumatra	2,400	5.7
Java	4,000	30.3
Borneo	670	0.9
Sulawesi	1,200	6.3
Bali	600	79.7
Lesser Sundas	600	9.1
Maluku	160*	2.2
Luzon and Visayas	800	4.0
Mindanao and Sulu	150	1.5
Total Southeast Asia	**23,300**	**5.8**

The basis for these estimates is set out in my *Age of Commerce*, I. 12–14; and in a little more detail in my 'Low Population Growth and Its Causes in Pre-Colonial Southeast Asia', in Norman Owen, ed., *Death and Disease in Southeast Asia*, Singapore, 1987, 33–47. The surprisingly high figure for Laos, not listed in the earlier publications, is based on counts of the corvéable population reportedly taken in 1376 and about 1640, covering a much larger area than the present state. The first yielded 300,000 adult male Lao and 400,000 non-Lao under royal control; the second 500,000 adult male subjects of unspecified ethnicity. David K. Wyatt, *Thailand, A Short History*, New Haven, 1982, 83; G. F. de Marini, *Delle Missioni de Padri della Compagnia de Giesu nella Provincia de Giappone, e particolarmente di quella di Tumkino*, Rome, 1663, 450.
* This figure, lower than my previous estimate, is based on the assumption that the area covered by detailed Dutch population counts in the Ambon and Lease Islands then embraced a quarter of the total Maluku population, as it did at the 1930 census. Gerrit Knaap, *Kruidnagelen en Christenen. De Verenigde Oost-Indische Compagnie en de Bevolking van Ambon 1656–1696*, Dordrecht, 1987, 100–1.

AN ECONOMIC BOOM

Southeast Asia has never been able to isolate itself from international economic forces. It sat athwart the great arteries of world commerce, it produced many of the articles which dominated the global long-distance trade, and it was widely accessible by water. Hence it is not surprising that it shared in some of the notable economic cycles which we know to have affected Europe and China.

The period 1400–1620 was essentially one of boom in both those great markets. Following the trauma of the Black Death throughout Eurasia in the fourteenth century, populations rose steadily in both Europe and China. Prices also rose, almost doubling in England and France during the sixteenth century. This boom was most intense during the period 1570–1620, when new methods of smelting caused a massive increase in the export of silver both by Peru (Potosi) and Japan. In China, Japan, and Europe this relatively well-documented period saw a great expansion of cities and a build-up of the trade networks which gave them life. The same was true in Southeast Asia.

If there is a particular moment for the beginning of this sustained trade boom as it affected Southeast Asia, it should be sought around 1400. China was the largest market for Southeast Asian goods, and the abrupt changes of imperial policy towards foreign trade could have a marked effect in the south. There seems no doubt that the advent of a remarkably stable and prosperous Ming dynasty in 1368, its policy of vigorously encouraging lucrative 'tribute' missions during the subsequent half-century, and especially its exceptional initiative in sending out seven massive state trading expeditions between 1403 and 1433, had an enormous effect in stimulating Southeast Asian trade and commerce. Chinese copper cash became the basic currency of Java, Malaya, and Maluku (the Moluccas) during the fifteenth century. Although small quantities of pepper had been exported from Java in earlier periods, it was around 1400, in response to the great new demand from China, that the Indian pepper vine (*Piper nigrum*) was carried from South India to northern Sumatra, and began its career as the biggest export item of Southeast Asia. During the fifteenth century Indonesian pepper and Siamese sappanwood (used for dye) became for the first time items of mass consumption in China.[7]

Chinese state trading ceased abruptly in 1433, and private Chinese trade remained officially banned, but Southeast Asia's trade to the north remained lively. There were always secluded bays on the South China coast where the imperial ban on trade was ineffective. Furthermore the use of tribute missions to Peking (Beijing) as a way to circumvent the ban was at its peak in the fifteenth century, with Siam sending a total of seventy-eight missions between 1371 and 1503.[8] Finally the island kingdom of Ryukyu, between Japan and Taiwan, became a crucial commercial link between Southeast and Northeast Asia in the period 1430–1512, profiting from its tributary relations with both China and Japan to bring Southeast Asian produce to these theoretically closed kingdoms.

Although the expansion of Chinese demand in the fifteenth and sixteenth centuries was probably the biggest stimulus for Southeast Asian commercial growth, the trade to the west was also increasingly lively. Throughout the European Middle Ages some cloves and nutmeg, grown only in Maluku in eastern Indonesia, had found their way to western Europe, along an arduous trade route that passed by Java, Sumatra,

---

[7] T'ien Ju-kang, 'Chêng Ho's Voyages and the Distribution of Pepper in China,' JRAS, 2 (1981).
[8] Suebsang Promboon, 'Sino-Siamese Tributary Relations 1282–1853,' Ph.D. thesis, University of Michigan, 1971, 106–20.

southern India, the Red Sea and Alexandria (or the Persian Gulf and Beirut) to Venice, Genoa or Barcelona. In the 1390s, however, this trade appears for the first time to have become substantial and predictable. More than twenty tonnes of cloves were then arriving in Italian ports in an average year, and we must assume that the quantities which remained in India were far greater. Although only one small branch of Southeast Asia's export trade, the Maluku spices reaching Europe are the only branch which can be quantified over the whole of our period, and are therefore a precious indicator of overall trade levels. As illustrated for cloves in Figure 8.1, these exports show a rapid expansion in the fifteenth century, a disruption caused by the Portuguese intrusion after 1500, and then a still more rapid growth up till the time when the Dutch East India Company established its monopoly in the 1620s.

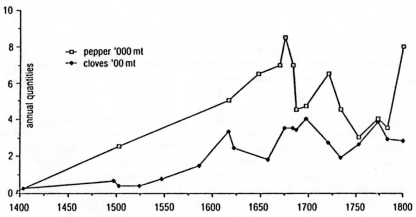

Figure 3.1 Southeast Asian pepper and clove exports, 1400–1800.[9]

[9] The data for cloves (in hundred metric tonnes) after the Dutch monopoly (1650) are based on accurate VOC reports of annual production in Gerrit Knaap, *Kruidnagelen en Christenen: De Verenigde Oost-Indische Compagnie en de bevolking van Ambon 1656–1696*, Dordrecht, 1987, 231, 235, and E. W. A. Ludeking, *Schets van de Residentie Amboina*, The Hague, 1868, 92–3. I have calculated these by decennial averages. Before 1650 what is presented in the graph is not production but my estimate of exports to Europe alone, which represent smaller shares of Moluccan production the earlier period. The pepper line (thousand metric tonnes) is my estimate of total Southeast Asian production, based on reports of amounts carried to Europe and to China, and total production estimated from the sources in notes 10 and 11. The major sources for clove and pepper quantities before 1600 are C. Wake, 'The Changing Pattern of Europe's Pepper and Spice Imports, ca. 1400–1700,' *Journal of European Economic History*, 6 (1979); Vitorino Magalhães-Godinho, *L'economie de l'empire portugais aux XVe et XVIe siècles*, Paris, 1969, 701–4; and Frederick C. Lane, *Venice and History*, Baltimore, 1966, 14. Pepper quantities carried by different agencies after 1600 are recorded in Kristof Glamann, *Dutch-Asiatic Trade 1620–1740*, 1958, 97–101; K. N. Chaudhuri, *The English East India Company, 1600–1640*, London, 1965, 148; G. B. Souza, *The Survival of Empire. Portuguese Trade and Society in China and the South China Sea, 1630–1754*, Cambridge, UK, 1986, 152–3; J. Kathirithamby-Wells, *The British West Sumatran Presidency (1760–85)*, Kuala Lumpur, 1977, 217, 220; J. de Rovere van Breugel, 'Beschrijving van Bantam en de Lampongs,' BKI, 5 (1856), 358–62. The 1800 pepper estimate is that of van Hogendorp, in *Encyclopaedie van Nederlandsch-Indië*. III. 385. For more detail on how the earlier figures were calculated, see Anthony Reid, 'An "Age of Commerce" in Southeast Asian History', MAS, 24, 1 (1990).

Although the exceptional number of hands through which Maluku spices passed on their long journey to the west and north made them far more important than the small quantities might suggest, it was pepper which became the great Southeast Asian cash crop of the sixteenth and seventeenth century. It is not mentioned as a product of Sumatra or Malaya until after 1400, but by 1510 these regions were producing about 2500 tonnes of pepper a year, in contrast to 3600 tonnes exported by the more ancient pepper centres of Kerala in South India.[10] In the course of the sixteenth century Southeast Asian production increased two or threefold—primarily in west, central and south Sumatra, and western Java. Banten (Java) alone exported an average of 2100 tonnes a year in the first two decades of the seventeenth century,[11] and total Southeast Asian production must have been close to 5000 tonnes. The quantities produced continued to increase to a peak of about 8500 tonnes around 1670 before falling off. Prices declined sharply after 1650, though it was another two decades before this was translated into reduced production. In terms of the returns flowing into Southeast Asia, the peak of the pepper boom occurred in the first half of the seventeenth century.

The increase in Southeast Asian production after 1500 almost all went to fill the growing demand in Europe. The initial impact of the Portuguese appearance in the Indian Ocean was to disrupt the existing Muslim-dominated trade routes, though this effect was most damaging for the established pepper-producers of Kerala. Prior to 1500 Indonesian pepper went almost exclusively to China (and other parts of Southeast Asia), but the Portuguese began bringing some to Europe during the first half of the sixteenth century. In the 1550s a major new Muslim trade artery was opened up between Aceh, at the northern tip of Sumatra, and the Red Sea, avoiding the areas of Portuguese strength on the west coast of India. For most of the second half of the century this route carried Sumatran pepper through the Red Sea to Alexandria in quantities at least as large as the Portuguese were taking from India to western Europe.[12] With the arrival of the English and Dutch, Southeast Asia became unquestionably the major source of the world's pepper and therefore the centre of competition between Portuguese, English, Dutch, Chinese and Indian buyers. Pepper, primarily from Sumatra, the Malay peninsula and southern Borneo, provided more than half of the invoice value of both English and Dutch return cargoes from Asia until 1650. Thereafter the proportion dropped sharply as pepper prices in Europe fell and more profitable cargoes were found in Indian cloths and indigo. Pepper had declined to only 10 per cent of the

---

[10] *The Suma Oriental of Tomé Pires*, ed. and trans. Armando Cortesão, London: Hakluyt Society, 1944, 82, 140, 144.

[11] Calculated from M. A. P. Meilink-Roelofsz, *Asian Trade and European Influence in the Indonesian Archipelago between 1500 and about 1630*, The Hague, 1962, 393 n. 80.

[12] Lane, *Venice and History*, 25–34; Fernand Braudel, *The Mediterranean and the Mediterranean World in the Age of Philip II*, trans. S. Reynolds, New York, 1976, 545–51; Charlex Boxer, 'A note on Portuguese Reactions to the Revival of the Red Sea Spice Trade and the Rise of Atjeh, 1540–1600,' JSEAH, 10 (1969).

value of English cargoes by the 1680s, and to 11 per cent of Dutch cargoes by 1700.[13]

These developments for the two Southeast Asian exports about which we know most (because they were the principal articles of European interest in Asia during this period) were paralleled by other indicators of Southeast Asian trade, both local and long-distance. The peak of the boom in Southeast Asia's trade occurred during the period 1580–1630, as a result of the coincidence of exceptional demand from China, Japan, India, and Europe. Price levels were high throughout the world during this period, largely as a result of unprecedented exports of silver from the Americas and Japan, and competition for Southeast Asia's valuable products was intense.

In China this period represented the 'late Ming boom', when trade, urban growth and prosperity were at high levels. In 1567 the emperor Mu-tsung for the first time lifted the Ming ban on private trade to the south. Fifty junks were initially licensed to leave from the southern Chinese ports each year, and this figure grew rapidly to 88 in 1589 and 117 in 1597. A roughly equal number of unlicensed junks appear to have continued the age-old 'smuggling' trade. Roughly half of these junks were licensed for the 'eastern seas', meaning the Philippines and northern Borneo, but especially the flourishing Spanish port of Manila, founded in 1571. Other major destinations for the Chinese ships were western Java (8 ships a year in the 1590s), southern Sumatra (7 ships), the Nguyen-ruled kingdom of what is now central Vietnam (8 ships) and Siam (4 ships).[14] From the records of ship movements kept by the Spanish in Manila and the Dutch in Batavia, it is clear that Chinese shipping to Southeast Asia remained at high levels through the 1630s, but thereafter dropped to only one-third or less until the 1690s.[15]

For Japan the period 1570–1630 was a unique moment when the country was unified, cities prospered as the nuclei of a flourishing internal trade, and exceptional quantities of silver were extracted from the mines to form the basis of a vigorous trade with Southeast Asia. Japanese vessels were still forbidden to trade directly with China, so the exchange of Japanese silver for Chinese silk and other goods had to take place in Southeast Asian ports, notably Manila and Hoi An (known to Westerners as Faifo, central Vietnam). Throughout the period 1604–35 about ten Japanese vessels a year were licensed to trade with the south, the largest numbers going to Vietnam (124 ships during the thirty-one years), the Philippines (56), and Siam (56). In 1635 this activity stopped abruptly when the shogun Iemitsu prohibited Japanese from travelling abroad. Japanese external

[13] K. N. Chaudhuri, *The Trading World of Asia and the English East India Company, 1660–1760*, Cambridge, UK, 1978, 529; J. R. Bruijn, F. S. Gaastra and I. Schöffer, *Dutch-Asiatic Shipping in the 17th and 18th Centuries*, The Hague, 1987, I. 92.

[14] Zhang Xie, *Dong xi yang kao* [Studies on the East and West Oceans, 1617], new edn, Beijing, 1981, 131–3; R. L. Innes, 'The Door Ajar: Japan's Foreign Trade in the seventeenth century,' Ph.D. thesis, University of Michigan, 1980, 52–3.

[15] Pierre Chaunu, *Les Philippines et le Pacifique des Ibériques*, Paris, 1960, 148–75; Leonard Blussé, *Strange Company. Chinese settlers, mestizo women, and the Dutch in VOC Batavia*, Dordrecht, 1986, 115–20.

trade remained high throughout the rest of the century, but only through the tightly controlled Dutch and Chinese trade at Nagasaki.[16]

The enormous increase in output of the silver mines of Spanish America in the 1570s also had its effect on Southeast Asia. Some of this silver was carried directly to Manila from Acapulco, to buy Chinese products and Southeast Asian spices. A larger amount crossed the Atlantic, where first the Portuguese and Venetians, and after 1600 the Dutch, English, Danes and French, carried some of it eastward to buy the precious products of Asia. Magalhães-Godinho has calculated that Europe as a whole was sending precious metals to the equivalent of seventeen tonnes of silver per year to Asia in the 1490s, but that this suffered a 'sensational' drop to only three tonnes in the early 1500s, as a result of Portugal's resort to plunder rather than purchase in the Indian Ocean. The old level was regained by the mid-sixteenth century, as the Portuguese adjusted to more peaceful trade and the Muslim–Venetian route through the Red Sea revived. After 1570 New World silver began pouring into Europe, and the union of Portuguese and Spanish Crowns in 1580 gave the Portuguese ready access to it. Both Portuguese and Venetians were sending unprecedented amounts of silver to the east in the last two decades of the century, when a total treasure equivalent to seventy-two tonnes of silver was being annually shipped to Asia.[17] With the added competition of Dutch, English and French buyers, the amount of silver flowing east from Europe reached a temporary peak in the 1620s. Since Southeast Asian products were then the major goal of the Europeans, by contrast to the situation after 1650, much of this treasure must have served to enrich Southeast Asia during that busy half-century before 1630.

CASH-CROPPING AND COMMERCIALIZATION

Before this long post-1400 boom, most Southeast Asian exports had consisted of the natural products of the forest and the sea—that exotic inventory of medicines, delicacies, perfumes and aromatic woods described in Chinese manuals of the T'ang and the Sung. No doubt there were ups and downs in the trade in such items, but such swings would not have altered the way of life of the majority of Southeast Asians. After 1400 such forest products as camphor, sandalwood and sappanwood were gathered on an increased scale, but they were increasingly dwarfed in importance by cultivated crops grown specifically for export. Whole communities devoted themselves to cultivating pepper, clove, cotton, sugar, and benzoin, and became dependent on the international market for their livelihood. 'This one product with which they abound must furnish them with everything

---

[16] Iwao Seiichi, Kaigai Koshoshi no Shiten. 2: Kinsei [Views on Overseas Contacts, vol. 2: Modern Times], Tokyo, 1976, 300–1. Innes, 'Door Ajar', 51–66. Innes, 376–432, has effectively shown that the overall value of Japan's foreign trade did not fall after 1635, as previously thought. In fact the highest levels were reached in the three periods 1636–8, 1659–62 and 1696–9.

[17] Magalhães-Godinho, L'economie, 316, 334–5.

else; this is why . . . these people [of eastern Indonesia] are constrained to keep up continual intercourse with one another, the one supplying what the other wants.'[18]

The spectacular growth of pepper production drew particularly large numbers of people in Sumatra, the Malay peninsula and southern Borneo into this kind of insecure prosperity through cash-cropping. Judging by eighteenth-century calculations that a family pepper farm delivered on average 200 kilograms of pepper a year,[19] the 8500 tonnes of pepper produced at the peak of the boom must have required the labour of 40,000 families or at least 200,000 individuals. These cultivators would have represented about 5 per cent of the total population of Sumatra, Borneo and the Malay peninsula at that time. If we add the people who depend indirectly on this export item as traders, port workers, city-dwellers and dependants of the merchants and officials who drew the largest profit from the trade, the total proportion whose economic livelihood was dependent on cash-cropping would be at least twice as great.

Pepper and the other items in the long-distance trade to Europe and China have left us the best data. They were also crucial in bringing wealth and shipping into the region as a whole and thereby stimulating a vast range of local trade routes which brought provisions and consumer goods to the cash-croppers and the cities. In terms of the overall level of commercialization in the region it was this local and regional trade which was most important, though impossible to quantify. In the sixteenth and seventeenth century the bulk of Southeast Asian cargoes were certainly in foodstuffs, textiles, ceramics and metalware, not the high-value pepper and spices of the long-distance trade.

Cotton was an even more widespread cash crop than pepper, though marketed less far afield and frequently grown alongside rice. Since only those parts of Southeast Asia with a substantial dry season could grow cotton, it was exported around the region both as raw cotton and as cloth. Around 1600 the eastern parts of Java, and Bali, Lombok, Sumbawa and Buton supplied cloth to Maluku, Sulawesi, Borneo and the Malay peninsula. The dry areas of Luzon, Cebu and Panay provided cotton for wetter parts of the Philippines. Cambodia exported cotton as far afield as Pattani on the Malay peninsula. Some Southeast Asian cotton and cloth was even taken back to China by returning traders from ports in Java, Luzon and Vietnam. At least in the eighteenth century, and perhaps for some time earlier, there was a large-scale cotton trade from the dry regions of central Burma up the Irrawaddy and along caravan routes into Yunnan.[20]

Sugarcane, although native to Southeast Asia, was used primarily for chewing as a confection until the seventeenth century, when Chinese refining methods were introduced to Java, Siam, Cambodia and the Quang Nam area of central Vietnam. In Banten around 1630 cultivators were shifting from pepper into sugar, which was more profitable as an export to China. Japan, which grew no sugar of its own, was an even bigger market,

[18] *The Voyage of Francis Pyrard of Laval to the East Indies, the Maldives, the Moluccas and Brazil,* trans. A. Gray, London: Hakluyt Society, 1887–90, II. 169.
[19] Kathirithamby-Wells, 61, 70.
[20] Reid, *Age of Commerce,* I. 90–2.

importing over 2000 tonnes a year in the second half of the century. After Taiwan, the major exporters to Japan were central Vietnam and Siam, each providing several hundred tonnes a year for Chinese and Dutch shippers to take to Nagasaki.[21]

Another important cash crop of the period was benzoin (the resin of the tree *Styrax benzoin*, used for incense), grown wild but also in large plantations in northern Sumatra, Siam, northern Cambodia and Laos. The Mekong valley was exporting 270 tonnes a year through Cambodia in the 1630s, primarily to Asian ports—Persia alone took about 60 tonnes.[22] Tobacco and indigo, on the other hand, were grown primarily for markets within the Southeast Asian region. Seventeenth-century Batavia drew its substantial tobacco needs primarily from the Javanese north coast, but also from Madura, south Sulawesi, Amboina and Mindanao.[23]

Cash-cropping brought wealth, international contacts, and social changes on a considerable scale. Some growers undoubtedly became very wealthy, but the principal beneficiaries were the rulers of the port-cities which marketed these goods, the traders, and the intermediaries who financed the new frontiers of cash-cropping. Since population was scarce relative to land, the key figure in developing new areas was the entrepreneur who could mobilize labour through a sufficient advance of capital and could control access to a market. Those who received an advance of money or goods to set them up as pepper-growers on a new frontier would remain dependent on the financier, and in particular would be obliged to market their harvest through him or her. Sometimes this dependence was akin to slavery, as in the case of the jungle frontier around Banjarmasin (south Borneo), which imported from Makassar and elsewhere 'male and female slaves fitted for labour in the pepper-gardens'.[24] In all cases a large share of the profit would go to this intermediary financier and broker, who might in time become the chief of a small river-system; a percentage would also go as tribute to the ruler of the city-state where the international market was located.[25]

The cash-cropping centres and the cities which they helped to stimulate relied for much of their livelihood on imports. Taking Southeast Asia as a whole, the largest single item of import in the sixteenth and seventeenth century was undoubtedly Indian cloth. Personal adornment and clothing were the principal items of non-essential expenditure for most Southeast Asians, so that any increase in income was likely to show first in expenditure on cloth. As one observer pointed out for the Burmese, they were

---

[21] Innes, 'Door Ajar', 504–8; Yoneo Ishii, 'Seventeenth Century Japanese Documents about Siam,' JSS, 59, 2 (1971) 170.

[22] W. Ph. Coolhaas, *Generale Missiven van Gouverneurs-Generaal en Raden aan Heren XVII der Verenigde Oostindische Compagnie*, The Hague, 1960–76, I. 592.

[23] Thomas O. Höllman, *Tabak in Südostasien: Ein ethnographisch-historischer Überblick*, Berlin, Dietrich Reimer, 1988, 145–50.

[24] 'De Handelsrelaties van het Makassaarse rijk, volgens de notitie van Cornelis Speelman uit 1670', ed. J. Noorduyn, in *Nederlandse Historische Bronnen*, Amsterdam, 1983, III. 112.

[25] The system of pepper-growing is much better known in the nineteenth century, though these essentials probably remained unchanged. See James Siegel, *The Rope of God*, Berkeley, 1969, 17–21; James Gould, 'Sumatra—America's Pepper-pot, 1784–1873,' *Essex Institute Historical Collections*, 92 (1956).

parsimonious in food and housing, but 'splendid and extravagant in their dress. They have always in their mouths that their dress is seen by everybody; but no one comes into their houses to observe what they eat and how they are lodged.'[26] The conversion of most of the island world to Islam or Christianity in the fifteenth to seventeenth centuries brought new styles of dress using much more cloth, particularly on the upper body. In addition sumptuous cloths were used to decorate houses and public buildings, as a store of wealth, an item of ritual exchange at weddings, and to shroud the dead in burial.

For all these purposes Indian cloth was preferred to the local product because of the much brighter colours Indians could fix in their dyes, the bold designs, and the fine weaving. The boom in Southeast Asian exports was matched by a rapid increase in imports of cloth. The last and wealthiest Malay ruler of Melaka (Malacca), Sultan Mahmud (r. 1488–1511), is credited in the chronicles with sending a mission to south India to acquire forty varieties of rare cloth. The Portuguese who conquered his capital gave estimates of the total value of cloth imports from Bengal, Coromandel (the modern Madras area) and Gujerat which could be conservatively totalled at 460,000 cruzados a year, equivalent to about 19 tonnes of silver.[27] In the period 1620–50, the heyday of Indian cloth exports to Southeast Asia, the Dutch alone carried cloth valued between 10 and 20 tonnes of silver (roughly 1 to 2 million guilders) each year from the Coromandel coast to Batavia.[28] The total Southeast Asian imports of Indian cloth in this period probably peaked at a value of about 50 tonnes of silver, representing more than 20 million square metres of cloth—almost a metre per person per year. Indian cloth was traded not only in the great maritime emporia: it reached the tiny spice-growing islands of eastern Indonesia on the one hand, and the land-locked kingdom of Laos on the other, where at least three months were needed for bullock-carts to haul it from Ayutthaya.

The commercial boom also made it possible for large cities and substantial populations to import their food by sea. The Malay capital of Melaka, without any rice-growing hinterland of its own, was supplied by fifty or sixty shiploads (varying greatly in size, but perhaps averaging 30 tonnes) of rice each year from Java, and about thirty each from Siam and Pegu (lower Burma). Pasai in north Sumatra, and its much larger successor after 1520, Aceh, also imported their rice from Pegu, Tenasserim, and South India, as well as Java. Pattani drew more than half its rice from Songkhla, Nakhon Sithammarat, Siam and Cambodia, and merchants from Pahang, further south, came to the Pattani market to buy their supplies of grain. Banten also imported its foodstuffs by sea from other parts of Java, from Makassar and Sumbawa, until Dutch blockades began to place these supplies in doubt. Other foodstuffs such as vegetables, dried fish and fermented fish-paste, coconut oil, salt, and palm-wine also travelled long distances by sea to feed the flourishing cities. During a two-month period

[26] V. Sangermano, *A Description of the Burmese Empire*, trans. W. Tandy, Rome, 1818, reprinted London, 1966, 159.

[27] *Suma Oriental of Tomé Pires*, 269–72.

[28] Calculated from Tapan Raychaudhuri, *Jan Company in Coromandel 1605–1690*, The Hague: KITLV, 1962, 140–3.

in 1642 the Dutch counted twelve ships arriving in Aceh from Java, carrying 'salt, sugar, peas, beans and other goods'.[29]

In bulk terms rice was the largest single item of trade. The bunded irrigated fields of Java and the flood-plains of Siam, Cambodia and Burma were able to generate large surpluses, which were regularly carried by river or pack-animal to the ports whence the grain was shipped in sacks to urban or rice-deficit areas. In the seventeenth century central Java was usually the largest single exporter, with quantities up to 10,000 tonnes being shipped from Japara in a good year. South Sulawesi under the able chancellor of Makassar, Karaeng Matoaya (r. 1593–1637), was one area where rice cultivation was deliberately expanded for export. Rice barns were built on royal initiative, and regulations framed to ensure that there was always a supply of rice to provide spice traders on their way to Maluku. Even in these circumstances, however, rice cannot be considered a true cash crop. It was grown primarily for local needs, and the surplus only was exported.

URBANIZATION

In Southeast Asia before 1630, maritime cities were probably more dominant over their sparsely-populated hinterlands than they were in most other parts of the world. Unlike the earlier period of Hindu-Buddhist states such as Angkor, Pagan and Majapahit, the capitals of this period were all accessible to ocean shipping. Rulers, and the circle of aristocratic officials around them, drew the bulk of their revenue from trade, participating in it directly as well as taxing it through import dues, gifts and impositions. The maritime capitals did not simply consume wealth from the hinterland and transform it into power: they generated most of the state's wealth through trade, and to a lesser extent manufacture. In most of the languages of Southeast Asia the state and the city were indistinguishable. The power and grandeur of the country essentially resided in its capital, and the ruler's military strength rested on that large proportion of his subjects who could be called to arms in a few hours from within and around it. What Bangkok was for Siam in the nineteenth century, Ayutthaya was to an even greater extent in the sixteenth and seventeenth: 'at once the seat of government, of religion, of foreign commerce, in short of nearly all public life. Bangkok is more to Siam than Paris to France.'[30]

These commercial capitals depended on the vagaries of international trade, and their populations rose and fell accordingly. The seasonality of the monsoons brought foreign traders and seamen who might add to the city's population for six months or more, while festivals and market days brought great crowds in from the hinterland. The Vietnamese capital Thang-long (Hanoi), in particular, became so crowded on the market days at the first and fifteenth days of each lunar month that some observers

[29] Reid, *Age of Commerce*, I. 21–31.
[30] Board of Foreign Missions, 1865, cited in L. Sternstein, 'The Growth of the Population of the World's Pre-eminent "Primate City": Bangkok at its Bicentenary', JSEAS, 15, 1 (1984) 49.

thought it then the most populous city in the world, with streets so crowded one could scarcely advance a hundred steps in half an hour.[31] The estimates of contemporary observers, the scale of food imports, and the physical dimensions of city remains, provide the basis for the following tentative estimates of the permanent populations of these Southeast Asian cities at their peak.

The extent of its walls confirms that the population of the Vietnamese capital of Thang-long was in excess of 100,000 throughout the period from the fifteenth to the mid-eighteenth century. Its population was the least dependent on international trade of any Southeast Asian capital, but it was the heart of the region's most centralized and populous state. It was also the major manufacturing centre of the country, with many of its quarters devoted exclusively to a particular craft. The fifteenth century was the golden age of the Vietnamese capital, when the vigorous Le dynasty extended its wall to ten kilometres and built many palaces and temples. Signs of decay were already evident in the seventeenth century.

For two or three decades before its conquest by the Portuguese in 1511, Melaka was the great trade-based city of the Malay world, with a population of around 100,000. It was reduced to about a quarter of that after the Portuguese occupation and the departure of most Muslim traders. In the mid-sixteenth century Ayutthaya and Pegu were probably the two largest cities of the region, until the Siamese capital was devastated by the Burmese in 1569, and Pegu in turn was largely depopulated in 1599. The archipelago cities were then probably somewhat smaller, with Aceh, Brunei (until the Spanish conquest of 1579), Demak and Tuban probably around 50,000 during the latter half of the century.

In the seventeenth century we have more frequent estimates of population, which also show a rapid growth of trade-based cities in step with the peak in the trade boom of 1570–1630. Ayutthaya must have recovered its former population by mid-century, at which point there were probably six Southeast Asian cities in the 100,000 class—Thang-long, Ayutthaya, Aceh, Banten, Makassar and Mataram. Other major cities having about 50,000 were Pattani, Surabaya (until its conquest by Mataram in 1621), the Cambodian capital near the junction of the Mekong and Tonle Sap rivers, the southern (Nguyen) Vietnamese capital at Kim-long, the restored and growing Burmese capital at Ava, and (to judge again from physical dimensions) the Lao capital of Vientiane under its 'sun-king', Soulignavongsa (1654–1712).[32]

Many of these cities were excessively large in relation to their hinterlands if compared with their counterparts in Europe. Numerous observers pointed out that the great Malay port of Melaka was surrounded by little but jungle, and had to import virtually all its rice by sea. Aceh was also dependent on imported rice in the seventeenth century, because it was trade and craft production that occupied the bulk of the population of the

---

[31] Samuel Baron, 'A Description of the Kingdom of Tonqeen,' in *A Collection of Voyages and Travels*, ed. A. and W. Churchill, London, 1703–32, IV. 3. Abbé Richard, *Histoire naturelle, civile et politique du Tonquin*, Paris, 1778, I. 28.

[32] For further details of these estimates see Anthony Reid, 'The Structure of Cities in Southeast Asia: Fifteenth to Seventeenth Centuries', JSEAS, 11, 2 (1980) 237–9; and Reid, *The Age of Commerce*, II. ch. 2.

Aceh river valley. Even in the relatively minor port of Kedah, surrounded by some of the best potential rice-land in the Malay peninsula, the town was said to have 7000 or 8000 inhabitants in 1709, and the whole country only 20,000, filled as it was with 'great forests, where one sees masses of wild buffaloes, elephants, deers and tigers'.[33]

European cities expanded rapidly in the prosperous sixteenth century, but most of them remained in a similar range to the cities above. Only Naples and Paris were in excess of 200,000, with London and Amsterdam rapidly approaching this. Tomé Pires had seen only the modest European cities of the Iberian peninsula when he declared that Melaka had 'no equal in the world', but later observers continued to make such comparisons. The English East India Company in 1617 thought Ayutthaya 'as big a city as London',[34] but it was the capital of a country with only a quarter of England's population. Even in the nineteenth century when the Thai capital was no longer a major international emporium it contained about 10 per cent of the country's population, and Ayutthaya can have had no less a share in the seventeenth century. The Dutch compared Banten in 1597 to 'old Amsterdam'; a French traveller in Burma a century later thought Syriam and Prome were the size of Metz (perhaps 25,000), and compared Pagan with Dijon and Ava with Rheims (both perhaps 40,000).[35] But the agricultural populations these towns served were very much less than those of the Netherlands and France. Their size was made possible by the capability of rice to produce very large surpluses in relation to labour input; by the ease of waterborne transport; by the relative importance of trade in this period; and by the desire of powerful statesmen to have the maximum of their followers around them for military and status purposes.

Southeast Asia in the period 1500–1660 should therefore be seen as highly urban, in relation both to other parts of the world and to its own subsequent experience. The European enclave cities which took over much of the lucrative long-distance trade of the region were much smaller than their predecessors. Portuguese Melaka never rose above 30,000, Dutch Makassar took two centuries to recover its pre-Dutch population, and even Batavia had scarcely 30,000 inhabitants within its walls in the second half of the seventeenth century when it dominated the maritime trade of Asia. The Dutch 'Queen of the East' was still smaller than the economically insignificant Javanese inland capitals in 1812, and Java's de-urbanization continued throughout the nineteenth century.[36] Similarly British Rangoon did not pass the population of the Burmese capital (successively at Ava, Amerapurah and Mandalay) until about 1890, long after it had defeated it economically and militarily. The reason was that these colonial cities discouraged an influx of people from their hinterlands, and played almost no role as political, cultural and religious centres of the regions which they

---

[33] Père Taillandier to Willard, 20 February 1711, in *Lettres édifiantes et curieuses, écrites des missions étrangeres*, new edn, Paris, 1781, II. 409.

[34] Cited John Anderson, *English Intercourse with Siam in the Seventeenth Century*, London, 1890, 69.

[35] P. Goüye, *Observations physique et mathematiques . . . envoyées des Indes et de la Chine à l'Academie Royale des Sciences à Paris, par les Pères Jesuites*, Paris, 1692, 73–4.

[36] Peter Boomgaard, *Children of the Colonial State*, Amsterdam, 1989, 110–11.

dominated economically. Southeast Asian societies themselves had few links with these international and 'modern' cities, and underwent a significant de-urbanization in the eighteenth century, becoming more isolated than before from the cosmopolitan and secular dynamism of city life.

The central features of the Southeast Asian city were the fortified palace or citadel, the mosque or temple, and the market. The citadel contained the residence of the monarch, his consorts and immediate dependants, and it was always surrounded by a high strong wall. This was the city proper, a place of cosmic power and centrality to the realm. Only Vietnamese cities emulated the Chinese model, with a wall around their entirety. In Siam the citadel and the city merged, with most of the important temples and the compounds of ministers contained within the walled and moated citadel, of which the royal palace was only the most important section. Yet even in such vast citadels as Ayutthaya, which embraced the seven square kilometres of an island in the river and contained much empty parkland, the foreigners were kept outside. Consequently much of the commercial life of the city was conducted outside the walled city proper. In Burma, Cambodia, and the Malay world the boundaries of the larger city were even less clear, since it was often only the royal enclosure which had any wall at all. Around this spread village-like assemblages of wooden houses shaded by trees, interspersed with the compounds of rich merchants and officials, the greatest of which replicated the citadel itself with their protective walls (often simply of bamboo, thornbushes, or earth), religious shrines, and accommodation for a large number of dependants.

In the sixteenth and especially the seventeenth century the example (and the threat) of the Europeans and Chinese encouraged more cities to build walls around the whole of the central area which had to be defended. Yet some of the largest cities in the archipelago, including Aceh and Mataram, never built walls except around the royal compound itself. In consequence there was no clear sense of the distinct character or autonomy of the city. Cities spread freely into the countryside, and were not constrained to build dense-packed permanent structures behind their protective walls as in Europe or China. To European visitors it appeared as if even a large Southeast Asian city was 'no more than an aggregate of villages', largely hidden by the profusion of trees.

Given their warm climate and exposure to frequent flooding, it was not surprising that Southeast Asians even in cities preferred to live in light and airy houses constructed on stilts out of temporary materials. There were also political reasons, however, for the scarcity of stone or brick buildings. Europeans were particularly anxious to build in stone, partly to avoid the danger of fire, but chiefly to be able to protect themselves effectively. After the Dutch had succeeded in making themselves impregnable in Jayakatra (Jakarta, which they renamed Batavia) in 1619, Southeast Asian suspicions hardened against this practice. Rulers in the seventeenth century forbade not only Europeans but also their own subjects to build in permanent, defensible materials. The only significant exceptions were the religious buildings which embellished all the cities and towns, and the half-submerged *gudang* (godowns or warehouses) which merchants were permitted to build to contain their flammable cloth and other merchandise.

Fire was a constant threat in these wooden cities. Sudden conflagrations were reported to have consumed 800 houses in Aceh in 1602 and 8000 in 1688; 1260 in Makassar in 1614, and 10,000 in Ayutthaya in 1545, while most of Pattani was burned during a revolt in 1613. For European and Chinese merchants this was a source of endless anxiety, but Southeast Asians appear to have accepted the essential impermanence of their houses, and to have kept what wealth they had in removable gold, jewellery and cloth. After a fire, whole sections of the city would be rebuilt in a matter of three or four days.

THE NATURE OF SOUTHEAST ASIAN COMMERCE

One of the reasons for the relatively large population of Southeast Asian maritime cities was the need of merchants and sailors to spend several months in port selling their wares, buying a return cargo, and awaiting a change of monsoon. The very regular nature of the seasonal winds meant that the most important shipping routes—across the Bay of Bengal, the South China Sea, or the Java Sea—were made at the period of most favourable winds, so that there was at most a single return voyage per year. Chinese and Japanese ships arrived in Southeast Asia in January to March, and returned at the earliest the following August. In many cases they spent a year and a half in the south visiting several ports to gain the best return cargo. Hence the Southeast Asian cities at their peak season were thronged with visiting traders from all over Asia.

The most numerous of these were the sailors and travelling merchants who accompanied their own merchandise. The sailors on Southeast Asian ships were not paid (though some received a food ration), but they were allocated a section of the hold in which they could carry their own trade goods. The officers—the pilot (*malim*), master, boatswains and helmsmen—received a full *petak* (small partition), freemen sailors received half a *petak*, and only slave members of the crew had no share. Since the large trading ships of the region carried 60 to 100 crew members, these allocations could amount to as much as a quarter of the ship's capacity. The travelling merchants, referred to in the Malay Code by the Chinese-derived word *kiwi*, negotiated with the *nakhoda* (supercargo) the number of *petak* they would occupy, and their price.[37]

Because he either owned the ship or represented the owner on shipboard, the *nakhoda* was the key figure on trading voyages and the truest

---

[37] The only discussion of these issues in English is in M. A. P. Meilink-Roelofsz, *Asian Trade and European Influence in the Indonesian Archipelago between 1500 and about 1630*, The Hague, 1962, 36–59, which pioneered the use of the *Undang-undang Laut*—for which see Sir Richard Winstedt, ed., 'The Maritime Laws of Malacca' JMBRAS, 29, 3 (1956). Since her work, important Portuguese sources on Southeast Asian shipping around 1520 have come to light—Luis Filipe Thomaz, *De Malaca a Pegu. Viagens de um feitor Portugues (1512–1515)*, Lisbon, 1966; Geneviève Bouchon, 'Les premiers voyages portugais à Pegou (1515–1520)', *Archipel*, 18 (1979).

Southeast Asian entrepreneur. An excellent picture of his role is provided by the Malay Maritime Code (*Undang-undang Laut*). Drawn up in about 1500 by a group of Melaka *nakhodas* to guide the conduct of business, it naturally underlines the power of the *nakhoda* at sea. The code likened his power to that of the ruler on shore, having the life and death of sailors and passengers in his hands. On arrival at port, when the market was at its most favourable, the *nakhoda* had first right to sell his merchandise, four days before the *kiwis* and six days before the sailors. Besides his own merchandise or that belonging to the ship's owner whom he represented, the *nakhoda* was responsible for the substantial share of the cargo entrusted to him by home-based merchants.

A system of commenda trade was well developed, whereby merchants would send goods in another man's ship, either in the care of some of his agents, travelling as *kiwis*, or entrusted to the *nakhoda* for a fixed return. The system was described for Malay Melaka about 1510 in this way:

> If I am a merchant in Melaka and give you, the owner of the junk, a hundred cruzados of merchandise at the price then ruling in Melaka, assuming the risk myself, on the return [from Java] they give me a hundred and forty and nothing else, and the payment is made, according to the Melaka ordinance, forty-four days after the arrival of the junk in port.[38]

The term 'junk' (Portuguese *juncos*) used here was routinely applied by European, Chinese, Arab or Malay sources to the large Southeast Asian trading ship. The word itself entered European languages from Malay, but its origins probably lie in Javanese. From their arrival soon after 1500 Europeans used this term for a ship of 100 to 600 tonnes, carrying two to three masts and two oar-like rudders on either side of a pointed stern. From modern excavations of wrecks as well as contemporary descriptions we know that a very similar type of ship sailed throughout the waters of Southeast Asia and the South China Sea. In fact it has been suggested that it should be labelled a hybrid 'South China Sea' ship, because its construction by joining the planks of the hull with wooden dowels, and its double rudders, were common to all other types of boatbuilding in Southeast Asia, whereas the ships also used supplementary iron nails and clamps, cargo partitions and other features characteristic of China.[39]

In the fifteenth century, and probably for some time before that, there was sufficient interaction among Chinese, Javanese and Malay shipbuilders and traders to explain such hybrid patterns. Many Chinese took up residence in the ports of Southeast Asia and built their ships there, and even traders based in South China sometimes had ships built in Southeast Asia because of the better and cheaper woods. The busiest shipyards were in the Mon (Pegu) port of Martaban, and Mon traders often sold both ship and cargo in Melaka after a trading voyage from their homeland.

At the time of the Portuguese arrival, these junks of several hundred

---

[38] *Suma Oriental of Tomé Pires*, 284.
[39] Pierre-Yves Manguin, 'Relationship and Cross-influences between Southeast Asian and Chinese Shipbuilding Traditions', *Final Report, SPAFA Consultative Workshop on Maritime Shipping and Trade Networks in Southeast Asia*, Bangkok, 1984, 197–212.

Figure 3.2   Vessels of the Java coast, 1596, as depicted in Willem Lodewycksz's account of the first Dutch voyage to the East Indies. Left: a Javanese junk; right: a Chinese junk; background, a Javanese *prahu*; foreground: a fishing boat.

From Lodewycksz's account of the first Dutch voyage in *De eerste schipvaart der nederlanders naar Oost-Indie*, vol. I, The Hague, Nijhoff for the Linschoten-Vereeniging, 1915.

tonnes dominated Southeast Asian maritime trade, and equalled the Portuguese vessels in size. In the course of the sixteenth century, however, the Portuguese vessels grew larger while the junks grew smaller. At the time of the earliest Dutch descriptions around 1600 only a few of the rice ships taking bulk cargoes from Java to Melaka exceeded 200 tonnes. In most areas the pattern was already established of thousands of small craft of less than 40 tonnes dividing up the cargo. By the middle of the seventeenth century the term 'junk' was no longer being used by either Europeans or Asians for the small Southeast Asian vessels, but only for Chinese vessels which continued to be of several hundred tonnes. The only large vessels remaining in Southeast Asian hands were the few European-rigged ships which the rulers of Siam, Banten and Burma had built for their long-distance trade.

The disappearance of the junk is one of the more spectacular demonstrations of the decline of Southeast Asian involvement with large-scale trade. It is not difficult to understand in light of the havoc the Portuguese wrought in the 1510s amongst these slow-moving vessels. Such large but unwieldy ships were highly profitable in conditions of relative security, but the attacks which Malay and Javanese shipping had to undergo from the Portuguese and later the Dutch made military factors more important. For trade purposes, faster vessels with less capital at stake were preferred. The largest Southeast Asian vessels built after 1640 were the heavily-armed war galleys that played a major part in the military tactics of Aceh, east Indonesia, Borneo, the Philippines, Siam and Vietnam.

It was an age when commerce was far easier by water than by land, and the whole region was remarkably well provided with waterways. All the states of Southeast Asia had access either to the sea or a major river artery. Sailing vessels ascended the Irrawaddy all the way to Ava, while the Red River, the Mekong and the Chao Phraya were navigable as far as the capital cities of Vietnam, Cambodia and Siam respectively. The Khone falls provided a natural frontier between Cambodia and Laos, passable only by disembarking all passengers and cargo, but the several hundred kilo-metres of navigable river higher up the Mekong provided the essential artery for the kingdom of Laos, centred on Vientiane. By contrast with these river routes, road transport remained extremely slow and dangerous throughout Southeast Asia. The only exceptions were those roads of great military significance to important kingdoms, such as the fine road from Mataram to the sea near Semarang and some strategic routes near the Burmese capital. The most important routes for bullock-carts—from Vientiane to Ayutthaya, from northern Burma and Laos into Yunnan, and across the Malayan peninsula from Tenasserim—had to be travelled in caravans for safety, at the excruciatingly slow pace of the most dilapidated cart.

The financial system of Southeast Asia, as of India, owed much to brokers of Hindu commercial castes—the Gujerati *sharafs* and South Indian *chettiars*—whose networks spread to the major trading cities of the whole Indian Ocean littoral. They had a developed system of saleable letters of credit (*hundi* in Hindi), which could be issued in one city and cashed in another, including such ports as Melaka, Banten, or Aceh. These mercantile caste groups were in the first instance moneychangers, a highly necessary occupation in cities where a score of types of coin might be current, but they also operated as bankers and brokers for merchants. The first Florentine merchant to visit Melaka acknowledged with astonishment that the resident Gujerati merchants there were as capable in every respect as Italian bankers;[40] European merchants in unfamiliar ports generally had to make use of them to avoid being cheated.

In the large international cities of the region there was a reliable money-market, in which the ruler and leading officials often lent their capital to the big merchants. In seventeenth-century Siam, Pattani and Jambi the interest rates were very similar, about 2 per cent per month, while in Iskandar Muda's Aceh interest was reportedly kept by law as low as 12 per cent per annum. Such figures, almost as low as in contemporary European or Indian cities, suggest a dependable and sophisticated money market. However there are also numerous reports of rates of interest as high as 100 per cent per annum or more, suggesting that the lower rates represent a privileged urban network of trusted large-scale borrowers, in which some rulers and the European companies were included.

[40] Letter to fra Zuambatista in Florence, 31 January 1513, in Angelo de Gubernatis, *Storia dei Viaggiatori Italiani Nelle Indie Orientali*, Livorno, 1875, 375–7.

Not surprisingly, the Malay word for capital (*modal*) used in the flourishing commercial transactions of the sixteenth century was a Tamil borrowing, while other concepts such as bankruptcy (*muflis*) and usury (*riba*) were taken from the Arabic language and Islamic law. Nevertheless a much older concept of credit and debt was deeply ingrained throughout Southeast Asia, sometimes expressed through the imagery of interest as the flower (Malay *bunga*; Tai *dòk*) and the capital as the plant or tree. The Indian, Chinese and European merchants who found they could invest money in local shipping ventures or advance money against crops, appear to have been less concerned about defaulting than they would have been at home. 'Their laws for debt are so strict that the creditor may take his debtour, his wives, children and slaves, and all that he hath and sell them for his debt.'[41] This was not because of sophisticated financial institutions, but rather the ingrained assumption that debt implied obligation, and particularly the obligation to labour. In every state of Southeast Asia, and even in the stateless tribal societies of the hills, defaulting debtors became the slaves of their creditors, obliged to serve them until the principal was repaid. Such slavery was not viewed as calamitous. On the contrary, every loan taken out already implied some form of obligation to the creditor, whose readiness to issue it implied a readiness to accept the borrower as a dependant. Some debts were contracted deliberately in order to become the dependant of a powerful figure, perhaps thereby escaping some more onerous obligation—for example of corvée due to the king.

The commercialization which undoubtedly marked the sixteenth and seventeenth centuries appears to have accentuated the importance of bondage of this type as the basis of labour obligations. The law codes originating from this period are certainly much concerned with slaves as the most important (and most legally complex) form of property. In the cities in particular, observers wrote as if the majority of the population were slaves and all manual work was done by them. This was true in the sense that there was no free labour market, and those who wanted work done had either to purchase slaves or to hire them from others. Much of the heaviest construction work, building forts, irrigation canals and palaces, was performed by captives regarded as slaves of the victorious king.

On the other hand bondage was not regarded as a pariah status except when it was associated with foreign, 'barbarous' captives, such as newly captured peoples from the hills or the easternmost islands. Even such low-status captives were quickly assimilated into the dominant population, because there was no state-backed legal system that set out to ensure that their slave status was permanent. Although slavery is an inescapable term for those newly captured or bought, because it correctly conveys the fact that they could be transferred without their will to another owner by sale, gift, or inheritance, it must be emphasized that this was an 'open' system of slavery which people moved in and out of almost imperceptibly. As was said of seventeenth-century Aceh: 'neither can a Stranger easily know who

---

[41] E. Scott, 'An exact Discourse . . . of the East Indians', 1606, in *The Voyage of Sir Henry Middleton to the Moluccas 1604–1606*, ed. William Foster, London: Hakluyt Society, 1943, 173.

is a Slave and who not amongst them; for they are all, in a manner, Slaves to one another.'[42]

Since traders from outside the region undoubtedly stimulated the boom in Southeast Asian commerce and contributed much to the life of the mercantile cities, the question may be asked how far commercialization and capitalist forms of exchange and production were simply alien enclaves in Southeast Asia, with as little effect on the surrounding societies as European capital had in the 'dualistic' colonial economies of the nine-teenth century. Chinese technology, weights and coins, Indian financial methods, Islamic commercial laws, and European technology and capital, all played a major part in creating the character of Southeast Asian urban and commercial life in this period.

The first point to be made here is that 'foreignness' was an undoubted asset for entrepreneurs in the region. There are numerous examples of the jealousy rulers felt towards their own subjects who became so wealthy that they appeared to pose a threat to the king himself. There were very few institutional curbs on the autocratic power of rulers to confiscate such private wealth. Foreigners were at an advantage in being both outside the local power system and able to move to another port in case of mistreatment from the ruler. Wealthy foreign merchants who remained for a number of years in one port naturally became influential, and might be drawn into the administration of commerce as *syahbandar* (harbourmasters), or even in some cases as virtual prime ministers or chancellors of the realm. In such cases they were useful to the ruler because of their knowledge of foreign merchants, their military skills, and above all their inability, as foreigners, to challenge the position of the king. When such figures or their descendants became so fully enmeshed in court affairs that they were no longer seen as foreign, like the Tamil-descended *bendaharas* in Melaka or the Persian-descended Bunnags in Siam, they were no longer immune from the periodic jealousy or wrath of the king.

However, these 'foreign' traders in any given port always included substantial numbers of Southeast Asians. In Melaka before the Portuguese conquest Javanese and 'Luzons' (Islamized Tagalogs) were among the largest-scale traders and shipowners. After the fall of Melaka its Malayized population of polyglot origins spread around the ports of Southeast Asia, so that 'Malays' (Muslim Malay-speakers) became a major element among the merchants of Banten (and later Dutch Batavia), Makassar, Cambodia and Siam, as well as in Malay ports such as Pattani, Pahang and Brunei. The Mons of Pegu (southern Burma) were shipowners and merchants in many of the ports on the eastern side of the Indian Ocean. The Dutch described the mix of merchants that greeted them in Banten in 1596 as follows:

> The Persians, who are called Khorasans in Java, are those who usually earn their living in [precious] stones and medicines . . . The Arabs and Pegus [Mons] are the ones who mostly conduct their trade by sea, carrying and bringing merchandise from one city to another, and buying up much Chinese

---

[42] William Dampier, *Voyages and Discoveries*, 1699, reprinted London, 1929, 98.

merchandise, which they exchange against other wares from the surrounding islands, and also pepper, against the time when the Chinese return to buy. The Malays and Klings [South Indians] are merchants who invest money at interest and in voyages and bottomry. The Gujeratis, since they are poor, are usually used as sailors, and are those who take money in bottomry, on which they often make one, two and three times profit.[43]

This picture indicates the importance of internationally-connected minority groups in Southeast Asia, as in Europe, in the early modern period. Not every group filled such roles, to be sure. There is little evidence of ethnic Burmans, Tais, Khmers or Vietnamese doing business outside their own regions, or taking to the sea on trading expeditions. If they did so, they presumably reclassified themselves as Malays, Chinese or Mons and associated with the urban enclaves of these groups. Ethnicity was probably as much a consequence as a cause of entrepreneurial minority status. Every major city had one or more quarters where traders congregated, designated as the 'Javanese', 'Malay', 'Chinese', 'Kling' or 'Portuguese' quarter, but traders who did not seem to qualify in terms of descent were assimilated in functional terms and perhaps eventually in language. When the Dutch arrived at the Cambodian capital to trade in 1636, for example, they were faced with five *syahbandar*, one each to look after the commercial interests of the Portuguese, Malay-Javanese and Japanese quarters, and two for the Chinese quarters. They chose the Japanese *syahbandar* since they were on their way to Japan, and lodged in that quarter.[44]

In considering the ways in which Southeast Asians responded to the commercialization of the 'long sixteenth-century boom', the role of women cannot be ignored. Commerce and marketing were considered predominantly the business of women by all Southeast Asian societies, as to a lesser extent they still are in rural areas. Foreign traders were surprised to find themselves doing business with women, not only in the market-place but also in large-scale transactions. Women frequently travelled on trading ships, to the surprise of Europeans, Chinese and Indians alike. While for males of high status it was considered demeaning to haggle over prices, at least in one's home territory, women had no such inhibitions. The business concerns of powerful men were typically managed by their wives.

For all but the most aristocratic and the most Islamic women, there was also a tolerant attitude towards marriages of convenience with foreign traders. In the busiest ports, therefore, traders in town to await the next monsoon frequently formed a sexual and commercial partnership with a local woman. Sometimes the relationship endured for many years, and many separate voyages by the foreign trader; sometimes it ended with his departure. There was no stigma preventing the woman contracting a subsequent marriage. From the commercial point of view these relationships gave foreign traders an enormous advantage in marketing their goods and obtaining the local knowledge they needed.

[43] W. Lodewycksz, 1598, in *De eerste Schipvaart der Nederlanders naar Oost-Indië onder Cornelis de Houtman*, ed. G. P. Rouffaer and J. W. Ijzerman, The Hague, Linschoten-Vereniging, 1915–29, I. 120–1.
[44] Muller, *Oost-Indische Compagnie*, 63–4.

Most part of the Strangers who trade thither [in Pegu], marry a wife for the Term they stay . . . They prove obedient and obliging wives, and take the management of affairs within doors wholly in their own hands. She goes to market for food, and acts the cook in dressing the victuals, takes care of his clothes, in washing and mending them; if their husbands have any goods to sell, they set up a shop and sell them by retail, to a much better account than they could be sold for by wholesale, and some of them carry a cargo of goods to the inland towns, and barter for goods proper for the foreign markets that their husbands are bound to, and generally bring fair accounts of their negotiations.[45]

The local women who made the most advantageous unions of this type occupied very strategic commercial positions. A woman of Mon descent in Ayutthaya, Soet Pegu, was able virtually to monopolize Dutch–Thai trade in the 1640s through her relationships with successive Dutch factors in the city, who in turn could not do without her access to the Thai élite.

In sum, there was a very marked commercialization of Southeast Asian life between the fifteenth and the seventeenth centuries. A large proportion of the population was drawn into the international market economy to some extent, and affected by its ups and downs. There were sophisticated methods for investing capital in trade and securing an adequate return on it. Southeast Asia differed markedly from early modern Europe, however, in its relative lack of legal security for capital and fixed property in private hands, as against the power of the state.

THE STATE AND COMMERCE

With the notable exception of the northern Vietnamese polity under the Le and the Trinh, which deliberately emphasized agriculture at the expense of commerce, all Southeast Asian states sought to woo international trade. As Melaka's illustrious Sultan Mansur wrote in 1468, 'We have learned that to master the blue oceans people must engage in commerce and trade, even if their countries are barren . . . Life has never been so affluent in preceding generations as it is today.'[46] Because no one state could expect to monopolize the countless waterways through which international shipping passed, ports typically competed with each other to attract trade by means of an open-door policy. The arrival of European trading enterprises, much more monolithic in the East than at home and anxious to use their military superiority to secure a monopolistic position in the market, put this free-trading policy under severe strains. Most rulers saw the dangers of succumbing to such pressures, and offered ringing declarations of the freedom of commerce: the ruler of Pidië (north Sumatra) told the Portuguese 'that his port was ever a free one where any man could come and go in safety'; his counterpart in Makassar a century later reproved the Dutch:

[45] Alexander Hamilton, *A New Account of the East Indies*, 1727, new edn, London, 1930, II. 28.
[46] Letter to King of Ryukyu, 1 September 1468, in Atsushi Kobata and Mitsugo Matsuda, *Ryukyuan Relations with Korea and South Sea Countries*, Kyoto, 1969, 111.

'God made the land and the sea; the land he divided among men and the sea he gave in common. It has never been heard that anyone should be forbidden to sail the seas.'

Impositions on trade and traders once they reached port were another matter. Trade offered a rich source of revenue, both public and private, but there was always the danger of squeezing it so hard that it was driven elsewhere. Where formal duties were fixed and regular, they fluctuated between 5 and 10 per cent on both imports and exports. Port officials met incoming ships in the roads and permitted cargo to come ashore only after its value for customs purposes had been determined. Only very occasionally were favoured groups (such as the English in Makassar) exempted from duties in return for some other service to the ruler. In every case, however, gifts had to be made to the king, the chief minister, and the *syahbandar*, as well as to numerous other influential figures in the state and port administration.

It is virtually impossible to assess the extent or even the proportion of revenues flowing to rulers through trade in its various forms. Much state revenue was in kind—the most striking case being the corvée owed to the rulers of Burma and Siam by their male subjects for up to half their total working time. In terms of the more convenient, disposable revenue in money, however, trade in one form or another appears to have provided the bulk of royal revenues in the first half of the seventeenth century except in Vietnam and perhaps Burma. Revenue flowed not only from the customs dues and associated charges. There were also royal monopolies on many of the most lucrative export items, tolls on internal trade, taxes on markets, and the personal trade of the ruler himself aided by his privileged position. Rulers often insisted that traders buy from them at exalted prices before being given access to the market.

It was alleged by indignant European traders that the practice of escheat, whereby the ruler inherited the property of both subjects and foreigners who died without heirs in his dominions, brought untold wealth to covetous rulers. While the practice undoubtedly existed, they probably exaggerated its importance. In Siam, Laos and Burma it appeared to be understood that the king was entitled to reclaim at the death of officials the property they had amassed in official service, but in practice only one-third usually went to the Crown, one-third or more to the heirs, and the rest to funeral expenses. The estates of foreigners dying in sixteenth-century Pegu were divided between the Crown, which took one-third, and the heirs, 'and there hath never been any deceit or fraud used in this matter'.[47] In the Islamic states it was rather a question of whether there were male heirs, without which all the estate could be forfeit. The more autocratic rulers such as Sultan Iskandar Muda of Aceh (r. 1607–36) undoubtedly enriched themselves by executing wealthy traders and subjects and confiscating their assets. Overall, however, this cannot have represented a substantial proportion of royal revenues.

[47] 'The Voyage and Travel of M. Caesar Fredericke', in Richard Hakluyt, ed., *The Principal Navigations, Voyages, Traffiques and Discoveries of the English Nation*, London, Everyman's edn, 1907, III. 268.

The cosmopolitan character of Southeast Asian cities meant that a wide array of coins was exchanged in the marketplace, as well as gold and silver by weight. The importance of Chinese demand in stimulating the commercial upturn is indicated by the vast influx of Chinese cash, beginning in the fourteenth century but much accelerating in the fifteenth and sixteenth. These were cheap copper coins with a hole in the middle, designed to be strung together in lots of 200, 600 or 6000 for ease of handling. In the late sixteenth century the outflow of such coins became so great that lead began to be substituted. Around 1500 these Chinese coins were already the principal currency used in the markets of Melaka, Java, Brunei and Maluku. Similar copper coins were minted in northern Vietnam for use there, as tin ones were in fifteenth-century Melaka and lead ones in seventeenth-century Aceh. In Siam and coastal Burma they did not play the same role because cowrie shells were accepted as a convenient low-denomination substitute.

Most rulers also issued their own higher coinage of gold or silver. In the Muslim states of the archipelago the small gold *mas* was the principal coin minted—by the north Sumatran kingdom of Pasai from the fourteenth century, and in the seventeenth by Aceh, Pattani, Makassar and Kedah. It was usually about a thousand cash or a quarter of a Spanish silver real in value. On the mainland silver was more important, in standard weights of a *tikal* (about 14 grams), known locally as a *kyat* in Burma and a *baht* in Siam. In Burma this was simply a standard weight of silver, which in the seventeenth century gradually replaced the previously standard heavy lumps of *ganza*, a copper-lead alloy. In Siam a cylinder of silver was bent into a kidney shape and stamped, halfway to becoming a true coin.

The increasingly complex tasks of government in dealing with the international trade of their ports, the influx of foreign ideas, the adoption of firearms and the need to confront formidable European trading companies, all called for more centralized and co-ordinated state structures. The loosely-integrated states of Southeast Asia had to develop larger and more sophisticated bureaucracies, codified and predictable legal systems, and professional armies, if they were to survive this robust period of competitive expansion. To some extent we can perceive such trends.

The writing of the Melaka legal codes in the reign of Sultan Mahmud (1488–1511), for example, was an explicit response to the needs of a polyglot commercially-oriented population for security of property and predictability of legal decisions in commercial matters. This code was copied and extended during the sixteenth and seventeenth centuries in other Malayo-Muslim centres such as Aceh, Pahang, Pattani and Kedah. In seventeenth-century Aceh there were four distinct courts sitting regularly, one dealing with offences against Islamic law; one with questions of debt and inheritance; one with theft, murder and other disputes; and the fourth with commercial disputes between merchants. The development of such courts in the Muslim sultanates drew on Islamic law not only in religious questions but also in order to deal with many novel problems in the commercial area. The trend towards ever heavier borrowing from Islamic models reached its peak in Aceh during the brief reign of Sultan Iskandar Thani (1637–41), when the ancient practice of trial by ordeal was ended in favour of the witnesses countenanced by Islam. The mid-seventeenth century also marked a high point in the application of Islamic law in Banten and Makassar.

Two contemporary fifteenth-century rulers, Paramatrailokanat in Siam (1448–88) and Le Thanh Ton in Vietnam (1460–97), were energetic centralizers who promulgated or codified laws which sought to assign every stratum of their subjects to their appointed place in a bureaucratically-organized and harmonious polity. Officials were allotted fixed areas of land in accordance with rank, as a remuneration which they lost at dismissal or death. Subsequent kings in both countries allowed centres of personal power to arise again and become hereditary, but both these states retained at least a theory of centralized bureaucratic rule in advance of their neighbours. With the much greater financial and military resources available to King Narai of Ayutthaya (r. 1656–88), the Thai state then impressed even visitors from Louis XIV's France as a model of authoritarian rule:

> All the officials can be made destitute at the pleasure of the prince who established them, he deposes them as he pleases; . . . in the distribution of responsibilities they pay most attention to the merits, the experience and the services that one has given, and not to birth; which ensures that everyone applies himself to earning the favour of the prince.[48]

In the early seventeenth century there were more widespread indications of bureaucratic development. In Burma Anaukpetlun (r. 1606–28) and Thalun (r. 1629–48) replaced princes by lower-ranking *myó-wun* (town governors) as provincial authorities, and also had them watched by centrally appointed military commissioners and 'royal spies'. In Aceh under Iskandar Muda hereditary rulers were replaced by ministeriales, recalled every three years, as governors of outlying districts on the west coast of Sumatra. In seventeenth-century Makassar a hierarchy was developed to supervise the work for military and state purposes of craftsmen of different types, while a unique court diary was begun to record the important decisions and events at the centre of the realm. In a number of states—notably Burma, both north and south Vietnam, Siam, and Aceh—the core of a professional army was established, with regular training and pay.

In fact the early seventeenth century saw a clear trend towards state absolutism, most marked in those Southeast Asian states which survived as vigorous trade centres into the mid-seventeenth century—Ayutthaya, Aceh, Banten, Makassar. Some of the causes of this trend were common to the 'age of absolutism' in other parts of the world, notably the introduction of firearms and heavily-armed ships, usually monopolized by the king, and the new wealth flowing from control of the port. Others were more specific: the aggressive approach to trade of the Europeans, forcing Muslim traders to seek powerful protectors against the Portuguese and Spanish, and all free traders to seek protection against the Verenigde Oost-Indische Compagnie (VOC, the Dutch East India Company); the growing

[48] M. de Bourges, *Relation du Voyage de Monseigneur L'evêque de Beryte*, Paris, 1666, 1581–9.

trend towards monopolistic trading arrangements, largely stimulated by the Dutch; and the use by rulers of the (always ambivalent) influence of the universalist religions to break free of traditional constraints on power.

In the heightened competitiveness of the seventeenth century, it seems as though the needs of trade for security and for freedom proved ultimately irreconcilable. On the one hand those pluralistic societies most congenial to competitive trade were the first to fall before the European onslaught—Melaka to the Portuguese in 1511 and Banda to the Dutch in 1621. On the other hand the more absolutist states which arose in reaction to this pressure sooner or later fell prey to excesses of personal power which destroyed or alienated the important shipowners and capitalists.

The sultanate of Aceh oscillated revealingly between these two dangers, and is especially interesting because it was the most important Southeast Asian port to survive the seventeenth century without major European intervention in its affairs. In the 1580s, if we can believe subsequent French reports, Aceh was dominated by a group of merchant oligarchs, the *orang kaya*, who had 'beautiful, large, solid houses, with cannons at their doors, and a large number of slaves'[49]—a situation not unlike Melaka in 1511 or Banten at the arrival of the Dutch in 1596. The ruler from 1589 to 1604, Sultan Ala'ud-din Ri'ayat Syah al-Mukammil, and his powerful grandson Iskandar Muda, saw these *orang kaya* as a critical danger and suppressed them ruthlessly. The new élite was tightly controlled by the requirement for constant attendance at the palace, a professional praetorian guard composed of foreigners, and a prohibition on building in brick or stone. Even so they continued to be terrorized by the king. In 1634 thirty-four of the leading men were castrated, mutilated or flogged for an alleged breach of palace etiquette. Iskandar Muda had kept the foreign threat at bay, but only by cowing his subjects and concentrating trade in his own hands. Consequently, after his death and that of his short-lived successor and son-in-law, the surviving *orang kaya* opted for a female ruler. Not once but four times in succession, between 1641 and 1699, this 'verandah of Mecca', as the sultanate liked to call itself, put a woman on the throne, as effective power passed progressively to an oligarchy of merchant-officials. Their régime was relatively benign, orderly and encouraging to commerce, but it lost the contest with the Dutch for the control of those former dependencies which produced the pepper and tin on which Acehnese prosperity had been based. In the long run, neither approach was able to prevent a gradual decline.

In Siam, Banten, Makassar, Jambi and Banjarmasin, the third quarter of the seventeenth century saw a steady expansion of royal monopolies, as rulers tried to cope with a less favourable economic climate and constant military threats. Foreign traders were restricted more and more to buying from the king and his agents, at prices above the market rates. Royal fleets were updated with European and Chinese help, and constituted the last challenge to European predominance in the large-scale shipping trade. In Sulawesi the dualism between the twin kingdoms of Gowa and Tallo

[49] Augustin de Beaulieu, 'Memoire du Voyage aux Indes Orientales', 110–11, in M. Thévenot, *Relations de divers voyages curieux*, Paris, 1664–6.

which had been at the heart of Makassar's thriving 'open society' was largely abandoned by Sultan Hasanuddin (1654–69). The pressures of the period were making it very difficult for open societies to continue to flourish, yet the more centralized régimes which replaced them were themselves brittle and full of embittered potential defectors.

A SEVENTEENTH-CENTURY CRISIS

Europeans came to Asia in pursuit of the spices popular in their home markets. They made it their business to use what military advantage they had to try to monopolize this trade. The Portuguese conquered Melaka in 1511 because it seemed to be the single port at which the whole of the Southeast Asian export trade was concentrated. 'The trade and commerce between the different nations for a thousand leagues on every hand must come to Malacca . . . Whoever is lord of Malacca has his hands at the throat of Venice.'[50] Yet the Portuguese incursion did no more than temporarily disrupt and dislocate Southeast Asian trade, dispersing the commerce and the merchants of Melaka to half a dozen different ports. The Portuguese could not in the long run impose a monopoly of any product; they became one more strand in the complex fabric of Southeast Asian commerce.

The Dutch onslaught on the key points of the spice trade was far more sustained and effective. The VOC was one of the most advanced capitalist institutions produced by seventeenth-century Europe, and proved able to operate as the world's first global commercial enterprise, sending six or more ships to the East every year and operating a world-wide trading network based on a number of key strongholds. First among these was Batavia, taken from its Javanese occupants in 1619 and defended definitively against a major Javanese counter-attack in 1629. The Company seized and depopulated Banda in 1621, repeopling this source of the world's nutmeg with slave-owning Dutch planters who delivered all their product to the VOC. The cloves of Maluku were more widely dispersed and took longer to monopolize, but the Dutch had succeeded by 1656 in destroying all the clove trees except those in the Ambon area which they directly controlled. They proceeded to conquer three of the crucial Southeast Asian entrepôts—Portuguese Melaka in 1641, Makassar in 1666–9 and Banten in 1682. Meanwhile Aceh had never recovered militarily from its disastrous failure before Portuguese Melaka in 1629, and the lengthy blockade by the Dutch in the 1650s deprived it of its control of Perak tin and west Sumatran pepper. Most other Indonesian trading cities were forced into monopolistic arrangements with the VOC by 1680. The Japanese decision in 1639 to refuse access to its market and its minerals to any but the Dutch and Chinese gave the Company great advantages in numerous other Asian ports.

[50] *Suma Oriental of Tomé Pires*, 286–7.

Figure 3.3   The first Dutch lodge at Banda Nera, to which the Bandanese brought nutmeg for sale. The nutmeg was weighed in units of a *kati* against cloth and other trade goods.

From *De tweede schipvaart der nederlanders naar Oost-Indie*, vol. II, The Hague, Nijhoff for the Linschoten-Vereeniging, 1940.

The retreat of Southeast Asian trade has usually been explained in terms of these military and economic successes of the Dutch. It should also be seen, however, against the background of the crisis facing most of the economically advanced world in the period between 1620 and about 1680. In Europe, Turkey and China, in particular, this period clearly marked the end of the 'long sixteenth-century boom', and was characterized by declining prices, crop failures, a stagnation or decline in population, especially urban population, and a series of major political crises—of which the collapse of the Ming dynasty in China, the religious wars in Germany and the English revolution were the most spectacular.

The most global explanation of this 'general crisis' is also the least understood—that is, the gradual decline in solar activity and in temperatures during the seventeenth century, which reached its nadir in many parts of the northern hemisphere in about 1690 before the modern warming trend began. Evidence has been mounting to link this cooling with reduced rainfall and crop failures in the northern hemisphere, and perhaps therefore with the mid-seventeenth century dip in population.

If this 'little ice age' affected the humid tropics at all, it was by reducing rainfall as a result of the larger share of the planet's water locked up in the polar ice caps, and by increasing the variability of weather. In Southeast Asia the only long-term index of rainfall is Berlage's remarkable series of tree-rings from the teak forests of east-central Java, which provides relative rainfall levels for every year between 1514 and 1929.[51] This shows the period 1600–79 to be below the long-term norms for rainfall in Java, and very markedly the worst substantial period in the whole series. In particular the period 1645–72 has not a single year reaching 'normal' modern levels of rainfall. If this phenomenon was more widespread than Java, the effect would have been most dramatic in lengthening the dry season dangerously in those areas of eastern Indonesia and the Philippines where survival depends on a delicate balance of wet and dry seasons. There may also have been crop failures in areas which depended on river flooding for their annual rice planting.

A number of famines and epidemics were reported in the seventeenth century, with epidemics killing substantial proportions of the population in parts of Java in 1625–6 and of Siam in 1659. Probably the worst epidemic of the century occurred in 1665, affecting many parts of Indonesia extremely severely. The fact that 1664 and 1665 were the two driest years in the whole of Berlage's 400-year series of Java tree-rings suggests that climate may indeed have had a significant effect in increasing mortality, presumably by a combination of crop failures and inadequate supplies of clean drinking water.

The only two substantial areas of Southeast Asia for which continuous population counts are available, the Spanish Philippines and the Dutch-controlled Ambon area of Maluku, both reveal a very significant drop in population in the mid-seventeenth century. Spanish counts of *tributos* in Luzon and the Visayas, from whom they claimed labour and tax, showed a spectacular drop from 166,900 in 1591 to 108,000 in 1655, before beginning a rapid rise. In Ambon and the adjacent Lease Islands, which the Dutch controlled tightly as their centre for clove cultivation, the population also dropped progressively from 41,000 in 1634 to a minimum of 34,000 in 1674. While wars and problems of accurate recording have been advanced to explain each of these population declines, the coincidence of the two series points to the need for a broader climatic or economic explanation.[52]

If climate was unkind to Southeast Asia in this period, the international economic environment was even more so. The general decline in prices in Europe and Asia was reflected in Southeast Asian export products. Pepper, the largest of these, sold in Indonesian ports for eight or nine reals per *pikul* on average throughout the period 1617–50 but then dropped precipitately, so that the Dutch usually paid less than four reals in the 1670s and 1680s. The amount of Japanese and American silver reaching Asia was at a long-term peak in the 1620s; thereafter the decline was spectacular in the two sources going directly to Southeast Asia. Japanese silver exports dropped from as much as 150 tonnes a year in the 1620s to only one-third of that amount by the 1640s, while the Spanish 'Manila galleons' from Acapulco in the period 1640–1700 never carried even a half the 23 tonnes of silver a year they had averaged in the 1620s. Even the Dutch and English,

---

[51] Conveniently set out in H. H. Lamb, *Climate: Present, Past and Future*, London, 1977, II. 603–4.
[52] The climatic and population data are more fully set out in Anthony Reid, 'The Seventeenth Century Crisis in Southeast Asia', MAS, 24, 4 (1990).

the 'winners' of the seventeenth-century crisis, took somewhat less bullion to the East in the middle of the century than they had in the 1620s.

Although most sections of the world economy faltered in the mid-seventeenth century, Southeast Asia was especially hard hit because its share in world trade dropped markedly. The imports of Manila averaged 564,000 pesos in value per year throughout the peak period 1616–45, but only 218,000 per year in 1651–70.[53] International competition for the products of the region was at its peak in the 1620s, when pepper and Maluku spices accounted for more than half of the value of Dutch, English and Portuguese imports from Asia, while much of the trade between China and Japan also took place in Southeast Asian ports. In the second half of the century Indian cloth and indigo became the most important Asian exports to Europe, and Maluku spices and pepper began to fall in volume as well as price. Most serious of all, the monopoly established by the VOC in Maluku, and its dominance in other major ports of the region, greatly diminished the extent of price competition among buyers. All the profits of handling clove and nutmeg now flowed to the Company, where once they had invigorated a string of Asian ports from Ternate to Suez.

The effect of this reduction in export revenue was apparent in the declining ability to buy imported Indian cloth in the latter part of the century. Although the Dutch gained a steadily increasing share of the Southeast Asian market for Indian cloth, especially through their near-monopoly in many Indonesian ports, the VOC was selling 20 per cent less in Indonesia in 1703 than in 1652.[54] VOC sales to Indonesian vessels visiting Batavia to buy Indian cloth dropped more precipitately, by 43 per cent between 1665–9 and 1679–81, and even more rapidly in the subsequent twenty years.[55] Since Gujerati, English and Portuguese trade declined much more drastically after the 1620s, there is no doubt that Southeast Asian consumption of Indian cloth dropped dramatically. This is borne out by the statements of Dutch officials in the last three decades of the seventeenth century, who complained that Southeast Asians were no longer buying the expensive imported cloth because they simply could not afford it. Instead they revived their own cotton-growing and weaving:

> since these countries flourished more formerly than now, most of these peoples sought Coromandel and Surat cloths [for everyday use], not as luxuries, and gave large amounts of money for that . . . Now most of the surrounding [Indonesian] countries are empoverished, and the [Coromandel] Coast and Surat cloths have become limited to the use of the wealthy.[56]

As prices for export products dropped and Dutch military pressures mounted on all who grew spices and pepper, there was also a reaction

---

[53] Calculated from Pierre Chaunu, *Les Philippines et le Pacifique des Ibériques (XVIe, XVIIe, XVIIIe siècles)*, Paris 1960, 78, 82.

[54] I owe this figure to Ruurdje Laarhoven, who has calculated that in 1652–3 the VOC sold 314,039 pieces of Indian cloth in Indonesia, and in 1703–4, 256,458 pieces.

[55] Combining the data in Gabriel Rantoandro, 'Commerce et Navigation dans les Mers de l'Insulinde d'après les *Dagh-Register* de Batavia (1624–1682)', *Archipel*, 35 (1988) 61, and those for Java only in Luc Nagtegaal, 'Rijden op een Hollandse Tijger. De noordkust van Java en de V.O.C. 1680–1743', Ph.D. thesis, Utrecht University, 1988, 181–2.

[56] Governor-General and Council report of 1693, in Coolhaas, *Generale Missiven*, 5. 639.

against cash-cropping. Each time a port was blockaded by the VOC in pursuit of a trade advantage, the inhabitants had no choice but to cultivate rice and other food crops in place of pepper. Where the Dutch succeeded in gaining the upper hand, pepper growers and dealers were forced to deliver at uneconomic prices. Even in some of the court poetry of the late seventeenth and early eighteenth centuries we find evidence of this disenchantment with the instability and ultimate ruin brought about by pepper-cultivation:

> Let people nowhere in this country plant pepper, as is done in Jambi and Palembang. Perhaps those countries grow pepper for the sake of money, in order to grow wealthy. There is no doubt that in the end they will go to ruin.[57]

The most dramatic long-term setback to Southeast Asian commerce cannot be attributed directly to the change in the international commercial or climatic environment, since it occurred at the beginning of the seventeenth century when other indicators were still booming. This was the virtual destruction of the base areas of two of the most dynamic actors in the region's maritime commerce—the Mons of Pegu and the Javanese of the *pasisir* (Java's north coast). Under the disastrous rule of Nandabayin (1581–99), the great wealth of Pegu and its ports in the Bay of Bengal was dissipated in ruinous campaigns to retain the overextended empire of his predecessor, Bayinnaung. In 1599 the city of Pegu finally fell before an alliance of Toungoo and Arakan, and both armies took home all that was moveable of the remaining population and wealth of the coastal region. The king of Arakan left behind one of his Portuguese mercenary captains, Felipe de Brito, to command the most important port of the region at Syriam. De Brito, however, fortified himself in the port and until 1613 held it as an independent city-state with a little help from the Portuguese in Goa. During this period trade with the interior appears to have almost ceased, and the control of the lucrative routes across the peninsula to the Gulf of Thailand to have passed to Siam and its Indian Muslim factors. Mon traders, who had been found in considerable numbers in Melaka, Aceh and Banten in the sixteenth century, ceased to travel significantly by sea.

The thriving ports of Java's north coast had exported Javanese rice and other foodstuffs throughout the archipelago, in exchange for Indian cloth from Aceh and Melaka and spices from Banda and Maluku. The systematic Dutch attempt to cut these commercial arteries to ensure their own dominance in Maluku and the isolation of Portuguese Melaka must have undermined these ports to some extent. In particular the VOC destroyed the shipping of Jepara in 1618 and burned most of the town. However, the major threat to the *pasisir* towns, as to the Mon ports in Burma, came from the interior. Sultan Agung of Mataram (r. 1613–46) was determined to establish a united polity centred on his capital near modern Yogyakarta. He conquered and devastated Lasem in 1616, Tuban in 1619, and the flourishing complex of Surabaya, Gresik and Sedayu in 1623–5. Agung

[57] J. J. Ras, *Hikajat Bandjar: A Study in Malay Historiography*, The Hague, 1968, 330.

himself was little interested in trade, except to the extent of monopolizing rice exports through Jepara as a political weapon against the Dutch. His successor, Amangkurat I (r. 1646–77), was bent on the destruction of all commerce not under his own control, since it could lead to potential opposition. Javanese traders of course transferred their operations to other centres such as Banjarmasin, Banten, Palembang, Pattani and Makassar, where they tended to assimilate to the 'Malay' community. In their homeland of east and central Java, however, it was reported in 1677 that the Javanese, 'besides their great ignorance at sea, were now completely lacking in vessels of their own'.[58]

EUROPEANS, CHINESE, AND THE ORIGINS OF DUALISM

The period 1400–1630 was one of economic expansion, in which Southeast Asia became an integral part of a dynamic system of world trade, and changed rapidly to incorporate new commercial techniques and social attitudes. Chinese, Indian and Arab traders married and settled within the maritime kingdoms of the region, and were part of the process of rapid borrowing and innovation which marks this period. To a somewhat lesser extent, even the Portuguese continued this tradition, as the numerous Portuguese or Eurasians who served Pegu, Arakan, Makassar and other states as soldiers, traders and technicians bear witness. The crisis which followed in the middle of the seventeenth century, however, drove a much deeper wedge between Europeans and Chinese on the one side and Southeast Asians on the other.

The Portuguese were in theory servants of their king in a way Asian traders had never been. In practice, however, the Crown could never control or pay all the Portuguese in the East, and still less the varied group of their descendants. In the ports which the Crown tenuously controlled, it badly needed the military support of locally domiciled Portuguese, and therefore encouraged them to marry Asian women, to settle within the walls as *casados*, and to gain their own livelihood through private trade— usually in partnership with Asians.

In the second half of the sixteenth century, therefore, the Portuguese behaved in most Southeast Asian ports very much like Asian traders. By contrast the Spanish in the Philippines, and still more the servants of the VOC everywhere, were relatively carefully controlled and centrally paid. After a tentative experiment in allowing Dutch private trade on the Portuguese model, this was forbidden in 1632 and in numerous subsequent decrees. Of course many Dutchmen married locally and produced a mestizo community of descendants, but these identified with the VOC and very seldom served or inhabited indigenous states. Moreover these states in turn were changing. Outward-looking port-dominated kingdoms like Makassar, Banten, or King Narai's Ayutthaya, where European languages and Arabic were widely spoken and ideas eagerly exchanged, had no successors after they fell in the period between 1669 and 1688. Subsequent

[58] Cited B. Schrieke, *Indonesian Sociological Studies*, The Hague, 1955, I. 79.

régimes were less involved with international exchange, less cosmopolitan, and therefore less in touch with 'modern' developments.

Indian and West Asian traders were among those who lost out in the crisis period. Turks, Persians and Arabs virtually ceased travelling 'below the winds' with the collapse of the spice route from Aceh to the Red Sea in the first two decades of the seventeenth century. Gujeratis continued to bring their cloth to Aceh until about 1700, though in much reduced numbers after the Dutch onslaught on Aceh's tin and pepper resources in the 1650s. Chulia Muslims from the Coromandel coast of Tamil Nadu were the only major group of Asians from 'above the winds' who continued their trade into the eighteenth century, and they too were losing out to European traders during that period. The primary reason was that the reduced amount of Indian cloth being consumed by Southeast Asia in the latter part of the century was now being carried primarily by Europeans, from the factories and fortresses which the Dutch, Portuguese, English, French and Danes established throughout the Indian cloth-exporting regions.

The only sector of the long-distance trade in Asia in which the Europeans failed to establish themselves was that to China. Apart from the Portuguese enclave at Macao, a minor factor in most periods, Europeans were resolutely refused access to the Middle Kingdom to trade. Even when Canton (Guangzhou) was finally opened to them in 1685, discriminatory tariffs against European-rigged ships ensured that Chinese junks continued to carry the overwhelming majority of Chinese trade for another century. In addition, with the closing of Japan to all but Dutch and Chinese shipping in 1635, the junk trade had a great advantage in access to Japanese minerals. For these reasons Chinese trade was largely unaffected by European competition. After a slump in mid-century as a result of the collapse of the Ming and the long struggle by the new Manchu dynasty to gain control of the southern maritime provinces, Chinese trade to Southeast Asia recommenced its rapid upward path in the 1680s.

From about the same period Europeans and Western Asians were almost squeezed out of the trade of Ayutthaya, Cambodia, and the two Vietnamese states. The Siamese 'revolution' of 1688 drove out the previously dominant French, who had earlier replaced Indian Muslims in influential commercial positions. In the Vietnamese states, Burma and Cambodia, the Dutch tried hard to consolidate their trade in the 1630s and 1640s, but towards the end of the century they, along with the English, appear to have found the rewards not worth the restrictions placed on trade by these régimes—particularly once the Europeans gained direct access to China. The international trade of these states was therefore dominated by Chinese throughout the eighteenth century.

Already in the early 1600s Chinese were the largest group of foreign traders in the Vietnamese states, the Philippines, Pattani and Banten. In Ayutthaya they were probably more numerous though less wealthy than the Indian Muslims at the beginning of the century, but by far the biggest foreign group at its end. Contemporaries estimated that there were about 3000 adult Chinese males in Ayutthaya and the same in Banten (Chinese females did not emigrate). In Manila numbers fluctuated in response to official policy, but were often far higher. In the Cochinchina port of Hoi An (near modern Danang) there were perhaps 5000 in the 1640s, and more at the end of the century. Numbers were swelled by those who had supported Zheng Chenggong (Coxinga) in his long sea-based resistance to the Manchu régime, and after 1685 by the relative ease of leaving China because of the opening of trade.

As the seventeenth century advanced, these Chinese who stayed behind in the ports of Southeast Asia penetrated further and further into the hinterlands of the great emporia. In Banten around 1600 the Chinese had already begun to buy up pepper in the interior after the harvest, to resell not only to their compatriots but to any other buyers who would pay a good price. By the 1630s the same thing was happening in Jambi and Palembang.

The Europeans initially resented this influence on the market, but quickly came to terms with the Chinese as indispensable middlemen. They increasingly advanced cloth to local Chinese who, aided by their Indonesian wives or concubines, carried it into the interior to exchange against pepper. Chinese middlemen were also found far in the interior of Laos and Cambodia in the 1640s, travelling by canoe or ox-cart to buy the local product more cheaply at its source.

In the cities Chinese residents also became highly valued as craftsmen. During the short period at the end of the seventeenth century when they were permitted to trade in Aceh, for example, Dampier described the numerous 'Mechanicks, Carpenters, Joyners, Painters, etc' who came with the Chinese ships and turned the Chinese quarter into the busy heart of the city during the two or three months they were there.[59] Chinese also came to the region as miners and smelters, of silver in northern Burma and copper in northern Vietnam. In the eighteenth century they began to dominate the mining of tin and gold in the Malay world, activities previously the preserve of locals.

Did this input of Chinese skills and energy serve to stimulate or to stifle the indigenous economy? It is a question which cannot be answered categorically, any more than in the case of Europeans. The answer appears to depend very much on the extent of assimilation, or the barriers to it. As shown by the example of the 'South China Sea junk' and by numerous other commercial and technical borrowings of the fifteenth and sixteenth centuries, Southeast Asian urban and commercial culture gained enormously from its encounter with emigrant Chinese. As long as Chinese married into the local society and adopted its religious and social norms, their skills became part of the new urban culture being built in Southeast Asia. The greater ease of traffic between China and the Nanyang after 1685, and the rapid increase in numbers of Chinese migrating, necessarily reduced this tendency to assimilate. It also discouraged Southeast Asians from continuing to mine, smelt and work metals which the Chinese could import more cheaply or produce locally more efficiently.

There is much evidence that the establishment of the Spanish in Manila and the Dutch in Batavia helped to make the interaction with outsiders

[59] Dampier, *Voyages and Discoveries*, 94–5.

more dualistic, so that the economic activity of Europeans and Chinese increasingly diverged from that of Southeast Asians. Certainly it is from the Philippines that the earliest European complaints can be heard blaming Chinese industry for the 'laziness' of both Filipinos and Spaniards.[60]

Both Manila and Batavia were dependent on Chinese traders for the import of consumer goods, but also on local Chinese as craftsmen, labourers, market-gardeners, bakers and practically every other productive role. In Batavia the Chinese were allowed to settle inside the city walls, where they represented 39 per cent of the inhabitants (3679 Chinese) in 1699 and 58 per cent in 1739; in Manila they were obliged to concentrate in the Parian outside the walls, where there were already 10,000 in 1586. The Dutch, and even more the Spanish who had experienced Chinese attacks, were profoundly ambivalent about their dependence on the industry of the Chinese colonists. Tensions erupted in horrific anti-Chinese pogroms in both cities (six in Manila, one in 1740 in Batavia). But as Morga noted after 23,000 Chinese had been killed in and around Manila in 1603, 'the city found itself in distress, for since there were no Sangleyes [Chinese] there was nothing to eat and no shoes to wear'.[61] The Europeans knew that their cities could not have been built, their trade maintained, nor their everyday needs supplied, without the Chinese. Chinese had the great merit of being not only industrious but peaceful. Northern Europeans immediately compared their deferential attitude to the proud Southeast Asian aristocracies to that of Jews in Europe— 'like Jews, [the Chinese] live crouching under them, but rob them of their wealth and send it to China'.[62]

For the Chinese, the attraction of the European-controlled ports was twofold. As the new centres of international trade they were convenient and lucrative, particularly as sources of the American and Japanese silver which was much needed in China. Second, they provided a relatively stable environment in which a few Chinese could grow very wealthy and influential without ceasing to be Chinese. The Spanish did, unlike the Dutch, expect the leading Chinese to become Christian and cut their hair short, making it difficult for them to return to China. But for both European régimes it was convenient that the Chinese should remain distinct from the majority populations around them, and therefore useful as intermediaries without the danger of becoming leaders of a combined resistance. Batavia, Manila, and their dependencies such as Dutch Melaka, Makassar and Semarang, and Spanish Iloilo and Zamboanga, became centres of extensive Chinese commercial networks, which served to encourage even those Chinese living in Asian-ruled states to maintain their Chinese identity.

The major concentrations of Chinese under indigenous control, in Ayutthaya and Fai-fo, were big enough also to remain culturally distinctive, but their leaders knew that they had to become to some extent Thai or

[60] Antonio de Morga, *Sucesos de las Islas Filipinas*, trans. J. S. Cummins, Cambridge, U.K., Hakluyt Society, 1971, 225, Emma H. Blair and James A. Robertson, *The Philippine Islands, 1493–1898*, Cleveland, 1903–9, VI. 270–1; H. de la Costa, *Readings in Philippine History*, Manila, 1965, 41.

[61] de Morga, *Sucesos*, 225.

[62] Scott, 'An exact Discourse', 174.

Vietnamese and take office as court officials in order to protect and develop their interests. The ethnic identification of Chinese with trade and Southeast Asian with office-holding was therefore never so sharp under indigenous rule, but it did slowly take hold nevertheless.

The farming of revenues by Chinese appears to have begun in the Dutch ports, and spread from there to Asian-ruled states. Whereas the *syahbandar* in the previous system was nominally expected to deliver all revenue to the king (though he kept numerous gifts and advantages to himself), the tax-farmer kept the port duties, market tax, or salt, opium and gambling revenues as his own return after having offered in advance to the ruler a fixed sum—often by competitive bidding. The Dutch were familiar with this farming system in Europe, and immediately introduced it in Batavia. It proved a brilliant means to leave the Chinese to their own commercial habits while extracting a heavy tax from them. Within two decades of Batavia's foundation, a system had developed whereby the monopoly right to operate tolls, markets, weigh-houses, gambling-dens, theatres, taverns and numerous other remunerative city services was bid for annually by the leading Chinese. As the Dutch extended their sway to other ports in the archipelago, this system went with them, and the British in due course emulated the practice.

This model of the financial relationship between political authority and Chinese business also offered great advantages to native rulers whose bureaucratic apparatus was even less adequate than the VOC's for levying such taxes directly. Chinese began to carry the system along the north coast of Java at least by the last decades of the seventeenth century. In most ports still under Javanese control, Chinese became not only *syahbandars* but also farmers of the port revenues, the weigh-house, alcohol and gambling, and frequently of particularly lucrative articles of trade. Around 1700 the Javanese rulers began establishing internal toll-gates and farming them out to Chinese, as a further device for raising revenue. In eighteenth-century Siam port revenues, gambling, tin-mining, and even the governorships of productive provinces in the south were farmed by Chinese in return for an annual payment to the Crown.

Combined with the retreat of Southeast Asian states from direct involvement with trade in the late seventeenth century, this development made it easier for rulers to withdraw entirely from commercial concerns. The Chinese revenue farmers became valued visitors at court, and to that extent had to acquire the dress, language and politenesses acceptable in high society. They were classic cultural brokers who also needed to retain their connections with the Chinese communities in the cities in order to continue their trade. They did not offer a direct threat to indigenous rulers as wealthy and talented members of the local community did. In the long term, however, this development of Chinese revenue farming undoubtedly widened the gulf between the indigenous population and large-scale commerce. It may be significant that the peoples of Southeast Asia among whom the entrepreneurial spirit best survived were those very little affected by Chinese tax farming, either because of remoteness, like the Minangkabaus, Bataks and Torajans, or religious and cultural hostility, like the Acehnese, Bugis and Tausug.

THE TRADE IN NARCOTICS

Narcotics had long been a major trade item within Southeast Asia, but the eighteenth century greatly expanded this trade with the outside world. Chewing a mildly narcotic quid of betel was the age-old social lubricant of the whole region, essential for every ritual and social occasion as well as for coping with hunger and the other hardships of life. The narcotic properties of this quid were obtained by combining a small piece of the nut of the areca palm (*Areca catechu*), a fresh leaf of the betel vine (*Piper betel*), and a pinch of lime. Betel leaves must have been consumed on a vast scale (a Penang consumption estimate of the early nineteenth century[63] amounts to twenty leaves a day for every man, woman and child), but as it had to be fresh it was always grown close to local markets. The areca nut (or betelnut) was traded over much longer distances, Aceh (northern Sumatra) alone exporting about 2500 tonnes to India, China, and Malaya around 1800.[64] It was the newer additives and rivals to this betel quid, however, which had the largest effect on relations between Europeans and Asians.

Gambir, an astringent obtained from the gum of a shrub (*Uncaria gambir*) native to Sumatra, had occasionally been used as another ingredient in the betel chew. This became virtually obligatory in Java and elsewhere in the eighteenth century, and as demand increased a new centre of gambir plantations was opened through a mixture of Bugis and Chinese enterprise in the Riau archipelago (south of Singapore) in the 1740s. As a Malay chronicler put it:

> The Bugis and Malays planted the gambir, establishing several hundred holdings. The labourers who processed it were Chinese from China and with the cultivation of gambir, Riau became even more populous. Trading boats arrived from such eastern areas as Java and the Bugis homeland. Javanese goods were bartered for gambir . . . According to the description of the old people, 'Those days in Riau were good'.[65]

During the following century, gambir cultivation was spread chiefly by Chinese to Singapore and the southern Malayan peninsula. The new market for it was Europe, however, where its remarkable properties in tanning had meanwhile been discovered.

Tobacco was introduced by the Spanish, reaching the Philippines from Mexico in 1575. It spread very quickly, so that in the first decade of the following century the rulers of Java and Aceh were reported to be smoking it in long pipes. By the end of the seventeenth century cheroots of tobacco had become popular among men and women in the Philippines, Maluku, Burma and Siam, and in some parts of the Indonesian archipelago. It grew

---

[63] James Low, *The British Settlement of Penang or Prince of Wales Island*, Singapore, 1836, reprinted Singapore, 1972, 72, 125.
[64] George Bennett, *Wanderings in New South Wales, Batavia, Pedir Coast, Singapore and China*, London, 1834, I. 426–7.
[65] Raja Ali Haji ibn Ahmad, *The Precious Gift (Tuhfat al Nafis)*, trans. Virginia Matheson and Barbara Andaya, Kuala Lumpur, 1982, 90–1.

readily in most parts of the region, and typically was produced in small gardens for local consumption. Much was nevertheless traded by sea. Batavia recorded the entry of forty-four tonnes of Java tobacco in 1659, and in subsequent decades equally large amounts were imported from as far afield as Ternate and Mindanao.

In Europe tobacco was frequently taxed, since it was disapproved of in many quarters and moreover was easy to control. Europeans experimented with the same pattern in the East. In 1624 the Spanish attempted to establish a monopoly of all tobacco and betel supplies to Manila for the benefit of a new seminary, but this project soon fell before popular resistance and the difficulties of control. The Dutch had better success in 1626 in farming out the monopoly of tobacco sales in Batavia to some resident Japanese for a substantial fee. Much the most ambitious attempt in this direction, however, was the Spanish plan to finance the government of the Philippines, after the disaster of the British occupation of Manila in 1762–4, by the establishment of a royal monopoly on all sales of tobacco in the colony. The difficulties of policing the thousands of small tobacco farms seemed initially too great, but in 1782 means were found to place the production of all of central Luzon with a single royal contractor. A factory was built in Manila where 5000 women cut and rolled the tobacco into cigars—probably the largest single manufacturing enterprise in the region. By the 1790s the tobacco monopoly was reckoned to be earning the Crown more than 400,000 pesos per year, almost double the income from the old tribute system. Although Luzon was probably the biggest tobacco producer in Southeast Asia, relatively little was exported legally in the eighteenth century, mainly as a result of the severe Spanish restrictions on trade. The centralized tobacco monopoly nevertheless laid the basis for a major export industry in the nineteenth century.

Opium was a very minor element in the Southeast Asian narcotic scene until the late seventeenth century, when the Dutch and English found it an extraordinarily advantageous way to open up Southeast Asian markets. Southeast Asians no longer had the wealth from pepper and spice sales to buy Indian cloth as they had around 1600, so that the European companies had difficulty selling this ancient staple towards the end of the seventeenth century. Opium provided a substitute, with the added advantages of low transport costs and extraordinary profit margins. Once the Dutch had established control over Java's import trade by the conquest of Banten in 1682, they deliberately set out to make opium a new item of mass consumption in Java. The VOC monopolized its import from Bengal to Batavia, but then sold it at below the previous market price to Chinese dealers who spread it throughout Java. Imports to Batavia (to serve Dutch trade throughout eastern Asia) tripled in the next half-century, reaching seventy tonnes a year on average in the period 1728–38. The amount sold in the Java market rose with particular speed, from 4700 Spanish dollars a year in the 1670s to 83,000 dollars (equivalent to 1404 kilograms of silver) in the 1720s.[66] By the end of the century the quantity sold annually in Java had risen to thirty-five tonnes at a selling price of nearly two million

[66] Nagtegaal, 'Hollandse Tijger', 127–8.

Spanish dollars. John Crawfurd reckoned the supply to all the rest of the Indonesian archipelago as another 350 chests or twenty-two tonnes.[67] Poor Javanese sugar-mill workers and dock hands dug into their small earnings to buy a little opium to smoke in a mixture with tobacco. Only wealthier Javanese and Chinese could afford to become real addicts. For the Dutch and British companies who imported the opium, however, the profits were 168 per cent over the Bengal buying price, and 3000 per cent over the Bengal cost price.

EIGHTEENTH-CENTURY TRANSITIONS

By 1700 Southeast Asian entrepôts were no longer the centres of political and cultural life in the region. Two of the last of the great port-centred states, Aceh and Johor, were both thrown into internal chaos in 1699, which drove trade elsewhere. The mainland states least dependent on revenues from trade were the most successful in negotiating the commercial crisis. They achieved a certain stability, and probably increased in population after the terrible disruptions of the seventeenth century: Burma once the kings of Ava had stabilized a much reduced empire around 1634; Vietnam after the north and south wore each other out in wars by 1672; Siam during the relatively peaceful reigns of Thai Sa and Borommakot (1709–58). These mainland states became primarily reliant on Chinese commerce and rightly distrustful of the heavily-armed Europeans.

Even these states, however, were in the long run unable to operate the degree of centralization they had inherited from more prosperous times. In Siam, northern Vietnam and Burma, decrees repeatedly complained that manpower was falling into the hands of officials and monasteries, so that the Crown could not perform its task effectively. The Kyaukse ricebowl of upper Burma suffered increasingly frequent crop failure in the period 1661–1740, as royal authority was no longer sufficient to see that irrigation channels were maintained. In northern Vietnam the same failures of centralized power led to famines, revolts, and what Vietnamese historians consider 'a profound and irremediable crisis' in the eighteenth century.[68] European observers of these states in the period, on the other hand, tended to believe their peoples were kept exceptionally poor by a 'frightful tyranny' which deprived them of the fruits of any initiative.[69]

In short, the mainland states succeeded in retaining their coherence by withdrawing from international commerce and reasserting their bureaucratic control of agriculture. They did not, however, escape impoverishment and eventual collapse under the strain of a bureaucracy more complex than they could maintain without the revenues from trade.

In the archipelago there was also disenchantment with commerce and

---

[67] *History of the Indian Archipelago*, Edinburgh, 1820, 518–20.
[68] Nguyen Khac Vien, *Vietnam: une longue histoire*, Hanoi, 1987, 109. See also Lê Thanh Khoi, *Histoire du Vietnam, des origines à 1858*, Paris, 1987, 303–9.
[69] Most eloquently Pierre Poivre, *Les Mémoires d'un voyageur*, ed. Louis Malleret, Paris: EFEO, 1968, 54–8. Also Dampier, *Voyages*, 32–3; Marcel Le Blanc, *Histoire de la revolution du royaume de Siam, arrivée en l'année 1688*, Lyon, 1692, I. 7–13.

cash-cropping, and an attempt to assert 'traditional' hierarchic values, but it was scarcely possible to cut the troublesome reliance on the sea. Instead, power was diffused to smaller centres and more numerous ports. The VOC, having driven its European rivals from their important bases and helped to destroy the Asian entrepôts, found itself so committed to high administrative and military overheads that it was at a disadvantage in all sectors except where its own monopoly guaranteed a very high profit margin—and these were of dwindling importance. The eighteenth century therefore gave opportunities to a variety of independent traders relatively little beholden to the power centres, European or Asian.

The most successful of these were European and Armenian traders based primarily on the eastern coast of India, but sometimes establishing themselves in Southeast Asian ports such as Aceh, Kedah, Phuket (Junk Ceylon), Tenasserim, Mergui, and Rangoon. They co-operated with Indian merchants and seamen to carry Indian cloth and metals to the smallest Southeast Asian centres, wherever a small profit was to be made. Alongside them, and sometimes sharing cargoes with them, were Chulia Muslims from the Coromandel coast, who often became important figures in these ports. Both elements were active in sectors of the intra-Asian trade which generated less profit than the Dutch or English companies could tolerate. They profited, however, from the flow of English and Indian capital towards the eastern Indian seaboard to feed the enormous European demand for the cottons of this region.

Further east it was locally domiciled Chinese who played the larger role in inter-island trade, as they gained enough capital to own their own small Malay-style vessels to operate out of all the Dutch ports (Batavia, Makassar, Melaka, Semarang, Surabaya, Padang) and also Ayutthaya and Riau. Between 1722 and 1786 Chinese-owned vessels rose from 7 to 39 per cent of all arrivals in Makassar.[70] In 1700 there were still more Malay and Javanese than Chinese vessels in the trade of the north Java coast, but by 1731 Chinese owned 62 per cent of the vessels reaching Batavia from this region.[71] Moreover the direct trade between South China ports and the Nanyang grew ever more intense in the eighteenth century, extending in the 1730s into rice, which became the major Siamese export to China.

Of Southeast Asian traders, the most vigorous beneficiaries of the opportunities for small-scale enterprise were the Bugis of south Sulawesi. The campaign waged by the Dutch and their Bugis allies from Bone against Makassar in 1666–9 was a bitter one, which destroyed the city and drove out most of the merchants who had settled there. Among these were Bugis originating from Wajo, which remained loyal to Makassar to the end and was therefore also severely repressed by the victorious Arung Palakka of Bone. Wajo people fled Sulawesi in their thousands, forming new communities in Java, Sumatra, and especially the eastern coast of Borneo. From these bases they were eventually able to free their homeland from Bone control in 1737. Meanwhile they had become more successful as a commercial diaspora than they had been when operating from their homeland.

[70] Information from Heather Sutherland.
[71] Calculated from Nagtegaal, 'Hollandse Tijger'. 47.

They were welcomed into the small Malay ports of the region because they brought trade and wealth, but also because they were hardy warriors, accustomed to modern firearms and chain-mail. They became key factors in the power struggles of the Straits of Melaka area and Borneo. At the same time they occupied a crucial role in inter-island trade, losing out to Chinese in Dutch ports but more than holding their own in all the independent ports of the archipelago. They sailed as far north as Cambodia and Sulu.

Because they generally evaded the port charges imposed by the Dutch, the Bugis were able to operate at even lower profit margins than other independent traders. They had another advantage in the cotton cloths manufactured by the women of south Sulawesi. The decline in Southeast Asian purchasing power from the mid-seventeenth century had reduced sharply the import of Indian cloth, but boosted local production of cotton and cotton cloth. Java began its role as supplier of batik and other cloths to the other islands of Indonesia in this period, but the Bugis were even more successful in filling the gap. Cotton grown in the dry limestone soils of Selayar and the adjacent Sulawesi coast at Bira, or imported from Bali, was woven by the women of Selayar and Wajo into fine checked sarongs which were in demand all over the archipelago. Bugis traders sold these cloths at half the price of the comparable Indian cloths in VOC hands, enabling them to penetrate markets everywhere with very little capital.

VOC profits on its monopoly trade items were never so great in the eighteenth century as in the seventeenth. Where the seventeenth century had seen the Company exploring commercial opportunities in every corner of the world, including Ava and Vientiane far up the great rivers of Southeast Asia, the eighteenth century put it on the defensive as a worldwide trading enterprise. The profitable developments of its second century were in agriculture rather than trade, making use of its increasingly dominant position in Java as well as Maluku.

Sugarcane was already being grown for export in Banten and the Batavia area in the first half of the seventeenth century, mainly by Chinese. Once the VOC had demolished its Banten rival in 1684, it encouraged further planting of sugar by Chinese all along the north coast of Java, which the Company now bought for export to Japan, China and Europe. These Chinese entrepreneurs leased land and labour from the local Javanese authorities in north-central Java. About 1800 labourers were at work in the high season for the thirty-three mills in this area in 1719, effectively performing the corvée they were held to owe the aristocracy. In the environs of Batavia, where the largest number of mills were concentrated, the resident Javanese population had been driven out, and slaves proved too expensive for the task. A system of recruiting landless young labour on a seasonal basis from aristocrats in the eastern Priangan was therefore developed. These workers were not strictly free, but were paid a wage.[72] VOC exports of sugar reached a peak of about 4400 tonnes in 1718–19. For most of the rest of the century the figure was closer to 1000 tonnes,

---

[72] ibid., 134–6.

since slave-grown West Indian sugar could be delivered more cheaply to Europe.

The smaller sugar industries of Siam and Vietnam, though exporting primarily to Japan and China, also encountered problems in the eighteenth century. A dramatic increase began in the last decades of the century, however, partly for local consumption and partly to fill the growing demand in Europe and Japan. By 1800 sugar had probably replaced pepper as the major Southeast Asian export to the rest of the world. Dutch Java and the Spanish Philippines were each exporting about 4000 tonnes at the century's end, though this was but the beginning of a massive growth in the nineteenth century. In addition the smaller Siamese sugar industry was re-established under the new Chakri dynasty at about this time. In all three places the collection and refining of sugar was almost entirely in Chinese hands.

For the Dutch East India Company the other major success was coffee, the new fashion which swept through Europe in the eighteenth century. Prior to 1700 it grew only in the Yemen, and made famous that country's port of Mocha. The VOC introduced it to the Cirebon and Priangan areas of western Java in 1707, and within two decades Java had become the leading world producer. In this case it was not Chinese but Javanese and Sundanese aristocrats who took the initiative in having the trees planted and delivering the crop to the VOC at agreed prices. More than two million trees were planted in the Priangan highlands south of Batavia, and almost as many in the hinterland of Cirebon. But the boom peaked around 1725, oversupply reduced prices in Europe, and the Company lowered its demand to 2000 tonnes a year. Prices were also reduced to a level below that which interested independent cash-croppers, so that quotas were filled only with an element of force.

The experience of the VOC with coffee and sugar, and the Spanish with sugar and tobacco, provided a foretaste of the different quality of economic imperialism which was to dominate the nineteenth century. The VOC had begun buying each of the major Southeast Asian crops—pepper, cloves, nutmeg, sugar, coffee—at a time of commercial boom when prices were high enough to lure growers voluntarily into the international economy. As prices dropped or competition mounted, however, the European companies moved further towards enforcing delivery at prices which were still profitable for the companies, with their high overheads, but not for the growers. Such delivery contracts were always made through the medium of a local élite, for whose subjects it was often presented as a form of corvée. Driven out of Banten by the Dutch victory there in 1682, the British developed the same form of forced delivery of pepper in their new base in Benkulen (southwest Sumatra) as the Dutch were developing through the defeated rulers of Banten and Palembang.

In the eighteenth century these pockets of European-sponsored agricultural activity were marginal to Southeast Asian life. Chinese initiatives such as the gambir cultivation of Riau and Johor, the tin-mining of Bangka and gold-mining of western Borneo were almost equally so. Southeast Asians were not groaning under the effect of Western oppression or Chinese commercial penetration. Their lives were no more squalid, their health no more wretched, their physical stature no worse than those of eighteenth-century Europeans. In some respects they may indeed have been better off as a result of a benign climate, low population density, and sensible diet. Only around 1800, when European prosperity, health and stature began its upward course, did Southeast Asia begin to fall behind in these important measures of well-being.

Nevertheless it was already clear by 1700 that Southeast Asian states were not following the path of European ones. Cosmopolitan urban agglomerations, private concentrations of capital, craft specialization, a curiosity about the scientific world, were all less, not more, central to these states than they had been a century earlier. In order to preserve what they could of cherished values, comfortable lifestyles and familiar hierarchies, Southeast Asian states had disengaged from an intimate encounter with world commerce, and the technology and mind-set which went with it. When this commerce began its restless, almost uninterrupted growth from the late eighteenth century, it of course stimulated numerous new forms of economic life in Southeast Asia. The most vital of these were not the responses of the remaining Asian states, however, but of traders, raiders, cash-croppers, miners and manufacturers at the interstices of the Southeast Asian world. The states which had to confront the new Western onslaught now lacked the technology, the capital, the bureaucratic method, and the national coherence of their opponents, and would be made to pay dearly for it.

BIBLIOGRAPHIC ESSAY

Primary Materials

Although the inscriptions of an earlier period often have useful economic data on temple endowments, freedom from taxation and the like, the manuscript chronicles which dominate the indigenous record of this period are little interested in economic or social conditions, particularly in quantified terms. Surviving Burmese materials provide some exceptions. Many reports from local officials (*sit-tan*) have been translated in F. N. Trager and William J. Koenig, *Burmese Sit-tans 1764–1826*, Tucson, 1979. Than Tun, *The Royal Orders of Burma, A.D. 1598–1885*, 8 vols (Kyoto: Kyoto University Center for Southeast Asian Studies, 1983–8) translates a diverse collection of royal orders, which deal with everyday matters and revenue collection as well as the life of the court. The Vietnamese tradition of local administration also generated land registers and other data of great economic importance. Among texts which have been published but not yet translated, the most important source of pre-1800 economic data is probably the collected work of Le Quy Don, *Toàn Tập*, 3 vols, Hanoi, Nha Xûat Bân Khoa Học Xã Hội, 1977–8.

Chinese records are essential for understanding trade patterns. Among the most important is the 1433 description of Southeast Asia resulting from the Ch'eng Ho expeditions: Ma Yuan, *Ying-yai Sheng-lan: 'The overall survey of the Ocean's Shores'*, trans. J. V. G. Mills, Cambridge, UK: Hakluyt Society,

1970. Much relevant Chinese material is translated in W. P. Groeneveldt, *Historical Notes on Indonesia and Malaysia, Compiled from Chinese Sources*, Batavia, 1880, reprinted Jakarta, 1960, and in the works of Rockhill, Wheatley and Wang Gungwu. Not yet translated is the important work of Zhang Xie, *Dong xi yang kao* [Studies on the East and West Oceans, 1617], new edition, Beijing, 1981. All the Ryukyuan documents pertaining to trade with Southeast Asia in 1425–1638 are translated by Atsushi Kobata and Mitsugu Matsuda in *Ryukyuan Relations with Korea and South Sea Countries. An annotated translation of documents in the 'Rekido Hoan'*, Kyoto, 1969. Many Japanese documents on the Southeast Asian trade are reproduced in two books by Iwao Sei'ichi, *Shuinsen bōekishi no kenkyū* and *Shuinsen to Nihonmachi*, Tokyo, 1958 and 1966. Far richer are the series of reports of the Chinese junks arriving in Nagasaki in the period 1640–1740, the *Kai hentai* [Chinese Metamorphosis], compiled at the time by Hayashi Shunsai and his son Hayashi Hoko. The modern edition is by Ura Ren'ichi, *Kai hentai*, 3 vols, Tokyo, Toyo Bunko, 1958–9.

The standard Portuguese and Spanish chronicles all contain some economic data, though less than one would expect from the commercial interests of their countrymen. By far the best Portuguese source on Southeast Asian trade and economy is *The Suma Oriental of Tomé Pires*, trans. Armando Cortesão, London: Hakluyt Society, 1944.

With the arrival of the Dutch in 1596 there is a dramatic improvement in the quality and quantity of economic reporting. Dutch factors had instructions to report extensively on trade opportunities, shipping movements, prices, and export and import quantities. There is much useful information even in the journals of the early voyages, first collected for publication in *Begin ende Voortgangh van de Vereenigde Neederlandtsche Geoctroyeerde Oost-Indische Compagnie*, ed. I. Commelin (Amsterdam, 1646), and now being progressively edited in a professional manner by the Linschoten-Vereniging. Still more valuable is the systematic reporting of shipping movements in the *Daghregister gehouden in 't Casteel Batavia, 1642–1682*, 31 vols, Batavia and The Hague, 1887–1931. The extraordinarily voluminous correspondence of Jan Pieterszoon Coen, the founder of Dutch fortunes in the East, has been published first by H. T. Colenbrander and finally by W. Ph. Coolhaas as *Jan Pieterszoon Coen: bescheiden omtrent zijn bedrijf in Indie*, 7 vols in 8, The Hague, 1919–53. Although all these series make the period up to 1682 far more accessible than what follows, the most recent of the ambitious Dutch source publications has so far provided edited texts of the regular letters from the VOC Council in Batavia to Amsterdam up to 1735. This is W. Ph. Coolhaas, ed., *Generale Missiven van Gouverneurs-Generaal en Raden aan Heeren XVII der Verenigde Oostindische Compagnie*, 7 vols, The Hague, 1960–76. This series is also particularly rich in data on trade.

Secondary Sources

The biggest debates in this field have revolved around the relationship between the economic systems of the Asian region and the rise of capitalism in Europe. Two Dutch sociologists launched the debate into Indonesian waters before the war, in work which became more widely known in English translation in the 1950s: *Indonesian Sociological Studies: Selected Writings of B. Schrieke*, 2 vols, The Hague, 1955, and J. C. van Leur, *Indonesian Trade and Society: Essays in Social and Economic History*, The Hague, 1955. While Schrieke had pointed to the collapse of Javanese shipping in the seventeenth century, van Leur was more anxious to minimize the impact of the VOC and to argue for a continuity in Asian trade well into the eighteenth century. These themes were examined empirically by M. A. P. Meilink-Roelofsz, *Asian Trade and European Influence in the Indonesian Archipelago between 1500 and about 1630*, The Hague, 1962, who concluded that Asian traders were more varied than van Leur had allowed, and did decline in importance in the seventeenth century, but even at their height lacked critical features of their European counterparts such as the legal protection of property.

Subsequent work has had to become more sophisticated, more quantified, and more global in scope. Because of the nature of the sources and the problems, the best of this work has tended to treat Southeast Asia as part of bigger units. Outstanding examples are Vitorino Magalhães-Godinho, *L'economie de l'empire portugais aux XVe et XVIe siècles*, Paris, 1969; Pierre Chaunu, *Les Philippines et le Pacifique des Ibériques (XVIe, XVIIe, XVIIIe siècles). Introduction methodologique et indices d'activité*, Paris, 1960; K. N. Chaudhuri's two books on the English Company, *The English East India Company. The Study of an Early Joint-Stock Company 1600–1640*, London, 1965, and *The Trading World of Asia and the English East India Company, 1660–1760*, Cambridge, UK, 1978; Niels Steensgaard, *The Asian Trade Revolution of the Seventeenth Century*, Chicago, 1973; Kristof Glamann, *Dutch-Asiatic Trade 1620–1740*, The Hague, 1958; J. R. Bruijn, F. S. Gaastra and I. Schöffer, *Dutch-Asiatic Shipping in the 17th and 18th Centuries*, 3 vols, The Hague, 1979–87; R. L. Innes, 'The Door Ajar: Japan's Foreign Trade in the seventeenth century', Ph.D. thesis, University of Michigan, 1980; and G. B. Souza, *The Survival of Empire. Portuguese Trade and Society in China and the South China Sea, 1630–1754*, Cambridge, UK, 1986.

The interaction between Southeast Asia and the China trade has been well handled by Sarasin Viraphol, *Tribute and Profit: Sino-Siamese Trade, 1652–1853*, Cambridge, Mass., 1977; Wang Gungwu, *Community and Nation: Essays on Southeast Asia and the Chinese*, Singapore, 1981; John E. Wills, *Pepper, Guns and Parleys: The Dutch East India Company and China 1622–1681*, Cambridge, Mass., 1974; Leonard Blussé, *Strange Company. Chinese settlers, mestizo women, and the Dutch in VOC Batavia*, Dordrecht, 1986; and Chingho Chen, *Historical Notes on Hôi-An (Faifo)*, Carbondale: Southern Illinois University Centre for Vietnamese Studies, 1974. There has been even more recent work on the Indian Ocean as a sphere of economic activity, notably K. N. Chaudhuri, *Trade and Civilization in the Indian Ocean. An Economic History from the Rise of Islam to 1750*; S. Arasaratnam, *Merchants, Companies and Commerce on the Coromandel Coast, 1650–1740*, Delhi, 1986; A. Das Gupta and M. Pearson, eds, *India and the Indian Ocean 1500–1800*, Calcutta, 1987; Denys Lombard and Jean Aubin, eds, *Marchands et hommes d'affaires asiatiques dans l'Océan Indien et la Mer de Chine, 13e–20e siécles*, Paris: EHESS, 1988.

Such works have clarified Southeast Asia's interaction with the global economy, and demonstrated a long-term pattern of economic expansion and contraction. To understand the specific economies of the region, however, we must turn to scholars familiar with indigenous literary traditions and informed by field research. Especially useful regarding economic and social change are Victor Lieberman, *Burmese Administrative Cycles: Anarchy and Conquest, c. 1580–1760*, Princeton, 1984, and Nguyen Thanh-Nha, *Tableau économique du Vietnam aux XVIIe et XVIIIe siècles*, Paris, 1970. Some of the most interesting work in this area is being done by the group associated with the journal *Archipel* in Paris, notably Denys Lombard, Claude Guillot and Pierre-Yves Manguin. Important special issues of *Archipel* were devoted to commerce and shipping (no. 18, 1979) and to cities (nos. 36, 1988, and 37, 1989). The problem of slavery is addressed in Anthony Reid, ed., *Slavery, Bondage and Dependency in Southeast Asia*, St Lucia, Queensland, 1983. Finally, the Dutch archives are at last being mined in a number of theses on particular regions, of which the most notable for their economic data are: Gerrit Knaap, *Kruidnagelen en Christenen: De Verenigde Oost-Indische Compagnie en de bevolking van Ambon 1656–1696*, Dordrecht, 1987; Lucas Nagtegaal, 'Rijden op een Hollandse Tijger. De noordkust van Java en de V.O.C. 1680–1743', Ph.D. thesis, Utrecht University, 1988; Ito Takeshi, 'The World of the *Adat Aceh*; A Historical Study of the Sultanate of Aceh', Ph.D. thesis, Australian National University, 1984.

4

RELIGIOUS DEVELOPMENTS IN
SOUTHEAST ASIA c. 1500–1800

The present chapter, which continues the account of religious developments in Southeast Asia from about 1500, is divided into five sections. The
first draws on the European source material that becomes available in the
sixteenth century to survey important features of indigenous beliefs as
they were practised in areas then little touched by the world religions.
An examination of the advance of Islam and Christianity, destined to
have such fundamental effects on the evolution of island Southeast Asia,
makes up the second and third sections. It will become apparent that
the manner in which these newer religions adapted to the local context
in many respects resembles the previous infusion of Hindu, Buddhist
and Confucian ideas already discussed in Chapter 5. The fourth section
therefore takes up several themes common across the region as the world
religions extended and consolidated their position. The chapter closes
with an overview of the eighteenth century, identified as a time when
unprecedented pressures, both internal and external, created new
demands in Southeast Asia's religious environment.

INDIGENOUS BELIEFS

An important contribution to our understanding of indigenous beliefs
comes in the sixteenth and seventeenth centuries as European missionaries began to move into areas of eastern Indonesia and the Philippines
which had to this point been relatively isolated from external religious
ideas. Despite their obvious cultural bias, the accounts missionaries
compiled provide the historian with the first sustained contemporary
descriptions of native religious customs outside a court environment.
  Most striking in these early European sources is not the regional variation in belief which observers noted, but the similarities. All affirm that the
ordinary man and woman conceived of the natural world as animated by a
vast array of deities who inhabited trees, rivers, caves, mountains and who
were capable of great kindness or extraordinary malevolence. Otherwise
inexplicable events such as volcanic eruptions, earthquakes, epidemics, a

failure of the rains, were a sign that the spirits were angry and needed to be appeased with appropriate offerings. In arming themselves against the vagaries of fate, individuals could seek assistance from their ancestors and from past leaders and heroes who, after death, had become powerful spirits in their own right. Often they were believed to have entered the bodies of animals, like the tiger, the crocodile or the pig. In eastern Indonesia such beliefs were especially obvious, and one Portuguese account describes how the people of Maluku (the Moluccas) 'worshipped the celestial bodies, the sun, moon and stars, they made idols to the honour of their fathers and forefathers. These were made of wood and stone with faces of men, dogs, cats and other animals.'[1]

A key factor in communicating with the spirits was propitiation and ritual performed at designated sites like a sacred mountain or at the graves of ancestors. Offerings of food, drink, cloth, and certain symbolic items were most common, but on some occasions the spilling of blood was deemed necessary to allay anger, or ensure the fertility of the soil and the continuance of supernatural favours. After some animal—a goat, pig, or a buffalo—was slaughtered, its head was usually offered to the spirits while the participants ate the rest of the meat in a ceremonial feast. On special occasions a human being might be sacrificed, the victims usually obtained by raids into neighbouring territory or by the purchase of slaves. In the Visayas, for example, the people 'are in the habit of buying some Indios from other provinces to offer them as sacrificial victims to the devil'.[2] Ritual and offering were part of the lives of everyone, especially during the great life crises of birth, marriage and death, but the most elaborate ceremonial was often that associated with funerals. The careful preparation of bodies for burial, the dressing of the corpse, the provision of goods, food, drink, clothing and transport described in several societies, attest to a belief in life after death, where an individual would enjoy a status commensurate with his or her standing while alive.

Although men also assumed high ceremonial positions, early European observers were struck by the prominence of females in religious ritual. When the Spanish first arrived in the Philippines they saw old women (called *babaylan* in the Visayas and *katalonan* in the Tagalog areas) through whom the spirits spoke. Several societies accorded particular respect not only to women but to 'Indians dressed as women', a reference to the transvestites who symbolically combined the regenerative powers of both sexes. To a considerable extent the prestige of such figures was due to their ability to deal with both male and female sacral items and to provide a medium for spirit pronouncements. When they fell into a trance, induced by incantation, dance, and the music of bells, drums and gongs, they became more than human. Shamanistic skills were especially valued in times of illness because this was attributed to non-human agencies. Missionaries in the Philippines described curing sessions in which 'the woman leader can talk to herself with many posturings', anointing the

---

[1] Hubert Th. Th. M. Jacobs, *A Treatise on the Moluccas (c. 1544)*, Rome, 1971, 75.
[2] Cited in Pablo Fernandez, *History of the Church in the Philippines (1521–1898)*, Manila, 1979, 3.

head of the sick person with oil and telling him the *anito* (spirit) would give him strength.

The secret knowledge which set such individuals apart could not be obtained without instruction. In the late seventeenth century in Ceram the Dutch missionary Valentijn described how children were taken into the jungle for months at a time to be inculcated by magic rituals as 'devil priests'. Equipped with these secret skills, the shaman was able to help protect the community against witches and sorcerers who had somehow mastered the magic arts and were ready to use them in harmful designs. Some sorcerers could fly, some could kill without raising a hand, others could cast charms to make the most loving wife reject her husband. In Maluku these alleged 'witches' were called collectively by the Malay word *suangi* (ghost) and were frequently accused by a shaman in trance of having caused illness or other calamities. 'When kings, dukes or ministers fall ill, they order some *suangi* to be killed.'[3] On one occasion missionaries said that over a hundred people were put to death as *suangi* because the ruler had died.[4]

Surrounded by an army of supernatural beings, some kindly but capricious and others simply malevolent, and facing the added danger of hostile elements in human form, the communities depicted by the missionaries placed enormous importance on the possession of amulets and other objects believed to have protective powers. Among the most widely valued weapons against magic were bezoar stones (called by Malays *mestika galiga*), especially from a wild pig and deer. Similar attitudes were attached to other objects such as old spears, krises and cloth, possession of which gave to the owner an extra-human power. In Ambon, for instance, a very rare type of bracelet known as *mamakur*, together with holy stones, Chinese porcelain and clothes worn by deceased ancestors, were carefully preserved to ward off harm. Great credence was also given to dreams and omens, by which messages from the non-human world could be transmitted. If a sneeze on leaving the house was a warning of ill fortune, how much more did the eclipse of the sun or moon presage impending catastrophe? In Ternate, said the Dutch, people believed it was a portent of death, either of their own relatives or the king himself. It was in the hope of appeasing the mighty forces inherent in the heavenly bodies that the people of Makassar kept representations of the sun and moon in their homes long after the court had adopted Islam.

Evidence from this period relating to indigenous religious practices is not as extensive for the rest of Southeast Asia as it is for eastern Indonesia and the Philippines. It is nonetheless apparent that many of the customs described by missionaries in the island world were once common throughout the region. Animal and sometimes human sacrifices to the spirits, for example, could be found in Burma at least into the eighteenth century, despite Buddhist prohibitions against the taking of life. Although some observances have disappeared, students of the modern period will certainly discern much that is familiar in early missionary descriptions of

[3] Jacobs, *A Treatise*, 181.
[4] Georg Schurhammer, *Francis Xavier. His Life, His Times*, III, trans. M. Joseph Costelloe, Rome: Jesuit Historical Institute, 1980, 92.

native religions. Indeed, any study of Southeast Asian cultures will stress the tenacity of indigenous beliefs and will point out that for a number of societies they have remained a completely satisfactory means of explaining the world. Such studies will also emphasize that all the world religions which became established in Southeast Asia succeeded because they not only made some accommodation with existing attitudes but elaborated and enhanced them. In Burma, for instance, kings on behalf of their subjects continued to honour the spirits of their forebears before statues covered with gold in the belief that 'proper respect to the ancestors will bring prosperity'.[5] Significantly, these ceremonies came to be held on Buddhist holy days even though propitiation of the spirits of departed relatives receives no canonical sanction in Buddhist teachings. In Vietnam (Dai Viet) by contrast, the classical Chinese works of Confucianism elevated the indigenous veneration for deceased forebears into the central focus of household ritual. 'The piety they display towards the souls of their relatives,' said the Jesuit missionary Alexander of Rhodes, 'surpasses anything we could imagine in Europe. They go to incredible lengths to find suitable places for tombs . . . and spare no trouble or expense to lay out banquets for them after death.'[6]

Well before the arrival of Islam and Christianity, a dominant theme in Southeast Asia's religious development is thus already apparent. The major features of the indigenous belief system survived because for the most part they were able to coexist or to be engrossed by the ritual and teachings associated with the world religions. In a sense an alliance was struck between the new 'deities' and the old. A story found in Burma and the Thai areas describes how the earth goddess, wringing water from her hair, aids the Buddha to victory by flooding the armies of the evil Mara. In Burma this conjoining of indigenous and imported ideas is symbolized by the common depiction of the seated Buddha in the pose of touching the earth with his right hand, the signal to the earth goddess to witness the merit of his previous lives.[7] In much the same way the elaboration of ceremonial and the incorporation of awe-inspiring vocabulary had confirmed the importance of many existing customs. Beneath the formalized Confucian Oath to Heaven carried out in fifteenth-century Vietnam, for instance, can be seen traces of earlier allegiance rituals during which spirits were invoked, animals sacrificed and their blood communally drunk. For Buddhists the notion of kamma (karma) and the possibility of punishment for wrongful action extending into future lives imbued the oath-taking ceremony with added solemnity. A fourteenth-century inscription from the Thai kingdom of Sukothai thus describes a pact with a neighbouring king calling on the ancestors and guardian spirits of waters and caves to bear witness that all those who broke the oath were destined for hell and would 'never expect to see the Buddha, the Dharma or the

[5] Than Tun, trans., *The Royal Orders of Burma, AD 1598–1885*, Kyoto: Center for Southeast Asian Studies, Kyoto University, 1983–7, IV. 144.
[6] Solange Hertz, trans., *Rhodes of Vietnam*, Westminster, Maryland, 1966, 59.
[7] John Ferguson, 'The symbolic dimensions of the Burmese sangha', Ph.D. thesis, Cornell University, 1975, 24. The emphasis on the earth goddess legend found in Southeast Asia is absent in orthodox Theravāda Buddhist literature from India and Sri Lanka.

Sangha'. Similarly the amulets and talismans which provided such protection against harmful forces became even more effective as they absorbed the potency of beliefs from outside. In the Buddhist states such items were commonly made in the form of the Buddha or a revered monk, and larger Buddha images often became the palladium of the kingdom, special powers being attributed to them.

The persistence of spirits is the primary heritage of indigenous religious beliefs, but increasingly spirits became drawn into a world where the dominant religion was that patronized by the king and his court. In Burma the official abode of a pantheon of 37 *nats* (spirits) was the Shwezigon pagoda at Pagan, but the ruler gave each one a specific fief from whose inhabitants the *nat* received propitiation. In return for this royal patronage and the people's homage, spirits were expected to render service to the king and recognize the moral authority of the court religions. In Vietnam a fourteenth-century Buddhist scholar related how an earth spirit appeared to an earlier king in a dream, promising that his planned attack on Champa would be successful if he sacrificed to her. With the aid of a Buddhist monk the appropriate offerings were made, and subsequently a shrine was established for the 'Imperial Earth Lady' in the capital.

Legends suggest that this process of political and religious integration sometimes met resistance. This same scholar referred to 'depraved divinities' and 'evil demons' who had refused to act as guardians of religion and who were therefore ordered to 'quickly depart to another place'.[8] In Buddhist history across the mainland the subjection of spirits to the authority of Buddhism is a recurrent theme. The *Padaeng Chronicle* from the Shan state of Kengtung recounts how one demon, displeased at the construction of the city, 'went to haunt the golden palace, defying attempts by the ruler to expel him'. Monks were brought in to recite holy scriptures and strengthen the sacred religion. However, the demon 'came to haunt even more, the holy water putrified, the leaves of the magic trees withered, and the Bhikkus were defeated'.[9] The situation was rectified only when a learned monk was brought in to carry out the purification of the Buddha's religion and teaching (*sasana*). In 1527, the king of Lan Sang went so far as to ban spirit worship and order the destruction of all sanctuaries associated with the spirit (*phi*) cult, erecting a Buddhist temple in the capital where the shrine of the guardian spirit had previously stood.

Despite periodic questioning as to the extent to which they should be honoured, spirits never showed any sign of disappearing from Southeast Asia's religious life. The reason appears to lie in the relevance of spirit belief to human existence here on earth. Whereas the great religions were concerned with the future or, in the case of Confucianism, with questions of cosmic significance, the attention of spirits could be drawn to the most mundane matter whether it concerned illness or warfare, a trading venture or childbearing. In the early seventeenth century Tagalog Filipinos gave

[8] Keith Taylor, 'Authority and legitimacy in 11th Century Vietnam' in David G. Marr and A. C. Milner, eds, *Southeast Asia in the 9th to the 14th Centuries*, Canberra and Singapore, 1986, 139–76.

[9] Sao Saimong Mangrai, *The Padaeng Chronicle and the Jengtung State Chronicle Translated*, Michigan Papers on South and Southeast Asia, University of Michigan, 1981, 113–14.

Spanish missionaries a clear explanation of the relationship between the lesser *anito* and Bathala, whom they had named as supreme among the pantheon of spirits. 'Bathala', they said, 'was a great lord and no one could speak to him. He lived in the sky, but the *anito*, who was of such a nature that he come down here to talk to men, was to Bathala as a minister and interceded for them.'[10] A not dissimilar view of spirits is expressed in an early nineteenth-century Burmese chronicle which describes how a king of Pagan was once advised by a hermit to worship the Buddha when he looked to the future, but to the *nats* when he looked to the present.[11] The survival of spirit worship is particularly telling in the case of Islam and Christianity, both of which place a primary doctrinal stress on monotheism. These two religions were to become the dominant faiths in island Southeast Asia, and it is to their history that we shall now turn.

THE COMING OF ISLAM

An appreciation of the rapidity of Islam's spread in the sixteenth century necessitates a review of the historical context in which this advance occurred. The nature of the sources, however, makes it impossible to answer the most fundamental questions about the arrival of Islam in the archipelago. In the first place, there is no way of knowing exactly when and where the first significant local conversions occurred. Existing evidence suggests that it was in northern Sumatra, closest to India and the Islamic heartlands, where Islam established its first beach-heads. The evidence for the existence of local Muslim communities does not emerge until the late thirteenth century CE, although they may well have arisen earlier than this. The Venetian traveller Marco Polo mentions Muslims in Perlak in 1292 CE, and in neighbouring Pasai a royal gravestone inscribed with the date 697 AH (1297 CE) and the Muslim title Sultan Malik al-Salih ('the saintly king') has been found. It is apparent, however, that this new faith had not penetrated beyond the coast. A traveller from Morocco, Ibn Batuta, visiting Samudra-Pasai in 1345 on his way from Bengal to China, described it as Muslim in the port, but still 'pagan' in the interior.

The evidence from Java is also sparse. The tombstone of a Muslim woman discovered at Leran (near Surabaya) and dated at 496 or 475 AH (1102 or 1082 CE) is generally believed to mark the grave of a foreign rather than a locally born Muslim. By contrast, the shape, the decorative carving and the Old Javanese script on a number of Muslim gravestone inscriptions situated near the centre of the former kingdom of Majapahit in east Java clearly indicate that those buried there were of local origin. Most are from the fifteenth century, but one stone bears the Śaka date 1290 (1368 CE) while two others are inscribed 1298 and 1302 (1376 and 1380 CE). The proximity of the graves to the site of the Majapahit *kraton* raises the distinct

[10] Emma H. Blair and James A. Robertson, *The Philippine Islands, 1493–1898*, Cleveland, 1903–09, V. 144.
[11] Pe Maung Tin and G. H. Luce, eds and trans, *The Glass Palace Chronicle of the Kings of Burma*, Rangoon, 80–1.

possibility that there were already a number of Muslims in court circles
and possibly among the royal family at the time when Majapahit was at the
height of its power.

A third important discovery regarding the dating of Islam's arrival was
made in Terengganu on the east coast of the Malay peninsula. It consists of
a stone, apparently intended as a pillar, which records a royal order to
local officials. One side, enjoining them to uphold the Islamic religion and
the teachings of the apostle of Allah, has a hijra date which is incomplete
because of damage to the stone and which has therefore been read
variously between 702 and 789 AH (1303 and 1387 CE). Although the
inscribed laws on the remaining three faces cannot be completely deci-
phered due to surface flaking, several deal with the relationship between
creditor and debtor, while others are concerned with punishments for
sexual transgressions and perjury.

The available evidence on which to build any argument concerning the
date of Islam's first steps into the archipelago is thus hardly extensive.
Questions regarding the provenance of Islam are even more difficult to
answer, although there are some areas of general agreement. First, it is
obvious that Islam spread into Southeast Asia as Muslim traders moved
along established maritime trade routes. Later European observers who
complained that Islamic 'missionaries' were 'disguising' themselves as
traders failed to understand that there is no priestly class as such in Islam,
and that the religion itself grew out of a commercial urban environment.
Muslim merchants who had become accustomed to conducting their
business under the protective umbrella of Muslim law were the most
obvious transmitters of Islam's basic beliefs during these early stages.

In the second place, the known strength of the Indian trading presence
in Southeast Asian waters at the time when Islam began to move into
the region is convincing evidence for the role of Indian Muslims in the
diffusion of Islamic ideas. Over the years there has been a sometimes
heated debate about which region of India was the most influential in
bringing about the conversion of leading courts in the archipelago. Strong
arguments have been advanced in favour of Gujerat, Bengal, and the
Muslim areas of southern India, all of which had strong trading ties with
Southeast Asia. Gujerat came under Muslim rule in 1287 and much of its
trade was in Muslim hands. According to Tomé Pires, Bengali traders had
long frequented Pasai and in the latter part of the thirteenth century had
been responsible for placing 'a Moorish king of the Bengali caste' on the
Pasai throne. But later Malay texts from both Pasai and Melaka talk of
the coming of the apostle of Islam from Ma'bar, a name frequently given to
the Coromandel coast, and to this is added the fact that South Indian
Muslims, like Indonesians, are generally adherents to the Shāfi'ī school.
These apparently competing sources in fact suggest that one of the reasons
why Islam was so attractive in this early period was that influences were
coming simultaneously from a number of different areas, for India supplied not only teacher-traders but also acted as a stepping stone for
Muslims from other areas of the Islamic world.

Somewhat neglected in this discussion have been other possible sources of contact with Islamic teaching, such as Champa, where two Muslim gravestones dating from the early eleventh century have been located. The Chinese connection may also be significant. Trading contacts with Persia and Central Asia led to the development of Sino-Muslim communities in towns along the southeast coast of China, notably Canton (Guanzhou). The involvement of Muslim Chinese in ocean-going trade in turn fostered the growth of settlements overseas. In 1416, for instance, the Chinese Muslim Ma Huan remarked that most of the Chinese living in Java came from southern China, and that many of them were Muslim. While the dominance of the Hanafi school in China has made scholars reluctant to see Chinese Muslim traders as missionizers, the influence they wielded cannot be discounted. For centuries China had been regarded as the virtual overlord of most of Southeast Asia, and the seal of imperial approval given to Islam by an emperor such as Yung-lo (1402–24) must have aided its cause.

The degree to which Chinese contributed to the spread of Islam in Java remains debatable, although most scholars accept that the founders of several ruling families along the north coast were Chinese Muslims who had married local women. However, Chinese connections for Islam are much clearer elsewhere in the archipelago. In Jolo in the southern Philippines, for example, one of the founders of local Islam is said to have come accompanied by Muslim Chinese, while in about 1590 a Spaniard in Brunei was told that Islam had been brought by a Sultan Yusuf who had come from the Malay lands via China. There he had married a Chinese noblewoman and was confirmed as king of Borneo by the emperor of China 'whom he recognised as a superior king'. It was from this marriage that the rulers of Brunei were descended.[12]

Evidence regarding the arrival of Islam in Southeast Asia and its origins is thus incomplete and at times conflicting. Arabs had known of the region for generations, but only from the thirteenth century is there clear proof of local adoption of the Muslim religion. Even then Islamic influence was confined to scattered ports along coastal trading routes. While India was almost certainly the conduit for Islamic ideas, the first Muslim teacher-traders probably came from various parts of the then Islamic world. Future research may provide a more detailed picture of the way Chinese Muslims contributed to the prestige of the Islamic faith. It is clear, however, that despite continuing Shī'ite influences, it was Sunni Islam which was established in Southeast Asia, together with one of its four schools of law, the Shāfi'ī. We also know that, by the time Islam began to penetrate the region, the central structure of Sunni doctrine had assumed more or less its final form, and the text of the Koran and corpus of traditions relating to the Prophet had been established. Yet in their response to and interpretation of these new teachings, the peoples of the region were able to contribute to a process that was to give Southeast Asian Islam a distinctive character which it has retained to the present day.

---

[12] John S. Carroll, 'Berunai in the Boxer Codex', JMBRAS, 55, 2 (1982) 4.

The Conversion of Melaka

The decision of the ruler of the Malay port of Melaka to adopt Islam is a milestone in the history of Islam's expansion into Southeast Asia. Apparently founded by a refugee prince from Palembang around the beginning of the fifteenth century, Melaka grew from a small fishing village into a trading emporium which became the commercial hub of the archipelago. The increasing numbers of Muslim traders from India arriving in the region would also have helped raise Islam's prestige while they themselves conveyed the basic tenets of the faith. Indeed, according to a well-known Malay epic, Melaka's famed folk hero Hang Tuah was taught to recite the Koran by a trader from India's Coromandel coast.

Several dates for the conversion of the Melaka ruler, ranging from 1409 to 1436 CE, have been suggested, but the precise year is still subject to speculation. It is unlikely that the founder of the dynasty was himself Muslim, and it may have been the third ruler, Sri Maharaja Muhammad Syah (r. 1425–45) who made the decision to embrace the Islamic faith.[13] The great Malay description of Melaka, the *Sejarah Melayu*, recognizes the significance of this event, portraying it in terms of divine revelation, a formulaic account which is found repeatedly in other local versions of Islam's arrival. The Prophet himself appears to the ruler of Melaka in a dream, teaches him the profession of faith (*shahāda*, Indonesian *syahadat*), gives him the Muslim name of Muhammad and foretells the arrival the next day of a ship from Jedda. When the king wakes, he discovers that he has been circumcised. To the amazement of his servants, who believe he is possessed by a spirit, he continually repeats the confession of faith. That evening a ship from Jedda duly reaches Melaka carrying an eminent teacher, a Sayid, one of the Prophet's own descendants. He is received in honour by the ruler and it is on this occasion that the Melaka chiefs adopt Islam, while all the people 'whether of high or low degree' are ordered to do likewise.[14]

In the early sixteenth century Tomé Pires readily accepted the explanation that Islam's success was due to pragmatic rather than spiritual motives. According to his account the Melaka ruler was aware that Muslim Pasai owed its commercial vitality largely to the patronage of Indian Muslim traders. He therefore took active steps to emulate Pasai's success and himself attract Muslims to Melaka. Muslim merchants were granted commercial privileges, residences and mosques were built for them, and they were welcomed at court. Pires goes on to say that under the influence of Pasai and prominent Muslim merchants and mullahs, both from the Arab lands and Bengal, the ruler of Melaka adopted Islam at the age of seventy-two and married the king of Pasai's daughter.

Modern scholars, while accepting the importance of the trading connection, have been more concerned with explaining why Islam had such an appeal to Malay rulers. It is useful to remember that in the fifteenth

---

[13] The evidence is conflicting, but has been reviewed in C. H. Wake, 'Malacca's early kings and the reception of Islam', JSEAH, 5, 2 (1964).

[14] C. C. Brown, ed. and trans., '*Sejarah Melayu*, or Malay Annals', JMBRAS, 25, 2 and 3 (1952) 41–3.

century Muslim traders dominated a commercial network which stretched from Europe to Maluku. The kings of Melaka would clearly have gained by becoming part of a Muslim community that included rulers like those of Cambay or Bengal, Aden and Hormuz. The fifteenth century also saw a resurgence in Islam's temporal power. In 1453 the Ottoman Turks under their new ruler Mehmed II took Constantinople (Istanbul), rebuilding it into a centre of Muslim culture and scholarship. It is highly likely that stories of Mehmed's extensive victories percolated into the region, and certainly local traditions accord the same veneration to the rulers of 'Rum' ('Rome', i.e. Byzantium) as they do to the emperors of China. Furthermore, by this time the influence of Persian notions of kingship, stressing the monarch's sacral nature and elevating him to a place high above ordinary mortals, had spread throughout much of the Islamic world. Already regarded as possessed of supernatural powers, Melaka rulers were now able to assume other new and imposing Persian-style titles. The coins they minted proclaim the ruler as sultan and syah, thus raising him above all other princes in the area who, with the exception of Pasai, bore the simpler title raja. The ruler of Melaka was also termed 'Helper of the World and of the Religion' (*Nāṣir al-dunyā wa'l-dīn*), the deputy of Allah, to whom obedience was due as a religious obligation.[15]

It is therefore not surprising that the promotion of Islam in Melaka was carried out under royal patronage, with rulers themselves actively encouraging teaching and missionary work. Marriages between Muslims and infidels were arranged to attract new converts, and apostasy was forbidden. The performance of the obligatory daily prayers was constantly stressed, and to a considerable extent the legal system began to favour Muslims, especially as witnesses. Successive Melaka rulers also continued to promote Islam in neighbouring states, persuading or compelling their rulers to accept the new religion.

During the course of the fifteenth century, Melaka came to be regarded in the archipelago as a centre for Islamic scholarship, with religious teachers attracted by the patronage of the court and the possibility of acquiring pupils. Since Malay was the language of trade, and since Malay-speaking Melaka was the focus of regional commerce, the spread of Islam outwards along trade routes was a natural development. Indeed, so associated was Islam with Malay culture that in many areas the phrase *masuk melayu* (to become a Malay) came to mean the adoption of Islam. As the vehicle by which instruction in Islam was transmitted, the Malay language acquired a special status. In Bima, for example, the ruler in 1645 ordered that court notebooks should be written in the Malay language 'because this is the writing which has been approved by Allah Almighty'.[16]

Java's Role in the Spread of Islam

The rise of Melaka coincided with other important changes in Java. It appears that Majapahit rulers were aware of the advantages to be obtained from ties with Muslim courts in the region, for several legends mention

[15] ibid., 118; A. C. Milner, 'Islam and Malay kingship', JRAS, 1 (1981) 46–70.
[16] Henri Chambert-Loir, *Ceritera Asal Bangsa Jin dan Segala Dewa Dewa*, Bandung, 1985, 11.

high-born Muslim females who are taken into the Majapahit *kraton*. The grave of a Muslim woman found in east Java which dates from 1448 CE is even said to be that of a 'princess' who came from Champa (where leading merchant families were already Muslim) to marry the Majapahit ruler. Firmer evidence for the influence of Islam in the Majapahit court during the fifteenth century is provided by four Muslim graves near the site of the capital which date from between 1407 and 1475. These all bear a carving of the sun which, together with their proximity to the *kraton*, suggests that they mark the burial place of high-ranking nobles or even members of the king's family.

During this period the northern coast of Java, where Muslim communities may date from the last decades of the fourteenth century, was gaining importance economically as trade between Melaka and the Spice Islands of eastern Indonesia expanded. Pires attributes the adoption of Islam by the ruling families of these ports to the missionizing efforts of Sultan Muzafar of Melaka around the middle of the fifteenth century and even suggests that in some cases Muslims forcibly took control. He does not regard these Muslim rulers as Javanese of long standing, but as descendants of Chinese, Indian and Arab traders, many of whom had close links with Melaka. Javanese tradition, on the other hand, had at least by the seventeenth century attributed the coming of Islam to the efforts of 'nine' *walīs* (saints, those acting on behalf of God). At Gresik, which legends claim was with Surabaya the first Javanese port to adopt Islam, is a grave dated 822 AH (1419 CE), popularly believed to mark the burial spot of one of the most famous of these holy men, Malik Ibrahim.

Embedded in the stories of the miraculous deeds of the *walīs* are indications that several had studied or lived in Melaka and were involved in trade, and it was this commercial network which continued to foster Islam's spread. The trading routes from Melaka and north-coast Java brought Muslims naturally to the clove-producing islands of Tidore, Ternate, Makian, Bacan, Jailolo and Motir, where the kings became Muslim about the mid-fifteenth century. By the time the first Europeans arrived in 1512, the ruler of Ternate had established his superiority over his royal neighbours by assuming the title of sultan, and missionaries from Ternate were working to spread the faith in the southern Philippines.

During the fifteenth century, therefore, Islam made significant progress in the region. But while most ports along the major trade routes between Melaka and the Spice Islands had a community of Muslim traders, by no means all coastal rulers had accepted the faith, despite a long exposure to the Muslim presence. Islam's real advance did not occur until the sixteenth and early seventeenth centuries, when a number of factors combined to confirm its position in island Southeast Asia.

The Spread of Islam

There are several reasons for the accelerated pace of Islamization from around 1500 CE. In the first place, the conquest of Melaka by the Portuguese in 1511 closed that port to Muslim traders, who then began to patronize other places where the religious environment was more sympathetic. Aceh, on the northern tip of Sumatra, had apparently adopted Islam in the mid-fourteenth century and quickly developed into a centre for Muslim trade. Acehnese rulers became renowned for their patronage of Islam, and their campaigns carried the faith along both the east and west coasts of Sumatra. Another beneficiary of Melaka's fall was Brunei in northwest Borneo. Its ruler was converted to Islam sometime between 1514 and 1521, and the court soon acquired a reputation for sponsoring Islamic missionary activity, particularly in the Philippine archipelago. The chronology of Islam's advance in the southern Philippines is more difficult to establish, but well before the Spanish arrival in 1565 the courts of Sulu and Magindanao were under Muslim kings, and by this time a Muslim family related to the kings of Brunei had also assumed control in the Manila area.

A second development occurred around 1527 with the defeat of the Hindu-Buddhist kingdom of Majapahit by several north-coast Islamic states under the leadership of Demak. While the defeat of Majapahit does not signify a total break in the continuum of Javanese history, it does mark another stage in Islam's spread. Demak, whose ruler had taken the title of sultan around 1524, was already considered a patron of Islam, and its sacred mosque was regarded with particular veneration. Following the fall of Majapahit, Demak forces took to the field to assert supremacy over neighbouring ports. Under Demak's patronage, Banten in west Java developed into an important Islamic centre, and soon began to push out into the Lampung area of Sumatra. It was also from Demak that Islam spread to south Borneo. By the 1540s Demak's armies were moving into east Java, where Islam had not yet taken hold. Though Demak declined in the 1550s, other Javanese ports continued to foster Muslim missionary efforts. Of particular importance was Gresik, and teachers from here are frequently mentioned in stories of conversion from Lampung, Lombok, Makassar, Kutai and Maluku. In much of eastern Indonesia the 'priest king', the holy man of Giri who lived atop a mountain about half a mile from Gresik was revered as a source of supernatural power who could even bring the dead back to life.

A third milestone was reached with the conversion of the twin kingdoms of Goa-Tallo (better known as Makassar) in Sulawesi. While local chronicles convey an impression of sudden revelation, it is clear that the ruler's decision to adopt Islam was slow and considered. By the early seventeenth century Makassar was one of the few important courts where Islam was not established, despite the patronage given to Muslim traders and the missionary work of teachers from Aceh, Java, Pattani, and elsewhere. A crucial factor in the final decision appears to have been the acceptance of Islam by the ruler of Luwu, the oldest and most prestigious kingdom in Sulawesi, in early 1605. On Friday 9 Jumadilawal 1014 (22 September 1605) the ruler of Tallo, Karaeng Matoaya, recited the confession of faith, and assumed a new Arabic name which meant 'the first of Islam'. At the same time the ruler of Goa took the title Sultan Alauddin.

Makassar's patronage gave Islam a new base for missionary teaching in Sulawesi and eastern Indonesia. In conformity with Islamic custom, Makassar invited surrounding kingdoms to accept Islam. When their rulers refused, a series of campaigns was launched, known locally as the Islam Wars. By 1611 all southwest Sulawesi, including Makassar's Bugis rival Bone, had become Muslim. Only the mountainous area of Toraja did not succumb, primarily because the people here saw Islam as the faith of their traditional enemies. In 1618 Makassar undertook the first of several attacks on the island of Sumbawa to force recalcitrant local rulers to accept Islam. By the 1640s most neighbouring kingdoms had accepted Makassar's overlordship and with it the Muslim faith.

The growing attraction of Islam in the sixteenth century must also be seen in the context of developments in the wider Islamic world. The links with the Islamic heartlands appear to have considerably strengthened in this period, for local and European sources frequently mention the arrival of teachers from Mecca, Egypt and Istanbul. Such men would have brought news of the continuing advance of the Ottoman Turks, who now controlled the holy centres of Mecca, Medina and Jerusalem. Under the leadership of Suleiman the Magnificent (1520–66) Turkish armies proceeded to move into the Balkans, conquering Hungary and transforming the Mediterranean into a Muslim lake. By 1543 Suleiman had defeated the Habsburgs and had established an Ottoman provincial administration in Hungary. Not without reason did he style himself Sultan of Sultans and the Inheritor of the Great Caliphate. Reports of Turkish victories, filtering into Southeast Asia through the trade network, would have impressed local rulers and in about 1548 the ruler of Demak allegedly said that if he succeeded in defeating all Java he would consider himself a 'second Turk'.[17]

In the archipelago the presence of Turkish mercenaries and adventurers helped to reinforce Rum's legendary reputation. Not only were they active traders; in addition, they had particular command of military skills, specifically knowledge of muskets and large siege cannon. Local kings were quick to take advantage of this expertise. Turkish soldiers were incorporated into Aceh's armies and, according to Portuguese sources, were used in Aceh's campaigns against the Batak areas around 1537. They were also incorporated into several attacks launched on Portuguese Melaka by Aceh during the course of the sixteenth century. In the 1560s there were more direct contacts between Aceh and Istanbul as Acehnese rulers despatched missions to try to interest the Ottoman sultan in a military operation against the Christian Portuguese. While Turkey did not become involved on an official level, there were certainly messages of support and valued gifts such as banners and cannon.

Developments in India in the sixteenth century are equally significant, for here too the conquering power of Islam appeared to be amply demonstrated in the creation of a new Muslim dynasty, that of the Mughals (Moguls), in 1526. Gradually over the next fifty years, notably in the reign of Akbar (1556–1605), the Mughals proceeded to establish a kingdom which was to dominate the Indian subcontinent. Despite his eclecticism, Akbar was still formally a Muslim ruler whose incorporation of Hindu and

[17] H. J. de Graaf and Th. G. Th. Pigeaud, *De Eerste Moslimse Vorstendommen op Java*, The Hague, 1974, 76.

Persian traditions help to affirm popular veneration for Islamic kings in India and provides a persuasive example of the power with which Islam was associated. Iskandar Muda of Aceh (r. 1607–36) is thought to have been inspired by the 'Grand Mughal', and the panegyric recounting his deeds, the *Hikayat Aceh*, to have been modelled on the contemporary Indian work, the *Akbarnāma*.

The arrival of the Portuguese and Spaniards, who came determined not only to make Christian converts but to destroy Muslim trading dominance, was paradoxically another stimulus to the spread of Islam in the Indonesian archipelago. Decades of conflict between Christian and Muslim states in Europe and the Middle East had seen frequent recourse to notions of crusade and holy war which were imported into Southeast Asia. Albuquerque, who led the successful attack on Melaka, initially opposed any association with Muslims, and in the aftermath of the conquest the great mosque of Melaka was completely destroyed and all Muslim traders expelled. Local Muslims, for their part, could at times be persuaded that resistance to the Portuguese was enjoined by Allah. Sixteenth-century Javanese texts list obedience to the summons of holy war (*jihad*) as one of the duties prescribed by Islam, and remind Muslims that they should not befriend infidels, 'for this will be recorded against you as a sin in this world and the world to come'.[18] The struggle between Islam and Christianity seemed particularly marked in eastern Indonesia, where Jesuits reported the arrival of 'priests' from Mecca, Aceh, the Malay areas and elsewhere calling for a holy war. Towards the end of the century the atmosphere of confrontation was heightened as the Spanish, newly established in the Philippines, embarked on a push into the Muslim-dominated areas of the south. In 1578 the Brunei mosque was burned and the lord of Magindanao was told that the Spanish aimed to obtain his conversion to Christianity. To some extent, therefore, there was a 'race' between Islam and Christianity, as adherents of each tried to confirm their commercial, political and spiritual hold over particular areas.

While stressing the various stimuli to conversion, however, one should also emphasize the genuine appeal of Islam itself, and particularly the mystical strand known as Sufism (a term probably derived from *suf*, or wool from which the coarse garments of Muslim ascetics were made). Mysticism had been able to maintain a place in the Islamic mainstream because of the teachings of devout Sufis, pre-eminent among whom was one of the greatest Muslim theologians, Abū Ḥāmid al-Ghazālī (450–505 AH, 1058–1111 CE). From about the thirteenth century CE, mystical schools or *ṭarīqa* (Indonesian *tarekat*) had begun to develop, focusing on the teachings of one Sufi leader or *shaykh* which were transmitted to his disciples through a genealogical chain linking pupils and masters to the founder himself. With its willingness in certain forms and traditions to accommodate existing beliefs, Sufism developed into a significant vehicle for the movement of Islam outside the heartlands. Sufi teachers fanned out along trading routes where members of the *ṭarīqa* were often drawn from the commercial community. In India, which had a long tradition of

---

[18] G. W. J. Drewes, ed. and trans., *The Admonitions of Seh Bari*, The Hague, 1969, 69.

veneration for holy men, Sufism found a sympathetic environment. By the end of the fifteenth century a number of orders had gained a footing there, with some of the later but more influential being the Qādiriyya, the Shaṭṭāriyya and the Naqshabandiyya. These three orders also became the most popular in Southeast Asia.

Mystical thought was a part of Southeast Asian Islam from very early times, but not until the sixteenth century are there any contemporary textual sources. The few surviving Javanese mystical works of this period lie firmly within the framework of 'sober' or ascetic mysticism with one referring for its authority to al-Ghazālī's great work, *The Revival of the Religious Sciences* (*Iḥyā''ulūm al-dīn*). However, a number of other renowned Sufi teachers are also mentioned, and some of them, like Ibn al-'Arabī (560–638 AH, 1165–1240 CE) held more controversial views. Al-'Arabī is known especially for his formulation of the doctrine of *waḥdatu'l wujūd*, the Unity of Being, from which a myriad of aspects were revealed as the manifold forms of creation, and for his concept of the Perfect Man, the microcosmic figure who represents in himself the perfect attributes of the Divine Being. Ibn al-'Arabī's standing increased considerably during the fifteenth and sixteenth centuries, and Selim I of Turkey even ordered the rebuilding of his mausoleum in Damascus. It is not surprising, therefore, to find his name invoked as an authority in texts of this period. His influence is very clear in the writings of Hamzah Fansuri, a local teacher from Barus in western Sumatra known to have lived in the second half of the sixteenth century and to have been received into the Qādiriyya *ṭarīqa* while visiting Baghdad.

In Southeast Asia the Sufi aim of union with the Absolute blended easily with deep-rooted cultural attitudes that had long conceived of a constant interaction between the world of men and that of spirits. Many of the concepts presented in Sufi teachings thus struck a responsive chord in Southeast Asian societies. As Hamzah Fansuri put it,

> His radiance is a blazing glow
> In all of us
> It is He who is the cup and the *arak*
> Do not look for Him far away, child.

Or again, in the words of a Javanese text,

> there is no difference
> between worshipper and the worshipped
> both are He alone
> as the being of the universe
> cannot be divided.[19]

Southeast Asians would also have been drawn to Sufism because the methods used to achieve an ecstatic sense of unity with the Divine— dancing, singing, music, drumming, meditation, the recitation of *zikir*, 'magic' words in the form of Koranic passages or formulaic prayers—were similar to the religious practices to which they had been accustomed. Sufi

---

[19] *Arak* is rice wine. G. W. J. Drewes and L. F. Brakel, *The Poems of Hamzah Fansuri*, Dordrecht, Holland, and Cinnaminson, U.S.A., 1986, 8; G. W. J. Drewes, 'Javanese poems dealing with or attributed to the Saint of Bonañ', BKI, 124, 2 (1968) 225. Professor A. H. Johns suggested a slight change to the original translation.

emphasis on the close relationship between disciple and teacher, which is frequently compared to that of a parent and child or elder and younger brother, would similarly have found ready acceptance in traditional societies like those of Southeast Asia where kinship ties are considered fundamental in human interaction.

Available texts also suggest that an understanding of Sufism in Southeast Asia was facilitated because local teachers, drawing prestige from their links with Pasai, Minangkabau, Melaka, Java or Johor, used familiar images to explain the essence of mystical Islam. 'It is said', wrote one, 'that human sight may be compared to coconut milk, which in the long run will become oil; to an unripe banana, which gradually grows half-ripe . . . gradually human sight is perfected by the lord so that there is no doubt that the eye will behold the essence.'[20] Even so, we have no way of knowing how widely these works were read; one assumes they would have been studied only by the spiritual élite. Despite the obvious appeal of Sufism, its teachings were probably considerably simplified in oral transmission. One text warns against using Sufi terminology without complete understanding and quotes the *hadith* (tradition), 'Tell to the people what they understand; do you want to make God and his Prophet liars?'[21] Furthermore, while there were a number of erudite teachers in the courts, others involved in introducing Islam to the peoples of the archipelago may have had only a general understanding of mystic ideas. In the early seventeenth century, for instance, the Imam of Jambi on the east coast of Sumatra was a trader from Pahang, while in Ambon Javanese traders who could read and write often stayed over for a season to act as religious teachers. The first task of the Islamic schools established in the trading ports would have been to impart basic Muslim ideas, teach the ritual prayers and assist pupils to memorize passages from the Koran rather than to initiate deep discussions about exceedingly complex ideas. While one must be wary of generalizing from the few extant sixteenth-century texts, since they have survived purely by chance, they do provide evidence of this stress on the fundamentals of Islamic practice. Good Muslims should observe the precepts of Islam—perform the ritual prayers (*salat*) five times daily, recite the Koran, pay alms, fast during Ramadan, make the pilgrimage if possible, and respond to any call to join the holy war. Like the later Christian missionaries, Muslim teachers also developed a type of catechism designed to answer some of the most common queries, such as the meaning of unfamiliar words, the nature of paradise, and the fate of those condemned to hell. The condemnation of the pig as unclean received particular attention in eastern Indonesia where this animal had been accorded great veneration and was an important item of food at ritual feasts. In Maluku the Spaniards on Magellan's ships killed all the pigs they carried on board to please the king, 'for when those people happen to see any swine they cover their faces in order that they might not look upon them or catch their odour'.[22]

[20] Drewes, *The Admonitions*, 69.
[21] A. Johns, 'Dakā'ik al-Huruf by 'Abd al-Ra'uf of Singkel', JRAS (1955), 69, 72.
[22] Antonio Pigafetta, *Magellan's Voyage around the World*, ed. James A. Robertson, Cleveland, 1906, II. 29, 81.

At the same time the great triumph of Islam was its ability, within certain limits, to tolerate numerous pre-Muslim beliefs and practices. This was in turn due to the fact that the corpus of Islamic law and tradition, the *sharī'a*, allows for some local interpretation. Indeed, the legal codes of Melaka frequently include two penalties for the same crime, one following custom—now subsumed under the Arabic-derived word *adat*—and the other that of 'the law of Allah'. Much of the ritual associated with the great life crises survived, legitimized by Koranic verses and prayers recited by a person considered knowledgeable in the faith. The *Taj us-Salatin*, for instance, declares that after a birth it is the parents' duty to dress the child in proper clothes and then to have the call to prayer (*azan*) recited in the right ear and the following exhortation to prayer (*iqamah*) in the left. A new prominence was also given to circumcision, which was already practised for both sexes in many areas of the archipelago. In Islamic communities, however, it was elevated into an important rite of passage, especially for Muslim males. They and their families gained considerable prestige because the ceremony was performed by respected religious figures, frequently in the mosque itself. Islamic teachers could also be important in curing rites. In Makassar, for instance,

> if the sickness come to be never so little dangerous, they apply themselves no more to the physicians, but go straight to the priests because they do not think it then proceeds from any natural cause; and for that they imagine it is caused by some evil spirit, that is to be expelled by forces of exorcism and prayers.[23]

The new vocabulary offered by Islam, invoking the awe-inspiring authority of a supreme God and his designated spokesman, thus furnished another powerful weapon to defy potentially harmful spirits. In the words of an old incantation from Perak,

> Muhammad my shelter is beside me
> Only if Allah suffer harm
> Can I suffer harm
> Only if His Prophet suffer harm
> Can I suffer harm.[24]

At the same time the introduction of a whole range of angels, prophets and saintly teachers expanded the numbers of heroes and superhuman figures who could be invoked for help, advice and examples of proper conduct. For example, as elsewhere in the Islamic world 'Abd al-Qādir l-Jīlānī (470–561 AH, 1077–1166 CE), the founder of the Qādiriyya order, became an object of particular veneration, in part because of his descent from the Prophet. A manuscript from Banten dating from the early seventeenth century describes him as so pious that as a baby he even refused his mother's breast during the fasting month. This array of Islamic heroes was constantly augmented by the addition of revered locals, like Dato ri Bandang who legend claims brought Islam to Makassar and the surrounding areas, and who is said to have arrived in Kutai riding on a swordfish.

Through this kind of adaptation, Southeast Asian Muslims were already

---

[23] Gervaise, *An Historical Description*, 140.
[24] Richard Winstedt, *The Malay Magician*, Kuala Lumpur, 1982, 74.

coming to see Islamic beliefs not as imported but as an integral part of their own culture. In the western archipelago it ceased to be associated only with the coastal regions as internal trade and active proselytizing carried Islamic teachings into the interior. A poem written in Aceh in 1679, outlining the creation of the world and the implications of the Day of Judgement, was thus composed in Acehnese rather than Malay because 'few people [presumably in the interior] know the Malay language'.[25] Seventeenth-century chronicles may attribute the introduction of Islam to a holy man from overseas, from Mecca, Pasai, Melaka, Minangkabau or Java, but at the same time the acceptance of the new faith is symbolized by a marriage between this revered teacher and a local woman of high birth. In a number of cases he is associated with cultural features which helped distinguish a society from its neighbours. In Brunei, for instance, Sultan Yusuf was said to have discovered camphor, for which northwest Borneo was renowned; in Java *walīs* such as the great Sunan Kalijaga were often seen as adept in composing certain poetic metres, in kris making, in performing *wayang*—skills which lie at the very heart of Javanese culture.

By the time the Dutch East India Company established its headquarters at Batavia (Jayakatra) in 1619, Islam was clearly the rising faith in island Southeast Asia. The Spaniards themselves acknowledged that, had they not taken Manila in 1571, Islam would have penetrated the entire Philippine archipelago. A comment on the prestige of Islam is the fact that in the seventeenth century at least two mainland rulers converted, probably (like so many of their counterparts in the island world) in the hope of gaining some powerful ally. Some time between 1607 and 1676 the king of Champa, Vietnam's vassal, became Muslim, and Islam here spread to the extent that most Chams were at least nominal Muslims. In Cambodia, where the Thais presented a constant threat, the Muslim Cham and Malay merchant community was instrumental in a successful usurpation of power by a Khmer prince, who around 1643 adopted Islam and underwent circumcision. He took the reign name Sultan Ibrahim, but was called by the people Rama Cul Sas, or 'King Rama who embraced the religion [of Islam]'.

In general, however, Islam made little progress in mainland Southeast Asia, although there were substantial Muslim communities in the major ports. An obvious reason is the entrenched position of Theravāda Buddhism and its widespread integration into local culture, forming an all-encompassing belief system which seriously addressed questions regarding the afterlife as well as the problems of this one. But even in the island world Islam did not carry all before it. Attempts to persuade people to become Muslims not infrequently met with active resistance or simply indifference. The Badui of Sunda provide just one instance of a community which never adopted Islam, despite their proximity to Banten. Islamic ideas were also slow to spread in the scattered islands of eastern Indonesia because of their geographic isolation from trading routes and their very loose links with Muslim centres like Ternate. It is useful to remember that

[25] P. Voorhoeve, 'Three Old Achehnese manuscripts', BSOAS, 14 (1951–2) 337–9.

Islamization in contemporary Indonesia is still continuing and that in a number of societies indigenous beliefs still predominate.

Bali

The most obvious example of a society which was not caught up by Islam's advance is Bali. A glance at the historical background helps explain why this should be so. In Bali the sixteenth century had been a time of political consolidation. Conquest by Majapahit in 1334 had resulted in a union of the entire island, and following Majapahit's decline in the 1520s the tradition of unitary government had been assumed by the kingdom of Gelgel. Under Gelgel's leadership the Balinese extended their control not only over the entire island but into east Java on the one side and as far as Lombok and Sumbawa on the other. During this period the rich heritage of Majapahit was reshaped to create a uniquely Balinese social order characterized by the four basic divisions of the Hindu caste system, now enforced by rules punishing caste infringements. The *brahmana* (brahmins, the priestly caste), *satria* (warrior-kings) and *wesia* (nobles) were known collectively as the *trivangśa*, the three castes, standing apart from the bulk of the population, the *sudras*. There were also important developments in religion. Local temples, which can be seen as elaborated megalithic monuments, cult centres for the invocation of local divinities, the ancestors and the powers of fertility, continued to flourish, but the earlier Buddhism and the veneration of Indra were gradually overshadowed by rituals which stressed the worship of Śiva as manifested by the sun, the making of holy water, the recitation of mantra set down in the sacred scriptures, and ceremonial feasting (*galungan*). Temple priests (*pamangku*) who had survived from previous times were often relegated to commoner status, with the Śiva-worshipping high priests (*padanda*) coming exclusively from the *brahmana* caste and presiding over the ritual central to religious observances.

Bali thus faced the advance of Islam in the sixteenth century strengthened politically and invigorated religiously. In a society which had developed a complex and culturally self-sustaining means of explaining the cosmos and man's place in it, Islam made little headway. Nonetheless, Balinese were not opposed to Islam as such. Balinese who settled in Java tended to become Muslims, and in the eighteenth century Balinese Muslims in Batavia had their own mosque. Active resistance to Islam occurred when it was seen as a tool used by the Javanese or some other rival to lend legitimacy to a Muslim ruler's political ambitions. One tradition, for instance, claims that Balinese lances were smeared with pigfat during conflict between Gelgel and the staunchly Muslim Makassar over control of Lombok. Generally, however, the Balinese treated the new religion as they had done previous Javanese influences, incorporating some elements but merging them with their own culture. Mantras, for example, could include Islamic invocations, while in some areas people refrained from offering port to the gods. Balinese kings showed no opposition to the presence of Muslim communities descended from migrant Makassarese and Malays, as long as traditional customs and caste restrictions in marriage were not flouted. A few Muslim villages grew up at places such as Buleleng in the north, helping to promote a small body of Balinese literature dealing with Islam.

In the early seventeenth century the Balinese state under Gelgel's suzerainty was confident and united. Though Gelgel fell in 1651, the politico-religious base which had evolved over the previous 150 years proved well able to survive the fragmentation of the late seventeenth and eighteenth centuries. Indeed, it has been argued that this proliferation of competing Balinese kingdoms provided new centres of cultural enrichment, and that many of the rituals today associated with Bali in fact developed during this period. The vast array of alternative religious and artistic forms which was thus created has been a major factor in the continuing vitality of Balinese society.

THE ARRIVAL OF CHRISTIANITY

When dealing with the arrival of Christianity, the last world religion to arrive in Southeast Asia, we are on much firmer ground than in the case of Islam and the other major faiths. The motivations behind the spread of Christianity, the time of its arrival and the nature of the doctrine taught, are all well known. Catholic Europe in the late fifteenth and early sixteenth centuries was inspired by a zeal for missionizing which had been encouraged by tensions resulting from the protracted wars with Ottoman Turkey and the challenge of Protestantism, as well as by the excitement of recently discovered 'pagan' lands in Asia and the Americas. Foremost in the new endeavour were the Catholic monarchs of Spain and Portugal, who were strongly influenced by the apostolic idea of Christian kingship so prominent in the Middle Ages. In 1493 Papal Bulls made it an obligation for all Catholic kings to promote the spread of Christianity, and in the following year the Treaty of Tordesillas divided the world into two spiritual jurisdictions. One was assigned to the Portuguese Crown and the other to the Spanish. In actual fact, so little was known about world geography that the dividing line established by the Treaty of Tordesillas could not be satisfactorily identified and became a matter of bitter dispute between Spain and Portugal. Nonetheless, it effectively excluded proselytization by any other Catholic nation until the arrival of the French Société des Missions Étrangères in Vietnam in 1662. The royal patronage granted by the pope to the monarchs of Spain and Portugal made them responsible for the conversion of the 'heathen' and thus for the building of churches and monasteries, for appointing archbishops and lesser religious officials, and for financing the missionary effort. Unlike any other religion which came to the region, therefore, Christianity was shored up by the commitment of a secular government located on the other side of the world.

Under Spanish patronage, the first Christians reached the Philippines in March 1521, when Magellan's decimated fleet arrived in Cebu. There they were welcomed by the chief, Raja Humabon, who, together with his wife and eight hundred of his followers, agreed to accept Christianity. The decisive factor in Humabon's decision appears to have been the assurance that the power of Christianity and the association with the Spanish would help him overcome his enemies and protect him from harm. The new relationship with the Europeans was symbolized not merely by the ritual of holy baptism and the bestowal of Christian names, but by a ceremony in which Magellan and Humabon (now christened Don Carlos) drank each other's blood and thus became brothers.

Southwards, the Portuguese reacted to the Spanish expedition by strengthening their position in Maluku, where the king of Ternate had shown an interest in Christianity as early as 1512. In 1522, claiming that Maluku fell within the territory assigned to them for conversion by the Treaty of Tordesillas, the Portuguese accepted an invitation from the Ternate ruler to erect a fortress in his kingdom. In theory at least the king of Ternate had agreed to allow missionary work, while at the same time himself remaining a patron of Islam. Intent on maintaining their spice monopoly, the Portuguese were willing to live with this anomaly, and the preaching of Christianity was never accorded a high priority. A 'vicar' and a few secular clergy were appointed to the Ternate fortress, but while some baptisms were performed, neophytes received minimal instruction in religious doctrine and the so-called 'Christians' showed a disturbing tendency to apostatize.

The high point in the Portuguese mission in the Indonesian archipelago came in 1546 with the arrival of Francis Xavier, co-founder of the Jesuit order. He spent two years in the Maluku region and was said to have made thousands of 'converts', most of whom were among the Alifuru, the non-Muslim interior tribes. It was still apparent, however, that lack of proficiency in languages native to the eastern archipelago was a continuing obstacle to the explanation of Christian doctrine. Although Francis Xavier had undertaken translation of Christian works into Malay, it was found that this supposed lingua franca was unknown in the interior of many eastern islands. Only after the commitment of Jesuits to the region were efforts made to translate Christian texts and catechisms into local languages such as Ternatan and Siau. But Xavier's missionary efforts did stimulate a wider interest in Christianity, and by 1555 thirty villages on Ambon were considered 'Christian'. Even so, the lack of priests meant that whole communities could find themselves thrown back on their own resources. Furthermore, because the Portuguese never received effective support from the Crown, they were incapable of assisting local kings who had accepted Christianity against their (usually Muslim) enemies. The king of Bacan, for instance, was baptized in 1557 as Dom João, but Christian influence waned when the Portuguese could not protect him from Ternatan attacks. Under pressure from Ternate, Dom João later renounced Christianity and returned to Islam. The same experience was repeated elsewhere. In 1595 it was gloomily estimated that of about 40,000 Ambonese Christians, only 3000 had held to their faith. The situation was considered so hopeless that the Jesuits, who had been working in Maluku since the 1540s, even contemplated abandoning the field.

The mission in Maluku was further weakened after 1605 when the Dutch

East India Company (Vereenigde Oost-Indische Compagnie, VOC) took Ambon and drove the Portuguese from Ternate and Tidore. Surrounding islands fell progressively under VOC influence and the number of Jesuits stationed in the Indies steadily dropped. By 1624 only twelve Jesuits were left in Maluku. The capture of Portuguese Melaka by the Dutch in 1641 and the destruction of its numerous monasteries and churches represented a further blow to the Catholic presence in the Indonesian archipelago. With the departure of the last Spaniard from Ternate and Tidore in 1663, Catholic mission work in eastern Indonesia became confined to Solor, Flores and Timor where the Dominicans had been working since 1562.

The Christian impact on Indonesia was far less than in the Philippines, partly because the Catholic missions there never received a similar level of state support. The VOC domination of the area in the seventeenth and eighteenth centuries brought added changes, for the Dutch never considered conversion to be a goal in itself. Nonetheless, there was some attempt to woo converts away from Catholicism to Protestantism and to eradicate 'pagan' beliefs. In 1622, for example, the VOC governor of Ambon claimed that as many as eight hundred spirit houses had been burned and the offerings confiscated. On a number of occasions edicts were issued threatening the death penalty for anyone in whose garden images of the 'devil' were found. Furthermore, Christians in VOC areas were always favoured over Muslims, a practice which encouraged some conversions among eastern Indonesian groups. The attractions of Christianity were particularly evident after a landmark decision in 1729 when the governor-general laid down that a Christian chief could not be punished by his non-Christian lord. It appears to have been this decision which persuaded the first Rotinese ruler to become Christian, and a little more than a decade later seven hundred people in one area of Roti were said to be awaiting baptism. By the end of the eighteenth century Christianity was well established in many of the eastern islands, and for many groups it had become an important key to ethnic identification. The people of Roti, for example, attribute the advent of Christianity not to European missionaries but to one of their own culture heroes who also brought with him the art of distilling palm syrup, on which their economy is dependent.

The Establishment of Christianity in the Philippines

It was the Spanish colony of the Philippines which was destined to become the great Christian mission field in Southeast Asia. To a far greater extent than the Portuguese, the Spanish came to the archipelago seeing themselves as divinely appointed to spread the gospel among the heathen of the Americas and Asia. Although their encounter with Filipinos in Cebu in 1521 had ended in hostility and Magellan's death, the willingness with which so many people had accepted baptism held out a promise that the Philippines could become a rich source of Christian souls. In 1565, after several abortive attempts, another Spanish force under Miguel Lopez de Legazpi returned to Cebu carrying an Augustinian priest whose task was not only to submit a report on the expedition but 'to preach the Holy Gospel to the inhabitants of those new lands and to baptize those who accept our faith'.[26] However, during the years which had passed since Magellan's visit, acquaintance with the Portuguese had made local communities more suspicious of the intentions of white men. Two thousand Cebuans met Legazpi in full battle array, but their lances, shields, cutlasses and rope armour failed to sustain their courage when faced by Spanish musketry. Yet in the burning settlement Legazpi's men found evidence that the brief glimpse of Christianity offered by Magellan a generation earlier had not been totally forgotten. Among the charred remains they came across a statue of the Child Jesus which Magellan had earlier presented to the chief's wife. For over forty years it had been carefully preserved and held in veneration because it was a miracle-working *dewata* (god) of the white men.

In the aftermath of Legazpi's attack, the local community sued for peace. The legal basis of the Spanish endeavour was the fiction that the Cebuanos who had received baptism in 1521 had become Spanish subjects. As 'rebels' they were now asked to request pardon for killing Magellan and 'renew' an oath of loyalty to the Spanish Crown. Little missionary work took place during these early years, however, because the Spaniards were mostly concerned with survival. Besides, there were not enough priests to undertake sustained teaching, and it was still uncertain if Spain would in fact stay in the Philippines. Obviously it would be foolish to embark on a campaign of conversion if the neophytes were to be abandoned, and in the five years after the Spanish arrival only about a hundred people were baptized. But in 1570 Philip II made the important decision to commit Spain to the colonization and Christianization of the Philippine islands, despite the fact that they would obviously not yield the great wealth which had once been expected.

The Spanish capture of Manila in May 1571 marks a new stage in the spread of Christianity. Having seen his settlement reduced to ashes, the local chief agreed to a treaty by which he not only accepted Spanish protection but acknowledged the right of the Spaniards to propagate the Christian faith. In 1578 fifteen Franciscans arrived in Cavite to join the Augustinians, followed three years later by the Jesuits, then in 1587 by the Dominicans and in 1606 by the Recollects. By 1595 there were 134 missionaries working in the Philippines, and it was estimated that 288,000 baptisms had taken place. Each order was assigned to a specific area to evangelize, the aim being that newly converted areas were to be handed over to secular priests when the faith was well established. Because of resistance from the orders, however, the full secularization of parishes in the Philippines never occurred. During the seventeenth and for much of the eighteenth century it was thus the religious orders who not only brought in new converts, but took on the task of maintaining them as Christians.

The missionizing process in the Philippines followed precedents already set by the Spaniards in Mexico and South America, whence the orders drew many of their personnel. One of these precedents was the granting of *encomiendas*, which were held either by the Crown or by individuals

---

[26] Rafael Lopez, trans., *The Christianisation of the Philippines*, Manila, 1965, 255–6.

designated by the king as *encomenderos*. The latter had the right to collect tribute from a particular area, but in return were responsible for making the people aware of Spanish sovereignty and for giving them some basic knowledge of Christianity. In the Philippines the holding of private *encomiendas* was gradually abandoned, but in the early years the *encomenderos*, often former soldiers, played a significant role in blunting local resistance to the Spanish presence and preparing the way for the missionary orders to move in.

Another important aid to Christianizing was the policy of resettling the native population, which had also been followed in Spanish America. The indigenous Filipino pattern of independent kinship communities or *barangay* was changed to one where there was a main centre (*cabecera*) with a church where the Spanish priest lived, surrounded by a number of outlying hamlets (*visitas*). In these *visitas* small chapels were constructed where the priest periodically celebrated mass, and in his absence suitable Filipinos were sometimes selected to perform important Christian duties, such as baptism and preparing the seriously ill for death. For practical purposes, priests usually tried to combine several hamlets and to persuade people to move closer to the newly established town. But progress in this regard was slow, especially outside the Tagalog areas, and at the end of the seventeenth century there were fewer than twenty centres of more than two thousand people. This meant that priests in sparsely populated areas such as the Visayas had to move constantly between isolated settlements. Yet though some baptized Filipinos might see a priest only once a year, the Spanish commitment meant that Christian communities were very rarely abandoned.

The missionary orders did have their own character and concerns, but they shared many similarities because virtually all those involved were Spanish, because they were under the direction of the Spanish Crown and because they drew heavily on the collective Spanish experience of Christianizing in the Americas. Missionaries there had learnt, for instance, that it was vital to obtain the conversion of chiefs in order to win over their followers. In the Philippines local baptized leaders, grouped together as the *principales*, became the linchpin of the Spanish administration, helping to bring their following under the authority of the Church and the Spanish Crown. The people themselves remarked that 'If the father of them all became a Christian, how could they do otherwise?'[27]

Missionaries in New Spain had long since found that the most effective way of converting local leaders was to teach Christian ideas to their children, giving special attention to the sons of chiefs. In several places in the Philippines the orders established schools to instruct the young in Catholic doctrine, with each class concentrating on a particular topic such as the Hail Mary. When pupils had completed all the classes they were considered ready for baptism. Frequently an entire family was baptized together by using the children to prepare their elders, for priests would not baptize adults unless they could recite the basic prayers from memory and demonstrate some knowledge of the principal obligations of a Christian.

[27] Pedro Chirino, *The Philippines in 1600*, trans. Ramon Echevarria, Manila, 1969, 337.

To achieve this goal, much use was made of music, which had been an integral part of indigenous ritual. It was found that Filipinos, like the peoples of eastern Indonesia and the Americas, quickly learned to chant the Ten Commandments, the Lord's Prayer and other parts of the liturgy when these were translated into their own language and sung. Missionaries noted with delight how the people 'sang the doctrine' in their homes or while working in the fields; one father returning from Mass was amazed to hear a village woman 'singing' the sermon he had just given, which she had rendered into verse and put to a traditional tune. These sermons, which were given in the vernacular following the saying of the Latin Mass, generally dealt with one of four topics—the immortality of the soul; the existence of God; the rewards awaiting Christians in the next life; and purgatory, the place of perpetual pain. Explanations were often assisted by pictures, which were especially useful for priests whose knowledge of a regional language was limited.

An important factor in the success of Christianity was the fact that many aspects of worship struck a familiar chord in Filipino culture. Communion, the partaking of the body and blood of Christ, resonated with echoes of ritual feasting, and Tagalog translations of Christian texts spoke of the Eucharist as a source not only of sanctity but of courage, strength and potency. Another means of obtaining the power of Christianity was baptism. Water had always been an essential part of animist rites, and the holy water of the Christians was widely regarded as a cure for the body as well as for the soul. The priests themselves exploited this belief by deliberately making the baptismal ceremony as solemn an occasion as possible and by using holy water freely, especially in ministering to the sick. The sprinkling of water, the recitation of prayers in Latin, and the sign of the cross provided a compelling alternative to the curing rites of the *babaylan*. Even when Christian sacraments did not bring about recovery, faith in the efficacy of holy water remained. As one man said, 'I know that with the water which the Fathers pour on them [the sick children] will go to heaven.'[28] Baptism had additional advantages on earth, because by this means an individual acquired *compadre* or godparents who were charged with particular responsibility for his spiritual welfare. Filipinos, however, expanded this relationship to link the godparents not only with the child's father and mother, but with the rest of his family as well. Normally godparents of a higher social status were chosen and ritual co-parenthood (*compadrazgo*) thus evolved into a patron–client relationship, with both sides obligated to assist one another.

A further source of power inherent in Christianity was the vast family of holy figures it introduced into a society where the concept of spirit worship was deeply embedded. Saints, especially those to whom a local church was dedicated, came to be viewed as akin to sympathetic and approachable ancestors, whose assistance could be obtained by appropriate gifts and humble petitions and whose names could be invoked as a source of protection. 'Use this weapon [i.e. the names of Jesus and Mary]', says one commentary, 'and do not let it go, so that you may triumph against your

---

[28] Ana Maria Madrigal Llorente, *A Blending of Cultures: the Batanes, 1686–1898*, Manila, 1983, 60.

enemies.'[29] Blessed by the priest, rosaries, crosses, bibles and holy medals became potent talismans, and the priest's domain—his dwelling, the Christian burial ground nearby, and above all the church—a locus of extraordinary power. In one settlement where the church was moved to higher ground to avoid flooding, the people immediately moved their houses to the new site. The reason, they said, was their dread of the devils who nightly roamed the old town because it now had neither church nor cross.

In the meeting of local culture and Christian teaching there was a considerable degree of compromise. For example, Filipinos gradually came to accept the Christian idea of monogamy and the indissolubility of marriage, although this did cause some tensions in a society where divorce was relatively easy and where wealthy chiefs usually had more than one wife. At the same time, however, there was a steady Filipinization of many aspects of Christian worship. Some Filipinos believed, for instance, that one might not spit, or bathe oneself, or eat meat for three days prior to taking the Eucharist, while the occasion itself became an opportunity for women in particular to display their wealth in dress and jewellery as they had been accustomed to do in traditional *manganito* (spirit propitiation ceremonies) held for a betrothal or the gathering of the harvest. Firecrackers could even be set off during the raising of the host. Holy days in general were marked off for festivities and parties when the people of both sexes and all ages came together after saying the rosary, and observers in Manila noted how people 'diverted themselves by dancing, singing and bold and indecorous games'.[30]

There can be no doubt that this kind of compromise did give the missionaries cause for concern. The Franciscans and Dominicans were especially adamant that non-Christian cultures were the work of the devil, and that tolerance was a betrayal of Christian principles. As in the Americas, priests generally avoided translating key doctrinal concepts in an effort to avoid any confusion with native beliefs. The Spanish word 'Dios', for example, was used for God rather than any local equivalent, and the same principle was applied to other terms such as Trinity, Holy Ghost, grace, sin and hell. Particular efforts were made to root out spirit propitiation. One of the first steps in converting a village community was to insist on the destruction of any 'idols', old altars or places of worship, and when baptized Christians came to confession they were rigorously questioned as to whether they had been treated by sorcerers, or had sworn by dreams, or had made offerings to the spirits. Translated catechisms, like one sixteenth-century Tagalog text, directly addressed the issue of spirit worship: 'Christians, you have been baptized . . . why do you consult the *anito* when you get sick? Can the lifeless give life? Why do you make an offering when you work in the fields? Who else makes the rice grow if not God?'[31] But despite the efforts of the missionaries, the old beliefs

[29] Vincente L. Rafael, *Contracting Colonialism: Translation and Christian Conversion in Tagalog Society under Early Spanish Rule*, Ithaca and London, 1988, 120.
[30] Fernandez, *The Church in the Philippines*, 164.
[31] Antonio M. Rosales, *A Study of a Sixteenth Century Tagalog Manuscript on the Ten Commandments: Its Significance and Implications*, Quezon City, 1984, 35, 39.

remained. Rice seeds might be brought to the priest to be blessed, and the cross might stand guardian in the fields, but planting and harvest times were also the occasion for gatherings when pigs or chickens were presented to the spirits, and deceased ancestors were summoned up through prayers and sacred dances. Like other Southeast Asians, Filipinos continued to make offerings to ensure the co-operation of the supernatural whether they were gathering fruit, cutting wood, or collecting bamboo. In 1731 one friar complained that an accepted method of catching a thief was to place a pair of scissors upright on a screen in the shape of the cross of Saint Andrew, and hang a rosary on it. The name of those suspected was repeated and the shaking of the screen indicated the guilty party.

Caution should naturally be exercised in generalizing about the conversion experience of Filipinos, since cultural attitudes explaining the acceptance of Christian teachings in one area may not necessarily apply in another.[32] Yet regardless of the reasons underlying missionary success, it is clear that by the latter part of the seventeenth century the adaptation process had enabled Christianity to take firm root in the northern half of the Philippines. This in turn had encouraged the Spanish to proceed anew with missionary work in the south. In 1635 a fort was established in Zamboanga, and from this base the Jesuits were able to negotiate peace treaties permitting them to undertake Christian teaching in Muslim areas. But the extent to which force accompanied the Christian missions brought a hardening of Muslim opposition to the Spanish presence. During the 1650s Sultan Qudarat of Magindanao, a powerful centre on Mindanao, declared *jihad*, and his successor is still remembered in *khutba* (sermons given at the Friday prayers) as a ruler who fought the infidel Spaniards. Continuing attacks on Spanish-held areas by the Dutch, the loss of Ternate and Tidore, and the threat of raids on Manila by Koxinga led the Spanish authorities to close the Zamboanga fort in 1663. For half a century the Christian-Muslim division of the Philippine islands was implicitly accepted.

Missionary Work in Vietnam

Christianity had been known in Vietnam since the sixteenth century, for in 1533 there is mention of the religion taught by Ignatius, 'a man of the Ocean', presumably from Melaka. From 1580 representatives of several missionary orders passed through or spent some time in Vietnam. The first church was built in Danang by Father Francis Buzomi who had come from Macao in January 1615 and who in the first year of teaching gained three hundred converts. However, the beginning of the Christianizing effort is properly dated 1624, with the arrival of Alexander of Rhodes and several other Jesuits who had been expelled from Japan. Three years later Father Alexander was sent to the Trinh-ruled north to establish a mission. By the time it was closed three years later by the authorities, it had gained almost seven thousand Vietnamese converts. By 1640 there were said to be 39,000 Christians in the Nguyen territories and 82,000 in the areas under the Trinh.

[32] See Rafael, *Contracting Colonialism*, for a stimulating study of the role of language and textual translation in Tagalog acceptance of Christianity.

The process of 'conversion' in seventeenth-century Vietnam from a local perspective remains to be explored. There are, however, a number of reasons which at least in part explain the initial Christian success. As in the Philippines priests recognized the need to attract the high-born to Christianity, and there was much rejoicing when one of the foremost princesses in the southern Nguyen court was baptized and persuaded others to take the same step. More important, however, was the fact that the Jesuit missionaries, like their counterparts in the island world, placed great importance on learning the local language and preaching directly to the people. Father Alexander's romanization of Vietnamese into a form known as *quoc ngu* made it possible for missionaries to learn Vietnamese more quickly, although Christian material distributed to the faithful was still written in either Chinese characters or *nom* (Vietnamese demotic script). Furthermore in contrast to the Philippines, Jesuit priests in Vietnam argued that a strong native clergy was necessary for the promotion of the religion. By the middle of the century a seminary had been established which had a hundred members. Vietnamese catechists were also given elementary medical instruction and encouraged to move through the Vietnamese countryside spreading Christian teachings. Their rigorous training, understanding of Christian doctrine and religious devotion helped foster Christian conversions despite the very limited number of European priests. During one epidemic, for instance, six Vietnamese catechists supplied by the Jesuits with the weapons of Christianity—the cross, holy water, holy candles, blessed palm leaves and pictures of the Virgin—went to a stricken area to make war on the devil, whom they blamed for the suffering. When the epidemic abated, the local people were so convinced of Christianity's power that the local leader converted.

The growing hostility of both Nguyen and Trinh leaders to Christianity did not dampen missionary fervour; on the contrary, it raised the hope of dying for the faith and thus receiving the martyr's crown. The account given by Alexander of Rhodes on his return to France aroused keen interest there, not only among clerics but among those who hoped to extend French commerce in Asia. In the face of strong Portuguese objections at this incursion into the territory supposedly assigned to them in 1494, the Société des Missions Étrangères was formed in 1658. Some clerics, however, argued that without strong commercial relations evangelization would be unsuccessful. It is no coincidence that in 1664 the Compagnie des Indes et de l'Indochine was chartered to foster French commerce east of the Cape of Good Hope.

The first priests sent out by the Missions Étrangères left France in 1660, establishing a base not in Vietnam but in the more sympathetic environment of Ayutthaya. From here representatives were sent out to Vietnam, Cambodia and Laos. Like the Jesuits, the members of the Missions Étrangères were committed to fostering a native Vietnamese clergy, and in 1666 a seminary was opened in Ayutthaya to give formal training for the priesthood. By 1700 there were forty-five Vietnamese priests, and it was even suggested that in a short time some might be appointed as bishops. In the north a convent was set up for Vietnamese women, aiming to encourage a 'love and esteem for chastity' in this 'kingdom of darkness'.[33]

As elsewhere in Asia, a major concern of the missionaries was the degree of accommodation which should be made with local beliefs. In a foreshadowing of later debates in China, a synod convened by the Missions Étrangères in Fai-fo in 1682 roundly condemned the erection of *than* (private ancestral altars) within the homes of Christians. The synod thus overruled the pleading of Vietnamese catechists, many of whom had been converted by the more tolerant Jesuits. But such disputes were only one of several considerations which made the conversion process in the eighteenth century even more difficult than it had been in the seventeenth. In France sympathy for the missionizing effort was now waning, and without financial resources the Société's work was severely impeded. The situation was not helped by quarrels over religious jurisdiction, and to settle these disputes the Pope finally decided in 1738 that the Jesuits should work in the Trinh areas and the Société in the area under the Nguyen. The decisive factor, however, was the heightened animosity from Vietnamese authorities. Previously missionaries had been able to survive because of the desire of Vietnamese rulers to obtain commercial privileges or to take advantage of European military technology. Periodic persecution had thus been interspersed with liberal intervals when missionaries were well received. In 1682, for example, priests had commented on the freedom with which Christianity could be taught in the Nguyen domains. This was in fact a time when Christians were also welcomed at the Chinese court because of their scientific and technical knowledge. With changes in China missionaries in Vietnam were similarly confronted with a much more intransigent attitude, and in 1750 most were evicted. Though estimates of Christian converts at this time may be exaggerated, the attachment to Christianity found among many Vietnamese survived to re-emerge as a significant factor in the nineteenth century.

RELIGIOUS ISSUES

By the seventeenth century the religious map of Southeast Asia had assumed a shape which modern observers will recognize. Theravāda Buddhism was well established in Burma, Thailand, Laos, and Cambodia, while Islam and Christianity were well entrenched in the island world. In Vietnam a mixture of Mahāyāna Buddhism, Taoism and popular Confucianism continued at the village level, with small pockets of Christianity, while at the élite level there was a renewed emphasis on Confucianism. But although these developments resulted in the division of Southeast Asia into different religious spheres, the process of accommodation and consolidation reveals a range of common preoccupations, an examination of which may go some way towards drawing Southeast Asia's religious history together.

[33] Cited in Georges Taboulet, *La Geste Française en Indochine*, I, Paris, 1955, 35.

The Call to Reform

A feature of Southeast Asian religious history is the periodic call for reform. To an extent this reforming tradition stems from the fact that all the religions which came to the region based their authority on a body of revered texts which could be consulted by experts and invoked to support or refute a particular custom or idea. Added to these texts were the legends attached to sages, prophets, divinities, and scholars which had assumed a standing of their own and were frequently regarded as embodying immutable truths. The intermingling of textual authority and popular tradition meant that there was usually wide scope for debate on most issues, even when questions had theoretically already been resolved by religious scholars generations before. It was therefore possible for a commonly accepted practice to be condemned as contradictory to 'correct' religious interpretation. The recurring cycle of reform was encouraged because all the world religions to a lesser or greater degree shared a belief that society's spiritual and moral life was constantly threatened by declining values. They were also agreed that this process could only be averted or slowed by a return to the unadulterated teachings of the original faith as expressed in the holy texts. It could be argued, furthermore, that the period between 1500 and 1800 was a time of rapid change in Asia generally. In many areas the kinds of changes which occurred fed a belief that society was in a state of decay. In such cases the only remedy was felt to be a purification of religious belief.

The roots of the periodic movements for religious regeneration which occurred in Southeast Asia can thus be traced to a number of causes, and should be seen as a response both to wider developments and to specific events on the local scene. The example of Buddhism is a case in point. For Southeast Asian Buddhists, Sri Lanka (Ceylon) had long stood as the fount of religious orthodoxy and tradition. At various times when the *sasana* (the sum total of Buddhist teaching) was considered in need of restoration, kings despatched monks to Sri Lanka to be reordained into the purer tradition. Through their teachers many Buddhist monks in Southeast Asia were able to trace their spiritual lineage back to some saintly figure renowned in Sri Lanka or India for his wisdom and piety. The links with Sri Lanka were particularly strong in Burma, and were especially fostered by the Mon king Dhammaceti (r. 1472–92). From 1518, however, the maintenance of these links came under pressure as the Portuguese launched repeated attacks on the Sri Lankan coast, looting shrines, turning monasteries into centres of Catholic worship, and converting by highly questionable means. In 1560 they captured the holiest of relics, the Buddha's Tooth, publicly grinding it to powder. The situation was worsened because the Portuguese came to Sri Lanka at a time of internal conflict as rulers of different kingdoms took up arms against each other. By the last quarter of the sixteenth century it was impossible to locate even five properly ordained monks. Although the Buddhist kings of Kandy took up the struggle to unify the country and hold back the Europeans, an army commander could still say in 1630 that 'our religion is fallen'.[34]

---

[34] George Davison Winius, *The Fatal History of Portuguese Ceylon*, Cambridge, Mass., 1971, 28.

The degree to which Southeast Asian Buddhists were aware of the challenges to Buddhism in Sri Lanka is uncertain, although it is known that in 1568 the ruler of Burma, Bayinnaung (r. 1551–81) received a deputation of monks from Sri Lanka, whence he also received a wife. According to later chronicles he even sent some of his best soldiers to assist the prince of Colombo. However, it was the situation in Burma itself which was probably most disturbing.

Burmese chronicles remember the early years of the sixteenth century as a disastrous time, when prolonged warfare between rival groups led to destruction of monasteries and the loss of holy relics. In 1539 a Shan king went so far as to kill 360 monks in the area around Ava. Bayinnaung attempted to restore the strength of Buddhism by initiating the construction of religious buildings, the copying of texts, the collection of relics and the clarification of religious law. Particular attention was paid to the monkhood. While Bayinnaung sponsored mass ordinations, he also commanded that monks be examined to ensure they had an adequate knowledge of religious matters. Missionary work similarly received a high priority. Whenever a hill tribe area was conquered, monks were despatched to 'rectify corruptions' such as animal sacrifice. Though Bayinnaung's edicts show due respect for the *nats*, it is clear that they were expected to lend the king their assistance. In 1569 he called on them to help in 'a quick victory over the Chief of Bangkok, who is an arch enemy of the religion', and even told the principal guardian spirits (including Mahagīri, the 'king' of the *nats*) that if they did not assist him against the Thais, he would burn down their shrines.[35]

The rulers of Burma and Siam may also have felt urgent action was necessary because a critical point in religious history was imminent. Both countries had adopted a common calendar starting in March 638 and the thousandth year of this cycle was due to fall in 1638 CE. Political disruption in both countries towards the end of the sixteenth century may have served to fuel the sense that momentous times were at hand, and this would have increased as the millennium approached. In Ayutthaya, for instance, the end of the world had already been foretold and now disturbing omens were reported; deformed elephants were found, the tower on a famous wat collapsed, and brahmins foretold the king's death.

The ruler of Ayutthaya, Prasat Thong (r. 1629–56) saw a solution to the problem in a reordering of the calendar which would give 1638 a more auspicious name. The chronicles relate that when 'the vile Burman' refused to accede to his proposal, Prasat Thong turned to ritual to rectify time. A great model of the Hindu heavens was built outside the royal palace, depicting Indra and other gods seated atop Mount Mahāmeru. A statue of the Buddha and a copy of the Tipitaka were also placed on the summit: 'At the auspicious moment His Majesty . . . ascended Mount Meru . . . [and] paid obeisance to the three jewels [i.e. the Buddha, the Law and the *Saṅgha*] . . . imploring that his request might be granted. He then raised his hands and erased the writing of the old era.'[36]

[35] Than Tun, *Royal Orders*, II. 7–8.
[36] O. Frankfurter, 'A proposed change in the Siamese era Chulasakaraj 1000 (A.D. 1638)', *T'oung Pao*, Second Series 8 (1907) 99–104.

In the Burmese capital of Ava somewhat greater importance appears to have been placed on the purification of Buddhism as part of the administrative reforms being undertaken by Thalun (r. 1629–48). Concerned with the independence of certain monastic groupings and their growing control over property and manpower, Thalun ordered land titles to be registered, and he confiscated religious estates when ownership was unclear. Efforts were made to increase central access to religious revenues and to limit ordination to those who had given evidence of genuine religious leanings. At the same time these reforms may reflect the influence of the prestigious Mahāvihāra sect which had been introduced from Pegu around 1608 and which traced its origins back to the Mahāvihāra (the Great Monastery), the fount of orthodoxy in Sri Lanka. In 1637 orders were given for 'all noxious monks' to be driven from the monkhood, and efforts were made to discourage the involvement of monks in shamanistic activities or in business. There also seems to have been a renewed effort to limit spirit worship. One royal decree for example, notes that a lady could not receive the full merit which should come from the building of a monastery if she had allowed any propitiations to be made to spirits during its construction. All these efforts to purify the *sasana* were rewarded, for in 1638 two footprints of the Buddha were discovered near the capital Ava, a particularly auspicious sign. When Thalun survived the thousandth year he, like Prasat Thong, ordered public rejoicing.[37]

The emphasis on conformity with Islamic law and the strict observance of religious duties which many Europeans noted in the archipelago at the turn of the sixteenth century may also have been partially attributable to calendrical considerations as the millennium of the Prophet's death in 1011 AH (1602–3 CE) approached. In India, some sixteenth-century mystics believed that the Prophet would not remain in his grave longer than a thousand years, and that the coming of the Mahdi (the next Prophet) and the Day of Judgement, when each individual would be held accountable for his religious life, was imminent. Akbar himself is known to have commemorated the thousand-year anniversary of the Prophet's death. If anything, the passing of the millennium brought even greater stress on the need to rejuvenate the faith. The late sixteenth and early seventeenth century gave rise to the reformed Sufism of Shaykh Ahmad Sirhindi (970–1034 AH, 1564–1624 CE), whose call for a return to the *sharī'a* and reform of the Naqshabandiyya *tarīqa* earned him the title 'renovator [Mujaddid] of the second millennium'. The task of kings, he said, was to devote their energies towards a restoration of the pristine faith and a promotion of the teachings of the Prophet. Further stimulation to this stress on orthodoxy is given by the accession of the Mughal ruler Aurangzeb in 1658, who swore to bring the lives of his subjects more into accord with the Koran. 'For the first time in their history', one authority has written, 'the Mughals beheld a rigid Muslim in their Emperor.'[38]

Given the long-standing trading links, the sense of living at a momentous time prevalent in India must have penetrated to Southeast Asia. Indeed,

[37] Jeremias van Vliet, *A Short History of the Kings of Siam*, trans. Leonard Y. Andaya, ed. D. K. Wyatt, Bangkok: Siam Society, 1975, 96; Than Tun, *Royal Orders*, I and II, passim.
[38] Stanley Lane-Poole, *Mediaeval India under Mohammedan Rule*, Delhi, 1963, 254.

the Koranic stress on Judgement Day had not been ignored by Indonesian teachers. According to a sixteenth-century Javanese text, on this occasion all would be weighed in the scales and Allah would order all those found to have failed in their religious obligations to be bound and thrown into hell fire where they would be gnawed for a hundred years by a great *nāga*. 'Whoever does not believe this is an infidel.'[39] In the late sixteenth century several rulers, like Sultan Baabullah of Ternate, displayed their piety by dressing in Arab clothing, by patronizing religious teachers, by banning pastimes such as cockfighting and by active missionizing. An Englishman in Aceh in 1599 reported that every year the king and his ministers went to the mosque 'to looke if the Messias bee come'.[40]

In Southeast Asia it was in Aceh, in fact, where the reforming mood of the early seventeenth century became most apparent. Here Ibn al-'Arabī's concept of *wujuddiyya*, the grades of being from the Absolute, had been influential in shaping the thinking of Shamsuddin (d. 1630 CE), a teacher from Pasai in north Sumatra who obtained a high position in the Acehnese court during the reign of Sultan Iskandar Muda. However, the monism at the basis of Ibn al-'Arabī's theosophy attracted criticism among mystics like Syaikh Ahmad Sirhindi. With the arrival in 1637 of a Gujerati teacher, Nūr al-Dīn al-Rānīrī, Aceh too felt the impact of these debates. While al-Rānīrī mentions Ibn al-'Arabī's name reverently, he believed that the latter's teaching had been dangerously misrepresented by Shamsuddin and other Acehnese mystics. He therefore proceeded to launch a campaign against those whom he saw as *zindik* (heretics, especially those whose teaching endangers the state). '"I said to them," wrote al-Rānīrī, "you have claimed for yourselves divinity . . . but indeed you are of the unbelieving group [*kafir*]". [When they heard this] their faces betrayed a sour expression and they bowed their heads, for surely they are polytheists.'[41]

For a time al-Rānīrī's condemnation of this tradition of Sufi teaching was apparently supported by the Acehnese ruler, for there was wholesale burning of books, and reportedly executions of those who remained obdurate.[42] Not surprisingly, this campaign alienated many local Muslims, and in 1644 al-Rānīrī abruptly left Aceh, pressured by followers of the school of Shamsuddin at the instigation of Minangkabau.

No such controversy surrounded the return in 1661 of another Acehnese mystic, Abdulrauf (c. 1617–90 CE), who had studied for nineteen years in Mecca. Given authority to propagate the Shaṭṭāriyya *ṭarīqa* in the region, Abdulrauf remains an important figure because he was very aware of the concerns and questions of Southeast Asian Muslims. It was he who produced what is believed to be the first *tafsir* or commentary on the Koran

[39] Drewes, *The Admonitions*, 69.
[40] Sayid Alhar Abbas Rizvi, *Muslim Revivalist Movements in Northern India*, Agra University, 1965, 64–78, 262; Samuel Purchas, *Purchas His Pilgrimes*, II, Glasgow, 1905, 323.
[41] Syed Muhammad Naguib al-Attas, *Rānīrī and the Wujūdiyyah of 17th Century Acheh*, Singapore, 1966, 16.
[42] That al-Rānīrī was reflecting Islamic attitudes in India is suggested by an anonymous insertion of a panygyric extolling Aurangzeb into his most famous work, the *Bustan al-Salatin*. See Catherine Grinter, 'Book IV of the Bustan us-Salatin by Nuruddin al-Raniri: A study from the manuscripts of a 17th-century Malay work written in North Sumatra', Ph.D. thesis, University of London, 1979, 27, 51–2.

in Malay (actually a translation of a popular Arabic work), as well as Malay versions of a number of other Arabic texts. Above all, he deplored the accusations of unbelief which had caused such strains in local Islam. 'It is dangerous to accuse another of *kufr* [unbelief],' he wrote. 'If you do so, and it is true, why waste words on it, and if it is not true, the accusation will turn back upon yourself.'[43] Abdulrauf's influence continued long after his death, for one of his pupils, Shaykh Burhanuddin, is said to have brought knowledge of the Shaṭṭāriyya ṭarīqa to the west coast of Sumatra, whence it moved up into the Minangkabau interior.

Elsewhere in the archipelago there were other attempts to 'purify' Islam. In Sulawesi, La Maddaremmeng, Sultan of Bone between 1631 and 1644, unsuccessfully tried to apply *sharī'a* law literally, forbidding all superstitious practices, disbanding the *bissu* (indigenous priests, usually transvestites), and freeing slaves. When Alexander of Rhodes arrived in Makassar in 1646, he reported that women there veiled themselves in public. Across the seas in Kedah a formulation of law compiled in 1667 specifically notes that a register should be kept of 'gamblers, cockfighters, opium smokers, drunkards, worshippers of trees and rocks and those not attending the mosque'.[44] In Jambi it was said that the people were 'at present so religious that the ordinary man is half like a pope and the nobles wholly so'. The king himself asked Batavia for some 'clean, unbound books with gold margins on which to write his new laws and daily sermons'.[45]

The changed mood in Jambi probably mirrored that in the court of its overlord, the central Javanese kingdom of Mataram. Here the ruler, Sultan Agung (r. 1613–46), had assumed this Muslim title in 1641. He was described as regularly attending the mosque on Fridays and as a faithful observer of the Muslim fast. In 1633 he had taken the important step of combining the Javanese and Islamic calendar. Even more renowned for its sponsorship of Islamic orthodoxy was Banten, where the ruler received the title of sultan from Mecca in 1638. Sultan Agung of Banten (r. 1651–83) was also invested by Mecca, and his son made the pilgrimage twice. It was common in the court to wear Arab rather than Javanese dress and during religious ceremonies flags from Mecca were carried in processions around the city to cleanse it of evil influences. Sultan Agung forbade the use of opium and the drinking of alcohol, and was reputed to be so pious that he would not even use spices in his food. The strongly religious mood in Banten was enhanced by the arrival of the prestigious Makassar teacher, Shaykh Yusuf, a revered scholar and a vehement opponent of the Dutch. He had gone to Mecca in 1644 as a young man and is reputed to have also studied with Nūr al-Dīn al-Rānīrī. On his return to Sulawesi in 1678 he had been shocked by the extent of opium smoking, offerings to spirits, and other non-Islamic accretions, and after unsuccessful attempts to reform local observances he went to Banten.

[43] Johns, 'Dakai'k al-Huruf', 56.
[44] R. O. Winstedt, *A History of Classical Malay Literature*, Kuala Lumpur, 1969, 169.
[45] P. A. Tiele, *Bouwstoffen voor de Geschiedenis der Nederlanders in den Maleischen Archipel*, II, The Hague, 1890, 458 fn. 2.

The latter part of the seventeenth century also saw reforming tendencies in Vietnam with a revival of emphasis on Confucianism as the state ideology. In the north this was due in part to the desire of the effective ruler, Trinh Thac, to arrogate the symbols of political legitimacy in the face of the Nguyen challenge and to support a group of erudite people as a counter to the powerful warrior clans. The extent to which Trinh leaders were themselves personally committed to Confucianist teachings is not established, but it is apparent that they found in Confucianism a useful tool for government. In this they were supported by those Vietnamese literati who felt that Confucian scholarship had declined during the long years of civil war between the Nguyen and Trinh clans, which had resulted in the partition of the country into two administrative areas. A further source of concern for Confucian scholars was the growing popularity of Buddhism, not only among villagers. Le Thanh Ton, who reigned between 1619 and 1662, was a devout Buddhist. He was also known to be interested in Christianity, and the success of Christian missionaries in Vietnam was another trend which must have caused disquiet among the small circle of Confucian literati.

It is not yet known whether there was any interaction between the Confucian scholarship of China and that of Vietnam in the seventeenth century. Did Vietnamese educated in the classical tradition share the conviction of their Chinese counterparts that the fall of the Ming dynasty in 1644 was due to moral decline? Even if they did, would they have applied this lesson to Vietnam? It is apparent, however, that Vietnamese Confucian scholars saw themselves as part of a reforming process by which the bureaucracy would triumph over the military. In the Trinh-controlled north and to a lesser extent in the new régime which was evolving under the Nguyen, local administration was reorganized, departments were made strictly hierarchical, and the law was systematized in a manner which attempted (largely unsuccessfully) to reinforce Confucian values. Officials were instructed to wear clothing appropriate to their office and all men were urged to discourage their women from extravagant indulgence. There was increasing pressure to discourage villagers from 'bad habits' such as cockfighting, gambling, sorcery, promiscuity and betel chewing. The rulers of Vietnam also attempted to reaffirm their influence over popular religion. Efforts were made to stamp out Christian practices like the wearing of crosses, and Buddhism too became a target for attack. It was customary for local guardian spirits to be 'appointed' by the court; in 1722, for instance, 2511 village deities received royal sanction.

Religious Rivalry

Another issue which became more prominent in this period was religious rivalry. As old enmities resurfaced or new ones were created, the conflicts between different groups were often articulated in religious terms as each attempted to identify itself by delineating the boundaries between 'believers' and 'non-believers'. The most enduring conflicts took place between Christianity and Islam. A century after the fall of Melaka, Christians could still sound the battle cry in the name of religion. In 1634, for instance, the Portuguese epic *Malacca Conquistada* (The Conquest of Malacca) was published, depicting Portugal's conflicts in the archipelago as part of a continuing struggle against those 'hostile to Christ': 'And when the Turk, Persian and Muslim have been defeated, the Golden Age will return to the world.' Suspicion of Muslims had plagued Portuguese dealings with Indonesians; to a considerable extent this was inherited by the northern Europeans who arrived in the archipelago at a time when popular Christianity was imbued with a fear that a resurgence of Islamic strength would herald the end of Christendom. Even in England some astrologers were predicting a Turkish sweep from Germany to Cornwall which would signal the approach of Judgement Day. Certainly the Dutch tended to see their relations with Southeast Asian Muslims in terms of the meeting of two hostile traditions, and though they always presented themselves as simple traders the VOC was itself an outgrowth of a strongly Christian culture. Church ceremonies played a prominent part in the life of even the most isolated Dutch outpost, and any victory over local enemies was publicly celebrated in Batavia as direct proof of the power of the Christian God.

Dutch military strength became apparent in 1628, when Sultan Agung of Mataram launched an unsuccessful attack against Batavia. When his campaigns failed, there was some attempt to persuade Muslim rulers to set aside old enmities and work together against a common enemy. In 1652 influential Muslim teachers persuaded Agung's son, Amangkurat I (r. 1646–77) to abandon his plans for an attack on Banten and to ally instead with Banten and Makassar against the VOC. At approximately the same time a prophecy foretelling the eviction of the Dutch from Java was reported in eastern Indonesia, and some Indonesian states took up the Islamic tradition that any peace between Muslims and Christians could be only temporary. In 1659 the ruler of Banten told the governor-general of an oath he had made to an envoy from Mecca by which he had sworn to wage war against the Christians every ten years. Sultan Amsterdam of Ternate, whose very title had been adopted as a symbol of his close association with the VOC, attempted to organize an Islamic union against the Dutch, telling neighbouring Muslim rulers that they had intended to introduce Christianity into Sulu, Mindanao, and Banten and elsewhere.

These efforts to build up a grand anti-Dutch alliance failed completely. Hostilities between Banten and Mataram began again in 1657, and Makassar was also unable to gain support against the VOC. Throughout the seventeenth century Dutch victories mounted. In 1659 the VOC attacked and defeated Palembang, an important trading port on the east coast of Sumatra; in 1667–8 expeditions quelled Acehnese expansion; 1669 saw the conquest of Makassar, an event which sent shockwaves throughout the archipelago. The ruler of Jambi expressed the feelings of many local Muslims as he wept 'to hear of the terrible defeat of the famed motherland of Islam'. The *Syair Perang Mengkasar* depicts the battle with the Dutch as a holy war, and the poet's greatest condemnation is reserved for the 'heretics', especially the Bugis and Butonese, who fought on the Dutch side against their traditional enemies.

The Christian presence in the archipelago undoubtedly contributed to the heightened consciousness of religious affiliation in the seventeenth century. A similar mood is apparent in Vietnam. The reasons for Christianity's appeal here are not altogether clear, although the dislocation caused by civil war and the resulting neglect of Confucian scholarship may provide part of the answer. The numbers of converts to the new religion concerned many Vietnamese Confucians, who felt these foreign practices would lead to a decline in devotion to the ancestors and neglect of filial piety. This would have serious implications in a state where a subject's relationship to the emperor was equated to that of a son and his father. Furthermore, there were real fears that Christianity might be a pretext for the Europeans to take over Vietnam, as they had done in the Philippines.

Distrust of Christian missionaries, who were often accused of being sorcerers, was present in Vietnam from the outset, but hostility soon extended to those who had chosen to follow the new teaching, despite the conversion of several high-born individuals. The Nguyen and the Trinh both attempted to limit the spread of Christianity by periodically banning missionaries, proscribing preaching, and enacting anti-Christian measures. At first converts were simply forbidden to display their faith by wearing images, crosses and rosaries around their necks, but penalties soon grew more severe. In 1645, for instance, two catechists were executed by the Nguyen.

Notwithstanding their suspicion of Christianity, Vietnamese rulers made it clear that they welcomed commercial exchange with Europeans. They were also eager to acquire technical skills, and Europeans of various nationalities were employed in both courts to advise on the production of arms. The perception of Europeans as bearers of both useful knowledge and a dangerously subversive ideology explains the fluctuating fortunes of the missionaries as recipients of official favours or targets of extreme displeasure. But the effort to detach trade and secular knowledge from other aspects of European culture proved quite impracticable. As we have seen, the Société des Missions Étrangères was supported by commercial interests, and missionaries were often actively involved in trade. In later years Jesuits were frequently accused of disguising themselves as traders in order to exploit the leniency shown toward the commercial presence. Discovery of this kind of subterfuge simply fuelled Trinh hostility towards all Christians, wherever they came from, and in 1712 it was ordered that the words 'student of Dutch religion' be carved on the foreheads of convicted Vietnamese converts.

The growing anti-Christian feeling in Vietnam in the early eighteenth century should also be seen against the background of wider developments in East Asia. In Japan Hideyoshi's 1587 proscription of Christian teaching had been far more rigorously enforced by the Tokugawa, while in China from around 1600 a number of anti-Christian treatises were written. Following the fall of the Ming in 1644 the Chinese court was increasingly suspicious of new ideas, primarily because of the Qing emphasis on neo-Confucian orthodoxy of the Chu Hsi school. In 1724 the imperial edict of toleration was abruptly withdrawn, and Christianity was henceforth considered a heterodox cult. In Vietnam, which received so much intellectual and religious influence from China, distrust of Christianity also gained the upper hand and even covert proselytising proved increasingly impossible. When missionaries were again expelled by the Nguyen in 1750 it was partly because of fears that Europeans, perhaps in conjunction with the Trinh, might be planning an attack. However, according to another account it was also as a result of a letter received from 'a famous Chinese priest' exhorting the Nguyen to emulate the example set by the Emperor of China.[46]

The relationship between Theravāda Buddhism and other major religions in Southeast Asia provides something of a contrast. Bayinnaung, it is true, forbade Muslims to sacrifice animals and wanted them to listen to Buddhist sermons, but observers were generally struck by the relaxed attitudes of Buddhists towards other faiths. In the words of an English sea captain, 'They hold all religions to be good that teacheth men to be good . . . and that the deities are pleased with variety of worship.'[47] Outsiders mistook this tolerance for a lack of commitment to Buddhism and periodically through the sixteenth and seventeenth centuries entertained hopes of converting them to Christianity or Islam. In 1686, for example, there was an abortive rebellion in Ayutthaya led by Makassarese mercenaries who aimed to place the ruler's half-brother on the throne as long as he would accept Islam. But the case of the Cambodian ruler who adopted Islam around 1643 is exceptional. At the end of the sixteenth century Khmer Buddhism appears to have been flourishing, and the first Portuguese missionaries who visited Cambodia in 1555–6 found a well-organized *sangha*. Forty years later a Spanish Dominican estimated that there were 1500 Buddhist monks in Phnom Penh alone. However, attacks by the Thais had made Khmer military weakness apparent. The ruler had earlier indicated he might be willing to adopt Christianity in return for assistance, and it is probably in this context that his conversion to Islam should be considered. It is obvious, furthermore, that Khmers had difficulty explaining why the king should have taken this action, and the chronicles attribute it to his overwhelming love for his Malay wife and the spells cast by Malay magic. The consequences, they continue, were serious, for the ruler's failure to carry out his royal duties and protect the *sangha* caused Khmer Buddhism to decay. It was only restored when a coup brought about the installation of a Buddhist king once more.

Other Theravāda Buddhist kings might have looked on alien religions with interest and tolerance, but they were never persuaded to set Buddhism aside. A good instance of the environment which fostered this tolerance is found in Ayutthaya, where Catholic missionaries had been permitted to preach since the early sixteenth century. More than a hundred years later Ayutthaya was chosen as the headquarters of the Société des Missions Étrangères, and French records acknowledge with appreciation the provision of building materials by Narai (r. 1656–88) for the construction of a church on the city outskirts. Reference is made to the opening of a seminary and schools where religious instruction was given

---

[46] Taboulet, *La Geste Française*, 99.
[47] Alexander Hamilton, *A New Account of the East Indies*, ed. William Foster, London, 1930, II. 30.

to 'the children of Cochin Chinese and Tonkinese', while the clergy studied Siamese and Pāli, the scriptural language of Theravāda Buddhism. In 1667 a court official and his wife were baptized.[48] It is even possible that contact with missionaries may have influenced a new type of historical writing in Thai. Known as *phongsawadan*, this is more secular in its orientation than the traditional *tamnan* literature, and depicts the history of kingdoms as part of a universal environment rather than a purely Buddhist one. But such developments should not cloud the fact that the kings of Ayutthaya never doubted Buddhism's superiority to Christianity, whose priests drank wine and condoned the taking of animal life. A ruler like Narai could well take a lively interest in both Christianity and Islam, but any hope of conversion was a chimera.

Religion and Kingship

A third theme which runs through the religious history of Southeast Asia is the relationship between religion and kingship. All the religions which came to Southeast Asia from outside were closely connected with the ruler and the court, and thus became an integral part of the constellations of political power which had emerged by the mid-seventeenth century. Indigenous concepts of a leader as an elder kinsman, whose 'luck', possession of powerful objects, and relationship with supernatural forces set him above his fellows were reinforced by the ideas and the vocabulary of the imported religions. Among Malays, for example, the special power of kings which would punish those guilty of treason, previously subsumed in the Sanskrit word *śakti*, was now conveyed by the Arabic term *daulat*. In Java, too, it was an Arabic-derived word *wahyu*, meaning 'revelation from Allah', which Javanese used to refer to the dazzling light which denotes the legitimate king. In addition the world religions brought with them a formidable body of opinion amassed over centuries concerning the duties of rulers and the criteria by which a 'good' or a 'bad' reign could be judged. While traditions and vocabulary differed, there were underlying similarities. All kings, Christian or Muslim, Buddhist or Confucian, should ideally act not only as supporters of religion but as exemplars of moral and spiritual piety. By so doing they maintained an order in the mundane world and a harmony with the unseen one which merited the loyalty and obedience of their subjects. The Buddha's teachings thus stressed that a king should gain the favour of his subjects 'by the four elements of popularity', which were liberality, affability, justice and impartiality. Throughout his kingdom the religion and the people should be nurtured, no wrongdoing should prevail, and wealth should be given to whomsoever was poor.[49] Southeast Asians were taught that devout rulers who governed wisely would be rewarded, but a king who failed in his duties would ultimately be punished, either by the rejection of his subjects, by reincarnation as a lesser being, or by damnation on Judgement Day. The

[48] Adrien Launay, *Histoire de la Mission de Siam 1662–1811*, Documents Historiques, I, Paris, 1920, 17.
[49] Cited in Robert Lester, *Theravada Buddhism in Southeast Asia*, Ann Arbor, 1973, 62–5.

most important religious thinker of medieval Islam, al-Ghazālī, expressed the Muslim view thus: 'The man closest to God is the just Sultan, and the man most hateful and contemptible is the unjust Sultan . . . The harshest torment at the Resurrection Day will be for the unjust Sultan.'[50]

Nevertheless, what amounted to a kind of contractual relationship between ruler and subject was often obscured by the enhanced status assumed by Southeast Asian kings, to which religion itself made a direct contribution. Theravāda Buddhist rulers inherited the politico-religious notion of *cakkavatti* or Universal Monarch who would prepare the world for the coming of the next Buddha. All Burmese kings in the seventeenth century were honoured at their death with the funeral of a Universal Monarch, and the refusal of a ruler to recognize his neighbour's *cakkavatti* claims was often the prelude to prolonged warfare. The reign names assumed by Buddhist rulers also proclaimed them as *dhammarāja* or king of the [Buddhist] law, and they could similarly be compared to Hindu gods such as Śiva, Viṣṇu, and Indra. The 'Three Worlds Cosmology' composed by a Thai prince in the fourteenth century was in no doubt that pious kings 'are called *devata* [divine being] by common agreement'.[51] In a similar mode Muslim kings in Southeast Asia, like Akbar of India, may well have applied to themselves the mystic notion of the Perfect Man, the manifestation of Allah's desire to be known; a poem by Hamzah Fansuri thus speaks of the king of Aceh as 'one of Allah's elect, perfect in communion with Him'. Rulers took a leading role in public worship, and the names of the sultans and a recitation of their deeds were included in sermons during the Friday prayers and on religious holidays. In Vietnam the tendency to attribute special powers to kings may have compensated for the limitations which Confucianism placed on the sacral status assigned to rulers, and for their exclusion from a political role during the shogun-type government of the seventeenth and eighteenth centuries. The devout Buddhist king Le Thanh Ton, for example, was commonly believed to be the reincarnation of a pious Ly ruler who had lived four hundred years earlier.

Language, symbols and ritual derived from religious traditions all formed part of the arsenal of kingly prestige. Sacred texts, religiously potent items like a white elephant, a banner from Mecca, holy water, became part of the royal regalia, and he who possessed them was imbued with supernatural powers. Court ceremonial was in many respects a form of religious ritual. A Dutchman living in Ayutthaya in the seventeenth century described the royal acts of religious piety which reaffirmed the king's legitimacy. 'Once every year . . . the king of Siam shews himself by water and land in state to his people, going to the principal Temple of the Gods, to offer there for the welfare of his Person and Kingdom.'[52] In Burma and Siam a number of the functions previously performed by brahmins were assumed by Buddhist monks; in 1693 a French ambassador referred to an 'Oath of

---

[50] F. R. C. Bagley, trans., *Ghazāli's Book of Counsel for Kings (Naṣīhat al-Mulūk)*, London, 1964, 14–15.

[51] Frank E. Reynolds and Mani B. Reynolds, trans., *Three Worlds According to King Ruang*, Berkeley, 1982, 217.

[52] Joost Schouten, *A Description of the Government, Might, Religion, Customs, Traffick and other Remarkable Affairs in the Kingdom of Siam*, Bangkok: Siam Society, 1986, 128.

Fidelity' at the Ayutthaya court that consisted 'in swallowing the water, over which the Talapins [i.e. monks] do pronounce some imprecations against him, who is to drink it, in case he fails in the Fidelity which he owes to his King'. In Vietnam a Confucian scholar was similarly responsible for organizing the construction of altars dedicated to ancestral spirits before which the oath of loyalty to the ruler was sworn. *Ulamā*, the learned men of Islam, were equally evident in archipelago courts. An eighteenth-century description of royal Malay *adat*, for example, describes the prominent place given to the *kadi* (cadi, principal Islamic authority) at such ancient rituals as the rocking of the queen's abdomen in the seventh month of pregnancy (*melenggang perut*).

The religious scholars who surrounded the ruler dominated areas of government where literacy was essential. It was they, for instance, who drew up the law codes, adapting Indian, Chinese or Arab models to the local scene and arguing with those who defended traditional custom. The Mons, the Burmans, the Thai, the Lao, the Lan Na Thai and the Khmer all had their version of the *dhammathat*, the Laws of Manu derived from Hinduism, and a Burmese edict of 1607 specifies that judges should consult these when a punishment is to be determined. While functioning *sharī'a* courts in Muslim states may not have been common, a sixteenth-century Javanese text roundly states that 'it is unbelief when people are involved in a lawsuit, and [refuse to] settle the dispute according to the Law of Islam . . . and insist on taking it to an infidel judge'. Specialists in religion were also the major producers of the chronicles which recorded the country's history, tracing its links to the great faraway centres of religion and sometimes to the founder himself. The nineteenth-century Burmese text, the *Glass Palace Chronicle*, thus sees Burma's kings as directly descended from Buddha, and in the same fashion al-Rānīrī's *Bustan al-Salatin* places Aceh firmly within the history of the Islamic world. In these accounts of the past, rulers and their ancestors are depicted as playing a crucial role in the propagation of the religion. In one text from Sulawesi, for instance, it is the king and not his saintly teacher who is favoured by a vision of the Prophet commanding him to 'embrace Islam and bring others to the same faith, and wage war on those who oppose me in this'.[53]

Support from the religious hierarchy gave the ruler practical assistance in the exercise of government. Perhaps the most forthright instance of this alliance is the relationship between Church and state in the Christian areas of the Philippines. The governor in Manila was the ultimate authority of the colony, as the representative of the Spanish king, but the archbishop and the heads of the religious orders were all members of the *Junta de Autoridades*, a committee appointed to advise him. On a number of occasions the archbishop even acted as governor when the position fell vacant. At the provincial level the religious orders worked with the Spanish *alcalde mayor*, while the Filipino *gobernadorcillos* were expected to co-operate with the parish priest. Because relatively few lay Spaniards

---

[53] Cited in Russell Jones, 'Ten conversion myths from Indonesia' in Nehemia Levtzion, *Conversion to Islam*, New York and London, 1979, 150.

lived outside Manila it was the priest who represented the authority of the
Spanish Crown. He was the local schoolteacher, he compiled the records
and helped collect taxes, supervised the repairs of bridges and roads, drew
up grammars, and directed the defence of the town against attacks by hill
tribes or by Muslims from the south. But elsewhere in Southeast Asia the
religious hierarchy was normally just as supportive of the ruler, who was
after all the chief sponsor of religious activity. In the Islamic areas high-
ranking Muslim officials, credited with superior knowledge and usually
linked to the ruler through marriage, became leading figures in government. In Makassar where there was a special religious council called the
sarat, Sultan Hasanuddin (r. 1653–69) received the Dutch surrounded by
his *ulamā*, and in 1699, when it was decided that a queen could no longer
rule in Aceh, it was the son of the *kadi* who succeeded as Sultan. In normal
circumstances a king could count on the support of his religious appoin-
tees. A Spanish observer in Brunei in the late sixteenth century described
how the *kadi besar* (great judge) charged all nobles to obey the heir who
would inherit the kingdom, 'being greater than the others'.[54]

In the Buddhist kingdoms rulers similarly relied heavily on the services
of monks, who acted as royal teachers, envoys, scribes, and advisers. In
return, they were granted various privileges, including exemption from
taxes. Royal edicts in Burma also freed the family of a monk from corvée
duties, and a French visitor to Ayutthaya in the late seventeenth century
remarked that it was favours of this kind that contributed to the large
number of men entering the monkhood. The extensive network of monasteries and religious institutions set up by successive kings effectively
extended the arm of central government across the country, with monks
and novices accorded *sakdina* grades like any other Ayutthayan subject.[55]
Royal endowments to religion also acted to reduce the power of regional
lords, as in the southern Siamese province of Phattalung where Ayutthayan
kings granted a considerable measure of land and people to support
ecclesiastical establishments. Religion could equally be used to create or
strengthen ties between patron and client. A king of Laos, for instance,
anxious to expand his control over settlements distant from the capital,
sponsored the ordination ceremonies of the sons of local notables in order
to obtain the allegiance of their fathers.

Royal authority in the religious sphere could be further reinforced as
rulers were called upon to settle disagreements between different religious
groups. This mediating role assumes particular importance in Burma and
Siam, where apparently no acknowledged patriarch of the Buddhist monkhood emerged until the eighteenth century. Instead, there seem to have
been a number of *saṅgharāja*, or 'rulers of the *saṅgha*', senior monks who
apparently had some localized following. Because of the lack of a single
religious authority, disputes between (for example) the 'village-dwelling'
and 'forest-dwelling' monks regarding practices and behaviour often
required royal mediation. In Burma one source mentions a village monk
who incited his followers to burn the books of forest dwellers, but was

---

[54] Carroll, 'Berunai in the Boxer Codex', 11.
[55] These *sakdina* grades reflected a theoretical apportioning of rice lands, based on an
individual's social distance from the king.

stopped by the king's intervention. Even among the more orthodox 'village' monks, questions as to correct language, dress, deportment, could give rise to deep schisms. In the early seventeenth century one royal edict from Burma refers to further disputes between 'drum-beating monks' and 'lantern-turning monks' as well as arguments over the kind of robe which should be worn. The ruler apparently tried to effect a compromise by stating that monks could wear robes of any style and that as long as they led a good life sects were unimportant.[56]

This normally symbiotic relationship between royal and religious spheres nonetheless contained an inherent tension because as established religions extended their spiritual hold they also acquired control over people and territory. They could therefore be simultaneously co-operating with the ruler and potentially in competition with him. In turn this raised the issue of how far a king's authority extended into the religious domain. At times strains between rulers and the religious leadership could become so acute that they erupted into open confrontation. In such cases the ruler could be accused of neglecting his religious obligations, and the responsibility of the religious to a higher authority or greater principles be evoked. The *Taj us-Salatin*, the seventeenth-century Acehnese text on statecraft, thus argues that the king who does not follow the law of Allah is the enemy of Allah, and it was obligatory to oppose him. Vietnamese Confucian scholars could turn to the writings of the philosopher Mencius (372–289 BC), who insisted that the ruler's task was to provide 'benevolent government' and that if he failed to do so regicide was justified.

While the circumstances underlying each instance of conflict obviously varied greatly, one could argue that the ability of kings to curb the power of religious authorities was particularly problematic in the Islamic areas, where there was no 'priesthood' as such and where local centres of religious activity maintained a strong tradition of autonomy. An extreme case of royal frustration occurred in Mataram in 1648 when Amangkurat I moved to suppress opposition by killing about two thousand Islamic 'popes' who had allied with his younger brother. In so doing, of course, he merely fuelled opposition to himself. In the Buddhist states and in the Philippines, on the other hand, religious establishments were generally more integrated into a network responsive to supralocal authorities. Buddhist rulers, invoking their status as protectors of religion, could thus issue orders for the purification of the *sangha*, enabling them to strip monasteries of land and property, evict senior but uncooperative monks from the order and regain control over lost manpower. In 1684, for example, King Narai ordered that any Ayutthayan monk who could not read a certain Pāli text should be expelled. A few days later a French observer noted 'thousands of men still wearing the robe of the priesthood but working on the land, in the brickyards and bearing the trouble brought upon them through their ignorance'.[57] The Spanish Crown, faced by recurring disputes between church and secular authorities concerning the boundaries of civil and

---

[56] Than Tun, *Royal Orders*, II. 9.
[57] Nicolas Gervaise, *Histoire Naturelle et Politique du Royaume de Siam*, Paris, 1688, reprinted Bangkok 1929, 83.

religious jurisdiction, was able to take even more drastic action. In 1768 the Jesuit order was expelled from all Spanish domains because of suspected disloyalty. Overall, however, the Church in the Philippines proved well able to hold its own against the government, and in 1781 a French visitor commented on the great influence of the clergy. 'These friars are the masters of the country and are more absolute in the Philippines than the king himself.'[58]

Religion and Rebellion

The above remarks lead on to a fourth consideration—the manner in which religion, normally supportive of lay authorities, could also provide the inspiration for popular rebellion against them. In our period significant threats to the ruler's position came not from the formal religious establishment, with whom his ties were usually strong. The real challenge came from individual religious leaders who stood at the periphery of the officially sponsored order, whose status was often derived from indigenous traditions and who at times of social disruption could be seen as an alternative and legitimate authority. Throughout Southeast Asia the belief that even a person of humble origins could acquire extraordinary powers and claim a special relationship with the supernatural could give rise to sudden eruptions of localized religious movements when prophecies, dreams, magic, amulets, claims of invulnerability and secret revelations provided a potent weaponry. Thus in Vietnam at a time of dynastic decline in the early sixteenth century a miracle-working pagoda keeper claiming to be a descendant of the Tran and a reincarnation of Indra led a rebellion involving many thousands of people. So potent was his appeal that he was for a short time able to call himself king of Dai Viet. In 1581, when Ayutthaya had fallen under the overlordship of the Burmese, a holy man led a rebellion which broke out in the nearby countryside. Again, following the 'palace revolution' in Ayutthaya in 1688 a Laotian styling himself a 'man of merit' or *phu mi bun* succeed in convincing the governor of Korat that he was possessed of such magical power that it would be futile to attempt his arrest. According to the royal chronicles, over four thousand men, eighty-four elephants and more than a hundred horses were collected on behalf of the rebel forces before the latter were finally forced to submit.

Such figures could also be nurtured by the Messianic tradition which was found in all the world religions. In Buddhism, for instance, it was believed that the future Buddha, Metteiya, would one day descend to the earth to preach the final sermon, enabling all those who listened to attain *nibbāṇa* (nirvana) in this life rather than after an infinite number of rebirths. Although Buddhist texts specified that aeons must pass before the Metteya's appearance, there were recurring rumours that this might occur much earlier than originally foretold. The Mahdi, the next Muslim prophet, is most associated with Sh'ia Islam, but popular beliefs among

---

[58] Cited in Peter Gowing, *Islands under the Cross: the story of the Church in the Philippines*, Manila, 1967, 72.

Sunnī Muslims also incorporated numerous *hadith* which held out the promise of a great religious leader or perhaps a series of leaders who would unite Muslims and revive the faith. In desperate times these hopes were readily attached to individual holy men who predicted the advent of a new age when the tribulations of the present would be at an end.

There are numerous references to rebellions led by 'holy men' in the island world from the late sixteenth century onwards. In part this is a function of the Dutch and Spanish sources, for Europeans were more likely to notice and record such events than were the royal chroniclers. However, it also seems probable that uprisings of this type were in fact more common in maritime Southeast Asia at this time because the arrival of the Europeans had fostered extensive economic and social changes and because the European presence gave popular discontent a new focus. The Philippines, where a sometimes imposed Christianity was linked with other more onerous demands from the colonial government, is the most obvious example. As early as 1574, during an attack by a group of Chinese on Manila, local people turned on a church in the nearby settlement of Tondo, destroying or stealing sacred ornaments, vestments and relics. The practitioners of the ancient beliefs, the *babaylan*, who found themselves the direct target of Christian propaganda, retaliated by leading localized raids on convents and churches, often from places of refuge in the hills. By the 1660s a number of rebellions had already broken out against the Spanish, many of which were led by traditional religious leaders. What is interesting about these movements is the extent to which Christian symbols had been incorporated into the vocabulary of resistance. The leader of one rebellion which broke out in Bohol, for instance, claimed that he too could perform Christ-like miracles, change water into wine, rejuvenate old people, and bring the dead to life. Another uprising in Panay was led by an indigenous transvestite priest, described by the Spanish as 'a noted sorcerer and priest of the demon' who dressed in the clothes of a woman. Claiming that his instructions came from the ancestors, he entitled one of his deputies Son, another the Holy Ghost, and a 'shameless prostitute' (presumably a female shaman) 'Maria Santisima'. His movement had its own apostles, bishops and popes, and he himself took the title 'Eternal Father'.[59]

The goals of these localized rebellions in the Philippines during the seventeenth century were only vaguely articulated but they clearly rejected the payment of tribute, the rendering of corvée labour and subservience to Spain. In effect, their leaders were seeking to turn back the clock, to restore society to what it had been prior to the Spanish arrival. Yet, while attacks might be made on friars and religious buildings as symbols of Spanish rule, there was rarely a rejection of Christianity as such. The leader of a Pangasinan uprising in 1660–1, one of the *principalia* named Don Andres Malong, saw to it that his followers heard Mass and received the sacraments. He said they 'had no desire to abandon the faith of Jesus Christ which they had professed at baptism . . . and would give their lives

---

[59] Eric Anderson, 'Traditions in conflict: Filipino responses to Spanish colonialism, 1565–1665', Ph.D. thesis, University of Sydney, 1977, 146–7.

in its defense, and with the help of God they would be faithful sons of the Church until death'.[60]

One of the reasons behind the failure of this and other rebellions was the lack of co-ordination between neighbouring areas. Malong's revolt coincided with others in Pampanga and Ilocos, but the Pampangans came to terms with the Spanish without his knowledge. Secondly, only extraordinary conditions of hardship and exceptional leadership could maintain effective resistance. The Spanish remarked that the typical rebellion began to fade after less than a month and, as supporters melted away, local *principalia* themselves began to contribute troops to the Spanish forces. When Malong himself was captured, it was with the aid of native spies. The quelling of such movements was therefore not difficult. Several hundred Filipinos might be involved, but a company of Spanish soldiers supported by native levies was sufficient to put down resistance.

Independent movements were usually regarded with suspicion by established religious leaders. In 1681, for instance, two men returned to Ambon from Batavia with a new Islamic teaching focused on the telling of the *tasbih* (rosary), which consisted of two hundred beads each corresponding to a specific Arabic prayer. Devotees were told that by praying in a certain ritually prescribed way they could gain heaven, not only for themselves but for their ancestors. Neophytes had their heads shaved, were given new names, bathed in the river, and were then admitted to the community. But the new movement aroused the ire of local *ulamā*, who declared it to be contrary to Islamic tradition. Supported by village heads, they appealed to the VOC. The Batavian Council considered that the movement's 'undue' stress on prayers imperilled not only ordinary work but the performance of corvée duties. In consequence, it was declared heretical and its leaders banned.

On Java, where the impact of the European presence was strongest, the rebellions of the seventeenth and early eighteenth centuries had far-reaching effects. The long tradition of holy men, ranging from guardians of sacred graves to hermits and wandering teachers, provided a pool of potential leaders of dissent. If they and their followers allied with discontented relatives of the ruler, they could mount a serious challenge to his authority. In 1630, for example, a rebellion broke out in central Java with adherents of local holy figures supported by a branch of the royal family. This uprising, which aimed to replace Sultan Agung, was put down by force, but the growing Dutch influence on Java meant that popular unrest frequently took the form of an 'anti-kafir' movement to which was added specific Javanese ideas, such as the concept of a just king, the Ratu Adil, who would usher in a new age of peace and prosperity.

These factors came together in the 1670s during the rebellion against Amangkurat led by a Madurese prince, Trunajaya, who had allied with Mataram's crown prince. Much of Trunajaya's popular support can be traced to his marriage to a daughter of Panembahan Kajoran, a revered holy man, and to the support he received from the Sunan of Giri, another

---

[60] Rosario Mendoza Cortes, *Pangasinan, 1572–1800*, Quezon City, 1974, 155.

religious authority from east Java. Prophecies foretold Trunajaya's eventual victory, in accordance with Allah's will, and identified the Dutch as a
principal enemy. Sunan Giri even said Java would not prosper until the
infidels were evicted. The sense of impending crisis was deepened by the
approach of the Javanese year 1600 (1677 CE), for there was a common
belief that the end of a Javanese century would witness major events such
as the fall of a dynasty. Omens, like the eruption of Mount Merapi, were
interpreted as a sign that Judgement Day was at hand, and the crown
prince of Banten, then in Mecca, himself sent back a message to say that
the Javanese war was a sign that the end of the world was near. In this
atmosphere Trunajaya was readily perceived as the harbinger of a new age
at the expected fall of the dynasty, and there can be little doubt that
Amangkurat would have been defeated had it not been for Dutch support.
The succession of Amangkurat II in 1677 did little to resolve popular
opposition to the dynasty, and the following year he was attacked by a
holy man credited with invulnerability, together with forty armed followers.

The sense of crisis infected other areas of the archipelago, although here
protest was more clearly directed against the Dutch than the rulers who
had allied with them. To the west, a Minangkabau 'saint' appeared near
Melaka in 1677 with a force of nearly four thousand men from Rembau,
Naning and other areas. The VOC intercepted several letters here and in
Sumatra calling on all Muslims to take up the sword against the infidel
Dutch and promising that all those who died in the strife would
be immediately transported to heaven. Of more concern was another
Minangkabau-led movement under a Sultan Ahmad Syah, the so-called
Rāja Śakti, a prince who in 1685 claimed he was commissioned by Allah to
expel all Dutchmen. What sets him aside from other holy men is his vision
of an archipelago-wide alliance: letters were sent to Siam, Aceh, west
Sumatra, Borneo, and apparently he also attempted to establish links with
Amangkurat and Surapati, a former Balinese slave himself regarded as a
holy man who between 1686 and 1707 maintained his own independent
domain in eastern Java.

While religion played an important part in the articulation of popular
protest in the Islamic areas of the archipelago, it was never sufficient to
gain undivided support against the Europeans and the local rulers they
supported. The imprisonment or death of a leader could quickly see the
disintegration of his following. Nonetheless, such movements were rarely
taken lightly. An object lesson came in 1735 in Surabaya, where a holy man
called Mangunjaya lived on a hill outside the town with about twenty
followers. Believing he had been given the responsibility to take over
Surabaya and protect Islam, Mangunjaya began to plan an attack on the
VOC officials. Hearing of the conspiracy, the Dutch Resident in alliance
with the Javanese regent of Surabaya ordered Mangunjaya's hilltop residence to be stormed. Nine hundred men were used in the attack, during
which Mangunjaya was killed. So convinced were these Javanese troops of
his invulnerability that his body was stabbed more than a hundred times.[61]

---

[61] Luc Nagtegaal, 'Rijden op een Hollandse tijger. De noordkust van Java en de V.O.C.
1680–1742', Ph.D. thesis, Utrecht University, 1988, 211.

The Status of Women

Yet another consideration which emerges from an examination of religious developments up to 1800 is the retraction of the public role of women. None of the world religions which came to Southeast Asia provided any textual basis for female participation in religious rituals at the highest levels. The Le law codes of Vietnam might have accorded females more rights than did their Tang counterparts, but the legal status of a woman was always below that of a man from the same social class. Thus the Trung sisters, who led a rebellion against the Chinese in 43 CE and were popularly regarded as goddesses with their own temple cults, were in Confucian historiography overshadowed by their husbands. In the Buddhist countries of Southeast Asia it was also accepted that women were inferior to men and must be reborn as males before they could aspire to the higher stages of being. Early Buddhism did allow an active religious role for women, but the tradition of higher female ordination was lost early in the present millennium. In fifteenth-century Burma one of the *sangharāja* was a woman, but two hundred years later observers in Ayutthaya noted that while there were women who led secluded lives and followed a discipline similar to that of monks, they were not full members of the *sangha*.

Christianity had remained true to the Pauline tradition which enjoined submission on women, both because females were created after males and as a punishment for the sin of Eve. While Christian missionaries in Southeast Asia did insist on monogamy as a prerequisite to baptism, they were equally sure that only in paradise would women gain spiritual equality with men. For a devout native woman opportunities to develop a fuller religious life were few, although the first Spanish nuns had arrived in 1621. One initiative in this direction occurred in 1684 in Manila, when a Chinese mestizo founded a *beaterio*, a foundation for pious native women (*beatas*) who wore a religious habit and pursued a devotional life patterned after that of Saint Ignatius of Loyola. Despite a lesser status, it remains clear that female participation made a significant contribution to the evolution of popular Christianity in the Philippines. Missionaries often commented on the piety of Filipinas who took a prominent role in Christian celebrations and church festivals. During the Easter Sunday procession in one parish in Nueva Segovia, for example, it was customary for women to carry the image of the Blessed Virgin. Finding this custom difficult to eradicate, the religious authorities finally specified that at least the devotees should be clothed in a seemly fashion.

Islam too stressed the subordinate position of women. Man had authority over women because Allah had made the one superior to the other, and a wife's duty was therefore to bear children and remain a loyal helpmate to her husband. A Malay manuscript, describing a particularly faithful wife, exhorts its hearers to pattern themselves after her. 'That is how women who love their husbands behave. We women believers should be devoted to our husbands, in the hope that we shall obtain the mercy of Allah the Exalted in the hereafter.'[62] It is certainly true that Muslim women in

---

[62] Russell Jones, ed. and trans., *Hikayat Sultan Ibrahim bin Adham*, Berkeley: Center for South and Southeast Asian Studies, University of California, 1985, 173–5.

Southeast Asia were much freer than their sisters in India or the Arab
lands, but the prominence of females in indigenous religious ritual which
had caught the attention of early missionaries became progressively less
apparent as communal worship came to be dominated by males. Thus in
sixteenth-century Brunei, 'the common people go to the mosque and the
women never go but it is the men'. In Makassar, where the women had
their own mosque, the wife of one of the leading *ulamā* had the effrontery
to go to the public prayers on a fast day, but her husband deemed the
mosque so profaned that 'he took his wife by the hand and publicly
divorced her, as unworthy to be the wife of a priest of the Law'.[63]
     The traditional place of women in religious ritual in Southeast Asia was
not easily taken away. But increasingly they tended to be relegated to the
domain of shamanism and spirit propitiation, while the high positions
of the dominant faiths were reserved for males. In the process the status of
the shaman, both female and transvestite, declined. Islam and Christianity
took strong exception to the homosexuality which was often associated
with indigenous religious figures such as the Bugis-Makassar *bissu*, and
spirit mediums are among those specifically excluded from the Burmese
State Council or *hlutdaw*. An English sea captain in the early eighteenth
century described how women and 'hermaphrodites' at a Burmese feast
'danced a dance to the gods of the earth',[64] but there is a significant
absence of any *nat kadaw* (*nat* wives) in spirit appeasement at the court
level, where brahmins and monks were in charge of ritual. Because
women were now the principal practitioners of 'village' as opposed to
'court' magic, they were far more likely to be accused of unacceptable
practices such as witchcraft, and a Burmese law of 1785 provides extensive
instructions for immersion of a woman in water 'to find out if she is
a witch'.[65]
     The redefinition of female status had obvious implications for the
exercise of political authority. Sparse though the evidence is, the sources
suggest that the idea of a male–female duality which comprises the whole
had permeated concepts of power in much of early Southeast Asia. Hindu
ideas of kingship had in many respects reinforced this notion, and in
the early Indianized kingdoms the sexual union of a king and his queen,
the bearer of his *śakti*, was regarded as a mystic ritual essential to the
fertility of the realm. In a number of early societies it also appears that
kingship was seen as properly belonging to the man who gained possession of the community's highest-ranking female, whose body symbolized
the land itself. One scholar has been led to speculate that in early Burma
'political power, though held by men, was transmitted through women'.[66]
While less common, it was at times possible for a woman (usually a widow
or dowager queen) to reign in her own right. During our period this is
no longer evident in the mainland states, but in the archipelago a number
of seventeenth-century kingdoms, notably Aceh, were under female rulers.

[63] Gervaise, *A Historical Description*, 158–9.
[64] Hamilton, *A New Account of the East Indies*, II. 31.
[65] Than Tun, *Royal Orders*, IV. 102.
[66] J. S. Furnivall, 'Matriarchal vestiges in Burma', *Journal of the Burma Research Society*, 1,
    1 (1911) 21.

In Islamic courts this must have led to some criticism from *ulamā* who accepted the prevailing Muslim view that 'women cannot be allowed to assume power, for they are wearers of the veil and have not complete intelligence'.[67] In 1699 the annals of Aceh allege that a *fatwa* arrived from Mecca decreeing that no women should now be permitted to rule, since this was against the law of Allah. Though a historian can still document the continuing influence of women at all levels of Southeast Asian society, it does not appear that their status has been improved by the spread of the major world religions into the region.

THE EIGHTEENTH CENTURY

To some extent periodization is always arbitrary, but there is some argument for regarding the eighteenth century as a time of special interest in the evolution of Southeast Asia's religious history. Disruptive economic changes, civil wars, dynastic collapse, the expanding European presence have contributed to a view that this period is largely one of fragmentation, if not positive decline. Yet an examination of religious developments suggests that Southeast Asians saw in these apparent forces of disintegration a call for renewed religious activity. Accordingly, the eighteenth century witnessed not merely a reaffirmation of the commitments of the past but the formulation of new solutions to deal with unprecedented social and economic pressures.

In Vietnam the Trinh court was steadily losing its hold in the north, and to a lesser extent central government under the Nguyen was also weakening in the south. Throughout the eighteenth century rebellions proliferated. The popularity of Buddhism and Christianity is indicative of peasant dissatisfaction with élite efforts to strengthen Confucianism, and during this period Buddhist temples frequently served as foci of discontent, with monks sometimes organizing their followers into armed militia. Rebels often questioned accepted Confucian values, mocked scholars, abused mandarins and even made fun of the emperor. The educated bureaucracy, however, generally considered that the cause of the prevailing social ills was a collapse of properly ordered human relationships which neo-Confucianism had raised to cosmic principles. Many scholars also felt the only solution was rebellion since, said one, 'for a long time all idea of hierarchy and values has disappeared'.[68] The Tayson brothers who led the great revolt which broke out in 1771, though themselves of peasant background, adopted as their model the ancient sage emperors praised in Confucian writings. Their chief mentor in fact compared himself to Yi Yin, the famous reformer of classical texts who had said he could assist any ruler to become a sage king. In the following century court-sponsored Confucianism flourished anew in Vietnam, yet the Tayson's emphasis on the importance of the people in the functioning of the state and their declaration of the equality of rich and poor alike augured the ultimate end

---

[67] John A. Williams, *Themes of Islamic Civilization*, Berkeley and London, 1975, 105.
[68] Cited in Thomas Hodgkin, *Vietnam. The Revolutionary Path*, London, 1981, 80.

of the old order. It is significant that of all the imported belief systems it was Confucianism, whose village roots were the most shallow, which was finally to disappear despite hundreds of years of élite patronage.

The eighteenth century was also a critical time in the history of Islam. With the decline of the Ottoman empire the holy cities of Mecca and Medina had reasserted their independence, and their ability to act as the major centres for Islamic study was enhanced. As international shipping expanded, growing numbers of Muslims were able to visit Mecca and Medina, 'the two sanctuaries' (Haramayn), as pilgrims or for longer periods of study. Here they could choose to study under various Haramayn scholars, men from several Muslim countries who were linked by close student–teacher ties and who shared a similar view of religious matters. One of the prime concerns of several Haramayn teachers was to encourage the re-examination of early Islamic sources, rather than merely accepting the judgment of previous scholarship. Like most reformers, they were also especially concerned with purifying society by eliminating accretions not approved by the Koran or Muslim law. Opposing the more monistic forms of mysticism, they were affiliated with *ṭarīqa* known for their commitment to reform of Sufism. Several of the leading teachers in the Haramayn were members of the Naqshabandiyyah, which continued its role as exponent of strict adherence to the *sharī'a*.

The environment of Mecca and Medina clearly had a formative effect on many of the overseas Muslim students who studied with them. A notable example was Shaykh Waliyullah of Delhi (1113–76 AH, 1702–62 CE) who returned from Mecca to continue in the same tradition as Ahmad Sirhind. He condemned the decadence he saw in contemporary Islam, but also envisaged a purifed Sufism which would foster the *sharī'a* as an integral part of Muslim life. In Southeast Asia a strong influence derived from the teachings of the vigorous but puritanical leader from Arabia, Muḥammad ibn 'Abd al-Wahhāb (1115–1201 AH, 1703–87 CE) who had also studied in Mecca. There he became a controversial figure because of his call for a complete social and moral reconstruction of Muslim society, his condemnation of many Sufi teachings and practices such as the worship of saints and veneration for holy graves, and his attack on the unquestioning acceptance of established authority in religious matters. The pristine law was to be the basis of the rejuvenated Muslim faith.

The influence of Wahhābism has been traced in Minangkabau in the early nineteenth century, but the traffic between Southeast Asia and the Islamic heartlands had been steadily growing throughout the eighteenth century. In part this was because of improved communications and shipping connections, but another important factor was the greater number of Arabs now settling in the region. Foremost among these migrants were Sayids from the Hadramaut. Moving out from the arid coastal strip of the Yemen, members of the foremost Sayid families became established from East Africa to Southeast Asia. Since they continued to maintain strong connections with their homeland, they provided links between scholars in many parts of the Islamic world.

The Sayids who found their way to the archipelago had always been received with honour because of their descent from the Prophet, their command of the holy language Arabic, and their assumed expertise in all things Islamic. From the mid-eighteenth century, however, mention of Arab Sayids appears more frequently in the records. Much desired as husbands for high-born women, they quickly acquired an influence which far surpassed their numbers. Now it was Sayids who frequently assumed the position of *kadi* and acted as envoys and royal advisers. By the end of the eighteenth century, most royal families in the western archipelago had some Sayid blood, and Arab communities had grown up in the port towns of Aceh, Kedah, Melaka, Batavia, north-coast Java, Riau, Palembang and in the new British settlement of Penang. In Mempawa, Matan and Pontianak in west Borneo, and in Siak in Sumatra, the founders of dynasties were themselves Sayids.

The growing Sayid presence was to have a considerable effect on the development of Indonesian Islam. While they usually came to the archipelago as traders rather than missionaries, many were recruited as teachers and the strictness with which they observed Islam could not fail to impress. In Melaka, for instance, the Arabs had their own mosque so that they could maintain their own traditions of worship.

A full study of how Indonesia responded to these new influences in the eighteenth century remains to be written. The study of law was always the basis of Islamic education, but by the 1780s it seems that Islamic schools in Minangkabau were giving increased emphasis to the teaching of Muslim law and its application to daily life. During this period another important centre for reformist teaching emerged at Palembang, where a wealthy court sponsored a number of Muslim scholars who expressed concern at what they considered the degeneration of local Islam. Among these the best-known is Abdulsamad, said to be the son of a *shaykh* from the Yemen who had become *mufti* (expert on Muslim law) in Kedah, and a Palembang noblewoman. He went to Mecca as a young man and, although it is not known whether he returned to Palembang, his writings in Malay, summaries of lectures given by Meccan scholars and translations of well-known Arabic works made him an influential figure. It was through Abdulsamad that the Samaniyyah *ṭarīqa* was introduced to the archipelago.

Abdulsamad directed much of his energy towards improving the practice and understanding of Islam among his countrymen. One of the works for which he is most renowned is his Malay rendering of the abridgement of al-Ghazālī's *The Revival of the Religious Sciences*. Another, entitled 'A gift addressed to those desirous of an exposition of the essence of the Muslim faith', devotes considerable attention to a definition of 'faith', reiterating that anything deviating from the Koran or the traditions attached to the Prophet or his Companions is an unacceptable form of *bid'a*, or innovation. He deplores the widespread custom of spirit propitiation, arguing that it is wasteful and of no avail, since there is no evidence that the ancestors are still alive. The authority of old stories, or even the pronouncements of the elders, cannot be taken as proof. Those who claim to be possessed by spirits have simply fallen under the control of evil forces. They should not be called upon in cases of illness, since their 'remedies' have nothing to do with medical treatment. He singles out for particular condemnation those men who wear women's clothes and do women's work, an apparent reference to transvestite groups which had survived from earlier times.

The encroachment of European powers in the Middle East as well as in Southeast Asia probably lies behind the contemporary Muslim interest in the holy war, and Abdulsamad himself produced a tract on this topic in Arabic. By this time central Java had been divided into two kingdoms, Yogyakarta and Surakarta, each a vassal of the VOC. The evidence suggests that the Javanese were themselves trying to resolve the tensions inherent in the deepening association with the VOC. In 1774, at the beginning of a new Javanese century, the crown prince of Yogyakarta composed a poem which sees Javanese culture as eventually absorbing the Dutch who ultimately adopt Islam. Although evidence from the central Javanese courts suggests a self-conscious adherence to accepted Islamic norms, their co-operation with the Dutch had apparently been a source of disappointment to many Muslims. In 1772, in a letter of introduction for two travellers returning to Java, Abdulsamad reminded the sultan of Yogyakarta of the Koranic tradition that those who fall in the holy war are not dead but alive, while the writer of another letter sent at the same time despatched a banner from Mecca which the Sultan could use against his enemies 'and all unbelievers'. A letter from Mecca to Surakarta some years later accuses the ruler of being nothing less than 'the Devil's king' and an apostate. 'Shall the Europeans then indeed be more powerful than Allah?'[69]

The reiteration of the call to holy war sounded by many eighteenth-century reformists aroused a strong response outside Java. The early years of the thirteenth Muslim century, which began in 1785, witnessed a number of serious attacks on Europeans, several of which drew their inspiration from religion. Raja Haji, a Bugis prince from Riau who was regarded even during his lifetime as *keramat*, a living saint, laid siege to Melaka. A Malay text describes how he went into battle reading religious works and, following his death in the fighting, was received into the company of the blessed 'as a martyr . . . in Allah's war'. Six years later, in 1790, a call went out from Penang to 'all Muslims' to drive out the English from Penang, while Malay ships were said to be massing on the east coast for an attack on Dutch Melaka. But it was not only Europeans who were the target of Islamic feeling; at the same time it was reported that several hundred hadjis led by a *shaykh* from Mecca were gathering in Kedah to make war on the infidel Siamese. Growing confrontation was also apparent in the southern Philippines, where enmity between Muslims and Christians had continued throughout the eighteenth century as Spanish priests again tried to push their missionary activities into the southern areas subject to the sultan of Sulu. The more militant mood of Islam combined with Sulu's expanding economy saw an increase in raiding for Christian slaves in the Visayas, adding further fuel to the ongoing Christian–Muslim animosity.

Unlike Islam, Filipino Christianity remained isolated from outside influ-

---

[69] Ann Kumar, 'Javanese Court Society and Politics in the Late Eighteenth Century: the Record of a Lady Soldier', Part I, *Indonesia*, 29 (April 1980) 69.

ences in the eighteenth century. It was therefore largely untouched by the reformism in Bourbon Spain which had begun to question the superstition and ignorance that had often characterized Spanish Catholicism. The absence of liberalizing trends was also due to the fact that the Spanish clerics who entered the missionary orders during this period generally lacked the commitment and training of their predecessors, and the high purpose of the early years of Christianization was clearly fading. But in addition the Church in the Philippines resisted change because it had flourished in the colonial environment. In the past the friars had often been allied with the Filipinos against government officials, but now their growing acquisition of land, demand for corvée labour and abuse of religious authority meant they were often themselves seen as oppressive. In 1745 an agrarian revolt erupted in the Manila area, notable because it was the first large-scale display of Filipino resentment towards the monastic orders. The revolt was shortlived, but Filipino anger fed into other areas of discontent, primarily that relating to the issue of native ordination. Although the Church had long recognized that one of its major responsibilities was to train a native clergy, no progress had been made in this regard during the seventeenth century. By the 1750s, however, the continuing lack of clergy combined with pressure from the Crown and a few liberal priests compelled the friars to employ some Filipino assistance. Outside the orders, Filipinos had also begun to receive training as secular priests, and by this time there were at least four institutions in Manila training local candidates for the priesthood. Of 569 parishes, 142 were headed by native seculars. But the regular Spanish orders consistently refused to grant full ordination to local priests, partly because of a desire to protect their own positions and partly because of an entrenched conviction that Filipinos were congenitally unfit for full clerical duties. As a result, while the secular priests were almost all Filipinos, the missionary orders remained unrepentantly Spanish. Provincial governors were still unable to act without their co-operation; *principales* needed the support of priests to be confirmed in office; and in numerous cases complaints were received of abuse by the orders of their traditional privileges.

In a climate of growing anti-Spanish feeling, the British capture of Manila in 1762 was hailed by some Filipinos as marking the end of the Spanish era and the hold of the Spanish-controlled Church. People rejoiced, they said, because now there was 'no more king, priest or governor'. Diego Silang, the main figure in the anti-Spanish rebellion which now erupted, had worked for the Spanish authorities and had become convinced that the time was right for the Filipinos to reclaim political control of their country. By the end of 1762 he had established his own government near the town of Vigan and announced a programme which included removal of oppressive officials and freedom from tribute. Initially he attempted to win the friars over to his cause, but the latter regarded Silang as a sorcerer and accused him of condoning the 'pagan' excesses of his allies from the hills. The animosity of the religious was also aroused when Silang claimed to be under the patronage of Jesus of Nazareth with himself as *Cabo Mayor* (Sergeant Major). Furthermore, Silang had his own interpretation of a Christian's duties. He could not be persuaded to confess, for instance, and as far as the Church was concerned could never fully participate in the Mass since he was never in a state of grace. Because of his own attitudes, Diego Silang apparently failed to understand the hold that the friars had over Filipinos, and their ability to use the refusal of communion as a means of enforcing obedience. When he was finally killed in 1762, it was by the orders of a group of friars who had given their appointed assassin a holy relic to ensure the success of his mission.

In 1764 the Treaty of Paris restored the Spanish administration in the Philippines, but the events of 1762–3 in the Philippines did produce some results. From 1767 attempts were made to place native secular priests in charge of parishes formerly controlled by the orders. The experiment, however, was a failure because too many illiterate, untrained Filipinos were suddenly placed in positions of authority. Indeed, at the time Manila wits quipped that there were no oarsmen to be found for the coastal vessels because 'the archbishop had ordained them all'.[70] There were endless complaints from Filipinos themselves about the conduct of the newly appointed clergy—that they favoured their relatives, that they used the rectory for parties, that they exacted large stipends and fees. The most unfortunate result of this venture was its apparent confirmation of the claim that Filipinos did not have a true vocation and could not be permitted to take on greater religious responsibilities. The hardening of Spanish attitudes in turn contributed to a more pronounced hostility among Filipinos towards the Spanish grip on Christianity. A Samarino secular priest in 1775 went so far as to develop his own religion in which he said Indios would be ordained even if they could not read or write, and that the Spanish sacraments would be abandoned. One Spanish friar was ready to regard the Moro raids on Samar as a blessing in disguise, for otherwise, he said, neither royal orders nor warnings from the priests could have persuaded the people to remain settled near the town.

The eighteenth century similarly stands out as a significant period in the Theravāda Buddhist world. In Sri Lanka, the *sangha* had deteriorated during the two hundred years of Portuguese and Dutch occupation, and a lack of proper ordination ceremonies meant that many monks had reverted to virtually lay status. Indeed, it was said that on the entire island only one still knew Pāli. Against this background a Sinhalese revivalist movement developed which emphasized piety, poverty and scriptural knowledge and was led by the *samanera* (senior monk) Valivita Saranamkara. Inspired by the hope of re-establishing the lost tradition of higher ordination (*upasampada*) in Sri Lanka, Valivita Saranamkara persuaded the ruler of Kandy, Kirti Sri Rajasimha (1747–82) to send a mission to Siam.

In itself this decision is a comment on the health of the Thai *sangha*. When Alexander Hamilton visited Siam in 1720 he remarked on the numbers of 'temples and priests', and he reckoned there could be as many as 50,000 'clergymen or Tallapoys' around Ayutthaya. Efforts had even been made to curb the activities of Catholic priests, possibly because Christians were claiming exemption from drinking the water of allegiance.

[70] J. L. Phelan, *The Hispanization of the Philippines: Spanish Aims and Filipino Responses, 1565–1700*, Madison, 1956, 84–9.

From 1730 it was at least in theory illegal to write a book on Christianity either in Thai or in the sacred language of Pāli; to preach Christian doctrine to Buddhists or attempt to lure them to conversion; or to criticize Buddhism publicy. The reign of Borommakot (1733–58) is still remembered as a golden age of royal Buddhist sponsorship, and so great was the king's piety that he refused to confer a noble title on someone who had not previously been a monk. The reputation which Ayutthaya had acquired in the Theravāda Buddhist world was clearly demonstrated when, after two abortive attempts, a mission finally left Sri Lanka in 1753 with a request that a chapter of Thai monks be sent to revive the discontinued *upasampada* tradition. One of the Sinhalese ambassadors described the splendour of their reception in Ayutthaya, when they were greeted by the leading monk, Upali Maha Thera, who was borne in a palanquin and accompanied by a procession in which a golden Buddha image was carried, together with flags, music, sacred books and offerings. Subsequently, a party of twenty-five monks headed by Upali Maha Thera was sent to Sri Lanka where they were received with great rejoicing. During his three-year stay, Upali Maha Thera performed seven hundred ordinations for monks and three thousand for novices, and Valivita Saranamkara was himself made Saṅgharāja, the Supreme Patriarch. This mission was followed by another when the Thai monks 'trained the [Sri Lankan] priests in many things relating to the religion, such as abstract meditation' which had been developed by the *saṅgha* in Siam. It was the exchange between Sri Lanka and Siam in the eighteenth century which laid the foundation for the development of the largest order in Sri Lanka today, known as the Siam Nikaya.[71]

However, the rapidity with which even a flourishing religious climate could deteriorate in times of political fragmentation soon became apparent in Ayutthaya. Indeed, it was already evident in Burma, where a divided *saṅgha* had suffered with the decline of the Toungoo dynasty and where contemporaries blamed the ruler's lack of virtue for the country's misfortunes. Inevitably this crisis period saw the rise of a number of charismatic leaders who held out the hope of some extraordinary resolution of mankind's distress. One monk claimed that those who became his followers and accepted his interpretations of Buddhism would automatically become a *sotapanna* (stream winner) with at most only seven reincarnations before reaching the state of *nibbāna*. Such movements were undoubtedly fostered by widely circulating prophecies predicting that a time of chaos would be followed by the rise of a king in Pegu who would usher in an age of utopian prosperity. The Buddha himself was reported to have said that a Bodhisattva would appear by at least 2290 of the Buddhist era (1746 CE), about the middle of the five thousand years predicted for the life of the religion. The emergence of an ex-monk, Smin Dhaw Buddha Kesi, believed to possess 'knowledge of spells, charms, magical incantations and exorcisms' and supernatural powers which gave him invulnerability, was

[71] P. E. Pieris, *Religious Intercourse between Ceylon and Siam in the Eighteenth Century. I. An Account of King Kirti Sri's Embassy to Siam in Saka 1672 (AD 1750)*, Bangkok, 1908, 37–8; Urmila Phadnis, *Religion and Politics in Sri Lanka*, London, 1976, 48; Rev. Siddhartha Buddharakhita Thera, *Syamupadasampada*, printed as *Religious Intercourse between Ceylon and Siam in the Eighteenth Century*, II, Bangkok, 1914, 66–7.

apparently regarded by many as a fulfilment of such prophecies and in 1740 he was proclaimed king of Pegu. His promise of a restoration of religion and a new life of wealth and comfort was for a time sufficient to attract a wide range of followers, but in 1747 he was deposed. Peguan forces, however, continued to apply pressure to Ava, and in 1752 the city fell. Following Ayutthaya's conquest by a rejuvenated Burma in 1767, Siam similarly provided a fertile breeding ground for new religious movements. In Sawangburi, one of the northern provinces, dissident monks led by a certain Phra Fang seized control and rejected some of the fundamental requirements of the *sangha*. Not only did they ignore the *vinaya* and live as laymen; they also adopted military ranks and sought worldly power, even attempting to extend into neighbouring Phitsanulok.

The great leaders who emerged in Siam and Burma in the mid-eighteenth century were a product of this environment. When the founder of the Konbaung dynasty in Burma took the title Alaung Mintayagi or embryo Buddha, and presented himself as a *cakkavatti*, a Universal Ruler, it imbued his campaigns with messianic significance. His wars against Ayutthaya were justified by the claim that the religion there was not 'blossoming nor shining', while his son Bodawpaya (r. 1782–1819) also presented his attack on Arakan as a crusade on behalf of Buddhism. In addition, Bodawpaya attempted to assert himself as the saviour for whom the Burmese had waited. Declaring that the five thousand years allotted for the religion had already passed, he proclaimed that he was not only the Metteyya but a *cakkavatti* as well. Events in Burma may have influenced developments in Siam where Taksin, who reunified the country after 1767, aspired to *cakkavatti* status, expressing a desire to be 'greater than the King of Ava'. In order to attain a more purified state through greater bodily discipline, he embarked on a study of mystical techniques and finally claimed to have reached the status of a 'stream winner', discerning on his own body several marks of the coming Buddha.[72]

Although little is known of developments in Lao and Khmer Buddhism during a period when their countries were increasingly subservient to more powerful neighbours, it appears some Lao princes responded positively to Taksin's vision of himself as the leader of a wider Buddhist community. However, it is clear that demands for the monks to acknowledge him as a spiritually superior being precipitated a major clash with the *sangha*. As a punishment for their refusal to pay him obeisance, Taksin ordered five hundred monks to be flogged and sentenced to menial labour. The hostility Taksin aroused among the religious hierarchy has been seen as instrumental in his downfall in 1782. Some years later, when Bodawpaya presented himself as the Metteya he too faced such opposition from the monkhood that he was largely forced to abandon his claim.

Such developments should not obscure the fact that in most respects these kings all supported Buddhism in traditional ways. Learned monks were honoured, sacred scriptures copied, monasteries built, ordinations

[72] Craig J. Reynolds, 'The Buddhist Monkhood in Nineteenth Century Thailand', Ph.D. thesis, Cornell University, 1973, 32–3. Dr Reynolds' research suggests that Taksin may even have been influenced by mystical Sufi practices learnt from Malay texts, and a monk from the south became his Supreme Patriarch.

sponsored. Alaungpaya attempted to reform Buddhist practice and eliminate deviant sects; he also ordered a revision of the *dhammathat* code which
tried to eradicate hierarchical inequalities before the law and to institute a
more ethical and humane approach in place of the Brahmanic ritualistic
injunctions of its predecessors. Bodawpaya too reaffirmed proscriptions
against gambling and intoxicants, and sent missionary monks out into
marginal areas. Like previous rulers, he was particularly concerned with
the unity of the monkhood. He tried to put an end to the robe controversy
by decreeing in favour of the two-shoulder party while at the same time
reorganizing the *sangha*, appointing monks he favoured to leading monasteries, naming his own teacher as Supreme Patriarch and creating a Council
of Elders to oversee religious affairs. An official was delegated to supervise
and keep records of monastic lands to limit the amount accumulated by
monasteries, and another post was responsible for the maintenance of
monastic discipline. Courses of study with set texts were prescribed for
monks, with monthly examinations to ensure that they were well grounded in knowledge of the *vinaya*. Those who failed were tattooed and
expelled. 'It is not right', declares one edict, 'that monks should remain
doing nothing except keeping away from sins and enjoying free food.'

Bodawpaya's efforts to repair the schisms in the monkhood were only
partially successful. He himself changed his opinion on several issues, and
does not seem to have provided the leadership necessary to overcome a
history of *sangha* factionalism. On occasion he was forced to expel quite
senior monks from the order. The restlessness in Burmese Buddhism is
suggested by the apparent blossoming of radical Buddhist sects during this
period. One such group was known as the Zawti: they rejected the
veneration of Buddha's statues and monks, denied reincarnation and
preached the existence of one supreme deity, the world creator. Though
the leaders were arrested, other sects continued to emerge at the village
level. In the early nineteenth century, faced by peasant discontent and
military setbacks, Bodawpaya appears to have become involved with
another lay group, the Paramat, which stressed meditation and a specula-
tive philosophy more akin to Mahāyāna Buddhism. But despite, or perhaps because of, this proliferation of different groups, Burma maintained
its reputation as a centre for Buddhist activity, and when people of low
caste were forbidden by the ruler of Kandy, the patron of the Siam Nikaya,
from entering the Sinhalese monkhood they sought ordination at the
Burmese capital of Amarapura.

Siam, on the other hand, provides something of a contrast, and Bodawpaya's contemporary, Rama I (r. 1782–1809), stands out as possibly the
greatest Buddhist reformer of the century. Convinced that moral degeneration had led to Ayutthaya's destruction, he reaffirmed the religious
duties of the laity, promoting Thai translations of important Pāli works
such as 'The Questions of Milinda' for lay Buddhists unable to read the
originals. Even more important was the restoration of monastic discipline.
A school of monks was opened at the royal temple of the Emerald Buddha,
with learned men from the Department of Royal Pundits as instructors. In
1801, 128 corrupt monks were disrobed, tattooed and put to hard labour as
punishment for deficiencies in conduct and knowledge. Another key

concern was to restrict the development of fringe groups. Laws were passed aiming at the control of wandering holy men and individuals who 'extolled supernatural power' in attempts to take the throne. Every monk was required to obtain a certificate bearing his name, monastery, and rank, and if he wished to travel to another principality for instruction he had to present this document as proof that he had been properly ordained. Rama I also addressed the potentially divisive issue of royal involvement in monastic disputes. Even though his ecclesiastical laws demonstrate continuing concern for the health of the *saṅgha*, he was clearly unwilling to become involved in questions of doctrinal interpretation. Accordingly, he decreed that the king should not intervene in religious disputes until the matter had been extensively discussed by the highest-ranking monks. In state ceremonies Rama I sought to emphasize the Buddhist aspects of ritual rather than Brahmanical and animistic ones, warning officials that, while they should pay due respect to the spirits, they should not place them above Buddhism. During the oath of allegiance, evidence of Buddhist devotion should always take precedence over homage to guardian spirits and past rulers. The worship of lingas, on the other hand, was not sanctioned in the scriptures and they should be destroyed.

A further measure sponsored by Rama I was the convening of a great Buddhist Council in order to produce a full revision of the Pāli Tipitaka, the Buddhist canon. The task was carried out in 1788–9 under the supervision of leading monks and with the financial support and active involvement of the king, royal family and court officials. The significance of this event can best be appreciated if it is realized that the last such Council had been held in Chiengmai in 1475, and that the texts which resulted from Rama I's endeavours are still among the standard works of Thai Buddhism. Added prestige came with the completion of a new rendering of the fourteenth-century *Traiphum*, the Three Worlds Cosmology, a version which gave an unprecedented prominence to mankind and the role of kings, placing the merit-making Universal Monarch 'at the apex of the world'.

Spanning a period of nearly thirty years, these refinements of the traditional order infused Rama I's reign with a sense of religious purpose, and imbued Thai Buddhism with a strength which has endured into modern times. Greater monastic unity and a more amicable relationship between rulers and monks meant that the Siamese *saṅgha* was less subject to internal divisions than its Burmese counterpart. It has been argued, moreover, that the religious reforms of this period are distinguished because they were not simply an attempt to return to the 'pure' traditions of the past. The greater stress on human rationality, the unprecedented exercise of critical faculties, and the re-examination of humanity's relationship to the universe represented a real intellectual shift, a 'subtle revolution' which provided a solid basis for the challenges that Thai society was to face in the nineteenth century.[73]

---

[73] David K. Wyatt, 'The "Subtle Revolution" of King Rama I of Siam', in David K. Wyatt and Alexander Woodside, eds, *Moral Order and the Question of Change: Essays on Southeast Asian Thought*, New Haven: Yale University Southeast Asia Studies Monograph no. 24, 1982.

CONCLUSION

The three hundred years surveyed in this chapter were a time of considerable change in Southeast Asia's religious development. The increase in source material, both European and indigenous, allows many of these developments to be discussed in greater detail than is possible for earlier periods. Missionary accounts, for example, make an important contribution to our understanding of indigenous beliefs, feeding into other sources from both mainland and island areas to throw light on the process by which the world faiths adapted to the local environment. The arrival of Islam predates our period, but for a number of reasons it was only in the sixteenth century that its expansion into the archipelago gathered pace. This coincided with the coming of Christianity, the last of the world religions to reach the region and the major challenge to Islam's penetration of the island world.

Despite their doctrinal differences, the imported beliefs were all caught up by similar concerns, several of which have been discussed here—the maintenance of basic religious principles in the face of continuing accommodation with indigenous customs, the relationship with other major faiths, the connection between religion and authority, the role which women should play. None of these questions could be fully resolved, and from time to time they still emerge as matters for debate. What the events of the eighteenth century demonstrate, however, is the capacity of Southeast Asian peoples to draw on inspiration from both inside and outside the region in order to formulate their own responses to contemporary challenge.

BIBLIOGRAPHIC ESSAY

There are numerous studies of religious developments in Southeast Asia in more recent times, but relatively few are specifically concerned with the period between 1500 and 1800. A good deal of relevant information is contained in the political histories of the period, for which the reader is referred to the bibliography for Chapter 7. We have given below a selected list of books and articles which expand material discussed above, but reference should also be made to the bibliographies for Chapter 4, and (in Volume II) for Chapters 4 and 9.

Christianity

It should be noted that the early missionary accounts also contain the most detailed descriptions of indigenous customs and beliefs. There is as yet no complete study in English of Portuguese missionary efforts in Indonesia. The basic contemporary source is Artur Basilio de Sá, ed., *Documentação para a história das missões do Padroado portugês do Oriente*, 5 vols, Lisbon, 1955–8. A general study of the western archipelago is Fr Manuel Teixeira, *The Portuguese Missions in Malacca and Singapore (1511–1958)*, 3 vols, Lisbon,

1961–3. The third volume of Georg Schurhammer, *Francis Xavier. His life, His Times,* trans. M. Joseph Costelloe, Rome: Jesuit Historical Institute, 1980, provides detailed material on the Jesuit founder's time in Indonesia. The Franciscan mission is described in Fr Achilles Meersman, *The Franciscans in the Indonesian Archipelago,* Louvain, 1967. See also C. Wessels, *De Geschiedenis der R. K. missie in Amboina vanaf haar stichting door den H. Franciscus Xaverius tot haar vernietiging door de O.I.Compagnie 1546–1605,* Nijmegen-Utrecht, 1926, and B. J. J. Visser, *Onder Portuguese-Spaansche Vlag: De Katholieke Missie van Indonesië 1511–1605* Amsterdam, 1925. J. Fox, *The Harvest of the Palm,* Cambridge, Mass., 1977, gives useful material on Christianity in eastern Indonesia in the VOC period, as does Gerrit Knaap, 'Kruidnagelen en Christenen. De Vereenigde Oost-Indische Compagnie en de Bevolking van Ambon 1656–1696', Ph.D. thesis, Utrecht University, 1985.

For the Philippines the secondary literature is extensive, although of variable quality. The best source of primary material for indigenous beliefs as well as for the missionizing process is E. H. Blair and J. A. Robertson, *The Philippine Islands, 1493–1898,* 55 vols, Cleveland, 1903–9. General studies are Peter Gowing, *Islands under the Cross. The Story of the Church in the Philippines,* Manila, 1967; Nicholas Cushner, *Spain in the Philippines. From Conquest to Revolution,* Quezon City: Ateneo de Manila University, 1971; Miguel A. Bernad, *The Christianization of the Philippines. Problems and Perspectives,* Manila, 1972; H. de la Costa, *Church and State: The Philippine Experience,* Manila, 1978; Pablo Fernandez, *History of the Church in the Philippines (1521–1898),* Manila, 1979. Gerald Anderson, ed., *Studies on Philippines Church History,* Ithaca and London, 1968, contains several articles on specific issues. H. de la Costa, *The Jesuits in the Philippines 1581–1768,* Cambridge, Mass., 1961, is an extremely detailed study of one of the major orders. Eric Anderson, 'Traditions in Conflict. Filipino responses to Spanish colonialism, 1565–1665', Ph.D. thesis, University of Sydney, 1977, contains interesting material on early rebellions which adopted Christian symbolism. Dennis Roth, 'The Friar Estates of the Philippines', Ph.D. thesis, University of Oregon, 1974, examines the background to the 1745 rebellion, and David Routledge, *Diego Silang and the Origins of Philippines Nationalism,* Quezon City, 1979, considers the relationship between Silang and Church authorities. An intriguing analysis of the vocabulary of conversion is Vincente Rafael, *Contracting Colonialism. Translation and Christian Conversion in Tagalog Society under Early Spanish Rule,* Ithaca and London, 1988. Antonio Rosales, *A Study of a Sixteenth Century Tagalog Manuscript on the Ten Commandments; its Significance and Implications,* Quezon City, 1984, provides a commentary on one translated document.

A useful contemporary account of Christianity in Vietnam is contained in the work of Alexander of Rhodes. See, for example, *Rhodes of Vietnam,* trans. Solange Herz, Westminster, Maryland, 1960. A selection of useful documents and commentary is Georges Taboulet, ed., *La Geste Française en Indochine,* Paris, 1955. See also Adrien Launay, *Histoire de la Mission de Cochinchine 1658–1823,* 3 vols, Paris, 1923–5, and *Histoire de la Mission du Tonkin,* Paris, 1927. His *Histoire de la Mission de Siam, 1662–1881,* 2 vols, Paris, 1920, covers Christian mission work in Thailand.

Confucianism

Much remains to be done in understanding the intellectual climate of Vietnam in this period. An important start has been made by Keith Taylor, 'The literati revival in seventeenth century Vietnam', JSEAS, 18, 1 (1987). Useful discussions of the interaction between China and Vietnam are found in Edgar Wickberg, ed., *Historical Interaction of China and Vietnam: Institutional and Cultural Themes*, Lawrence: Center for East Asian Studies, University of Kansas, 1969, and in Alexander Woodside, 'History, structure and revolution in Vietnam', *International Political Science Review*, 10, 2 (1989).

Islam

An indispensable reference book in several volumes and still in progress is H. A. R. Gibb, C. E. Bosworth et al., eds, The *Encyclopaedia of Islam*, new edn, Leiden and London, 1960– , which provides a ready source of specialized articles on virtually every topic and individual connected with Islam.

As far as Southeast Asia is concerned, there has been considerable debate about the nature and timing of Islam's arrival in the archipelago. A thoughtful synthesis of current views is in M. C. Ricklefs *A History of Modern Indonesia*, London, 1981. See also G. W. J. Drewes, 'New light on the coming of Islam to Indonesia?', BKI 124, 4 (1968), and S. O. Robson, 'Java at the crossroads; aspects of Javanese cultural history in the 14th and 15th centuries', BKI 137, 2 and 3 (1981). A general survey of the pre-modern period can be found in P. M. Holt et al., eds, *The Cambridge History of Islam*, II, Cambridge, UK, 1970. Raphael Israeli and Anthony H. Johns, eds, *Islam in Asia*, II, Jerusalem, 1984, contains useful essays on the region, as does M. B. Hooker, eds., *Islam in Southeast Asia*, Leiden, 1983. A number of valuable articles, including Merle Ricklefs, 'Six centuries of Islamization in Java' and A. C. Milner, 'Islam and Malay Kingship' are reprinted in Ahmad Ibrahim et al., eds, *Readings on Islam in Southeast Asia*, Singapore: Institute of Southeast Asian Studies, 1985.

The basic work on Sufism in the Indonesian archipelago is A. H. Johns, 'Malay Sufism as illustrated in an anonymous collection of 17th century tracts', JMBRAS, 30, 2 (1957). His publications over the last two decades cover numerous topics but have contributed particularly to our knowledge of the connections between Southeast Asia and the Middle East. See, for example, 'Islam in Southeast Asia; reflections and new directions', *Indonesia*, 19 (April 1975). G. W. J. Drewes has edited several early mystical Muslim texts which provide an insight into sixteenth-century teaching. See *Een Javaanse Primbon uit de Zestiende Eeuw*, Leiden, 1954; *The Admonitions of Seh Bari; a 16th century Javanese Muslim text attributed to the Saint of Bonan*, The Hague, 1969; *An Early Javanese Code of Muslim Ethics*, The Hague, 1978.

Islamic scholars in early seventeenth-century Aceh have been the subject of a number of studies. G. W. J. Drewes and L. F. Brakel, *The Poems of Hamzah Fansuri*, Dordrecht, Holland, and Cinnaminson, USA, 1986; C. A. O van Nieuwenhuize, *Samsu'l-din van Pasai, Bijdrage tot de Kennis der*

Sumatranaasche Mystiek, Leiden, 1945; Syed Muhammad Naguib al Attas, *Rānīrī and the Wujūdiyyah of 17th century Acheh*, Singapore, 1966, rejects al-Rānīrī's criticism of local mystics; A. H. Johns, 'Daḳā'ik al-Huruf by 'Abd al-Ra'uf of Singkel', JRAS (1955) 55–73, 139–158, and P. Riddell, ''Abd al-Ra'uf's *Tarjuman al-mustafid'*, Ph.D. thesis, Australian National University, 1984, consider the work of a leading Malay scholar of the period.

The Islamization process in Sulawesi has also been well studied. See J. Noorduyn, 'De Islamisering van Makasar', BKI, 112, 3 (1956); Leonard Andaya, 'Kingship-*Adat* Rivalry and the role of Islam in south Sulawesi', JSEAS, 15, 1 (1984); Henri Chambert-Loir, 'Dato ri Bandang. Legendes de l'islamisation de la région de Célébes-Sud', *Archipel*, 29, 1 (1985); Christian Pelras, 'Religion, Tradition and the Dynamics of Islamization in South Sulawesi', *Archipel*, 29, 1 (1985).

For Minangkabau, especially in the eighteenth century, see Christine Dobbin, *Islamic Revivalism in a Changing Peasant Economy, 1784–1847*, London and Malmö: Scandinavian Institute of Asian Studies, 1983. J. Kathirithamby-Wells, 'Ahmad Shah ibn Iskandar and the late 17th century "holy war" in Indonesia', JMBRAS, 43, 1 (1970), provides a case study of one holy man, as does Ann Kumar, *Surapati. Man and Legend*, Leiden, 1976.

A discussion of the environment in eighteenth-century Palembang is found in G. W. J. Drewes, *Directions for Travellers on the Mystic Path*, BKI, 81, The Hague, 1977. See also his 'Further data concerning 'Abd al-Samad al-Palimbani', BKI, 132, 2 and 3 (1976).

The most comprehensive book on the history of Islam in the Philippines is Cesar A. Majul, *Muslims in the Philippines*, Quezon City, 1973. On Champa, see Pierre Yves Manguin, 'The Introduction of Islam into Champa', JMBRAS, 58, 1 (1985).

Developments in eighteenth-century Islam are discussed in Thomas Naff and Roger Owen, eds, *Studies in Eighteenth Century Islamic History*, Carbondale and Edwardsville, 1977, and John O. Voll, *Islam: Continuity and Change in the Modern World*, Boulder, 1982.

Bali

For recent historical work on Balinese culture, see Adrian Vickers, *Bali: A Paradise Created*, Melbourne, 1989, and also his 'Hinduism and Islam in Indonesia. Bali and the Pasisir World', *Indonesia*, 43 (October 1987). To this should be added David Stuart-Fox, 'Pura Besakih: a study of Balinese religion and society', Ph.D. thesis, Australian National University, 1987.

Buddhism

There is considerable material on contemporary Theravāda Buddhism in Southeast Asia, but the selection below emphasizes works which include material directly relating to the period discussed in this chapter. Robert E. Lester, *Theravada Buddhism in Southeast Asia*, Ann Arbor, 1973, provides a concise but thoughtful introduction. Bardwell L. Smith, *Religion and Legitimation of Power in Thailand, Laos and Burma*, Chambersburg, 1978, contains a number of relevant essays. Milford E. Spiro, *Burmese Supernaturalism*, Philadelphia: Institute for the Study of Human Issues, 1967, is a wide-ranging introduction to spirit worship and its relationship to Burmese Buddhism, while Miharranjan Ray, *An Introduction to the Study of Theravada Buddhism in Burma*, University of Calcutta, 1946, is still a basic reference. E. Michael Mendelson, *Sangha and State in Burma: A Study of Monastic Sectarianism and Leadership*, Ithaca, 1975; Donald E. Smith, *Religion and Politics in Burma*, Princeton, 1965; John Palmer Ferguson, 'The symbolic dimensions of the Burmese sangha', Ph.D. thesis, Cornell University, 1975, can be consulted together to convey a sense of the evolving position of the monkhood in Burma. To these can be added the stimulating arguments advanced by E. Sarkisyanz, *Buddhist Backgrounds of the Burmese Revolution*, The Hague, 1965. On the periodic reforms of the monkhood, see Michael Aung-Thwin, 'The role of *sasana* reform in Burmese history: economic dimensions of a religious purification', JAS, 38 (1979), and the response by Victor Lieberman, 'The political significance of religious wealth in Burmese history: some further thoughts', JAS, 39 (1980). There are only a limited number of historical studies of Thai Buddhism devoted to the pre-nineteenth-century period. Yoneo Ishii, *Sangha, State and Society: Thai Buddhism in History*, Kyoto, Center for Southeast Asian Studies, 1986, offers a broad introduction. Prince Dhani Nivat's booklet, *A History of Buddhism in Siam*, Bangkok: Siam Society, 1969, gives a lucid picture of the evolution of Thai Buddhism, having been written for the as yet unfinished *Encyclopaedia of Buddhism*. Developments in the eighteenth century are discussed in depth by Craig J. Reynolds, 'The Buddhist monkhood in nineteenth century Thailand', Ph.D. thesis, Cornell University, 1972. The exchange of religious missions between Siam and Ceylon (Sri Lanka) in the mid-eighteenth century is the subject of P. E. Pieris, *Religious intercourse between Ceylon and Siam in the eighteenth century*, I: *An account of King Kirti Sri's Embassy to Siam in Saka 1672 (A.D. 1750)*, Bangkok, 1908, and II: *The adoption of the Siamese order of priesthood in Ceylon, Saka Era 1673 (A.D. 1751)*, Bangkok, 1914. The phenomenon of holy men is discussed by Charles F. Keyes, 'Millennialism and Theravada Buddhism', JAS, 26, 2 (1977), and Yoneo Ishii, 'A note on Buddhistic millenarian revolts in northeastern Siam', JSEAS, 6, 2 (1975).

CHAPTER
5

THE AGE OF TRANSITION: THE
MID-EIGHTEENTH TO THE EARLY
NINETEENTH CENTURIES

STATE RIVALRY AND CYCLICITY

Geographical, cultural and ethnic diversity renders any overview of Southeast Asia's history a difficult task. The same problems of diversity are met even in the study of individual components of the region, given, for example, the differences between Shan and Mon in Burma, Vietnamese and Khmer in the Indochinese peninsula, Tagalog and Moro in the Philippines, and coastal Malay and hill Batak in north Sumatra. What cultural and historical identity obtained between or within particular segments was, to a large extent, the dictate of geography. A Confucianist Vietnam and a Christian Philippines on Southeast Asia's fringes confirm the significance of geographical location. Beneath the striking overlay of differences, Southeast Asian societies shared a substratum of distinct traditions of lineage patterns, social structuring and belief systems which were related to the overarching concern over resource management within their particular environment. In time, the accommodation of these features with varying degrees of external influences added a second dimension to the identity of pre-modern societies. Burmese and Thai responses to Theravāda Buddhism were different, as were the responses to Islam in Java and in the Malay world. The European element added a third dimension to the evolution of these societies. European penetration has, in fact, been considered a watershed, with its earlier inroads into the maritime regions constituting a further distancing between developments there and the mainland. To what extent was this dichotomy between colonial and indigenous administrations real in terms of social impact?

From the mid-eighteenth century, Southeast Asian political régimes were strengthened by the vigour of new dynasties on the mainland and in central Java, and the increased pace of activity in the maritime region by the Dutch and Spanish colonial administrations. The new age was universally one of growth and expansion. The concomitant expansion of territorial frontiers, administrative control and economic activity was unprecedented. During the process, the rough outlines and the cultural and ethnic structuring of the future nation-states were imperceptibly settled. Simultaneously, the colonial territories and, uniquely among the independent powers, Siam, were brought within the mainstream of international economic developments. But internal social affairs in these territories were not necessarily different from those prevalent under indigenous despotism. The preoccupation of both indigenous and colonial authorities was primarily with the procurement of security and the management of scarce material and manpower resources for increased productivity and profit. Fulfilment of these aims was through the diverse methods of armed control, ideology, administrative ordering and improved communication. In the process, the Southeast Asian community moved into a period of transition leading into the modern era.

In island Southeast Asia, Western influence directly and indirectly stimulated development in the prosperous maritime centres before the end of the eighteenth century. Relative to these events, the forces which determined the cycles of change on the mainland remained, as yet, internal. The seventeenth-century dalliance of Toungoo Burma, Ayutthaya and Le Vietnam with merchant adventurers, commercial companies and missionary educators had, soon after the mid-century, provoked suspicion and caution, resisting Western involvement. This meant that just as indigenous power in the archipelago reached a point of overall stasis or decline about the mid-eighteenth century, the momentum of cyclic reintegration began to gain full force on the mainland. The new burst of energy was propelled by a complex array of forces. The cumulative impact of population growth and movement, with the related problems of resource mobilization and economic competition, the maturing and leavening of religious and political ideology and the importation of Western arms, launched mainland Southeast Asia into the most spectacular and expansive era of indigenous statehood and centralization.

During the decades straddling the foundation of the last autonomous dynasties—the Konbaung (1752–1885), the Chakri (1782–   ), and the Nguyen (1802–1945)—the inherent forces of integration and authority were stretched to their maximum limits of growth and geographical expansion. The push from within the Irrawaddy, the Chao Phraya and the Red (Hong) River valleys laid the ground for conflict among the kingdoms of Burma, Siam and Vietnam for political integration, involving expansion along roughly north–south valley and coastal orientations. Wedged between these geographically determined political configurations were the land-locked Lao principalities and Cambodia, suffering the humiliation and loss brought by shrinking borders and the perpetual insecurity of buffer status. The problems of inter-state conflicts were exacerbated and never permanently resolved due to the nature of Southeast Asian political authority, at the apex of a hierarchy of power based on patron–client relations. As power was fluid, the fortunes of the polity fluctuated with the expansion and contraction of its territories. In the absence of fixed boundaries, influence shaded out with distance from the centre. Loyalties in the peripheral areas were less secure than elsewhere, though during the period under survey they were drawn closer to the main centres of power than at any other time before. In the main, regional, economic and

Map 5.1   Mainland Southeast Asia during the early nineteenth century.

religious integration which came with territorial expansion superseded ethnic divisions such as those between Shan, Burman and Mon, or between Thai, Khmer and Lao. Here loyalty and vassalage were elicited more successfully than in the cultural and religious interface between Thai and Malay or Khmer and Vietnamese. The foundation of the three new dynasties of the mainland saw the primary contours of the region take shape, leaving the firming of boundaries to the approaching era of European imperialism.

FORCES OF INTEGRATION: RELIGION, CHARISMA AND RESOURCE CONTROL

Much as in island Southeast Asia, geo-economic and religious factors were essential ingredients for territorial expansion and integration in the Theravāda-influenced Irrawaddy-Salween and Chao Phraya valleys, from indeed at least the time of Pagan and Ayutthaya. This process of expansion and integration marked the gradual establishment of Burmese and Thai hegemony in the respective regions.

The essence of political authority lay in the ruler's effective control and utilization of resources at the centre. The Theravāda Buddhist ruler's role as the fountain of justice and power was idealized in the concepts of *dhammarāja* and *cakkavatti*. It was the duty of the ruler to enhance his *karma* (merit) through charitable acts (*dana*) and by instituting the laws of *dhamma* (Buddhist teachings). But intensification and extension of this function within a larger community of people obliged him to assume the role of *cakkavatti* or Universal Monarch. Within the framework of this philosophy, the Theravāda Buddhist rulers of the mainland managed the manpower and material resources of their environment. A successful interrelation of the spiritual and secular roles was an essential aspect of the ruler's charisma.

Given the ruler's central role in resource management, the recurrent economic calamities during the reigns of Pindale (1648–61) and Pyè (1661–72) in Burma were a logical outcome of diminished royal authority and administrative efficiency and, specifically, the neglect of agriculture. The downward spiralling persisted during the reign of their successors, culminating in the 1752 Mon conquest of Ava.[1] Simultaneously, Ayutthaya showed a clear but less dramatic downward slide in its internal politics. King Borommakot (r. 1733–58) was unable to check the loss of royal manpower (*phrai luang*), as against the growth of private manpower (*phrai som*) amongst the princes and ministers. This undermined the strength of the ruler and laid the court open to political intrigues.[2] Weakness at the capital unleashed centrifugal forces favouring diffuse centres of power and the assertion of subregional and provincial interests. Towards the mid-eighteenth century Ava was plagued by Manipuri and Shan raids, while

---

[1] V. B. Lieberman, *Burmese Administrative Cycles: Anarchy and Conquest, c.1580–1760*, Princeton, 1984, 142–55, 176–7.

[2] Akin Rabibhadana, 'The Organization of Thai Society in the Early Bangkok Period, 1782–1873', Data Paper no. 74, Southeast Asian Program, Cornell University, 1969, 36–9.

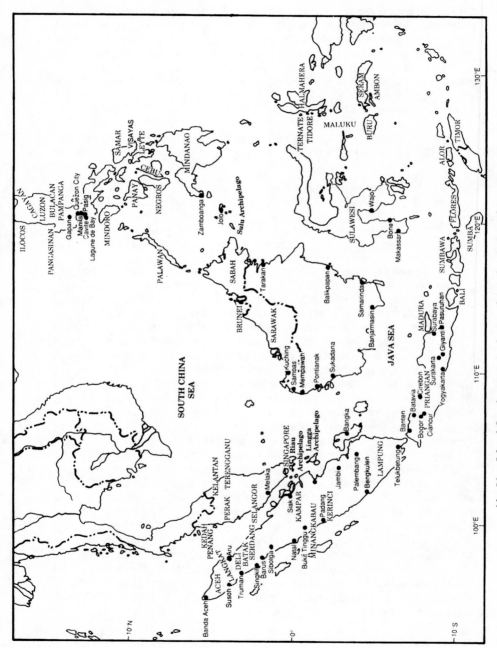

Map 5.2   Island Southeast Asia during the early nineteenth century.

Mon power achieved brief ascendancy in the south, centred on Pegu (1740–52). In Ayutthaya similar fragmentation of power befell the kingdom on the failure of King Suriyamarin (r. 1758–67) to defend his capital successfully against Burma's cataclysmic invasion. It resulted in the decentralization of power at Phitsanulok, Sawankhalok, Nakhon Sithammarat, Phimai and Chanthaburi.

Abandonment of *dhamma*, the universal laws of righteousness, justice and morality enshrined in the teachings of Buddha, was believed to bring dynasties to an end. Conversely, manifestation of the principle became the cardinal qualification for the initiators of new lines of kingship. In Burma and Siam no clear rules of succession were fixed in terms of pedigree or precedence of rank and seniority within the royal house; but male offspring of royal mothers or concubines had preference under normal conditions. When the dynasty's loss of credibility provoked challenge, however, there was provision for tapping new sources of leadership, setting aside ethnic and class boundaries. In Burma, the southern Mon reaction against Ava's decline was led by Smin Dhaw, a man of Gwei-Karen origins, with a polyglot following, who was acclaimed ruler at Pegu in 1740.[3] He was succeeded by the Shan elephanteer, Binnya Dala (r. 1747–57) who was ousted by Maung Aung Zeya, headman of the obscure village of Mok-hso-bo (Shwebo). The latter, as Alaungpaya (r. 1752–60), founded the Konbaung dynasty at Ava. In Siam, Phraya Taksin, the man who rose to power after Ayutthaya's fall in 1767 and founded a new capital at Thonburi, was the son of a wealthy and influential Chinese merchant. His successor, Rama I (r. 1782–1809), who moved the capital to the opposite east bank of Chao Phraya to Bangkok and founded the Chakri dynasty, shared similar ties with the important Chinese merchant élite originating from Ayutthayan times, through his mother Dan Ruang.[4] The Chakri dynasty's links with the foreign merchant community were reinforced through the mother of Rama II (r. 1809–24), Queen Amarin, a member of the prominent Bunnag family of Persian merchant origin.

While the physical prowess of Binnya Dala and Alaungpaya and the royal military commissions of Phraya Taksin and Phraya Chakri were important passports to leadership, enhancement of it through personal charisma was imperative for the mobilization of manpower and realization of the status of *cakkavatti*. It was said that heavenly signs at the time of his birth portended Alaungpaya's future greatness and, just before Ava's fall, in 1752, he was rumoured to have 'the smell of a king about him'.[5]

In the establishment of monarchical power, control over the nuclear resource base was a paramount consideration for the process of legitimization. Preceding Alaungpaya's rise, decline of the agricultural core region in the Kyaukse basin, through the neglect of irrigation and famine, had

---

[3] N. Brailey, 'A Re-investigation of the Gwe of Eighteenth Century Burma', JSEAS, 1, 2 (1970); Lieberman, *Burmese Administrative Cycles*, 217.

[4] K. Wenk, *The Restoration of Thailand Under Rama I, 1782–1809*, Tucson: Association of Asian Studies, University of Arizona, 1968, 1–2; D. K. Wyatt, *Thailand, A Short History*, New Haven, 1982, 161–2.

[5] Arthur P. Phayre, *History of Burma ... from the Earliest Times to the End of the First War with British India*, 1883, reprinted New York, 1969, 149–50; Lieberman, *Burmese Administrative Cycles*, 235.

driven population to the south and to Arakan. It was therefore at Shwebo, within the focus of the resource base in the Mu region, that the new ruler established his capital. Not until the unification with lower Burma and the return of relative stability was the prosperity of the traditional Burmese heartland at Kyaukse restored, motivating Ava's resurgence as the capital under Hsinbiyushin (r. 1763–76).

Similar considerations of resource control influenced the political reorganization and consolidation under the rulers of Siam. Faced with the devastation of Ayutthaya by the Burmese in 1767 and the depletion of the population through thousands being carried away as captives, Taksin sought to lay a stable resource base in Teochiu Chinese activity in the south. Labour shortage and a significant upturn in the trade with China since the decline of European commercial influence at the turn of the previous century led Taksin to cultivate the Chinese community on the opposite bank of Thonburi, having already established contacts with them in Rayong, on the Gulf of Thailand. They provided the labour force for draining the marshy region and for laying out new areas of cultivation, together with the skills for carpentry and building construction. The shifting of the capital by Rama I to the more strategic location on the east bank at Bangkok contributed immensely to immigration and trade, and an expanded market for Chinese bricks and tiles. A desperate shortage of rice at the start of the Bangkok era had made supplies from the Malay peninsula imperative. But by the 1780s Siam's double cropping enabled it to resume exports to China, with the Ch'eng-hai merchants assuming a dominant role in this sector of trade.[6]

In Burma, in the course of attempting a valley-wide integration of the Irrawaddy, Alaungpaya did not underestimate the importance of the delta region, the point of ingress for the two essential ingredients for consolidation—Theravāda Buddhism and Western arms. The delta was, moreover, the focus of Mon resistance. In founding the delta entrepôt at the holy city of Dagon, which he renamed Rangoon in 1755, he envisaged effectively undermining Mon power at Pegu and gaining ready access to Western arms at Syriam. Unsuccessful overtures to the British for cannons left Alaungpaya with no option but to fall back on manpower resources, drawn from among the loyal Burmans in the north, to subdue the Mons. Given the river silting which had closed off Pegu and was beginning to affect Syriam, Alaungpaya's move to shift the port to Rangoon was timely and pragmatic.[7] A simultaneous shift of capital to the south remained, nonetheless, out of the question. The delta continued to serve as an important frontier outlet for the dry zone; but economic incentives were insufficient to offset the ravages of malaria and political instability. Despite Burmese attempts at acculturation, Mon hostility remained evident in no less than six rebellions during Konbaung rule. Strategically as well, a centrally located capital in the northern plains was of prime importance.

[6] Hong Lysa, *Thailand in the Nineteenth Century, Evolution of the Economy and Society*, Singapore: Institute of Southeast Asian Studies, 1984, 47; Sarasin Viraphol, *Tribute and Profit: Sino-Siamese Trade, 1652–1853*, Cambridge, Mass.: Council of East Asian Studies, 1977, 109.
[7] B. R. Pearn, *A History of Rangoon*, Rangoon, 1939, 41–8.

Manipuri raids and symptoms of restlessness amongst the Shans did, in fact, force Alaungpaya to break off the expedition to the south in order to return to the north. Moreover, the capital's proximity to the important trade route to Yunnan and access to rice granaries—those of the Kyaukse and Mu valleys in the vicinity as well as Prome in the south—militated against a transfer to the coast.

The isolation from the coast of the Burmese core region in the north, except for a brief period during the reigns of Bayinnaung (1551–81) and his son Nandabayin (1581–99) when the capital was at Pegu, sharply contrasted with the Chakri dynasty's integration of its rice economy with external trade. The main disincentives to the early expansion of the rice economy in the delta would appear to have been the prohibition of rice exports and the diversion of supplies, collected as tax, to the northern dry zone where the escalation of war under the early Konbaung rulers effected a heavy depletion of manpower and food supplies. The lack of economic incentive, combined with the hazards of malaria in newly opened areas, limited rice acreage to clusters of settlements. By 1830 the total area under rice cultivation in lower Burma was no more than 260,000 hectares, as against 1 million hectares in the northern dry zone.[8] But, despite the contrast between coast and interior, there was effective valley-wide economic integration, evident in increased commercialization. Hence, during the period 1750–1830, about 97 per cent of the land sales were made exclusively in silver.[9] By the last decades preceding the British conquest in 1852, the economic disparity between coast and interior was less significant. There was considerable economic growth in the delta which emerged as the chief granary of the Konbaung dynasty.[10]

BUDDHIST IMPERIALISM

The imperial policies of Burma during this period, often challenging any economic and political rationale, were grounded in the philosophy that it was the ultimate end of the Buddhist state, through the ruler as its chief instrument, to extend the *dhamma*, if necessary by forceful conquest. While such acts of humanity as the respective efforts of Alaungpaya and Taksin at the beginning of their reigns to relieve hunger and the ravages of war had won wide loyalty, their later insensitivity and claims to Bodhisattva status alienated the *sangha* and the populace.[11] Standing before the gates of Ayutthaya, Alaungpaya made an appeal for surrender, claiming he was

---

[8] V. Lieberman, 'Secular Trends in Burmese Economic History, c. 1350–1830', paper presented to the Conference on Southeast Asia in the Fifteenth to Eighteenth Centuries, organized by the Social Science Research Council and Universidate Nova de Lisboa, December 1989, 7.

[9] ibid., 16.

[10] M. Adas, *The Burmese Delta: Economic Development and Social Change on an Asian Rice Frontier, 1852–1941*, Madison, 1974, 20–2.

[11] C. J. Reynolds, 'The Buddhist Monkhood in Nineteenth-Century Thailand', Ph.D. thesis, Cornell University, 1973, 32–4; J. G. Koenig, 'Journal of a Voyage from India to Siam and Malacca in 1779', *Journal of the Straits Branch of the Royal Asiatic Society*, XXVI (1894) 164–5; B. J. Terwiel, *A History of Modern Thailand 1767–1942*, St Lucia, Queensland, 1983, 56–7.

the *arimittiya* or the future Buddha, that brought ridicule and the loss of credibility in the eyes of the Thais.[12]

Quite apart from the need to quell border tribes, it could be argued that the military exploits of the early Konbaung rulers were aimed at securing submission and loyalty; but expeditions beyond the valley complex drained Burmese resources. The economic importance of the wet-rice Shan states and their contribution of manpower for the pacification of the Mons was a strong factor in favour of their reduction to vassalage. Similarly, the capture of Chiengmai in 1762 gave the Burmese the advantage of additional forces for the victorious assault on Ayutthaya in 1767. As it proved, the price that Burma paid for entanglement in the northeast was heavy. Interference with the Shan and Lao states brought the Burmese right up to the borders of China, culminating in friction with the Chinese viceroy over the status of Kengtung. The Burmese under Hsinbiyushin fought off four Chinese invasions, each larger than the last, and secured the Shan states. These events, however, interrupted the lucrative overland trade with Yunnan involving the exchange largely of cotton for silks. The conflict was also a heavy drain on resources, not least with investment in thousands of gold and silver images at the shrines at Shwezigon (Pagan) and Shwedagon (Rangoon) in order to avert the heavenly vengeance portended by the occurrence of earthquake at the time of the Chinese threat.[13] The ruler's control over manpower and natural resources during this period was attested in Hsinbiyushin's boast, recorded in a 1768 inscription at Shwezigon, that he could rebuild the royal city of Ava in 106 days.[14]

After the brief respite from war during the reign of the passive Singu (1776–82) who took refuge in religion, the government of Bodawpaya (r. 1782–1819) marked the high point of imperialist ambitions. Arakanese incursions were countered by conquest in 1784. But, by extending Burma's borders close to British India, Bodawpaya opened the way for later external intervention. At the termination of the war an estimated 20,000 captives were deported, transporting the gigantic Mahamuni image via the Arakan Pass. These barely compensated for casualties incurred by military expeditions. Of an estimated 200,000 men conscripted for the 1785 and 1786 expeditions against Siam, for example, about 40 per cent were lost to disease or desertion.[15] Regardless of the disruption to economic activity brought by war and the general population drain, forced labour was pressed from the Shans, Mons and the Burmese to satisfy the spiritual ambitions of the ruler. He commemorated his claim to future Buddhahood by the construction at Mingun of a bell, smaller only than that in the Kremlin, and an unfinished pagoda of fifty metres—one-third of the proposed height. The effects of labour mobilization reached crisis point in

[12] Maung Htin Aung, *A History of Burma*, New York, 1967, 169; J. P. Ferguson, 'The Symbolic Dimensions of the Burmese Sangha', Ph.D. thesis, Cornell University, 1975, 183–4.

[13] Phayre, 198.

[14] Ma Yi Yi, 'A Bibliographical Essay on the Burmese Sources for the History of the Konbaung Period, 1752–1885', paper presented to the First International Conference of Southeast Asian Historians, Singapore, 1961, 4.

[15] F. N. Trager and W. J. Koenig, *Burmese Sit-Tàns, 1764–1826: Records of Rural Life and Administration*, Association of Asian Studies Monograph, no. XXXVI, Tucson, 1979, 29–30.

1795 with a major expansion of the Meiktila tank and irrigation system which affected virtually the entire kingdom. Agriculture was seriously disrupted and, with successive seasons of drought, a prolonged famine set in during 1805 which lasted nearly a decade.[16] In 1809, at the height of widespread hunger, flight and banditry, Bodawpaya launched his five-pronged attack on Siam, the largest he ever mounted. It was largely a failure, apart from securing the ports of Mergui and Tenasserim against Rama I's attempts to continue in possession of them, and it brought Burmese imperialist efforts to a halt through the sheer drain of resources.

In converting the state into a vast war machine, Bodawpaya instituted more efficient collection of revenue through checking irregularities in the functioning of the *hlutdaw* administrative and judicial council. Towards the same end, surveys of population, boundaries and productivity were conducted during his reign.[17] The *sasana* reform, or purification of the *sangha*, also contributed towards increasing royal revenues by checking tax evasions where private property was held under the guise of glebe lands.[18] Military victories earned with the blood of the people were commemorated with architectural excesses executed with even more labour impressed from them. The burdens of labour, aggravated by the rapacity of local officials, drove the Arakanese to rebellion in 1794 and the flight of thousands to Chittagong, precipitating British diplomatic reaction. Others sought refuge in Thai and Shan areas. The opportunities for wage labour at Rangoon, from timber-felling for the growing shipbuilding industry in Calcutta, provided additional outlets for the disgruntled.

Bodawpaya's absolutism alienated him from other sectors of the community as well. It put Burma clearly on the path of decline from which it was unable to recover under more enlightened rulers like Mindon Min (r. 1853–78). Harsh measures were taken against restive commanders and unorthodox clergy alike. As part of the programme of religious purification, Bodawpaya put an end to the longstanding 'shoulder wrapping' controversy pertaining to the dress of monks, in favour of the 'two-shoulder' faction. The office of primate which Alaungpaya had created was modified so that the incumbent acted in consultation with a newly constituted ecclesiastical council. Bodawpaya's merit-making act of feeding thousands of monks, his construction of pagodas in about 250 towns, and his ascetic practices did little to absolve him from negligence of economic affairs. His sternest critics were a reformist lay group who postulated the revolutionary concept of de-emphasizing the material aspects of merit-making. They were punished, but Bodawpaya had no way of forcing the *sangha* to acknowledge his claims for divinity.[19]

Despite many points of similarity in their institutional foundations, and the comparable achievements of the contemporaneous Bodawpaya

[16] W. J. Koenig, 'The Early Kón-Baung Polity, 1752–1819: A Study of Politics, Administration and Social Organization in Burma', Ph.D. thesis, University of London, 1978, 87–8.

[17] Trager and Koenig, 53.

[18] M. Aung-Thwin, 'The Role of *Sasana* Reform in Burmese History; Economic Dimensions of a Religious Purification', JAS, 38, 4 (1979) 674; V. B. Lieberman, 'The Political Significance of Religious Wealth in Burmese History: Some Further Thoughts', JAS, 39, 4 (1980) 768.

[19] Ferguson, 202–4.

and Rama I in pushing the boundaries of their respective empires to their fullest limits, Burma and Siam were on different paths. The programme of Burmese expansion, along the finger-like valley and coastal configuration, as well as across Shan and Lao territories, found no natural focus in Ava. In contrast, Thai military activity fanned out from Bangkok with greater facility up the Chao Phraya and down the Gulf of Thailand to the isthmus. Unlike the Burmese who faced Mon challenge, the Thais had the further advantage of the absence of major ethnic conflict within the nuclear zone. Perhaps with a fresh memory of the unfortunate end to which Taksin's spiritual presumptions had led him, the Chakri rulers were content with a more modest interpretation of their role as *cakkavatti* than their Burmese counterparts. Their military initiatives, provoked largely by Burmese and Vietnamese expansion on the outer flanks, involved bringing under their vassalage the Laotian states of the north and northeast, Cambodia in the southeast and the northern Malay states.

Thai territorial expansion followed a systematic policy of consolidation, which was generally not the case in Burma. Begun by Taksin, who achieved integration of the core region by eliminating his rivals at Phitsanulok and Fang, a programme of pacification helped build up a complete circle of border provinces with strong administrative ties with the centre. The importance of Chinese economic activity in the Gulf of Thailand drew Taksin's attention first to the south where Nakhon Sithammarat and Songkhla were brought under Thai vassalage and were maintained as quasi-independent provinces, the latter headed by a Chinese governor.[20] In the north and northwest, the suspension of Burmese military activity during the reign of Singu allowed the Thais the opportunity to gain control over Chiengmai in 1776. Though seriously depopulated and depleted by frequent Thai–Burmese conflicts, it was to emerge during the reign of Rama I as the most influential *müang* (province), supervising the northern tributaries, as Nakhon Sithammarat and Songkhla supervised those in the south.[21] Bangkok appointed the provincial governors, whose sons, in their capacity as royal pages at the capital, were virtually political hostages.

Beyond the circle of the outer provinces, Champassak and Vientiane in the northeast and Siemreap and Attopeu in the southeast formed a buffer zone with local rulers under Thai vassalage. Vientiane and Luang Prabang, the strongest of the Lao states, were not wholly submissive, but their mutual rivalries were used to good effect by Siam. Luang Prabang terminated relations with Burma in 1778 and, as well as offering tribute to China, sent the 'silver and gold tree' to Bangkok. In 1791–2, suspicion of its loyalty caused Siam to reduce it to complete submission, using Vientiane forces. In 1797, 1799 and 1803 Vientiane provided Siam with support also against Burmese attempts to recapture the northern Lao states. Vientiane's buffer status, with expanding Vietnamese power on its eastern flank, led to its adoption of dual allegiance, much in the Cambodian

[20] Chenglo A. Cheng, 'Mac Thien Tu and Phrayataksin, A Survey on their political stand, conflicts and background', *Proceedings of the Seventh Conference of the International Association of the Historians of Asia*, Bangkok, 1977, 1538.
[21] L. M. Gresick, 'Kingship and Political Integration in Traditional Siam, 1767–1824', Ph.D. thesis, Cornell University, 1976, 126–7, 129.

manner. It allied with the Nguyen leader, Gia-long, against the Tayson and, between 1804–17, sent a triennial tribute of elephants, horses, rhinoceros horn, ivory and cinnamon.[22] The termination of Vientiane's tribute after this period could have been due to the preoccupation of the ruler, Chao Anu (Anuvong), with consolidating his power in the face of Thai domination and attempts at assimilation, such as the policy of tattooing enacted in 1824.[23]

Relations between Siam and Vientiane soon reached a crisis. Rebuffed by failure to secure the appointment of his son as ruler of Champassak, as reward for earlier assistance against the northern Lao principalities, Anu prepared for revolt. His audacious march against Bangkok in 1827 was calculated to coincide with an ill-founded rumour of a British attack on the capital. The fierce Thai retaliation that followed dealt a deadly blow to Laotian power. It depopulated virtually the whole left bank of the Mekong through massacre and mass transportation of captives. This episode, encompassing the destruction and abolition of Vientiane, became in time the major trauma of Lao nationalist memory. On the isthmus end of Siam's outer fringe, religious and cultural differences exacerbated the independent spirit of the distant vassals. Terengganu, Perak and Kedah paid tribute only under duress, and recalcitrant Pattani was subdued in 1791.

Excluding the outer rim of independent and semi-independent tributary states (*prathetsarat* or *müang khun*), Thai administration was based on manpower control. The size of provincial units was determined roughly in inverse proportion to the density of population, which decreased overall from the centre to the fringes.[24] Under Rama I, the territories were neatly classified in accordance with the degree of administrative power exercised over them by Bangkok. The tributary peninsular states on the peripheries of the kingdom, with Cambodia, enjoyed the maximum independence, holding the status of first-class *müang*. The remaining provinces were divided into second- third- and fourth-class *müang*. Songkhla, Nakhon Sithammarat and Battambang-Siemreap, as border capitals, enjoyed the status of second-class *müang*. The principalities of Chiengmai, Vientiane, Champassak and Pattani fell within the purview of the third-class *müang*. They owed tribute, manpower and military obligations and could expect arbitrary Thai interference in their internal affairs. The remaining core provinces of the original Ayutthayan kingdom, within the direct control of the capital, constituted the fourth-class *müang*. The degree of territorial integration achieved was evident, for example, in the demotion of Phitsanulok and Nakhon Sithammarat to the status of third- and second-class respectively, from being first-class *müang* during Ayutthayan times.[25] The administrative ordering of the kingdom, imperative for stability, ensured at the same time the mechanics for mobilizing resources. Enhanced centralization allowed for the systematic exploitation of proportionately increased

[22] D. K. Wyatt, 'Siam and Laos, 1767–1827', JSEAH, 4, 2 (1963) 27.

[23] B. Terwiel, 'Tattooing in Thailand's History', JRAS, (1979) 158; Mayoury and Pheuiphanh Ngaosyvathn, 'Lao Historiography and Historians: Case Study of the War between Bangkok and Lao in 1827', JSEAS, 20, 1 (1989) 58–9.

[24] L. Sternstein, 'The Distribution of Thai Centres at Mid-nineteenth Century', JSEAH, 7, 1 (1966) 66–72.

[25] Gesick, 25–6; Wyatt, *Thailand*, 158.

sources of wealth and manpower from the outer circle to the centre, committing the directly administered provinces to greater economic obligations than the vassal territories beyond them. Reinforcement of loyalties to the capital was institutionalized in the annual 'water of allegiance' ceremony for *müang* within the Siamese proper, while vassal states were additionally obliged to send, periodically, the 'gold and silver tree'.[26] Loyalties secured by force, rather than voluntary submission, were then carefully nurtured through military assistance and protection in times of crisis. Where conciliation failed coercion was inevitable, as frequently in the case of the northern Malay states.

BUFFER STATUS AND DOUBLE ALLEGIANCE

Shared affinities with a glorious Khmer past and Theravāda Buddhism accounted for Thai paternalism towards a weak Cambodia as the Vietnamese push into the Mekong gained momentum at the beginning of the eighteenth century. Thai influence at the Khmer capital at Udong had waned after the fall of Ayutthaya but was soon renewed with the diversion of Vietnamese attentions away from Cambodian affairs on the outbreak of the Tayson rebellion (1771–1802) (see page 588). By offering refuge to Prince Ang Eng, fleeing civil war in Cambodia, and the Nguyen prince, Nguyen Anh, who had escaped the Tayson rebels, Rama I won the allegiance of both. Ang Eng provided Rama I the means to restore Thai patronage in Cambodia. The ruler regarded the young prince as 'a priceless jewel' and raised him 'as his own adopted son', installing him at Udong when he came of age (r. 1794–7). In the meantime, backed by supplies and arms from Rama I for resistance against the Tayson, Nguyen Anh established himself in Saigon in 1788. He faithfully acknowledged vassalage with the sending of the 'gold and silver tree' in 1788, 1790, 1795, 1797 and 1801, which the Thai ruler reciprocated with rich gifts of silks, horses, saddles and gongs; this ceased abruptly, however, on his elevation to the throne at Hué in 1802 as Emperor Gia-long. He continued to show his deep gratitude to Rama I, sending lavish presents of gold and silver ingots to the Thai court. But these were in lieu of the 'gold and silver tree', a symbol of vassalage, which he was no longer prepared to offer. Gia-long's claim to equal status with the Thai ruler was evident in the advice he despatched to his former patron about the desirability of appointing a new heir apparent at Bangkok, following the death of the incumbent in 1804.[27]

The instability of Thai influence in Cambodia during the early nineteenth century demonstrated the fragility of tributary relations. In the political upheavals which followed the end of each reign in Cambodia, the military intervention of the suzerain power often established a semblance of stability. The peace was disrupted in time by internal forces of dissent, initiating a new cycle of change. Cambodian leaders lacked the economic options available to the Chakri and Nguyen rulers for rebuilding

---

[26] Gesick, 37–8.
[27] Chaophraya Thiphakorawong, *The Dynastic Chronicles, Bangkok Era, The First Reign*, ed. and trans. Thadeus and Chadin Flood, Tokyo, 1978, I. 272–3.

independent power. The region's commercial potential was seriously undermined by loss of the coast, south of Phnom Penh, to the Vietnamese. Its chief port, Kampot, was described during the mid-nineteenth century as totally lacking life and bustle, 'with only 300 houses at most'.[28] Cambodia, with its sparse population, was dependent largely on a subsistence economy without the necessary manpower, wealth and arms for effective centralized authority. Though more tolerant perhaps of the Thais with whom they shared cultural affinities, the Cambodians were resentful of the patronizing 'brother' image and civilizing mission of the Vietnamese in their attempt to impose a Confucianist model government. Vietnamese interference in Cambodian affairs, which had abated during the Tayson rebellion, came to a head with the powerful thrust southward under Emperor Gia-long. Caught between two poles of influence, Cambodia adopted a policy of dual allegiance or the image of the 'double-headed' bird, though its gaze fell more readily on Bangkok. Cambodia's leanings towards the Thai capital, by contrast to its uneasy feelings towards Hué, were succinctly expressed in the informal annual tribute to the one and the formal triennial missions to the other.[29]

The depth of anti-Vietnamese feeling found expression in the 1820 uprising led by a monk named Kai from Ba Phnom, which closely paralleled the anti-colonial revolts in contemporary Philippines and Java, spurred by forced labour and economic repression (see pages 597–8). The Kai rebellion had its origins in the recruitment of about a thousand Cambodians out of a total workforce of 50,000 for employment in the construction of the Vinh Te Canal, running some 40 kilometres from Hatien to the city of Chau Doc (Chau Phu). The exploitation of Cambodian labour by a powerful neighbour was not, however, without precedent. Thai chronicles of 1783 report the conscription of ten times as many Cambodians for the construction of the Ropkrung canal to the east side of Bangkok.[30] This would suggest that the Vietnamese recruitment of labour for the Vinh Te canal provided the occasion rather than the cause for the ensuing rebellion. Despite the wide following the movement attracted, Kai's eventual defeat was rationalized by a Cambodian narrative poem of 1869 for popular recitation in typically Southeast Asian terms, as resulting from the loss of merit and charisma.[31]

> [A]lthough his people still saw him as a refuge, the misdeeds they all had done were inescapable. In the same way Kai, when he had become a monk, had gained a large amount of merit. After what he had done, the merit had faded away, and now he had no special powers; he had become an ordinary man. His honour was no longer great; his skills were ineffective . . . [T]his time, when the enemy drew near, there was no merit to his blessings. His followers were unable to attack or fire their weapons . . .

[28] H. Mouhot, *Travels in Siam, Cambodia and Laos, 1858–60*, London, 1864, repr. Singapore, 1989, I. 180.

[29] D. P. Chandler, 'Cambodia Before the French: Politics in a Tributary Kingdom, 1794–1848', Ph.D. thesis, Michigan University, 1973, 64–8.

[30] D. P. Chandler, *A History of Cambodia*, Boulder, 1983, 120–1; Thiphakorawong, I. 58.

[31] D. P. Chandler, 'An Anti-Vietnamese Rebellion in Early Nineteenth Century Cambodia: Pre-colonial Imperialism and Pre-Nationalist Response', JSEAS, 6, 1 (1975) 21.

It, nonetheless, left an indelible memory in Cambodian folklore of Vietnamese misrule.[32]

Local reaction was again brought to a head in 1840 following the introduction of census and cadastral surveys aimed at more efficient taxation and military mobilization. These and other measures of Vietnamization were viewed as a threat to Cambodian kingship, Buddhism and social structure. The initiators of the popular anti-Vietnamese rebellion were the *okya* or high-ranking officials, who viewed themselves as the guardians of Khmer tradition. Vietnamese reforms relating to taxation and the maintenance of efficient records, including those pertaining to grain stocks, made heavy demands on the *okya* who administered the *sruk* (districts). Within the unchanging Cambodian context of political patronage, the withdrawal of Vietnamese interference in 1847 followed by the resumption of allegiance to Siam by Ang Duong, provided only a compromise for the messianic hopes of the peasantry and the apprehensions of the traditional élite. The installation of Ang Duong (r. 1848–60) by Thai ceremonial investiture at Udong and with a seal of authorization from Hué returned Cambodia, nominally, to dual allegiance, ushering in a brief 'golden era'.[33]

ECONOMIC AND CULTURAL CRISIS

Vietnamese economic and political exploits in Cambodia were a direct symptom of the agrarian crisis within Vietnam stemming from problems of land distribution, political instability and institutional weakness. Population growth and pressure on land were aggravated by the creation of latifundia and socio-economic instability stemming from civil war and resistance to the burdens of taxation; as of the fifteenth century, this combination of factors accelerated the push towards Cham and Khmer territories. Factionalism amongst rival clans and Trinh domination of the Le court at Hanoi led to Nguyen separatism in 1626 and the Nguyen bid to find an outlet for their ambitions in the frontier territories to the south. Establishing their capital in Hué, they supported the southern expansion through founding military colonies (*don dien*). By the eighteenth century the environmental constraints of the narrow Annamite coastal plain brought the focus of migration to the Mekong delta.[34] By 1760, six delta provinces came under Nguyen lords. Economic problems were evidently less severe in the south, where greater opportunities existed for opening up new lands and for commercial activity at Qui Nhon and delta towns such as Hatien and Vinh Long. Nonetheless, the burdens of seigniorial authority in the form of taxes, levies, serfdom and encroachment on communal lands were common to both Trinh and Nguyen territories. These grievances repeatedly fuelled peasant resistance, whether to internal oppression or Chinese domination, contributing to the overarching theme of liberation in Vietnamese history.

[32] Chandler, 'Cambodia Before the French', 103.
[33] Chandler, *History of Cambodia*, 128–36.
[34] M. Cotter, 'Towards a Social History of the Vietnamese Southward Movement', JSEAH, 9, 1 (1968) 14–15, 18–19.

Evasion was the universal means of avoiding tax burdens, and the 1725 census survey for more efficient collection of taxes resulted in a major insurrection. Oppressive taxes, neglect of irrigation, and natural calamities culminated in famine some ten years later, with the drift and dispersal of population and widespread mortality.[35] There was increased awareness of the ineffectiveness and decadence of seigniorial rule and the corruption of the bureaucracy, brought about by the purchase of offices by the mandarins. This fostered a new spirit of questioning and re-evaluation of traditional values. A succinct and cynical comment on Confucianist-mandarin ideology found expression in the poem, 'Passing by the Shrine of Ch'in', by Nguyen Du (1765–1820).[36]

> A tattered sheepskin on his back,
> he trudged and lugged his bundle home.
> His woman would not leave the loom.
> His sister would not cook for him.
> His parents gave him not one glance,
> treating him like a passerby.
> When fortune disregards a man,
> his flesh and blood ignore him, too.
> But then Su Ch'in's big moment came.
> Six seals of office jingled on his sash.
> Pairs of jade rings, ingots of gold—by tons
> his coaches carried them to his old door.
> His parents met him at the village gate.
> His wife, awestruck, admired him with shy eyes.
> His sister greeted him on bended knees.
> His lifetime's ambition he'd achieved.
> 'You all respect me now—why not before?' . . .

The emergence of new values based on Vietnamese, as opposed to a Chinese identity, was apparent in the use of the *nom* Vietnamese script for prose and poetry and a critical reassessment of human relationships, hitherto viewed from a Confucianist perspective. The assertion of female identity within Vietnamese society, for example, is evident in the eighteenth-century lament by the poetess, Ho Xuan Huong, on 'Husband Sharing':[37]

> One rolls in warm blankets,
> The other freezes:
> Down with this husband-sharing!
> You're lucky ever to have him,
> He comes perhaps twice a month,
> Or less.
> Ah—to fight for—this!
> Turned to a half-servant, an unpaid maid!
> Had I known
> I would have stayed single.

[35] J. Chesneaux, *Contribution à l'histoire de la Nation Vietnamienne*, Paris, 1955, 49; Thomas Hodgkin, *Vietnam: The Revolutionary Path*, New York, 1981, 79.
[36] Huỳnh Sanh Thông, ed. and trans., *The Heritage of Vietnamese Poetry*, New Haven, 1979, 53–4.
[37] Nguyen Ngoc Bich, ed. and trans., *A Thousand Years of Vietnamese Poetry*, New York, 1975, 118.

The quest for self-expression and a national identity accrued from the general socio-economic unrest which prevailed for nearly four decades (1730s–1760s). Localized but powerful insurrections broke out in the areas worst affected by poverty, in the heart of the Red River delta, in the provinces of Son Tay, Hai Duong and Son Nam. Disillusionment spread even among the non-peasant classes. The scholar Nguyen Huu Cau, for instance, led the rebellion in 1743 in Hai Duong. Merchant and minority communities swelled the tide of discontent due to the impositions on trade by the Trinh.[38] These included indirect taxes on minerals, salt, charcoal and saltpetre—commodities essential for local industries—and a direct tax on exports, which affected the production of lacquer and silk.[39]

Significantly, anti-mandarin sentiments coalesced in the central location at Tayson which serviced the areca-nut trade between Qui Nhon on the coast and Kontum in the region of the Muong and Bahnar minorities. The three Nguyen brothers who led the rebellion were, like the bulk of their following, men of diverse experience and different talents. The eldest, Nhac, a betel-nut trader, had previously been a tax collector, while the youngest, Lu, was a bonze. But it was Hue, the second, who was the military genius and charismatic figure, 'with a voice musical as a bell and a look bright as lightning'.[40] With its wide support, the rebellion soon gained momentum, undermining Nguyen power enfeebled by the maladministration of Chua Vo Vuong and the succession dispute following his death in 1765.[41] By 1778 the Tayson took effective control over the south, including Saigon. But victory was incomplete in that Nguyen Anh, a grandson of Chua Vo Vuong, escaped and laid the ground for a counter-revolutionary movement.

In the north a succession dispute amongst the Trinh, and an economic crisis aggravated by famine, won Nguyen Hue an easy victory in 1766. After almost two centuries of division Vietnam was effectively reunited, with the exception of some southern localities which still held out under Nguyen Anh. In 1788 Nguyen Hue repulsed a Chinese attempt in 1788 to take Hanoi on behalf of the Trinh before proclaiming himself emperor with the title of Quang-trung (r. 1788–92). Resumption of tributary relations with China was characteristic of Tayson reluctance to break completely with the past while seeking reform within the framework of existing traditions. Agrarian reforms were attempted through conventional land redistribution and by bringing fallow lands into cultivation. At the same time, communal registers were introduced in order to induce the large floating population to settle.[42] A compromise was attempted between tradition and the assertion of a new indigenous identity. Vietnamese manners, including betel-chewing and the wearing of long hair and local dress, were officially permitted except at court. Similarly, the traditional mandarin examination system was retained, but proficiency was required in the composition of prose and verse in *nom*.

---

[38] Chesneaux, 49; Hodgkin, 82–4.
[39] Hodgkin, 79; Le Thanh Khoi, *Le Viêt-Nam, Histoire et Civilisation*, Paris, 1955, 254–6.
[40] Hodgkin, 85.
[41] Le Thanh Khoi, 296–7.
[42] Hodgkin, 91.

An important aspect of Tayson reform was the liberation of commerce and industry. To facilitate trade, a unified currency system was introduced. Symptomatic of the increased circulation of cash and the development towards a monetary system was the growth of wage labour in the main commercial centres of Hanoi, Fai-fo (Quang Nam), Binh Hoa and Saigon, well in advance of parallel developments in Burma and Siam. Mining was activated and shipbuilding, military workshops, paper and printing-works established. These developments, in combination with the abolition or the reduction of taxes on local produce, as well as the liberation of the frontier and maritime trade with China, rendered the thirty-year régime of the Tayson an era of important commercial growth, with the emergence of a pre-capitalist merchant community.[43] Impressed by the scene of change and activity, the poet Nguyen Huy Luong wrote in 1802:[44]

> The smoke of the lime-kilns of Thach Khoi climbs in thick spirals.
> On the rapids of the Nhat Thieu the waves roll roaring on.
> Floating at the rim of the bar of Duoi Nheo the sails of merchant junks are
>   pressed close, like the wings of butterflies . . .
> In the village of Yen Thai the night mist throbs with the sound of pestles
>   pounding paper . . .

Despite the impressive beginnings of reform under Quang-trung, there was no radical restructuring of society so as to resolve the perennial agrarian problems. Trade and merchant activity were still in their infancy, and fundamental problems of agriculture remained. The lack of strong leadership after the death of Quang-trung, at the age of thirty-nine, in 1792, contributed to the success of Nguyen Anh's counter-revolutionary movement. Nguyen Anh gained his initial victories, however, with help from Chinese pirates and Cambodian mercenaries. Then, after the capture of Saigon in 1788, he was backed by French mercantile interests under the influence of the Catholic priest Pierre Pigneau de Behaine, Bishop of Adran. Qui Nhon was captured in 1799 and the Tayson capital, at Hué, in 1801.

To symbolize the unification of north and south for the first time under the name of Vietnam, Nguyen Anh took the title of Gia-long, derived from a combination of Gia Dinh (Saigon) and Thang-long (Hanoi). In terms of policy, the Nguyen administration represented a swing in the pendulum towards the reinstatement of the aristocracy and landed bureaucratic classes, on the Confucianist model, as supports for monarchical power. The resulting royal absolutism of Gia-long (r. 1802–20) and his successor Minh-mang (r. 1820–41) involved centralization to a much greater degree than in China. Under Gia-long two regional overlords, one in Hanoi and another in the person of the powerful Le Van Duyet at Saigon, wielded unrestrained local influence; but under Minh-mang the power of these overlords was removed. To increase the effectiveness of the administration, the country, with a population of about eight million, was divided into 31 centrally controlled provinces (*tinh*) and 283 districts (*huyen*). There

---

[43] Chesneaux, 61–2.
[44] Quoted Hodgkin, 91.

were provincial governors (*tuan phu*) who each supervised the administration of two or three provinces. In comparison with this extensive administrative machinery, Ching China, with roughly 350 million people, had an estimated 1500 districts.[45]

Though the Vietnamese were inspired by the Chinese model, resentment of Chinese domination was evident in their refusal to model themselves on any particular dynasty. Instead, the Nguyen administrative system was derived from an adaptation of those Chinese institutions which most contributed to monarchical power and centralization.[46] In reaction to the Tayson régime and the heterogeneous religious culture it had patronized, neo-Confucianism was central to the Nguyen administrative structure. Gia-long's edicts, in fact, stipulated severe punishment for Taoist and Buddhist practices.[47] The adoption of Chinese architectural styles for the royal palace complex and the building of Vauban-type citadels further insulated the ruling classes from the peasantry.

With the exception of the major cities and ports, the administrative centres did not develop into commercial urban centres, and a large amount of trade continued to be conducted at river confluences.[48] There were impediments to trade in the form of royal monopolies on high-value produce such as ivory, stag-horns, cinnamon, cardamom and gold-dust, raised mainly as tribute from the mountain people.[49] A similar royal monopoly affected the production of silk and bronze. The pervasiveness of the bureaucracy resulted in close government control over guilds and artisans, putting many out of business. Equally detrimental to private enterprise was the direction of skills and raw materials to the imperial workshop at Hué. These conditions, as well as the restrictive commercial taxes and licences for the export of rice, salt and metals, put a brake on earlier beginnings towards commercial development.[50] Mines were the monopoly of the state and were leased to favoured mandarins and Chinese entrepreneurs. The latter, estimated at around 40,000 in the 1820s,[51] continued to dominate the important trade with China. Indigenous merchants were confined to the less profitable internal trade.

In agriculture as well the lot of the masses remained unimproved. Despite Nguyen introduction of salaries and pensions to nobles and officials in lieu of land and taxation rights,[52] the problem of landlessness remained. The meticulous land registers (*dia bo*) and census records (*dinh ba*), compiled annually since 1807 as part of the administrative reforms, provided an important tax base. But the complex computation of taxation

[45] A. B. Woodside, *Vietnam and the Chinese Model: A Comparative Study of Nguyên and Ch'ing Civil Government in the First Half of the Nineteenth Century*, Cambridge, Mass., 1971, 23, 84–5, 142–6.
[46] D. G. Marr, *Vietnamese Anticolonialism, 1885–1925*, Berkeley, 1971, 19–20.
[47] Truong Buu Lam, *New Lamps for Old*, Institute of Southeast Asian Studies Occasional Paper no. 66, Singapore, 1982, 4–5; Hodgkin, 108.
[48] Chesneaux, 77–8.
[49] J. White, *A Voyage to Cochin China*, London, 1824; reprinted with an introduction by M. Osborne, Kuala Lumpur, 1972, 249–50; Chesneaux, 78.
[50] Hodgkin, 113; A. Lamb, 'Crawfurd's Report on the State of the Annamese Empire', *The Mandarin Road to Old Hué*, London, 1970, 263.
[51] Woodside, 31–2, 272–3; Lamb, 257.
[52] J. Buttinger, *Vietnam: A Dragon Embattled*, New York, 1967, 279–80.

on the Chinese model was not commensurate with the significantly smaller population and size of the Vietnamese hamlet.[53] Furthermore, increased revenues from more efficient taxation merely paid for the upkeep of the larger bureaucratic machinery. Greater bureaucratic efficiency augmented corvée and poll-tax demands, from which the nobility and mandarins were exempted, shifting the burden to the peasantry. Sixty days or more per head were taken up annually, involving roughly one-third of the male population.[54] The system was probably more exacting than that system in contemporary Siam, accounting for the conspicuous participation of women in all sectors of private enterprise, including cultivation, industry and commerce.[55]

Corvée labour, apart from being engaged for the building and maintenance of public works, served the important military programme of the Nguyen, involving the building of fortifications, warships and arsenals. Nguyen methods of military recruitment and technology were conservative. The traditional method of conscription for the army and navy, which took the peasantry away from cultivation and fishing, proved detrimental to the economy; it also denied the defence sector its professionalism—a prerequisite for modernization. There was no lack of interest on the part of Gia-long and Minh-mang in Western technology. Gia-long's large fleet at Hué consisted of some square-rigged galleys constructed in European style and mounted with guns. Minh-mang displayed a passion for steamships which led him to set up a factory to copy a Western model. The venture failed, exposing the inadaptability of a conservative Confucianist tradition of education geared to conditions and needs long outmoded. The Nguyen military was impressive, 'dressed, equipped and disciplined after the European manner', and so were its fortifications.[56] But tactically and technologically the Vietnamese were antiquated compared to contemporary Western armies. Their generals believed 'in static defence at a time when European gunnery technology was advancing by quantum degrees in terms of increased power, range and mobility . . .'[57] Military and technological developments were intended mostly to defend against internal opposition and to suppress peasant uprisings.

Within barely two decades of Nguyen rule Vietnam re-entered the inherent cycle of mass discontent, sparked off by famine and epidemic resulting from floods, drought and the ravages of locusts. The total of 73 uprisings during Gia-long's reign escalated to some 234 during Minh-mang's rule.[58] Internally insecure and aware of the country's incapacity to resist Western pressure, Minh-mang turned his back on the Europeans, rejecting the earlier French connections. By the reign of Thieu-tri (1841–7), when French imperialism had joined forces with the Catholic Church, Vietnam's plight contrasted sharply with Siam's security, initiated by the 'subtle revolution' of Rama I. The shortcomings of the Confucianist examination system, apparent to Minh-mang himself, precluded adaptation to

[53] Woodside, 163–4.
[54] Lamb, 266.
[55] ibid., 270; White, 215–16, 245.
[56] Lamb, 267–8.
[57] Marr, 23.
[58] Hodgkin, 114.

changing needs and growing challenges. As Nguyen Truong To, the Catholic priest from Nghe-an, observed in the 1860s:[59]

> Look at Japan and Korea . . . If, instead of directing our efforts and time to polishing our style or to embellishing our calligraphy, we were to study current affairs—battle plans, for example, or the methods of building citadels and firing cannons—we should probably be in a position to resist our enemy.

INTELLECTUAL REFORM AND MODERNIZATION

In striking contrast to Vietnam, the important period of intellectual re-orientation under Rama I has been described by one scholar as 'a sort of Buddhist "Reformation"', though in Siam, unlike Europe, the religious reform involved no institutional conflicts.[60] The problem of restoring the moral decay, believed to have brought the downfall of Ayutthaya, was shared by Taksin and Rama I, as the great elect or *mahāsammata* inherent in the role of a Buddhist ruler. Where Taksin in his attempt to fulfil this regal function transgressed traditional concepts of kingship by his claim to sanctity, Rama I successfully strengthened the spiritual role of the monarch by establishing rational ties with the Buddhist community at large. Within the context of a fast-changing world, Rama I secured the co-operation of the *sangha*, the custodians of education within Buddhist society, for casting aside aberrations in favour of the meaningful applica-tion of religious precepts. It was not unusual for Buddhist rulers, such as Alaungpaya and Taksin, to undertake the compilation of scriptures and religious laws. In the case of Rama I, it involved the critical appraisal and revision of the Tipitaka or Buddhist texts by 218 monks and 32 learned laymen at the Nipphanaram temple in the palace grounds. Also under-taken through his initiative was the compilation of a completely new *Traiphūm* or *Traibhūmi* (the Three Worlds), the Siamese cosmological trea-tise. There was also a complete rewriting of the *Rāmāyaṇa* as the *Rāmākian*, an adaptation of the Indian epic meaningful to the Thai environment. It is the subtle mental revolution initiated by Rama I which laid the ground for the impressive adaptation to Western influence undertaken later, by Prince Mongkut, during the reign of Rama III (1824–51). Mongkut, with the princely élite, took to the study of Western languages and sciences, while Buddhist scholars pioneered the critical appraisal of orthodox Buddhism in consort with Sinhalese Buddhists. The two streams of schol-arship were painlessly reconciled in the new Dhammayut sect, within the traditional *sangha* framework of Buddhist scholarship and education. With the aim of restoring Buddhism to its universalism, channels were inadvert-ently opened to the absorbing of Western scientific knowledge and ration-alism without sacrificing indigenous culture and tradition. Investigation into Western religion and science, involving dialectical exchanges with

---

[59] Quoted Hodgkin, 120.
[60] D. K. Wyatt, 'The "Subtle Revolution" of King Rama I of Siam', in A. B. Woodside and D. K. Wyatt, eds, *Moral Order and the Question of Change: Essays on Southeast Asian Thought*, New Haven: Yale University Southeast Asia Studies Monograph no. 24, 1982, 40, 42–3.

Westerners as recorded in the first Siamese printed book, the *Kitchanukit* (The Book Explaining Various Things), constituted an integral part of the intellectual transition.[61]

The importance of a stable political and economic environment for a resolution of the contemporary intellectual dilemma faced by Southeast Asian states was borne out clearly in the less successful attempts at reform by King Mindon Min (r. 1853–78) of Burma. With a background in monkhood similar to Mongkut's, the Burmese ruler strove to strengthen Theravāda Buddhist institutions. At the same time, he encouraged Western learning and technological innovation with the introduction of river-steamers, gun-boats and telegraph lines, at roughly the same pace as in Siam. But he failed to weld the programme of modernization to a reformation of Buddhist mentality. Mindon's intellectual gifts were limited compared to Mongkut's; he was also severely handicapped by circumstances. Among the important factors was the need for closer association between the official class and the nobility which would have allowed for the development, as in Siam, of a strong élite community. Further, lack of commercialization amongst the élite, with insecurity of tenure for officials, resulted in the precarious dependence of both upon the favour of the reigning monarch. This fostered perpetual intrigue and political instability. No less important were the mounting British threat and Anglo-Burmese diplomatic fiascos. Mindon's loss of control over fast-developing lower Burma and Rangoon and his own physical isolation in Mandalay stood in contrast to the spectacular achievements of the early Chakri rulers in the valley of the Chao Phraya.

The economic foundations laid by Taksin and Rama I were strengthened by Rama II (r. 1809–24) and fully developed under Rama III (r. 1824–51). The taxes and commercial restrictions laid by the former on European commercial activity allowed Chinese trade to develop to its fullest potential. Within the framework of the tributary trade, Siam augmented its exchange of rice, sappanwood, rosewood, tin, pepper, cardamom, gamboge, rhinoceros horn and beeswax for silks, porcelain, paper, tea and saltpetre. Simultaneously, by the introduction of cash crops, Siam kept pace with colonial economic developments in the Philippines and Indonesia. The production of sugarcane and pepper was expanded respectively to an estimated 35,000 and 40,000 piculs collected in 1822 as royal monopolies.[62] The newly introduced tobacco cultivation soon exceeded home consumption, allowing for export to Cambodia and Cochinchina.[63] In addition, sugar-milling and iron-smelting industries were developed. These activities, as well as tin-mining, were based on the enterprise of the Chinese, whose immigration was encouraged. Exemption from corvée and conscription, and the payment of an annual poll-tax, much less than the sum payable in lieu of corvée by Thai males,[64] allowed the Chinese the

[61] C. J. Reynolds, 'Buddhist Cosmography in Thai History, with Special Reference to Nineteenth-Century Cultural Change', JAS, 35, 2 (1976) 209–10, 214–15.

[62] J. Crawfurd, *Journal of an Embassy to the Courts of Siam and Cochin China*, London, 1828; reprinted with an introduction by D. K. Wyatt, Kuala Lumpur, 1967, 381.

[63] J. Crawfurd, *The Crawfurd Papers*, Bangkok, 1915, 112.

[64] Terweil, *History of Modern Thailand*, 116.

necessary freedom of movement and activity for cash-cropping and business enterprise. In the meantime, the addition to the Chinese trade of bulk goods such as pepper and sugar, besides rice, boosted the shipbuilding industry. Some eight to ten teak vessels were built annually; in size they were up to 1000 tonnes, nearly twice the size of the vessels which had been built a century earlier.[65] Though a substantial proportion of the produce that accrued from the new economic activities went to traditional markets in China, Cambodia and other neighbouring territories, an increasingly large amount of sugar, in particular, found its way into the world market through Singapore.

In addition to the recruitment of Chinese wage labour for reclamation, building projects and a variety of craft-oriented occupations, measures were taken to encourage the growth of a free labour market through modifying the traditional corvée system. The corvée obligation of free men or *phrai* was reduced from six to three months and this, with the government preference for payment in specie or produce in lieu of labour, loosened clientage.[66] On the foundation laid by his predecessors, Rama III built the superstructure of a modern economy by creating a merchant fleet and introducing larger square-rigged vessels. These changes signalled the demise of the Chinese junk trade and the gradual tailing off of tributary trade in favour of alternate lines of modern international commerce.[67] The new branch of trade with Singapore (founded 1819), stimulated by the need for Western arms and other factors of economic growth, contributed to increased monetization. By the mid-nineteenth century, Siam had the semblance of a modern state concerned with the efficient extraction of cash revenues. In contrast to Burma, where Mindon had a substantial hold on commerce, royal monopolies were gradually abolished in favour of tax farms leased to Thai officials and Chinese. These covered exports of all luxury goods and cash crops, internal trade, gambling and the consumption of arrack.[68]

Along with the growth of commerce came as well a crucial restructuring of society. Rama I's policy of encouraging royalty and the official class to supplement income with trade was given further encouragement by his successor, Rama II. Prince Chetsadabodin (later Rama III), in his capacity as *Phrakhlang* or minister in charge of foreign affairs, in partnership with the prominent Dit Bunnag, played a significant part in the development of trade with China, for official as well as personal profit.[69] Apart from reducing the burdens of maintaining the monarchy, such participation brought the court into the mainstream of the newly emerging commercial élite, whose influence was no longer derived solely from manpower but

[65] *Crawfurd Papers*, 117–18; Viraphol, 181, 323 n. 5.
[66] Akin Rabibhadana, 'Clientship and Class Structure in the Early Bangkok period', in G. W. Skinner and A. T. Kirsch, eds. *Change and Persistence in Thai Society: Essays in Honour of Lauriston Sharp*, Ithaca, 1975, 117–18; W. Vella, *Siam Under Rama III, 1824–1851*, New York: Association for Asian Studies, 1957, 19–21.
[67] Viraphol, 186–7, 229–30.
[68] Viraphol, 204–5, 207, 215–19, 234–5; Joseph P. L. Jiang, 'The Chinese in Thailand: Past and Present', JSEAH, 7, 1 (1966) 43–4; C. L. Keeton 3rd, *King Thebaw and the Ecological Rape of Burma*, Delhi, 1974, 7–8.
[69] Viraphol, 192.

also from wealth.[70] By the reign of Rama III the Chinese gained equal opportunity with the Thais for the purchase of land, property and vessels. They became, in the process, part of a settled community. Many inter-married with the Thais and found access to official positions, some rising to governorships.[71] Siam's steady entry into the modern economy was evident in the 1848 population census conducted for the regulation and more efficient extraction, not of services, but of cash revenues. The essence of Ayutthayan glory, drawn from a synthesis of tradition and change, was imaginatively recreated by the Chakri rulers within the context of a new age.

DECLINE OF TRADITIONAL AUTHORITY

In the Dutch-administered territories of Indonesia where the colonial economy was based on the export of produce mainly for the European market, the introduction of coffee as a monopoly at the beginning of the eighteenth century saw the extension of forced cultivation. In Java, the cession by the dying Pakubuwana II (r. 1726–49) of the sovereignty of Mataram in 1749 gave the Vereenigde Oost-Indische Compagnie (VOC, the Dutch East India Company) opportunity to increase coffee, timber, indigo and rice supplies in the form of contingencies and forced deliveries, utilizing the influence of the regents. Besides the low price paid for coffee, the VOC tried to cope with the vicissitudes of the coffee market through a policy of alternate extension and extirpation. This proved economically disruptive. Evasion of forced cultivation constituted an important reason for a drift of population to the urban centres of the north coast to engage in small-scale commercial activity, smuggling and wage labour such as timber-felling. Population movement away from the war-torn west and interior would, nonetheless, appear to have abated with the relative peace which prevailed between 1757 and 1825.[72] The Javanese rulers paid a heavy price for the termination of war. The *mancanagara*, or the outer districts of the Mataram kingdom, were ceded to direct Dutch control. What remained of the inner core, constituting the princely states or *kejawen*, was divided by the 1755 Treaty of Giyanti between Yogyakarta and Surakarta, with a further division later, entailing the creation of the subsidiary courts of Mangkunegara (1757) and Pakualaman (1813).

Although under the influence of the VOC the Javanese economy of the north coast quickly adapted to cash-crop cultivation for the world market, traditional links between the coast and the interior remained crucial to the resolution of political and economic rivalries. The challenge which Sultan Agung (r. 1613–46) had faced from the regents of the prosperous commer-cial ports of the *pasisir* (north coast) was superseded during the reign of Amangkurat I (1646–77) by VOC attempts to seize control over them. The cession of commercial rights by Amangkurat II (r. 1676–1703) to the

[70] Rabibhadana, 'Clientship and Class Structure', 117–19.
[71] G. W. Skinner, *Chinese Society in Thailand, An Analytical History*, Ithaca, 1957, 19, 21–2.
[72] M. C. Ricklefs, 'Some Statistical Evidence on Javanese Social, Economic and Demographic History in the Later Seventeenth and Eighteenth Centuries', MAS, 20, 1 (1986) 29–30.

VOC, in exchange for political alliance, marked the beginning of a new cycle of internal conflicts in Mataram in the form of the Java succession wars, revolving around the question of Mataram's territorial integrity. Ironically, Mangkubumi, the man opposed to the leasing by his brother, Pakabuwana II (r. 1726–49), of the north coast to the VOC, shared in this partition of the old kingdom to become Sultan Hamengkubuwana I (r. 1749–92) of Yogyakarta.

The new sultanates, particularly Yogyakarta, enjoyed progress and prosperity, and problems arising from the division of territory, pertaining to boundaries, laws and jurisdiction, were gradually resolved. The adoption of a regular succession procedure ensured the general stability of the courts, but rivalries amongst them precluded any possibility of a reunification. At the same time, ideological acceptance of a permanent division of the kingdom, under Dutch protection, proved difficult. It was in the court of Hamengkubuwana I that the resolution of this crisis was attempted through the familiar method of literary myth. While earlier the Mataram court had initiated a mythological accommodation to the beginning of Dutch relations with Java through the *Sěrat Baron Sakendher* text, the *Sěrat Surya Raja*, written in 1774 by the crown prince of Yogyakarta (later Hamengkubuwana II, r. 1792–1810, 1811–12, 1826–8), professed the reunification of the kingdom and the conversion of the Dutch to Islam.[73] Neither Javanese text acknowledged submission to the Dutch. The *Sěrat Surya Raja's* prediction of Yogyakarta's conflict with them, backed by the spiritual forces of Islam and Kangjeng Ratu Kidul or Nyai Lara Kidul, the Goddess of the Southern Sea, was uncannily prescient of the impending Java War (1825–30).

Despite the difficulty in accommodating to the changes brought by Dutch intervention, the termination of wars promoted productivity and population growth. In Java and Madura, the population is estimated to have tripled from 1.5 million during the mid-eighteenth century to 4.6 million in 1815.[74] This far exceeded the figure of 3 million for roughly the same period for Siam,[75] and 2.5 million for Burma, and was exceeded only by Vietnam, which had an estimated population of 7–8 million, but in at least twice the area of Java.[76]

[73] T. G. Th. Pigeaud, *The Literature of Java*, The Hague: Koninklijk Instituut voor Taal-, Landen Volkenkunde van Nederlandsch-Indië, 1967, I. 162–3; M. C. Ricklefs, *Jogjakarta Under Sultan Mangkubumi, 1749–1792*, Oxford, 1974, 188–211; *A History of Modern Indonesia*, London, 1981, 97.

[74] M. C. Ricklefs, 'The Javanese in the Eighteenth and Nineteenth Centuries', in D. G. E. Hall, *A History of South-East Asia*, London, 1981, 509; Sir Stamford Raffles, *A History of Java*, London, 1817, reprinted with an introduction by J. Bastin, Kuala Lumpur, 1965, I. 63.

[75] Jiang, 41.

[76] H. Burney, 'On the Population of the Burmese Empire', *Journal of the Burma Research Society*, 31 (1941), reprinted 1977, 343; Koenig, 'The Early Kón-Baung Polity', 97–8; Lieberman, *Burmese Administrative Cycles*, 20–1; Woodside, *Vietnam and the Chinese Model*, 158–9. According to Widjojo Nitisastro, *Population Trends in Indonesia*, Ithaca, 1970, Raffles' figures though more accurate than others were 'a gross underestimate'. For 1820, much higher figures of 4.6 million for Thailand and 13.7 million for Indonesia have been estimated by Kees van der Meer. See 'A Comparison of Factors Influencing Economic Development in Thailand and Indonesia, 1870–1940', in A. Maddison and Gé Prince, eds, *Economic Growth in Indonesia, 1820–1940*, Verhandelingen van het Koninklijk Instituut voor Taal-, Land- en Volkenkunde, 137 (Dordrecht-Holland, 1989) 280.

FORCED CULTIVATION

Force contributed in no small measure to increased productivity in Java. Compulsory cultivation introduced by the VOC to counter the lack of incentives for cultivation was in itself not a new idea. Such a system, requiring every adult male or nuclear family to cultivate a stipulated number of pepper vines, was enforced by the rulers of Banten during the second half of the seventeenth century. Surveillance of cultivation and punishment for noncompliance, as well as the collection of and payment for produce, were vested in the indigenous administrative hierarchy. This provided the model for the forced cash-crop cultivation introduced during the eighteenth century by the Dutch in Java and by their British rivals in Benkulen. The imposition of European supervision through inspection surveys, conducted by Company officials, increased the efficiency of the indigenous mechanism but, at the same time, removed the customary safeguards against oppression. West Sumatra, Lampung and Banten, areas originally under swidden agriculture and a subsistence economy, were brought within the ambit of international market exchange, resulting in serious socio-economic dislocations. The cultivation of cash crops for the purchase of imports, such as cloth and salt, and the rotation of *ladang*, or hill-paddy, became increasingly difficult under forced cultivation which obliged many to settle permanently. Cultivation of cash crops, by and large, boosted rice production and population increase in those areas suited to *sawah*. However, in areas with poorer soils unsuited to *sawah*, such as west Java and British west Sumatra, the population came to depend more heavily on rice purchased with the meagre returns earned from cash-cropping for the Company. In these areas indebtedness and the flight of population were more common. In Java, as a whole, rice production did not keep pace with the increase in population and export crops during the periods 1795–1810 and 1830–50. Despite the extension of *sawah* cultivation in the principalities (see page 601), and the overall increase in rice production per unit, *sawah* acreage per household and consumption per capita actually decreased.[77]

Contrasting with the simple tribal socio-economic structure found in west and south Sumatra, which came under the protection of the British and Dutch respectively, the indigenous state authority for the extraction of produce and services that existed in Java contributed to the creation of a more efficient colonial machinery on that island. Nonetheless, at all stages of indigenous development in the past, patron–client relations had guarded individual rights and social cohesiveness. These ties of interdependence between *kaula* (servant) and *gusti* (master) in Java, and *anak buah* (dependant) and *ketua* (chief) in the Malay world were gradually undermined as indigenous chiefs and officials became agents of European control. The weakening of these traditional ties was in proportion to the increased extraction of services by the chiefs on behalf of the Company. It is calculated, for example, that at the beginning of the nineteenth century

---

[77] P. Boomgaard, 'Java's Agricultural Production, 1775–1875', in *Economic Growth in Indonesia*, 109–17.

in the district of Pasuruhan in east Java, one-fifth of the manpower which was committed to coffee cultivation was engaged in public service. The latter included the threshing of rice for Company supplies, police and postal duties, and personal services to an entire hierarchy of Javanese officials.[78] The Javanese, who initially had found coffee production lucrative, soon discovered it to be a burden which they bore with resentment. Attitude to the Company monopoly was no different in the British-administered territories in west Sumatra. Transportation of pepper either manually over rough terrain, or by raft down hazardous rivers, was generally unprofitable to cultivators. These hardships were aggravated by the engrossment of the internal trade in provisions by Company officials, with consequent indebtedness and, in Java, by the penetration of the Chinese into the new economic infrastructure.

In Siam the Chinese were accommodated socially; by contrast, in Java religious difference, and Dutch efforts to use them as apolitical agents in substitution for the traditional agents of commerce, encouraged their development as an alien community. Chinese ascendancy in the inter-island and internal trade under VOC patronage laid the ground to some extent for the problems of economic disparity and ethnicity which have continued into the present century. The commercial capital which they accumulated found investment in a major share of the lands leased out by the Dutch administration in west and north Java, with a labour force necessary for the planting and processing of sugar and the cultivation of coffee. The trade involved in supplying the needs of this workforce became the virtual monopoly of the Chinese, who were in universal control also of toll-gates and tax, opium and gambling farms. The Dutch officials, the Chinese and the Javanese *priyayi* (officials) were partners within the hierarchy of exploitation, with the indigenous chiefs placed last in the pecking order.[79]

Movement of population to areas where conditions were relatively easier—for example, in the Buitenzorg district which offered better communication and warehouse facilities—or where soil conditions were superior, was not uncommon. In times of severe distress, originating from oppression or the outbreak of disease such as smallpox, mass flight was customary. Cultivators working under the European forced cultivation system in west Sumatra and Java often sought refuge in the economically precarious interior, awaiting improved conditions. Kerinci was a common place for flight from the British-administered Benkulen districts. In 1840 Eduard Douwes Dekker, who then served in west Java, noted refugees from the notoriously oppressive Lebak district in the Priangan region of west Java.[80] With the expansion of cultivation and the dramatic rise in Java's population by the end of the eighteenth century, however, recourse to flight became less practical.

---

[78] Raffles, I. 150–1.
[79] James R. Rush, 'Social Control and Influence in Nineteenth-Century Indonesia: Opium Farms and the Chinese of Java', *Indonesia*, 35 (1983) 53–61.
[80] Multatuli, *Max Havelaar*, New York, 1927, reprinted with a foreword by J. Kathirithamby-Wells, Kuala Lumpur, 1984, 133.

FAILURE OF REFORM: REBELLION AND WAR

Directors of both the Dutch and English East India Companies were not unaware of the corruption in the system of forced cultivation, and its debilitating effects on peasant enterprise. Injunctions from the respective metropolitan powers to improve the system of payments through the adoption of greater honesty and regularity went, in the main, unheeded. The efforts of Governor-General G. W. Baron van Imhoff (1743–50) at regulating payment and reducing exploitation were, in the long term, as ineffective as the more rigorous attempts at reform during the 1770s in the Benkulen presidency. In Java it was the Napoleonic Wars which provided the occasion and a new conceptual framework for serious attempts at reform. But, whether amongst administrators in the East or liberal thinkers in Europe, the new humanitarian concerns were viewed strictly in terms of increased productivity and profit. In line with this objective, the provision of suitable incentives for greater industry was advocated by Dirk van Hogendorp, as member of the 1803 commission for reform. It became, in effect, the cardinal principle of nineteenth-century reformers such as Sir Thomas Stamford Raffles, when he was Lieutenant Governor of Java (1811–16), and W. R. Baron van Hoëvell who spearheaded the move in the Netherlands, some fifty years later, to abolish the *cultuurstelsel*. The freedom of cultivation and sale of produce, which lay at the crux of the liberal policy, pointed to radical socio-administrative changes and financial risks which colonial officials could ill afford to commit themselves to. A compromise struck by the reform commission under S. C. Nederburgh and, later, by Governor-General Herman Willem Daendels (1808–11) was the attempt to eradicate abuses in the system of forced cultivation. For Daendels, a strongly military man, the new policy meant stricter supervision through direct administration and improved communications, assisted by the construction of a coast road from Anjer in the west to Pasuruhan in the east. In the end, the seemingly different ideologies of Daendels, the pragmatist, and Raffles, the visionary, found common ground in the maintenance of forced deliveries, the sale and lease of lands to Europeans and Chinese, and interference in traditional institutions through reducing the power of the regents.[81]

Policies to increase revenue were a natural concomitant of territorial expansion and consolidation whether in European-administered or independent territories in Southeast Asia. The turn of the century witnessed census and cadastral surveys conducted by governments as disparate as the *ancien régime* of Bodawpaya in Burma and the centre for liberal economic experimentation spearheaded by Batavia. Though the latter, under Raffles, attempted to achieve a fair assessment of tax obligations, the practical difficulties involved were probably common to both. Raffles'

---

[81] J. Bastin, *The Native Policies of Sir Stamford Raffles in Java and Sumatra*, Oxford, 1957, 39–40, 63; *Raffles' Ideas on the Land Rent System in Java and the Mackenzie Land Tenure Commission*, Verhandelingen van het Koninklijk Instituut voor Taal-, Land- en Volkenkunde, XIV, The Hague, 1954, 74–92; H. R. C. Wright, *East-Indian Economic Problems of the Age of Cornwallis and Raffles*, London, 1961, 71, 81, 86–7.

policy of individual settlement with the cultivators, through the *desa* (village) chiefs was, in fact, as alien to traditional practices as the efficiency of taxation imposed by the Nguyen in Cambodia. In eliminating opportunities for corruption, the regents were dissociated, in principle, from revenue collection and were compensated with land and salaries. In practice, the 'defeudalization' process proved less practicable than contemporaneous Nguyen attempts at converting the mandarins into salaried officials.[82]

It is ironical that the residuum of French revolutionary zeal which to a degree infected European administration in Java, resulted in the perpetuation and, in some cases, the increase of forced cultivation and labour. This was exactly at the same time that corvée obligation, the basis of the traditional economy, was halved in Siam in favour of paid labour. The construction of the Puncak Pass between Bogor and Cianjur, in Java, is estimated to have taken a toll of 500 lives from a single district,[83] and the heavy labour services extracted for teak-felling on the north coast is calculated to have increased from 1600 males in 1776 to 5050 in 1809.[84] These conditions bear some comparison with the forced labour pressed by Bodawpaya from the Shans, Mons and Arakanese for the construction of the pagoda at Mingun. The end of the Napoleonic Wars and resuscitation of markets for tropical produce saw the restoration by the Dutch colonial government of the economic structure inherited from the VOC. But the foundations for direct rule laid by Daendels and Raffles provided for government interests to be pursued with greater vigour and thoroughness. It was only a matter of time before sporadic protest and rebellion against interference by an external agency in political and economic affairs escalated into the last major war in Java.

Succession disputes, an inherent feature of Southeast Asian politics, arising from the lack of clear rules of primogeniture, had among other factors facilitated Dutch ascendancy in Java. The political manipulations of the Dutch and the military support they afforded local allies provided for greater stability, but economic exploitation gave rise to new sources of discontent, which gradually gained momentum. In areas such as Banten and Cirebon, worst affected by compulsory cultivation, the forces of social and political dissatisfaction brought the variegated strands of society into a voluntary alliance earlier than elsewhere. Discontent against the Company ally, Ratu Sarifa, in Banten caused commoner and élite alike to take up the banner of rebellion under the religious leader, Kiai Tapa. The movement was crushed in 1751, but discontent spread to Lampung and to the Batavian highlands where European plantations were destroyed. The introduction of the forced cultivation of coffee, in lieu of pepper which the Bantenese were long accustomed to planting, and the heavy corvée services demanded by Daendels, brought another revolt culminating in

[82] Woodside, *Vietnam and the Chinese Model*, 79–80.
[83] E. S. de Klerck, *History of the Netherlands East Indies*, Rotterdam, 1938, reprinted Amsterdam, 1975, II. 25.
[84] P. Boomgaard, 'Forest Management and Exploitation in Colonial Java', *Journal of Forest History*, in press.

the sultan's abdication in 1813.[85] In Cirebon, problems of maladministration were compounded during the second half of the eighteenth century by recurrent epidemics, with resulting depopulation at a time of unprecedented upswing in the island's population as a whole. In 1800, the disgruntled peasantry joined forces with a disinherited local prince. Later, in 1811, they were led to revolt by an aristocrat, Bagus Rangin, venting their anger specifically on European and Chinese plantation owners.

In the Javanese principalities, as a whole, there was initial prosperity, particularly under the enlightened rule of Sultan Hamengkubuwana I. The area shared the island's overall population increase, accounting for roughly one-third of the total number of inhabitants during the second half of the eighteenth century. Given demographic growth and central Java's traditional role as the island's chief granary, cultivation expanded at an unprecedented rate. It is calculated that during the ten years between 1796 and 1806, *sawah* cultivation expanded by about 25 per cent around Yogyakarta.[86] It was not long, however, before these developments were countered by burdens of taxation and corvée. Apart from the heavy labour demands for his extensive building projects, in 1802, Hamengkubuwana II took measures to increase revenues by reducing the unit measure of land, or *caca*, allowed per family, without a proportionate reduction in taxes. Daendels' annexation of the north coast in 1811 and the resulting loss of Company rent paid since 1746 created the ruler's need for alternate sources of revenue. Many dignitaries similarly lost their income from appanages with the appropriation of *mancanagara* (outer-territory) lands by Raffles.

A more general problem, arising from the efforts of both the European and Javanese authorities to boost their respective share of revenue earnings, was the proliferation of Chinese-controlled toll-gates and tax farms. Internal trade was affected, with resulting price inflation. A poor harvest in 1821 and contemporaneous outbreak of cholera—originating from India and affecting equally Siam, Cambodia, some Lao states and Cochinchina[87]—brought the agrarian crisis to a head. Governor-General G. A. G. Ph. van der Capellen's efforts to end the abuses connected with the private leasing of land in central Java, and the consequent loss of revenue and burdens of indemnification this brought to the aristocratic landlords, only widened disaffection. Adding to the general instability was the weakness of the two courts, through moral corruption and political intrigues in which the Dutch had no small part. The eye of the impending storm settled on Yogyakarta. Here, a prince of the court, Dipanagara, rose to champion the cause of justice and the return to the ideals of tradition and religious virtue.

Succession wars in agrarian societies often had their origins in peasant unrest, where the emergent leadership assumed a charismatic mantle woven out of popular myth and religious beliefs. In the Java war, Dipanagara, who drew amply from the spiritual forces of Javanese mythology, was conceived as the *ratu paneteg panatagawa* or royal protector of religion,

[85] Raffles, II. 241–3; de Klerck, I. 381–4; II. 15–17, 44.
[86] P. B. R. Carey, *Babad Dipanagara, An Account of the Outbreak of the Java War (1825–30)*, Monograph 9, Malaysian Branch of the Royal Asiatic Society, Kuala Lumpur, 1981, xxxviii.
[87] Crawfurd, *Embassy*, 455.

and won the support of the *santri* (religious élite), under the leadership of Kiai Maja. Increased contacts with Arabia during the early nineteenth century brought Java, much as the rest of the Muslim world, under the reformist Wahhābi movement, turning the Java war into a *jihad* (holy war), aimed equally at the Dutch and *murtad* or apostate Javanese. It was five years before Dutch military power and strategy outdistanced the spiritual strength of the rebellion. With the introduction of the 'Cultivation System' at the end of the war in 1830, unenlightened Dutch economic policies in Java entered their final phase. In the meanwhile, in the highlands of Minangkabau, still free of Dutch control, the voices of social and religious discontent found expression in the Padri movement of the early nineteenth century.

COMMERCE, POLITICAL FRAGMENTATION AND MORAL DILEMMA

If in Java unrestrained interference by the Dutch had forced a reaction in the form of the Java War, their inactivity elsewhere allowed penetration by British commercial enterprise producing, curiously, conditions for a comparable social reaction. Since the English East India Company's expulsion from Banten in 1682, its activities in the archipelago had been confined to Benkulen and the west Sumatran coast. At the same time, British private trade and the Country Trade, of which Company servants in Madras and Benkulen had a considerable share, maintained a substantial presence in the commerce of the region, mainly in the importation of Indian piece-goods in exchange for spices, tin and pepper. The expansion of the China trade and the availability, after the victory at Plassey in 1760, of Bengal opium for barter for archipelago produce such as tin, pepper, birds'-nests and trepang (sea-cucumbers or holothurians) suitable for Canton, brought the Country Trade into increased prominence. Riau and Terengganu in the west and Sulu in the east of the archipelago were conveniently located on the route to China. They rose and prospered on the basis of this trade, stimulating internal lines of commerce with the Malays and the Bugis. In addition to the distribution of piece-goods and opium, there was an important trade in arms, particularly with Sulu, where it supported the slave-raiding activities of the Iranun seeking labour for the collection of sea-produce. The extent of the growth of this trade is evident in a single order made at Jolo for arms and ammunition in the 1780s, which included one dozen swivel guns and cannons, 600 muskets, 100 pistols and one thousand 25-pound (11-kilogram) kegs of gunpowder. Equally impressive was the rise in the importation of opium, from six chests per annum at the beginning of the nineteenth century, to some thirty-five after a period of only two decades.[88]

In the face of Dutch monopoly restrictions and Malay–Bugis dissensions in the Malay peninsula, the upsurge in the activities of the English Country Traders provided a new impetus for indigenous powers in the

[88] J. F. Warren, *The Sulu Zone, 1768–1898*, Singapore, 1981, 48–9.

western archipelago. Like Sulu, Riau and Terengganu were brought to
the peak of commercial growth through their role in servicing the Country
Trade. Piece-goods and opium imported by the Country Traders at Riau
were exchanged for Bangka and peninsular tin, Sumatran pepper and
forest produce, as well as gambir cultivated locally. Aceh, Selangor and
Kedah were other ports which benefited from the Country Trade. In
1767, for example, a total of about 500 chests of opium was distributed in
the Straits of Melaka at Aceh, Kuala Selangor and Riau by private traders
operating mainly from Calcutta.[89] As opposed to the free trade fostered at
Riau, trade in the hinterland and outlying regions was often engrossed by
European syndicates operating in collusion with local rulers. In Aceh,
commerce in the 1770s is alleged to have been the monopoly of the sultan
in partnership with the Madras syndicate of Gowan Horrop. It was with
the hope of winning for the Company this lucrative trade that the search
began for a British settlement, resulting in the founding of Penang in 1786
by Francis Light, a leading Country Trader. Following the Dutch take-over
of Riau two years earlier, Penang stepped in to fill the role of chief
distributor of Company opium consumed in the archipelago, amounting to
some 1000 chests at the beginning of the nineteenth century.[90] Like the
west Sumatran ports of Natal and Tapanuli which served as lucrative
centres for English private trade and Company servants at Benkulen,
Penang became the focus of innumerable commercial-cum-political part-
nerships between British traders acting as Company representatives—
such as Francis Light—on the one hand, and local rulers with their native
and European agents on the other.

To furnish the Country Trade, Terengganu's pepper cultivation was
greatly expanded and by the 1780s the state produced between 13,000 and
17,000 piculs annually, for which the main commodity of exchange was
opium.[91] Due to the importance of commercial contracts for revenue
and the supply of arms for security, the local rulers valued their contacts
with the Country Traders who had influential links with the Bengal
government. Faced with insecurity because of the Thai threat from the
north, deep-seated Malay–Bugis rivalry and Dutch monopoly restrictions
in the straits, local rulers quickly began to view the British as potential
allies. It became increasingly apparent, as with the Sultan of Kedah's
appeal for protection against Siam, that the British would not be forthcoming with military assistance. But their growing commerce, particularly with
the founding of Singapore in 1819, bolstered fragmented Malay power in
the peninsula and east Sumatra.

For the east Sumatran states—particularly Siak, Inderagiri and Kampar—
Penang and Singapore provided attractive outlets for produce from the
Minangkabau interior, evading Dutch monopoly controls at Padang. So
attractive, in fact, was this trade that it stimulated the cultivation of coffee

---

[89] J. Kathirithamby-Wells, *The British West Sumatran Presidency, 1760–85: Problems of Early
Colonial Enterprise*, Kuala Lumpur, 1977, 145–6.
[90] Wright, 170.
[91] Shaharil Talib, 'The Port and Polity of Terengganu during the Eighteenth and Nineteenth
Centuries: Realizing its Potential', in J. Kathirithamby-Wells and J. Villiers, eds, *The
Southeast Asian Port and Polity: Rise and Demise*, Singapore, 1989, 215.

and gambier in the hill regions of Agam and Limapuluh Kota, as well as the expansion of pepper cultivation on the east Sumatran coast, between Langkat and Asahan and, on the west coast, from Susoh to Singkel. These coastal areas were under the nominal authority, respectively, of the sultans of Siak and Aceh; but the weakness of royal authority and the new commercial opportunities unleashed a rash of political adventurism, supported by European capital, arms and vessels. Enterprising local chiefs opened up new plantations, attracting Minangkabau and Batak populations from the interior to the east coast, and there was a parallel movement of Acehnese migrants from further north to the west coast.

The lucrative trade involved purchase of cash crops and sale of cloth, opium and other provisions for the plantations; it provided British private trade with a vested interest in maintaining the independence of coastal ports and their chiefs in defiance of central authority. An outstanding case was Leubè Dapa, the Acehnese chief at Singkil and Truman, and his collusion with the British Resident at Natal, John Prince, a partner of the wealthy Calcutta merchant, John Palmer.[92] Shortly after the founding of Singapore, there was actually an attempt by the Acehnese territorial chiefs or ulëëbalang, in league with a Penang merchant faction, to depose Sultan Jauhar al-Alam (r. 1819–23) in favour of Syed Alam, son of Syed Hussein, a wealthy local merchant. The plan miscarried, but it spoke amply of the bankruptcy of indigenous sovereignty.

Dissolution of Malay political authority with the Dutch capture of Riau in 1784 threw up opportunities for merchant and entrepreneurial activities on an unprecedented scale. But the many petty rajas, and the pepper kings who rose from amongst them, secured their profits and their status at great risk through management of dubious contacts and alliances. In the absence of legitimized armed power, the orang laut (sea people) reverted to marauding activities. They preyed on vessels and the isolated communities of cash-croppers on the Sumatran coasts and at Banjarmasin and the tin mines of Sambas and Bangka, taking captives whom they sold as slaves. The orang laut formed an important political force in the interplay of local rivalries, the significance and magnitude of their activities enhanced by alliances with displaced princes or anak raja. Political instability at Siak, arising from succession disputes as of the mid-eighteenth century, afforded opportunity for intrigue and marauding, sometimes in partnership with Arab political adventurers. In 1787, to avenge humiliation by the Dutch, Sultan Mahmud of Riau turned to the Iranun for assistance, just as four years later the hapless Sultan Abdullah of Kedah sought their aid in taking revenge against the British in Penang.

The innumerable European trading vessels which ran the gamut of archipelago ports were better armed and therefore at less risk than the small native vessels; they thrived on insecurity. They found ready opportunities for cultivating the friendship and alliance of local chiefs and the heads of piratical lairs for profitable commerce, including the exchange of arms for slaves. Illicit trade, developed largely to escape Dutch monopoly

---

[92] Lee Kam Hing, 'Acheh's Relations with the British, 1760–1819', M.A. thesis, University of Malaya, 1969, 80–7.

restrictions, became the life-blood of Penang's contraband trade with the pirates of Lingga.

Regulation of trade and suppression of piracy, which Raffles began to advocate, ushered in a whole new order, based on fuller commitment of British official interest in the region. For the Dutch, Java, Sumatra and Bangka continued to remain the main areas of endeavour. The territories beyond, which suffered political fragmentation and internecine rivalry, posed no serious challenge to Dutch interests; but the inroads there of rival European activity and freebooting, in defiance of monopoly restrictions, claimed Batavia's attentions. Residual centres of local power in Bali, Borneo (Pontianak, Mempawa, and Sambas), south Sulawesi, Palembang and Jambi were accordingly brought under Dutch rule.

In the absence of strong indigenous authority outside the areas of direct Dutch control, the multitude of thriving chiefdoms proved ideally suited to the commercial adventurism of the period. Despite the marauding of coastal settlements and shipping, the decline of royal monopolies created unprecedented opportunities for private enterprise. The pepper planta-tions of the east Sumatran coasts and the coffee and gambier estates of the Minangkabau interior became new sources of wealth. Quite apart from those who prospered from the smuggling of tin from Bangka, the develop-ment of the plantation economy created a significant merchant community involved in the transportation of produce to Penang and Singapore. The attendant prosperity, enjoyed by cultivators and merchants, was double-edged. The increased circulation of wealth brought dependence on a market economy dominated by the indiscriminate sale of opium and arms with piece-goods and other provisions. The availability of cash and the erosion of traditional values had widespread social implications. These rendered the migrant population of plantation workers and itinerant traders susceptible to corrupting influences: the many urban centres servicing the plantations offered gambling and opium-smoking.

As traditionally, increased international trade opened up the mental vistas of the religious élite within Malay society. Greater wealth and the steady inroads of the *sayid* of Hadramaut brought the Arab world closer to the archipelago. For all his dabbling in the opium trade, the ruler of Selangor, for instance, was keen on doing his bit for religion by finding passage on English vessels for Muslim *ulamā* set on the pilgrimage.[93] A belief that moral corruption was affecting the Malay world gained poignancy under the reformist Wahhabi influence which currently swept the Muslim world. The Acehnese poem, *Hikayat Ranto*, for example, lamented the loss of Islamic values among the pepper-growers of the coastal regions.[94]

> Though engaged in trade many pious people practice usury.
> They traffic in opium and in money, so that they always
>   make a profit.

[93] W. Marsden, *A Grammar of the Malayan Language*, London, 1812, 150–1.
[94] G. W. J. Drewes, *Two Achehnese Poems: Hikajat Ranto and Hikajat Teungku Di Meuké'*, Biblio-theca Indonesica, 20, Koniklijk Instituut voor Taal-, Land- en Volkenkunde, The Hague, 1980, 15.

> Though having a security in hand, they take interest,
>   and this is usury, my brother.
> They cut off a part of the opium they already weighed
>   out, and this is a great sin.
> Among the shopkeepers there is much breaking of
>   the law. All the world has gone astray . . .
> Once arrived at the *ranto* they neglect the ritual
>   prayer and completely forsake the Lord.

There was an increasing awareness amongst the Malays of their role within the Islamic community at large. The Padri movement, which began in 1803, was a fully-fledged attempt at social reform. It advocated the eradication of gambling, cockfighting, opium-smoking, the consumption of alcohol, betel-nut and tobacco, and even banned the wearing of gold ornaments. Quite unlike the Buddhist reforms successfully engineered by Prince Mongkut which achieved a reconciliation of Thai religious beliefs with Western rationalism, Padri orthodoxy was opposed to any compromise. Through alienating the ruling house and lineage heads or *penghulu* at Tanah Datar, the Padri inadvertently facilitated Dutch intervention which led, at the termination of the war (1821–38), to the introduction of indirect rule in the interests of a coffee monopoly.[95] The Java and the Padri wars left indigenous forces enfeebled and their moral dilemmas as yet unresolved. Just as the remnants of Java's traditional policy sought refuge in an internalized cultural renaissance, the residuum of Malay political culture at Riau indulged in a recreation of the old order of *adat* and Islam.[96]

ECONOMIC DUALISM

The Philippines was affected just as profoundly as the rest of Southeast Asia by the socio-economic changes of the 'era of transition'. These important decades witnessed the gradual erosion of its isolation from the mainstream of developments in the region. Up till this time, any identity which the Philippines and Dutch Indonesia had shared as colonies was more superficial than real. Spain's commitment to the Philippines, like that of the Dutch in Java and eastern Indonesia, was adapted to the siphoning of profits to the metropolitan power in Europe. There was the important difference, however, that while Dutch profits were drawn predominantly from the organization and export of monopoly produce, Spanish preoccupation in the Philippines was from 1565 almost exclusively with the Acapulco–Manila trade. This left the internal economy isolated and undeveloped.[97] It is calculated that over two hundred years preceding the final collapse of the galleon trade at the beginning of the nineteenth century, no

[95] C. Dobbin, *Islamic Revivalism in a Changing Peasant Economy: Central Sumatra, 1784–1847*, Scandinavian Institute of Asian Studies, no. 47, London and Malmö, 1983, 136–7, 228.
[96] B. Andaya and V. Matheson, 'Islamic Thought and Malay Tradition: The Writings of Raja Ali Haji of Riau (1809–c. 1870)', in A. Reid and D. Marr, eds, *Perceptions of the Past in Southeast Asia*, Kuala Lumpur, 1979, 121–3.
[97] W. L. Schurz, *The Manila Galleon*, New York, 1939, reprinted 1959, 38–43.

more than five or six Spaniards owned landed estates (*haciendas*) at any one time.[98] A greater similarity with Dutch-administered territories became evident only with the move in Spain, at the turn of the century, for economic reforms in the colonies. The new policy was impelled partly by the revolutionary spirit in Europe, and partly by financial exigencies which made for economic reorientation.

The dichotomy between the growth of external commerce and internal economic stagnation in the Philippines emanated from the nature of the galleon trade. It was concerned exclusively with the exchange in Manila of Mexican silver for Chinese silks, porcelain, combs and bric-à-brac destined for markets in New Spain and Europe, with the addition of only a small amount of local gold, cotton and wax.[99] While the Chinese controlled the Canton–Manila arm of the trade, the Manila–Acapulco sector was the privilege of the Spanish official class (*peninsulares*) resident in Manila. Under this structure the Philippines had no direct part in international commerce.

Outside the capital, affairs were left in the hands of the *alcaldes mayores* or provincial governors, and the Christianizing endeavour of Spanish ecclesiastical agents, mainly in the form of 'regulars' or friar curates. Large tracts of communal or *barangay* land had been sold by Christianized village chiefs (*datu*) and their relatives (*principales*) to the clergy. These were absorbed into *encomienda*, the original territorial leases made as reward for service to the Spanish Crown. Conversion brought the guarantee for the *datu* of hereditary status and exemption from tax, in return for holding the loyalty of the *barangay*. Inhabitants of the *barangay*, in turn, paid tribute usually in the form of food and provisions, and rendered labour services in exchange, ostensibly, for protection and spiritual ministration by *encomienda* holders. The system of labour and tribute extraction generally resembled that which subsisted in traditionally administered areas in other parts of Southeast Asia. There was a difference, however, in the absence under Spanish rule of reciprocal relations between patron and client for the protection of mutual interests as, traditionally, between *datu* and members of the *barangay*. The *alcaldes mayores*, though entrusted with the overall supervision of the provinces and enjoying virtual autonomy, were unsympathetic to local interests. Involved in the political and commercial affairs of Manila and the Iberian world at large, they were oblivious to internal corruption in the provinces. From the late sixteenth century the sale of communal lands to Chinese mestizos and private Spaniards aggravated problems. The excesses of tribute and corvée extractions, as well as the high interest charged on monetary loans, were comparable to the burdens suffered by the peasantry under Dutch rule in Java.

Resentment against encroachment on Tagalog lands came to a head in a violent revolt in 1745 in the Augustinian estate of Meysapan, north of Laguna de Bay. Spreading to Cavite, Tondo and Bulacan, it involved over 6000 armed men in a bid to secure the restoration of communal lands

[98] D. M. Roth, 'The Friar Estates of the Philippines', Ph.D. thesis, University of Oregon, 1974, 33.
[99] C. Benitez, 'Philippine Progress Prior to 1898', with Tomas De Comyn, *State of the Philippines in 1810*, trans. W. Walton, Filipiniana Book Guild, XV, Manila, 1969, 183.

which they considered ancestral property. In negotiating for a settlement, the sympathy shown to Tagalog demands by Pedro Calderón Henríquez, a judge of the *Audiencia* of Manila, showed the validity of the rebel cause. The inevitable forces of economic change which followed after the mid-century, nonetheless, were to aggravate rather than alleviate the problems of the peasantry.[1]

ECONOMIC REORIENTATION

Ironically, though external influence and direct rule went much deeper in the Philippines than in Dutch-administered regions, the internal economy could not have been less related to Spain's commercial development. The British occupation of Manila (1762–4) and the capture of the outward-bound *Santisima Trinidad*, carrying about three million pesos,[2] exposed the vulnerability of an economy which rested entirely on the annual arrival and departure of no more than a couple of galleons. The opening of Manila to foreign trade during this period did, on the other hand, demonstrate the potential for the development of local exports.[3] The British occupation, in addition, gave release to a long-simmering peasant resentment of corruption, monopoly and perfidy amongst the Spanish official class and of the apathy and insensitivity of the clergy in the provinces. *Indio* rebellions broke out in about ten provinces, the most serious led by Diego Silang in Ilocos.[4] Damaging Spanish prestige, it forced a reappraisal of policy in order to ensure a successful restoration of power. The reforms were anticipated by Governor Don Pedro Manuel de Arandia (1754–9), with the backing of Charles III (r. 1757–88) and his enlightened mercantilist philosophy.

The two important reforms singled out by the Spanish government were the reduction of the powers of the friar curates and greater economic self-reliance of the islands. The first was vigorously championed by Governor Don Simón de Anda y Salazar (1762–4, 1770–6) and resulted in the indictment of the friars for oppression and neglect of spiritual duties and educational responsibilities, including the teaching of Spanish to the *indios*. These reforms were in tune with the anti-clerical sentiments of Charles III. In 1767 he expelled Jesuits from the entire Spanish empire.[5] The lack of sufficient priests from other orders gave rise to a policy of secularization. By 1770 nearly half the parishes were in secular hands.[6] Swiftly promoted *indio* and mestizo clerics, who were ill prepared for their tasks, offered no improvement over their predecessors. The prejudices this created contributed to a gradually increasing gulf between the *indio* and

---

[1] N. P. Cushner, *Landed Estates in the Colonial Philippines*, New Haven: Yale University Southeast Asian Studies Monograph no. 20, 1976, 59–66; Roth, 118–21.

[2] Schurz, 189.

[3] K. Lightfoot, *The Philippines*, London, 1973, 84.

[4] E. H. Blair and J. A. Robertson, *The Philippine Islands, 1493–1898*, Cleveland, 1907, XLIX. 300–5; G. F. Zaide, *Philippine Political and Cultural History*, Manila, 1957, II. 13, 16.

[5] Blair and Robertson, L. 269–77.

[6] Roth, 56.

Spanish clergy which had serious political overtones, especially after 1826 when Ferdinand VII returned most of the parishes to friar control.

In the economic sphere, loss of the galleon trade dictated a policy that constituted a cleaner break with the past than in the ecclesiastical field. As of the beginning of the eighteenth century the galleon trade was already showing signs of weakening. This was brought about partly by the increasing popularity of English and Indian cottons and a proportionate decrease in the demand for Chinese silks, which had hitherto constituted a major item of trade. To improve the climate of trade, Governor José Basco y Vargas (1778–87) established a corporation of merchants (*consulado*) to supervise all commerce. In 1785 the *Real Compania da Filipinas* (Royal Company of the Philippines) was based on the recommendations made twenty years earlier by Francisco Leandro de Viana. Its aim was to develop the economic potential of the Philippines and foster direct commercial links with Spain. Liberalization of trade met firm resistance from the Manila merchants. The Royal Company was excluded from the Acapulco–Manila trade, and the opening of Manila between 1789 to 1794 to foreign ships was restricted to those carrying Asian goods.[7] It was the Mexican revolution in 1820 that dealt the *coup de grâce* to the ailing Manila–Acapulco trade, the Philippines being opened fully to world commerce in 1834.

Crucial to the improvement of the internal economy was agricultural reform. As a basis for this the agricultural society founded by Governor Basco in 1781 disseminated information on agronomy and offered incentives for distributing seed, farm implements, and spinning machines. It fostered the cultivation of cash-crops, such as indigo and pepper, and the production of silk and hemp. By the investment of capital the Royal Company of the Philippines gave further encouragement to the large-scale production of cash-crops, particularly sugar, and to infant industries such as textile manufacture. Revocation of the ban on Chinese immigration in 1778, admitting those who were a source of potential labour, did much to help the expansion of agriculture. Between 1786 and 1800 more than 240,000 piculs of sugar were exported. Cultivation, though concentrated in Pampanga and Pangasinan, continued to expand elsewhere and, in 1854, exports rose to 762,643 piculs.[8]

Surveillance of the Chinese population by the Spanish government, allowing privileges of free movement, lower poll-tax and land leases only to those who embraced Christianity, had encouraged the emergence of a substantial mestizo community. Culturally it had no parallel in Dutch Indonesia and was comparable perhaps only to the large community of Thais of Chinese descent in Siam. A shared religion and Hispanic culture gave the mestizos a shared identity with the *indios*, though their economic status set them apart. Unlike the Chinese whose residence was restricted to Manila where they engaged in commerce, retail trading and various crafts, the mestizos utilized their privileges for extending their commercial enterprise beyond the main city into the provinces. They leased lands for

[7] Benitez, 190–2.
[8] N. P. Cushner, *Spain in the Philippines: From Conquest to Revolution*, Quezon City, 1970, 192, 201.

agriculture, mainly rice, sugar and indigo in the central Luzon provinces of Tondo, Bulacan and Pampanga, either subletting them to *indios* or cultivating them under the *kasamahan* system in which the tiller was allowed a percentage of the crop.[9] Money-lending to *indio* for seed, machinery and labour to tide over the period between planting and harvesting, brought ready opportunities for acquisition of land through confiscation of property for unsettled debts. The mestizos also played a major role in the purchase and transportation of crops to the capital, successfully competing in this line of trade with the provincial governors.[10] Apart from gaining a monopoly of the gaming and opium farms, they locked into the developing international capitalist economy, involving American and British investment in the plantation enterprise.

British commercial interests in the Philippines had been given a head start in the late seventeenth century when Country Traders began the importation into Manila of Coromandel cottons, using the cover of Asian trade in order to avoid Spanish restrictions.[11] From the mid-nineteenth century, agricultural entrepreneurs such as Nicholas Loney of Ker and Company provided advances for crops and machinery for the production of sugar, copra, coffee and hemp. The financial facilities they offered in the form of monetary advances for wholesale business aided mestizo commercial activity involving the purchase, transportation and distribution of goods between Manila and the provinces. The Spanish government's persistently anti-foreign policies—such as the edict passed in 1828, prohibiting foreign merchants from the provinces—were thereby circumvented. Mestizo and European commercial entrepreneurs enacted complementary rather than competitive roles, with the latter gaining pre-eminence in banking and international commerce. By 1859 there were fifteen foreign firms in Manila, including seven British and three American.

Successful private enterprise brought the Filipinos little benefit. Capitalist exploitation in the privately managed plantations, with compulsory cultivation for the government, contributed to widespread economic distress among the peasantry. A system of forced cultivation, introduced in the Cagayan valley, Gapan in the province of Pampanga and the island of Marinduque, supported a Spanish tobacco monopoly, so lucrative that by the mid-nineteenth century it rendered the Philippines financially independent. Under this system each family was required to raise 40,000 plants annually, for sale exclusively to the government. Shortfalls were subject to a fine, while anything in excess of the stipulated quota was systematically destroyed. Government inspections ensured that no part of the crop was held back, even for personal consumption. Pilfering from the homes of cultivators while conducting searches for concealed tobacco, and substitution for cash payment of promissory notes which were never honoured, were commonplace. Poor returns to the cultivators from tobacco, and also production of *vino y nipa* (toddy) for the government monopoly established in 1786, with reliance on staples purchased on the open market, contribut-

[9] E. Wickberg, *The Chinese in Philippine Life, 1850–98*, New Haven, 1965, 23–30.
[10] ibid., 29–30; J. Larkin, *The Pampangans, Colonial Society in a Philippine Province*, Berkeley, 1972, 51–4.
[11] H. Furber, *Rival Empires of Trade in the Orient, 1600–1800*, Minneapolis, 1976, 217–20.

ed to smuggling and black marketeering. Many took flight, mainly to Manila, in search of wage labour.[12]

Life was not vastly different even for *indios* outside the forced cultivation system. Under Spanish administration, each family was liable to payment of a tribute or poll-tax, collected in produce, and the system was open to many abuses. In Pampanga, until the early nineteenth century when sugar gained dominance, the tax was paid in the form of rice, supplied to Manila. Incentives for peasant agriculture, in general, were poor due to the *vandala* system which obliged cultivators to sell produce for token payments and promissory notes, as well as render *polo* or corvée services. Periodic floods and the ravages of locusts which destroyed the paddy were other factors that affected peasant welfare.[13]

EVOLUTION OF A 'NATIONAL' IDENTITY

Economic discontent went much further than peasant grievances. The arrival of many *peninsulares* or Iberian-born Spaniards expelled from Latin America, and their failure in large-scale European entrepreneurial activity, set them in competition with the *indio* and mestizo populations. The latter had traditionally staffed the lower echelons of the bureaucracy, but found themselves displaced by the *peninsulares*, who considered themselves socially superior. Similar friction developed between the friar community taking refuge in the Philippines from an anti-clerical Spain and the local clergy bidding for equality with their Spanish counterparts. Tensions increased within the broadening stratum of educated mestizos and *indios*, who evolved a new élite group, the *ilustrado*, claiming equal opportunity with the Spanish. Dissatisfaction pervaded the entire realm of life amongst the indigenous communities, including the army, and spearheaded anti-foreign sentiments. The smallpox epidemic of 1820 in Manila, which was particularly severe in the Pasig River valley, triggered a backlash aimed largely at the life and property of the Chinese.[14] In 1841, the powerful rebellion led by Apolinario de la Cruz, thwarted in his ambition of entering a monastic order, also bore a racial complexion.[15]

The articulation of discontent and the fostering of a new Filipino identity by the small but influential class of *ilustrados* gained momentum during the latter part of the century. This element, more than any, lent new cohesion to a society plagued by divisive economic forces which separated the moneyed and landed, of various origins, from the mass of poorer *indios*. The socio-economic ferment which grew out of Spanish rule—by contrast to the more effective control of colonial affairs by the Dutch in Indonesia— contributed to the early development of a popular movement based on a

---

[12] Blair and Robertson, LVII. 118–19; Comyn, *State of the Philippines*, 55–63.
[13] Lafond de Lurcy, 'An Economic Plan, from "Quinze Ans de Voyages autour du Monde"', in *Travel Accounts of the Islands, 1832–58*, Filipiniana Book Guild, XXII, Manila, 1974, 28, 32.
[14] Blair and Robertson, LI. 39.
[15] ibid., LII. 92–3 n. 37, 101.

shared Filipinized Hispanic culture. The importance of this cultural phenomenon is made particularly clear in the exclusion of the Moro, by way of their different religious and economic orientations, from the same historic process.

CONCLUSION

By the early decades of the nineteenth century Southeast Asia stood on the brink of the final phase of the European onslaught; indigenous forces were far from subdued and, in some cases, were actually stronger than during the initial encounter with the West. On the mainland, the assertion of Burman, Thai and Vietnamese cultures and their territorial expansion achieved a modicum of administrative centralization and cultural unification through the fostering of religious and cultural ideology. Though assisted to an extent by Western arms, this was achieved largely through local initiatives and the culmination of internal growth. With the political maturing and the evolution of statehood towards nation status, an awareness grew amongst the rulers of Burma, Thailand and Vietnam of rapidly accelerating change in the external world. Internal developments and external policies were determined, to a large degree, by rulers concerned about the nature of their own responses. Thai accommodation and adaptation and Vietnamese mistrust of the West were positive reactions. Burma under Mindon faltered between isolation and ineffectual efforts at modernization, while Cambodia and the Lao states found little room for initiative and were forced into isolation by their powerful neighbours.

In island Southeast Asia, Javanese and Balinese power, emasculated by the Dutch, adopted introversion and myth-making epitomized in the grand ideal of the 'theatre state'. In areas such as the Javanese *mancanegara* and the Philippines which had long been under colonial rule and had suffered the rigours of its monopoly systems, economic burdens gave new meaning to religious and cultural identities, ushering in an age of protest, rebellion and war. At the same time, it was the insular areas close to the main lines of commerce that witnessed the emergence of the new spirit of merchant enterprise, its flowering aborted by factors internal as well as external. Each component part of the region, for better or worse, clearly articulated a response to the inevitable forces of modernization and Western encroachment.

BIBLIOGRAPHIC ESSAY

Burma

The importance in Burma of clientage, bondage and taxation, both crown and glebe, makes M. Aung-Thwin's 'Hierarchy and Order in Pre-Colonial Burma', JSEAS, 15, 2 (1984), essential reading for an understanding of the interrelation between politics and socio-economic affairs. Comparison of the ideas and institutions of bondage in Burma and Thailand are found in

F. K. Lehman, 'Freedom and Bondage in traditional Burma and Thailand', JSEAS, 15, 2 (1984). A detailed account of the organization and influence of the monastic order is found in J. P. Ferguson, 'The Symbolic Dimensions of the Burmese Sanga', Ph.D. thesis, Cornell University, 1975. Problems relating to the administration of the *sangha* are discussed in Aung-Thwin, 'The Role of *Sasana* Reform in Burmese History: Economic Dimensions of a Religious Purification', JAS, 38, 4 (1979), and V. B. Lieberman, 'The Political Significance of Religious Wealth in Burmese History: Some Further Thoughts', JAS, 39, 4 (1980).

A general history of the period with an economic emphasis is found in W. J. Koenig, 'The Early Kón-Baung Polity, 1752–1819: A Study of Politics, Administration and Social Organisation', Ph.D. thesis, University of London, 1978. In respect of much of Southeast Asia the lack of hard data from indigenous sources has impeded detailed studies of administrative and economic systems of the pre-colonial period, but the Burmese administrative records or *si-tàn* are an important exception. These have been made accessible in the English translation found in F. N. Trager and W. J. Koenig, eds, *Burmese Si-Tàns, 1764–1826, Records of Rural Life and Administration*, Tucson, 1979. The significance of Mon–Burmese rivalry with reference to population and economic disparities is imaginatively interpreted in M. Adas, 'Imperialistic Rhetoric and Modern Historiography: The study of Lower Burma before and after conquest', JSEAS, 3, 2 (1972).

Thailand

Studies of the socio-economic organization of Siam for this period are found in A. Rabibhadana, 'Organisation of Thai Society in the Early Bangkok Period, 1782–1873', Data Paper, no. 74, Cornell Southeast Asia Program. A more concise statement is 'Clientship and Class Structure in the Early Bangkok period', in G. W. Skinner and A. T. Kirsch, eds, *Change and Persistence in Thai Society, Essays in Honour of L. Sharp*, Ithaca, 1975. A more recent intepretation is B. Terwiel, 'Bondage and Slavery in Nineteenth Century Siam', in *Slavery, Bondage and Dependency in Southeast Asia*, ed. A. Reid, St Lucia, Queensland, 1983.

The subject of fundamental reform within the *sangha* as a prelude to modernization is discussed in C. J. Reynolds, 'Buddhist Cosmography in Thai History, with special reference to nineteenth century cultural change', JAS, 15, 2 (1976), and D. K. Wyatt, 'The "Subtle Revolution" of King Rama I of Siam', in *Moral Order and the Question of Change*, A. Woodside and D. K. Wyatt, eds, New Haven: Yale University Southeast Asia Studies Monograph no. 24, 1982.

Studies of individual reigns are found in K. Wenk, *The Restoration of Thailand under Rama I, 1782–1809*, Tucson: Association of Asian Studies, 1968, and W. F. Vella, *Siam Under Rama III, 1824–1851*, New York: Monograph for the Association of Asian Studies, no. 4, 1957. An in-depth study of the structure and workings of Thai monarchy as an administrative institution during the period under survey is L. Gesick, 'Kingship and Political Integration in Traditional Siam, 1767–1824', Ph.D. thesis, Cornell University, 1976.

The standard work on the Chinese in Thailand is G. W. Skinner, *Chinese Society in Thailand: An Analytical History*, Ithaca, 1957. In addition, J. Jiang concerns himself with the role of the Chinese in Thai economy in 'The Chinese in Thailand: Past and Present', JSEAH, 7, 1 (1966), complementing S. Viraphol's definitive study, *Tribute and Profit: Sino-Siamese Trade, 1652–1853*, Cambridge, Mass., 1977, and J. Cushman's 'Fields From The Sea: Chinese Junk Trade with Siam during the late eighteenth and early nineteenth centuries', Ph.D. thesis, Cornell University, 1975. Of the European travel accounts for the period, there is considerable information on the commerce and economy of Thailand in *The Crawfurd Papers*, published by the Vajirañāṇa National Library, Bangkok, 1915, and the same author's *Journal of an Embassy to the Courts of Siam and Cochin China*, London, 1828, reprinted Kuala Lumpur, 1967. A more reliable source for tax and revenue figures is E. Roberts, *Embassy to the Eastern Courts of Cochin China, Siam and Muscat during the years 1832–34*, New York, 1837. A critical appraisal of these early sources is found in B. J. Terwiel, *A History of Modern Thailand, 1767–1942*, St Lucia, Queensland, 1983. Hong Lysa, *Thailand in the Nineteenth Century: Evolution of the Economy and Society*, Singapore: Institute of Southeast Asian Studies, 1984, uses Thai sources to present a comprehensive account of the important economic changes of the early Bangkok period involving the expansion of trade, the increased circulation of currency and the evolution of a new tax and revenue structure.

The best account of Siam's relations with vassal states during the first half of the nineteenth century is W. F. Vella, *Siam Under Rama III, 1824–51*, New York, 1957. An invaluable Thai perspective on politics and interstate relations is presented in Chaophraya Thiphakorawong, *The Dynastic Chronicles, Bangkok Era, The First Reign*, trans. and ed. Thadeus and Chadin Flood, I, Tokyo: Center of East Asian Studies, 1978. For an account of Thai–Lao relations leading to the destruction of Vientiane, see D. K. Wyatt, 'Siam and Laos, 1767–1827', JSEAH, 4, 2 (1963). The latter episode receives a nationalistic perspective in a recent study, Mayoury and Pheuiphanh Ngaosyvathn, 'Lao Historiography and Historians: Case Study of the War between Bangkok and Lao in 1827', JSEAS, 20, 1 (1989).

Cambodia

D. Chandler, *A History of Cambodia*, Boulder, 1983, provides the standard work. There is a more detailed analysis of the period under review in the same author's 'Cambodia Before the French: Politics in a Tributary Kingdom, 1794–1848', Ph.D. thesis, University of Michigan, 1973, and 'An Anti-Vietnamese Rebellion in Early Nineteenth Century Cambodia', JSEAS, 6, 1 (1975).

Vietnam

J. Chesneaux, *Contribution à l'histoire de la Nation Vietnamienne*, Paris, 1955, Le Thanh Khoi, *Viet-Nam, Histoire et Civilisation*, Paris, 1955, and Nguyen Khac Vien, *Histoire Du Vietnam*, Paris, 1974, provide good basic reading.

T. Hodgkin, *Vietnam: the Revolutionary Path*, New York, 1981, offers a more modern account with peasant sympathies. A. Woodside, *Vietnam and the Chinese Model*, Cambridge, Mass., 1971, is a scholarly analysis of Chinese bureaucratic and cultural influence on Vietnam.

As a result of the increased pace of British interest in the mainland during the beginning of the nineteenth century, journals and reports of missions provide rich eye-witness accounts of commerce and society. A handy compilation of these reports is found in A. Lamb, *The Mandarin Road to Old Hué*, London, 1970. The articulation of popular feelings on politics and social problems in verse lends ready access to the Vietnamese perceptions. Huynh Sanh Thong, *The Heritage of Vietnamese Poetry*, New Haven: 1979, provides a good annotated anthology in English.

The Philippines

An integrated history of socio-economic developments during the eighteenth and nineteenth centuries remains to be written. A good account of the administrative history of the period is E. G. Robles, *The Philippines in the 19th Century*, Quezon City, 1969. W. L. Schurz, *The Manila Galleon*, New York, 1939, reprinted 1959, still offers the most vivid and detailed description of the Manila–Acapulco trade. A statistical account of its decline is found in W. E. Cheong, 'The Decline of Manila as a Spanish Entrepôt in the Far East. 1785–1826: Its Impact on the Pattern of Southeast Asian Trade', JSEAS, 2, 2 (1971).

On the agrarian front, the friar estates and the related problems of the peasantry, leading up to the 1745 revolt, are discussed in D. M. Roth, 'Friar Estates of the Philippines', Ph.D. thesis, Oregon University, 1974. N. P. Cushner, *Landed Estates in the Colonial Philippines*, New Haven, 1976, focuses on the problems relating to the province of Tondo. Studies of agrarian problems in another area are found in J. A. Larkin, *The Pampangans: Colonial Society in a Philippine Province*, Berkeley, 1972. For an account of the organization of the government tobacco monopoly see E. C. de Jesus, *The Tobacco Monopoly in the Philippines: Bureaucratic Enterprise and Social Change 1766–1880*, Quezon City, 1980.

Documentary sources in E. H. Blair and J. A. Robertson, *The Philippine Islands, 1493–1898*, 55 vols, Cleveland, 1903–9, lend interesting insights into key events. Travel accounts include translations from the French and Spanish published by the Manila Filipiniana Book Guild (FBG). The most relevant for the period are Tomas de Comyn, *State of the Philippines in 1810*, FBG, XV, Manila, 1969; J. Bowring, *A Visit to the Philippine Islands*, London, 1859, and relevant sections from J. White, *A Voyage to Cochin China*, London, 1824, reprinted Kuala Lumpur, 1972.

The early phase of Chinese penetration into the Philippines is traced in E. K. Wickberg, 'The Chinese Mestizo in Philippine History', JSEAH, 5, 1 (1964); M. C. Guerrero, 'The Political Background', M. L. Diaz-Trechuelo, 'The Economic Background', both published in *The Chinese in the Philippines 1770–1893*, ed. A. Felix, Manila: Historical Conservation Society, XVI, 1969. For a later period a more substantial account is found in E. Wickberg, *The Chinese in Philippine Life, 1850–98*, New Haven, 1965.

Java and Madura

Sir Stamford Raffles, *History of Java*, London, 1817, reprinted Kuala Lumpur, 1965, 2 vols, and J. S. Furnivall, *Netherlands India: A Study of Plural Economy*, Cambridge, UK, 1939, reprinted 1967, are standard references for this period. Representative of modern scholarship are the overviews of M. C. Ricklefs in 'The Javanese in the Eighteenth and Nineteenth Centuries', published in D. G. E. Hall, *History of Southeast Asia*, London, 1981, and chapters 9 and 10 in the same author's *A History of Modern Indonesia*, London, 1981. A more detailed study is his monograph, *Jogjakarta under Sultan Mangkubumi, 1749–1792*, London, 1974. Surveys of socio-cultural aspects are available in the stimulating writings of D. H. Burger, *Sociologisch-Economische Geschiedenis van Indonesia*, intro. J. S. Wigboldus, 2 vols, Amsterdam, 1975; *Structural Changes in Javanese Society: The Village Sphere/The Supra-Village Sphere*, trans. L. Palmier, Ithaca: Cornell Indonesia Project, 1956–7; and the controversial work of C. Geertz, *Agricultural Involution: The Processes of Ecological Change in Indonesia*, Berkeley, 1963.

For the British period the main ground is covered in J. Bastin, *The Native Policies of Stamford Raffles in Java and Sumatra*, Oxford, 1957; 'Raffles' ideas on the land-rent system in Java and the Mackenzie Land tenure commission', VKI, 14 (1954); and H. R. C. Wright, *East-Indian Economic Problems of the Age of Cornwallis and Raffles*, London, 1961.

The mass of Dutch literature on the Java War (1825–30) has been meticulously researched in the modern studies of P. B. R. Carey. See 'The Origins of the Java War', *English Historical Review*, vol. XCI, no. 358; 'The Cultural Ecology of Early Nineteenth Century Java: Pangeran Dipanagara, a case study', Occasional Paper, no. 24, Institute of Southeast Asian Studies, Singapore, 1979; and *Babad Dipanagara: An account of the Outbreak of the Java War (1825–1830)*, MBRAS Monograph, no. 9, Kuala Lumpur, 1981.

Early studies of the culture system have been superseded by C. Fasseur, *Kultuurstelsel en Koloniale Baten: De Nederlandse exploitatie van Java 1840–60*, Leiden, 1975; Robert Van Niel, 'Measurement of Change under the Cultivation System in Java, 1837–51', *Indonesia*, 14 (1972), and 'The Effect of Export Cultivation in Nineteenth Century Java', MAS, 15, 1, (1981). For studies of specific areas see R. E. Elson, *Javanese Peasants and the Colonial Sugar Industry: Impact and Change in an East Javanese Residency, 1830–40*, Singapore, 1984, and C. Fasseur, 'Organisatie en sociaal-economische betekenis van de gouvernements-suikerkultuur in enkele residenties op Java omstreeks 1850', BKI, 133, 2–3 (1977). *Indonesian Economics: The Concept of Dualism in Theory and Practice*, The Hague, 1960, is concerned with the debates on the theory of 'dual economy'. For a recent statistical reassessment of production and a re-evaluation of some aspects of Geertz's theory of 'agricultural involution' see Peter Boomgaard, 'Java's Agricultural Production, 1775–1875', in *Economic Growth in Indonesia, 1820–1940*, VKI, 137, Dordrecht, 1989. *Changing Economy in Indonesia*, I: *Indonesia's Export Crops, 1816–1940*, initiated by W. M. F. Mansvelt, re-edited and continued by P. Creutzberg, The Hague, 1975, provides statistical information on Java's exports.

For accounts of Chinese enterprise in Java see J. Bastin, 'The Chinese Estates in East-Java during the British Administration', *Indonesië*, 7 (1954); Onghokham, 'The Peranakan Officers' Families in Nineteenth-Century Java', in *Papers of the Dutch-Indonesian Historical Conference, Lage Vuursche, The Netherlands, June 1980*, Leiden and Jakarta, 1982, and J. R. Rush, 'Social Control and Influence in Nineteenth Century Indonesia: Opium Farms and the Chinese in Java', *Indonesia*, 35 (1983).

Sumatra and the Malay World

J. Marsden, *History of Sumatra*, London, 1811, reprinted Kuala Lumpur, 1966, and E. M. Loeb, *Sumatra, Its History and People*, Vienna, 1935, provide important ethno-histories. Most modern studies are concerned largely with European political and commercial activity on the island. These include J. Kathirithamby-Wells, *The British West Sumatran Presidency (1760–85): Problems of Early Colonial Enterprise*, Kuala Lumpur, 1977; J. Bastin, 'Palembang in 1811 and 1812', in *Essays on Indonesian and Malaysian History*, Singapore, 1961; Lee Kam Hing, 'Acheh's Relations with the British, 1760–1819', M.A. thesis, University of Malaya, Kuala Lumpur; and J. W. Gould, *Americans in Sumatra*, The Hague, 1961.

C. Dobbin strikes a new path in her admirable study of the Padri War: *Islamic Revivalism in a Changing Peasant Economy, Central Sumatra, 1784–1847*, London and Malmö, 1983. Her seminal article, 'Economic Change in Minangkabau as a Factor in the Rise of the Padri Movement, 1784–1830', *Indonesia*, 23 (1977), traces the revived commercial links between central and east Sumatra and the Malay peninsula. For an account of early Minangkabau migrations see T. Kato, *Matriliny and Migration: Evolving Minangkabau Traditions in Indonesia*, Ithaca, 1982. E. Graves, *The Minangkabau Response to Dutch Colonial Rule in the Nineteenth Century*, Cornell University Modern Indonesian Project, Monograph Series, no. 60, Ithaca, 1981, is an account of the impact of early colonial rule on Minangkabau society.

Compared to those on Aceh and the Minangkabau, historical writings on other areas of Sumatra are few. There is a good contemporaneous account of east Sumatra in J. Anderson, *Mission to the East Coast of Sumatra*, reprinted Kuala Lumpur, 1971. A. C. Milner, *Kerajaan: Malay Political Culture on the Eve of Colonial Rule*, Tucson, 1982, is also relevant. L. Castles, 'Statelessness and Stateforming tendencies among the Bataks before Colonial Rule', in *Pre-Colonial State Systems in Southeast Asia*, ed. A. J. S. Reid and L. Castles, MBRAS Monograph, no. 6, Kuala Lumpur, 1975, is a discussion of socio-political organization. There is little on Lampung apart from mid-nineteenth century accounts of *adat* and administrative structure in W. R. van Hoëvell, 'De Lampoengsche distrikten op het Eiland Sumatra', *Tijdschrift voor Neerlands-Indië*, 14, 1 (1852), and H. D. Canne, 'Bijdrage tot de Geschiedenis der Lampongs', TBG, 11 (1862). Interest in 'ship cloth' has in recent years attracted the attention of scholars to this area and southwest Sumatra. See Tos van Dijk and Nico de Jonge, *Ship*

Cloths of the Lampung, South Sumatra, Amsterdam, 1980, and M. Gittinger, 'A Study of Ship Cloths of South Sumatra', Ph.D. thesis, Columbia University, 1972.

Tuhfat-al-Nafis, ed. V. Matheson and B. Andaya, Kuala Lumpur, 1982, is indispensable for the history of the Malay world centred at Johor-Riau. Apart from this, the publication in recent years of a number of Malay verse chronicles on Sumatra are of relevance. These include M. O. Woelders, 'Het Sultanaat Palembang, 1811–1825', VKI, 72 (1975); G. W. J. Drewes, ed. and trans., *Hikajat Potjut Muhamat: An Achehnese Epic*, Bibliotheca Indonesica, 19, The Hague 1979; *Two Achehnese Poems: Hikajat Ranto and Hikajat Teungku Di Meuké'*, Bibliotheca Indonesica, 20, The Hague, 1980; J. Kathirithamby-Wells and Muhammad Yusoff Hashim, ed. and trans., *The Syair Mukomuko: Some historical aspects of a nineteenth century Sumatran court chronicle*, MBRAS Monograph no. 13, Kuala Lumpur, 1985; and D. J. Goudie, ed. and trans., *Syair Perang Siak*, MBRAS, Monograph no. 17, Kuala Lumpur, 1989.

For the growth of commerce and piracy in the Malay world N. Tarling, *Piracy and Politics in the Malay World*, Melbourne, 1963, provides a good general background. D. K. Bassett, 'Anglo-Malay Relations, 1786–1795', JMBRAS, 38, 2 (1965); 'British Commercial and Strategic Interest in the Malay Peninsula during the late eighteenth century', *Malaysian and Indonesian Studies*, Oxford, 1964; and D. Lewis, 'The Growth of the Country Trade to the Straits of Malacca, 1760–1777', JMBRAS, 43, 2 (1970), point to the importance of British trade in the area. H. R. C. Wright, 'Tin, Trade and Dominion', in *East-Indian Economic Problems of the Age of Cornwallis and Raffles*, London, 1961, offers interesting insights which remain to be fully explored.

Histories of individual Malay states referred to in the bibliographic essay for Chapter 7 emphasize their growing political insecurity and fragmentation, except at the important commercial nodules of Terengganu and Riau where Malay socio-cultural forces converged. See Shaharil Talib, 'The Port and Polity of Terengganu during the eighteenth and nineteenth centuries', in *The Southeast Asian Port and Polity: Rise and Demise*, ed. J. Kathirithamby-Wells and J. Villiers, Singapore, 1990; E. Netscher, *De Nederlanders in Djohor en Siak, 1602 tot 1865*, Batavia, 1870; 'Bijdragen tot de Geschiedenis van het Rijk van Lingga en Riouw', TBG, IV (1855); V. Matheson, 'Mahmud, Sultan of Riau and Lingga (1823–64)', *Indonesia*, 13 (1972), and B. W. Andaya and V. Matheson, 'Islamic Thought and Malay Tradition: The Writings of Raja Ali Haji of Riau (c. 1809–1870)', in A. J. S. Reid and D. Marr, eds, *Perceptions of the Past in Southeast Asia*, Singapore, 1979. C. Trocki, *Prince of Pirates: The Temenggongs and the Development of Johor and Singapore, 1784–1885*, Singapore, 1979, provides a useful account of early Chinese enterprise in Johor.

The Eastern Archipelago

E. S. de Klerck, *History of the Netherlands East Indies*, Rotterdam, 1938, reprinted Amsterdam, 1975, gives fair attention to the 'Outer Islands', focusing on the eastern half in chapter XIV, though from a colonial viewpoint. For a conceptualization of the area as part of the Indonesian cultural entity see G. J. Resink, *Indonesia's History between the Myths: Essays on Legal History and Historical Theory*, The Hague, 1968. T. Forrest, *A Voyage to New Guinea, and the Moluccas, from Balambangan . . . 1774–1776*, London, 1779, reprinted Kuala Lumpur, 1969, and H. T. Fry, *Alexander Dalrymple (1737–1808) and the Expansion of British Trade*, London, 1970, provide contemporary views of the region.

For modern studies of west Borneo see J. Jackson, *Chinese in the West Borneo Gold Fields: A Study in Cultural Geography*, Occasional Papers in Geography, no. 15, University of Hull, 1970; Wang Tai Peng, 'The Origins of the Chinese *Kongsi* with special reference to West Borneo', M.A. thesis, Australian National University, 1977; and J. van Goor, 'Seapower, Trade and State-Formation: Pontianak and the Dutch', in *Trading Companies in Asia, 1600–1800*, ed. J. van Goor, Amsterdam, 1986. Knowledge of Sulu has been greatly enhanced by the fascinating study by J. Warren, *The Sulu Zone, 1768–1898*, Singapore, 1981. Other modern studies of individual components of the region include H. J. de Graaf, *De Geschiedenis van Ambon en de Zuid-Molukken*, Franeker, 1977; J. Fox, *Harvest of the Palm: Ecological Change in Eastern Indonesia*, London, 1977; and C. Geertz, *Negara: The Theatre State in Nineteenth Century Bali*, Princeton, 1980.

INDEX

Printed in the United States
55878LVS00004BA/28-57

9 780521 663700